DOCUMENTARY TESTIMONIES

Documentary Testimonies explores the varying forms, institutions, and practices of audiovisual testimony: the "moving testimonies" that compel us to bear witness, stir us to anger or tears, and possibly mobilize us to action.

Comprising ten new essays and a substantive introduction, this interdisciplinary volume provides an in-depth analysis of archives of social suffering tied to particular locales: Cambodia, Chiapas, Darfur, India, Indonesia, Korea, New Orleans, Norway, Rwanda, South Africa, and Washington, DC. Topics include technologies of capture, storage, and circulation; problems of historical veracity/frail memory; limits and potentialities of documentary as public record; architectonics of memory; and ethics of witnessing. Focusing on the generation and use of testimonial archives by documentary filmmakers, public administrators and institutions, and others with interest in social and environmental justice and genocide commemoration and prevention, the volume aims to investigate, from a critical and translocal perspective, testimony as social practice.

Bhaskar Sarkar is Associate Professor of Film and Media Studies at the University of California, Santa Barbara. He is author of *Mourning the Nation: Indian Cinema in the Wake of Partition.*

Janet Walker is Professor and former chair of the Department of Film and Media Studies at the University of California, Santa Barbara. She is author of *Couching Resistance: Women, Film, and Psychoanalytic Psychiatry* as well as *Trauma Cinema: Documenting Incest and the Holocaust*; she is co-editor of *Feminism and Documentary* (with Diane Waldman) and editor of *Westerns: Films through History*.

Previously published in the AFI Film Readers series
Edited by Edward Branigan and Charles Wolfe

Psychoanalysis and Cinema
E. Ann Kaplan

Fabrications
Jane M. Gaines and Charlotte Herzog

Sound Theory/Sound Practice
Rick Altman

Film Theory Goes to the Movies
Jim Collins, Ava Preacher Collins, and Hilary Radner

Theorizing Documentary
Michael Renov

Black American Cinema
Manthia Diawara

Disney Discourse
Eric Smoodin

Classical Hollywood Comedy
Henry Jenkins and Kristine Brunovska Karnick

The Persistence of History
Vivian Sobchack

The Revolution Wasn't Televised
Lynn Spigel and Michael Curtin

Black Women Film and Video Artists
Jacqueline Bobo

Home, Exile, Homeland
Hamid Naficy

Violence and American Cinema
J. David Slocum

Masculinity
Peter Lehman

Westerns
Janet Walker

Authorship and Film
David A. Gerstner and Janet Staiger

New Media
Anna Everett and John T. Caldwell

East European Cinemas
Anikó Imre

Landscape and Film
Martin Lefebvre

European Film Theory
Temenuga Trifonova

Film Theory and Contemporary Hollywood Movies
Warren Buckland

World Cinemas, Transnational Perspectives
Nataša Ďurovičová and Kathleen Newman

DOCUMENTARY TESTIMONIES

GLOBAL ARCHIVES OF SUFFERING

EDITED BY

BHASKAR SARKAR AND
JANET WALKER

First published 2010
by Routledge
270 Madison Ave
New York, NY 10016

Simultaneously published in the UK
by Routledge
2 Park Square
Milton Park, Abingdon
Oxon OX14 4RN

Routledge is an imprint of the Taylor & Francis Group, an informa business

Typeset in Spectrum by Keyword Group Ltd.
Printed and bound in the United States of America on acid-free paper by Edwards Brothers, Inc

Library of Congress Cataloging in Publication Data
Documentary testimonies : global archives of suffering / edited by Bhaskar Sarkar and Janet Walker.
p. cm. – (AFI film readers series)
Includes bibliographical references and index.
ISBN 978-0-415-99663-1 (hardback : alk. paper) – ISBN 978-0-415-99664-8 (pbk. : alk. paper) – ISBN 978-0-203-88341-9 (e-book : alk. paper) 1. Documentary films–Production and direction. 2. Documentary films–Social aspects. I. Sarkar, B. (Bhaskar) II. Walker, Janet.
PN1995.9.D6D5775 2009
070.1'8–dc22 2009020054

ISBN 10: 0-415-99663-5 (hbk)
ISBN 10: 0-415-99664-3 (pbk)
ISBN 10: 0-203-88341-1 (ebk)

ISBN 13: 978-0-415-99663-1 (hbk)
ISBN 13: 978-0-415-99664-8 (pbk)
ISBN 13: 978-0-203-88341-9 (ebk)

contents

illustrations

acknowledgments

But for an airport layover, this book might never have been. While we work in the same department with our esteemed series editors, it took this serendipitous meeting on the way back from the Society for Cinema and Media Studies Conference in Philadelphia to discover where our long-standing interests in documentary studies had been leading of late. On the other hand, the sheer experiences that motivate this book are much bigger than any academic exchange. We write in solidarity with people's continuing struggles to make their experiences known through documents, documentaries, and audiovisual archives.

Warmest thanks to Edward Branigan and Charles Wolfe for their editorial wisdom, and to Charles Wolfe for the provocations that helped us explain in the introduction that the crux of the volume is the relationship among individual testimonies, local archives, and global ethical communities. Matthew Byrnie and Stan Spring at Routledge offered their enthusiastic support, making possible this collective endeavor.

Dean David Marshall of the Division of Humanities and Fine Arts provided not only research funding but also strong encouragement of our work in this area. The UC Santa Barbara Interdisciplinary Humanities Center with its Research Focus Groups enabled us to form a "trauma unit"; we thank the members, especially Maurice Stevens. UC Santa Barbara colleagues have continued to provide a local atmosphere in which ideas flourish and colleagues from further afield have extended the conversation; for this volume we thank Bishnupriya Ghosh, Cristina Venegas, Michael Berry, Suk-Young Kim, Lucia Ricciardelli, Regina Longo, Liz Constable, and Julia Lesage. Another true inspiration for Janet was the experience of working on *Video Portraits of Survival* with Kwame Braun, Elizabeth Wolfson, and the project participants. For office and editorial assistance, we thank Kathryn Carnahan, Vikki Duncan, Andrea Fontenot, Fintan Power, and Alfred Symons.

We learned so much from each of the contributors' situated and meticulous essays; together they helped us realize the overarching connections of the volume. We thank our authors doubly for their collegiality and generous responses to what they must have thought were interminable email queries.

A special thanks to our family members, Bishnu, Steve, and Ariel. Bhaskar thanks Janet for inviting him to the project and Janet replies that she couldn't have done it without him.

introduction

moving testimonies

bhaskar sarkar and janet walker

The will to contribute audiovisual testimony about catastrophic events and social suffering is readily observable across the globe. Tens of thousands of people have delivered on-camera attestations of shocking experiences to local or broadly affiliated visual archives. These archives, in turn, are benefiting from the emergence of new media technologies for the capture, assembly, storage, and circulation of the gathered materials. In our latter twentieth and twenty-first century "era of the witness,"[1] media testimonial initiatives—be they official, grassroots, guerrilla, transitory, insistent, or any combination thereof—participate in the creation of ethical communities by bringing testifiers and testimonial witnesses together at the audiovisual interface.

The "documentary testimonies" this volume studies take various forms: from unedited video recordings to documentary films, from one-on-one reminiscences to site-specific public presentations and perambulations. Cobbled together, "documentary" and "testimony" signal the migration of the testimonial scene from documentary film, where it has been since the coming of sound a staple of advocacy and historical filmmaking,[2] to the humanitarian digital video archive[3]—and back again.

But while "documentary" and "testimony" are certainly related, they also possess distinct disciplinary genealogies. Through the analysis of their affinities and disjunctures, we seek to challenge some of the maxims of documentary studies as a sub-field of media studies, and, concomitantly, some of the presumptions that structure the sites where testimony is administered. For instance, while documentary scholars have tended to view the "talking head" as evidence of a lack of imagination on the part of film and filmmaker, now, nearly fifty years after the advent of direct cinema dimmed the luster of direct address,[4] official, non-governmental, and upstart entities—and documentary practitioners—are tapping the expressive, ethical, and activist potential of audiovisual testimony to further human rights and transitional justice initiatives. Here we seek to register the restrictiveness of documentary studies scholarship where it has neglected the policy considerations and wider networks through which individual documentary films make meaning.

Conversely, we seek to make available to archivists and other curators of public memory documentary studies' invaluable emphasis on the constructedness of non-fictional as well as fictional media texts. "If we consider the imaginary realm of fiction as having a metaphoric relation to history and lived experience," writes Bill Nichols, "as a kind of carefully shaped, translucent cloud that displays contours and shapes, patterns and practices that closely resemble the ones we encounter in our own lives, we might think of documentary as a mode where this fictive cloud has settled back to earth."[5] Quite a few of the chapters in the current volume proffer compelling close textual analyses of specific documentary works. And they do so always with a view to the wider landscape where these texts "settle back to earth" and form the pages of a volume conceived to enable a relational dynamic, within and among the chapters.

Media studies' nuanced debates about the vicissitudes of representation and subjectivity have this and more to offer archivists and institutions grappling with practical issues, including the veracity (or frailty) of testimony, the image ethics of victims and perpetrators, and, more generally, the use of audiovisual materials for the amelioration of social suffering. Whereas literary, history, and other non-media specialists often misconstrue the medium-specificity of audiovisual testimony, seeing it as residing in the "dimension of *the real*," "shorn of 'literary' ornaments,"[6] or, alternately, as somehow less indexical or historically valid than printed documents, we feel prepared to inject a note of constructive criticality into testimonial projects by speaking up around the hushed tones with which atrocious images are often met in order to facilitate a diversity of opinion and action about the complicated construction and uses of video testimony in the furtherance of agendas that vary.

Of course, we media scholars are also vulnerable, in the rush to construct a meta-archive of suffering (this book, for example), to the tendency to ignore the specifics and underlying conflicts of testimony's mechanisms of self-presentation. Aptly, these formations are given serious attention by our contributors and, we hope, in this introduction as well. All of the book's chapters are original to this volume, with each being a closely analytical and thickly contextualized study of an archive of social suffering tied to a particular locale: Cambodia, Chiapas, Darfur, India, Indonesia, Korea, New Orleans, Norway, Rwanda, South Africa, and Washington, DC. Together, these individually expert and informative studies inspire the multiplication of perspectives and queries: what are some of the cultural differences in bearing emotional reactions, in institutional prescriptions and proscriptions, and in the distinct kinds of knowledge enabled by testimonies in various media forms? How can we differentiate between and among televised public hearings and activist videos in terms of the kinds of archives they generate? Are these archives official? Renegade? Ephemeral? What does the comparative project lead us to discover about the limits and potentialities of documentary as public record? To what extent can or should aggregated testimonies be used to garner tangible reparations or enact social change? What are the corporeal and performative dimensions of testimony? And how do they compensate for or exacerbate the frailty of memory? The current planetary salience of documentary testimonies raises further questions regarding the politics of knowledge production, and the underlying cognitive, moral, and policy frameworks that are fast congealing into regulative global structures.

This introduction is one place—in addition to the crucial intellectual spaces of the classroom, center, archive, library, museum, and mind of the individual reader—where such compelling questions may be addressed at some length. And indeed, a number of consistencies and differences in the creation and use of testimony have become apparent as we have explored, along with our contributors, its cultivation by public administrators and institutions, human rights activists and organizations, documentary and ethnographic filmmakers, and other individuals and groups to serve the interests of environmental justice, human rights, social advocacy, and the commemoration and prevention of genocide. These differences and similarities will be broached as the introduction proceeds. Here, at the start, we do wish to highlight one profoundly significant tension that informs many of the individual chapters as well as this study of "global archives of suffering" as a whole: that is, the tension between the local and the translocal. While grassroots creators may strive to realize the existence, meaning, and import of collected testimonies in a local context, there may be certain instances when it would behoove even the most committed community activists to orchestrate their testimonial projects for a global audience. But then, when does local testimony's intricate play of meaning get usurped by universal and universalizing templates for the legitimation of suffering? And what do we mean, after all, by the global?

Even as we subtitle our book "Global Archives of Suffering"—hoping, frankly, for a wide audience—we resist the universalizing gesture that establishes the West at the epicenter of a globalized world, or, perhaps even worse, the mechanism of othering that construes everything but the West as a global-out-there where suffering occurs. Here too, we maintain a critical tension: expanding our geographic reach while realizing that there is plenty of suffering and there are plenty of good testimonial projects right here in the US. We hope that any loss of specificity from global hop-scotching can be mitigated to a large extent by the potential of the anthology form and will be mitigated by the consummate expertise of our contributors, specialists on diverse subjects and regions who have eagerly embraced this joint analytic enterprise. Recognizing testimony's relational essence, we attend to its disconnections as well as its affiliations and, while celebrating existing and emerging, small- and large-scale audiovisual testimonial projects around the world, we assess the complexities of the mode and the manifest idealism of the "see it, film it, change it" formula.[7]

Two key analytical positions underlie our editorial work (without, of course, becoming a litmus test for contributors) and result from it. First, out of respect for social protest and commitment to the continuance of individual and collective life beyond devastating experiences, we follow the critical shift from a politics of "victims" and victimhood to one of "survivors" and agency. Whereas to stress victimhood even from an empathetic perspective is to disregard survivors' resolute resourcefulness, turning them into hapless pawns of geopolitical maneuvers doubling as philanthropy,[8] testimony is one of the most tenacious expressions of a desire to overcome adversity, to keep on living, to secure the future of a community. And yet, the opinions of our contributors make for a multivocal text; we take this opportunity to signal Bjørn Sørenssen's intriguing critical and etymological discussion of "victim" in the Scandinavian context ("From 'Super Babies' and 'Nazi Bastards' to Victims Finding a Voice").

Second, we invoke social suffering as a necessary supplement to the trauma paradigm or, indeed, as an inherent aspect of the particular understanding of trauma theory that is ours. Refreshing the debate by moving away from a polarization of trauma's tortuous psychodynamics on the one hand and its messy sociological and political negotiations on the other,[9] Arthur Kleinman and Veena Das, with various collaborators in their trilogy on "social suffering," break down disciplinary boundaries around the fields of health, welfare, law, morality, and religion in order to reestablish "the collective and intersubjective connections of experience" and the salubrious subjectivity that social suffering damages.[10] Without undertaking an exhaustive explication of an area of critical studies that is both beyond the scope of this volume and the subject of our respective other works,[11] we too recognize the embeddedness of trauma's psychic structures and mechanisms within broader intersubjective networks and public transactions.

Reflecting on the theory and practice of Cuban documentarist Víctor Casaus, Michael Chanan remarks that "the vocation of documentary is testimonial."[12] Here we acknowledge that insight and extrapolate two others as foundational to our project: the vocation of testimony is archival, and, jointly, the vocation of the archive is ethical. This is the series of interlocking concepts and practices that structures our approach to the project as a dynamic whole, and organizes the introduction to this volume as it pieces together section by section. The contemporary social purchase of documentary practices motivates us to engage with testimony as, all at once: the most intimate manifestation of the survivor-witness relationship and the product of intercalated institutions and practices; profoundly human and incontrovertibly cyborgian; a performative act continually in the making; and, at the level of methodology, both a circumscribed object of documentary studies and the gold standard for global human rights initiatives.

This volume aims to study, therefore, what we think of as *moving testimonies*: the faces and voices that emanate from close or distant locations; the sounds and images that animate our ubiquitous screens; the archives we establish and the histories we resuscitate. These are the new assemblages that compel us to bear witness, move us to anger or tears, and possibly mobilize us to action for social justice.

I. talking heads

Imagine a length of film or video footage—or a ration of bytes on a hard drive—onto which a certain scene has been recorded: a seated individual speaks with conviction, eyes directed to an off-camera listener (stationed slightly to the left and below the lens) whose quality of attention is nevertheless palpable in the intensity of the speaker's gaze. The account of abuses survived and atrocities witnessed flows more or less without halting and in chronological order. The media object that houses this testimony may be pulled from the shelf or selected from the digital bank where it is stored, and played for an audience of one or more. Video is "a powerful, accessible and affordable medium that ... will become more and more vital as a form of witnessing current events and therefore of future historical evidence," writes Roxana Waterson.[13] Or, as the group WITNESS explains, the strength of human rights defenders is enhanced when "the power of visual images and the reach of emerging communications technologies" are united "to transform personal stories of abuse into powerful tools for justice."[14] Indeed, as we have indicated above and will continue to discuss below, the testimonial act has become "a crucial mode of our relation to events of our times," a mode increasingly germane to the construction of global civil society.[15]

However, this imagined triangular *mise-en-scène* of speaker, listener, and camera, with its distributive and motivational qualities in the public theater, is highly idealized. Would that we lived in a world where the act of speaking truth to power were purely achieved and politically transformative.[16] In our more complex (and perhaps, after all, more deeply satisfying) reality, testimony is a precious, horrifying, faceted, institutionally related, liminal force that, through its address to the other and its temporal multiplicity in reflecting on past actions for present and future purposes, constitutes the human symbolic—though not necessarily the human listener—as politically and historically attuned. There is a quality of abjection in testimonies of suffering (where they exist at all) in that paradoxically, uncannily, and necessarily they raise "what human life and culture must exclude in order to sustain themselves."[17]

Testimony is rare. Even though this volume is spurred by the proliferation of audiovisual testimonial projects, including those (such as the USC [University of Southern California] Shoah Foundation Institute for Visual History and Education) that have cultivated tens of thousands of testimonies and those (such as the videotaping of South Africa's Truth and Reconciliation Commission) that have been instrumental to state policies and even state formation, we wish nevertheless to recognize situations where ongoing human rights abuses include the suppression of testimony. For example, restrictions on Chinese media, including the Internet, limit mention of the unarmed civilians killed by the People's Liberation Army in Tiananmen Square on June 4, 1989 to the officially sanctioned characterization of these protestors as "counter-revolutionaries."[18] To this day, researchers, relatives, and survivors struggle even to count and name the dead, let alone engage in public mourning and remembrance.[19] The filmed testimonials by exiled Chinese dissident leaders in Michael Apted's 1994 documentary *Moving the Mountain* contribute greatly to the film's discursive power. To take another example, because Yong Kim is the only prisoner known to have escaped from North Korea's labor camp #14, his testimony to the Human Rights Committee of the US Congress in April 2003 and in the book *The Long Road Home* is both unique as such and representative of those who remain incarcerated. In response to Janet Walker's query as to whether he had ever observed fellow inmates writing down their experiences, Kim mimed the neck of a jar with one hand while gesturing with the other as if to stash a slip of paper. Yes, there are buried written testimonies; but they may never be retrieved, he stated, let alone the prisoners freed to express their testimonies in audiovisual form.[20]

Where testimony does occur, the presence of a given story sharer—a survivor of Hitler's Holocaust, for example—highlights the absence of others who are not, or are no longer, present.[21] Just as the poet Paul Celan has emphasized the solitude of (literary) witnessing, "no one bears witness for the witness," it is simultaneously the case, continues Shoshana Felman, that the "*appointment* to bear witness is, paradoxically enough, an appointment to transgress the confines of that isolated stance, to speak *for* others [whose testimonies we may lack] *to* others."[22]

Moreover, the presence of a story sharer may attest, again paradoxically, to "the impossibility of telling,"[23] or to the unavoidable incompletion of testimony itself. Shoshana Felman and Dori Laub's magisterial *Testimony: Crises of Witnessing in Literature, Psychoanalysis, and History* has been for us and many others the germinal work on testimony. We depend on these authors' articulation of the (literary, psychoanalytic, and historical) "*practice of the testimonial*" as a form of retrospective public witnessing of shattering events of a history that is "essentially *not over*" and is in some sense brought into being by the (itself interminable) process of testimonial witnessing.[24] As a concept drawn from its "traditional, routine use in the legal context," testimony is called for, Felman reminds us, "when the facts upon which justice must pronounce its verdict are not clear, when historical accuracy is in doubt and when both the truth and its supporting materials are called into question."[25] Its presence, therefore, signals not the attainment of knowable truths about the past, but rather a "crisis of truth" or an "accident" of witnessing that nevertheless is profoundly important to the reintegration, working through, or even the liberation of psychic and social life (17–25). These are the insights of psychoanalytically informed studies of the written form of testimony that we, as film and media studies scholars, wish to hold onto and not ignore. While we heartily agree that the medium specificity of video testimony relative to its literary counterpart is deeply significant—for example, Noah Shenker points out that the gestural reenactment in a woman's description of a hanging she witnessed cannot be rendered in written form[26]—still we would attribute the perceived rawness of videotaped testimony to *an impression* it conveys rather than an inherent quality of the video testimonial mode. As with a literary work, the audiovisual representation of a person, animal, object, or geographical setting is ontologically distinct from the creature or thing itself; video testimony visits but does not inhabit the traumatic past anymore than it does "the real."

Audiovisual testimony, like documentary film, does, however, participate in what Bill Nichols has termed "the discourses of sobriety," "systems" such as "science, economics, politics, foreign policy, education, religion, welfare" that "regard their relation to the real as direct, immediate, transparent."[27] But the apparently constative mode also shares the multidimensionality of "representing reality" (Nichols' apt title) that this introduction introduces and the chapters develop. Audiovisual testimonial utterances are always already mediated at the level of the speaking subject whose personal narrative is a product of selection, ordering, interpretation, partisanship, prohibition, character, reflection, and the vicissitudes of memory; and at the level of the media text. As James Young has insisted, "a survivor's memories are necessarily unified and organized [at least] twice-over in video testimony: once in the speaker's narrative and again in the narrative movement created in the medium itself."[28]

We are interested not only in the ingredients but also in the (Lévi-Straussean) cooking process of video and cinematographic testimony. In this respect we concur with Frances Guerin and Roger Hallas, who reject both the mimetic presumption that a moving or still photographic image is an authentic representation of the world it depicts and that images therefore speak for themselves, *and* the iconoclastic notion that all images are false and their claims to truth and value must be shattered.[29] As Guerin and Hallas indicate, citing the work of Bill Nichols and Michael Renov, documentary studies has long ago made the conceptually productive shift "from a narrow focus on questions of truth and referentiality in documentary film to a theoretical and historical concern with its complex discursive construction."[30] Guerin and Hallas call on documentary studies to recognize, as they so eloquently put it, "the specific ways that the material image enables particular forms of agency in relation to historical traumas across the globe."[31] Discussing the "collective symbolic forms" of narrating traumatic experience, Veena Das and Arthur Kleinman, in a Levinasian vein, articulate a philosophically complex form of subjectivity: "the appearance of the face through which communities torn asunder by violence begin to accord mutual recognition to each other."[32]

As scholars steeped in documentary studies and engaged with audiovisual testimony, we are invested in the images, voices, faces, and also the sounds, archives, times, and places. In nominating retrospective "talking head" documentaries and other assembled interviews as our main focus, we emphasize the audiovisual testimonial scene as one of the most common and geopolitically significant—but as-yet-under-researched—venues for the attestation, reception, and mitigation of social suffering. Thus we adapt with all due criticality cinema studies' psychoanalytically informed "apparatus theory" so as to conceive of testimony as a kind of ideological, institutional technology—a "testimonial apparatus"—that produces the details and emotion of suffering in and through the constitution of the spectator subject.

The "talking head" is an effect of this particular apparatus, at the basic level, with the head, according to convention, selected for framing and inclusion in an ordered sequence or hypertextual archive. In fact, the "talking head" (into which anatomical designation users generally throw a supporting neck and shoulders) only *seems* bodiless because the torso, hips, legs, and feet have been framed *out* by the film's compositional imperative. And the head *only seems* to be alone.

The interlocutor is also there, just beyond the frame; beside, below, or behind the camera, which latter device, like the projector, is invisibly necessary and necessarily invisible. And the meaning-making function of this physically present listener as actant and proxy for future media spectators is both significant in and of itself and key to a comparison with: 1) literary narration as *testimonio* (where, convention would have it, the writer is alone in a room although s/he will likely invoke "an absent polyphony of other voices, other possible lives and experiences");[33] 2) audiovisual or written autobiography in a confessional mode (again, the conceit is that the narrator stands alone); and 3) audiovisual or written oral history (where the balance of rhetorical power shifts to the social scientist recorder who, as a kind of midwife[34] of the audiovisual testimonial interlocutor, is more forceful than the latter in affixing his own stamp on the testimony).[35]

Moreover, as Chon Noriega has so succinctly stated, "the 'talking head' must always belong—at some level—to a body politic."[36] Where political urgency has motivated the practice of spoken and literary *testimonio*[37] in Latin America and Latin American studies, so too "*cine-testimonio*," in Michael Chanan's apt term, has arisen in contexts of struggle by marginalized and terrorized peoples.[38] These movements are part of the history and context for testimonial efforts on behalf of anti-colonial, feminist, and other egalitarian, reparative, and counterhistorical efforts around the world. The *testimonio* is a "counterdocument," Noriega writes, "intimately tied to the need to legitimize the postrevolutionary nation or struggles against state terror."[39] Drawing on literary *testimonio* studies also helps qualify our appropriation of an apparatus theory widely criticized for its monolithic notions of the powerless "interpellated subject" of Althusserian Marxism and the "inscribed spectator" of screen studies.[40] While not wishing to underestimate the subjugation of social subjects to state terror or ethnic fundamentalisms, we assert our belief in individual and collective agency as a motive force of social justice. The "testimonial apparatus" of this volume is ideologically conjunctural but not deterministic, technological but not mechanistic, structured but not unvaried.

But where do questions of truth in testimony fit into this interdisciplinary topography? Various well-publicized debates about the veracity of autobiographical testimony pertain. For example, factual inaccuracies in *I, Rigoberta Menchú*,[41] the celebrated book transcribed from taped interviews with indigenous political activist and Nobel Peace Prize winner Menchú (edited by anthropologist Elizabeth Burgos-Debray), have been analyzed by Ana Douglass, who writes that Menchú's "gesture to see her story as emblematic of the story of all indigenous peoples of Guatemala opens up a critical space in which the reader can then come into some proximity to 'strangeness,' optimistically into some proximity of 'truths' about an intolerably inhumane situation."[42] (But Douglass also makes it a point to avoid conflating the category of literary testimony with the form of testimony given in a court proceeding [73].)

Truth may also be "proximate" in the cases of misremembering. As Dori Laub has famously described, "knowledge in the testimony is ... not simply a factual given that is reproduced and replicated by the testifier, but a genuine advent, an event in its own right." Analyzing the case of a woman's verbal testimony as an eyewitness to the Auschwitz uprising in which inmates attacked the crematoria with explosives, testimony that was later recognized by historians to be exaggerated since only one chimney, rather than the three she recalled, was actually blown up, Laub argued that historians have much to gain from attending to the "subtle dialectic between what the survivor did not know and what she knew." Reading back and forth among testimony and other forms of historical evidence, an analyst may come to understand "not merely [the testifier's] subjective truth, but the very historicity of the event, in an entirely new dimension."[43] In fact, the eminent Holocaust historian Christopher Browning too has raised the question of how conflicting or even clearly mistaken testimonies might be used "to construct a history that otherwise, for lack of evidence, would not exist."[44] And then, reading back and forth among perpetrator, investigator, and survivor testimonies, in written form and on videotape, he has proceeded to do just that in his 2003 book *Collected Memories: Holocaust History and Postwar Testimony*.[45]

All of this is to say that the "testimonial apparatus" is performative with regard to the truths and memories of testifying and witnessing. Yes, certainly, there is a "receding horizon"[46] of truth that the testimonial apparatus, like the documentary film, fixes in its sights while grounded by its force. But audiovisual testimony—inevitably staged in that it wouldn't exist at all if not for the midwifery of the testimonial apparatus—is also at pains to enact, to bring into being, to perform, a world of hurt.[47]

With the imaginative and material constitution of the testimonial scene as a backdrop, we can now proceed to enumerate in a descriptive vein (not purporting to summarize the theses of the chapters) some of the varieties of audiovisual testimony our contributors explore. What Barbara Martineau has taught us about "synchronized sound close-ups, or 'talking heads,'" applies in spades to the testimonial scene: it "can be used in different ways to achieve very different results."[48]

It is the individual videotaped testimonies that comprise the foundational, enormous, partially digitized, and globally dispersed archives of suffering known in aggregate as "Holocaust testimony" that are most apt to be (mis)taken for the ideal type. Framing is in close or medium shot, the interviewer—usually a professional psychologist or layperson with sensitivity training—is off-screen, and the interviewee's glance is at an oblique angle just past the camera lens. And yet, what Noah Shenker makes clear from the start and throughout his chapter—and what has motivated us to place this chapter at the start of our volume—is the enormous value of understanding how the individual testimonial scene as a "*process* of witnessing" is mediated by the interrelationship among "individual practice," "institutional practices," and the architecture of testimony. The latter, as Shenker demonstrates through the case of the United States Holocaust

Memorial Museum (USHMM), includes the architectural space of the museum itself.

The four chapters that follow Shenker's inaugural analysis of a landmark video archive take up the case of filmed (or videotaped) testimony as a foundational trope of the social issues documentary film. The groupings of documentaries identified by Bishnupriya Ghosh, Janet Walker, Bjørn Sørenssen, and Hye Jean Chung all feature sympathetic advocates for change in discriminatory public consciousness and unjust policies and actions: for the modification of massive dam-building projects that are displacing hundreds of thousands of people along the Narmada River in western India (Ghosh); for racial and environmental justice in post-Katrina New Orleans (Walker); for an end to the legal and cultural discrimination against Norwegian women and children whose wartime connections with the German soldiers of the Nazi occupation turned them into social pariahs for four decades to follow (Sørenssen); for an unqualified official apology from the Japanese government for the military involvement in the sexual enslavement of Korean women (Chung).

But *how* do these films employ testimony to channel their respective "demand[s]" (Ghosh) in keeping with, in spite of, or to recuperate the iconicity of testimony? Bishnupriya Ghosh and Janet Walker explicitly study the documentary creation of what the latter calls "situated testimony": reflective interviews delivered *in situ* from the very place where catastrophic events occurred and, in some cases, while the situation continues to unfold. Ghosh expressively analyzes how testimonies from heterogeneous constituencies, such as indigenous activists, resettled camp-dwellers, and subsistence farmers pushed upstream to less fertile ground, are combined with moving camera shots of people living on the banks of the river to create what she calls an "immersive cinema." Chest deep in water, with hands tied in Gandhian protest, or on high ground in front of the Sardar Sarovar Dam, people articulate their sense of loss and activist commitment as would-be agents of change. Walker writes of testimonies delivered by returning evacuees from the rubble maw of New Orleans' Lower Ninth Ward.

Testimony *in situ* is also featured in the two documentaries discussed by Deirdre Boyle and the documentary cycle discussed by José Rabasa. But now the content of the attestations harks decades back to events that have in a literal sense come to a close, while living on in people's psychic and bodily memories and, in these particular cases, in continuing initiatives and rituals in the present. To create *S21: The Khmer Rouge Killing Machine*, filmmaker Rithy Panh (himself a survivor of Cambodia's Pol Pot regime) returned to Tuol Sleng prison (code named S21, where an estimated 17,000 men, women, and children were killed between the years 1975 and 1979), taking along former guards, interrogators, a clerk-typist, a photographer, a "doctor," and two of the seven surviving prisoners. There, Khieu Ches, a guard from the age of 12 or 13, not only reenacted but actually "re-live[d]," argues Boyle, his past actions and trained behaviors. Unlike other critics who are uncomfortable with the film's departure from the verbal testimonial mode, as well its/our exposure to perpetrators and perpetrator testimony, Boyle identifies in the films she analyzes an embodied form of testimony. "By reviving memory of this traumatic past," she states, "[Panh] makes the past present to engage public consciousness about the evil done in the name of the state." José Rabasa also has his own reasons, in dialogue with films about the Acteal massacre in Chiapas, for enlarging what might qualify as testimony beyond survivor, witness, and expert reportage of past events. Because revisionists, including former president Ernesto Zedillo Ponce de León, also testify, it behooves us, Rabasa argues, to develop a "poetics of testimony" capable of reconceiving the "politics of truth."

Reading back and forth among Rabasa's, Boyle's, and Chung's chapters in the context of the volume as a whole, our intuition that rhetorical strategies in documentary testimony are grounded in regionally specific practices is confirmed. But the significant formal differences one may therefore expect to find among geographically disparate sites of testimony often pale next to their affinities as grassroots practices against the grain of official or would-be official institutions and historiographies. While the United States Holocaust Memorial Museum archivists seek—through the means Noah Shenker so insightfully analyzes—to establish their large assemblage of sober direct address testimonies as the royal road to historical truth, independent filmmakers throughout the world are engaging in alternative testimonial practices that are expanding the modalities of testimony and its capacity to incorporate a diversity of voices and views.[49] Deirdre Boyle has observed that "documentary as embodied memory" (or vice versa) "seems more acceptable to Asian documentary makers than to most Western audiences." And indeed, we are struck by the applicability of her discussion to Hye Jean Chung's finding that Byun Young-joo's "*Murmuring* trilogy" brings testimony into existence through the sensate choreography of filmmaker, camera, and subject. In this latter case, filmmaker Byun herself is even audible and at times visible, "sharing the ... space within the frame," and attempting, like Panh, actively, physically to form an impression and influence policy through the *mise-en-scène* of documentary practice. But if we consider as well José Rabasa's explication of reenactment and commemorative practices in the documentaries of the Chiapas massacre, it would appear that broadly cross-regional and transnational *continuities* in testimonial modalities may well exist, especially where previously suppressed views or countercultural patterns are being cultivated by testimonial works against the dominant values of the relevant state formation.

The next two chapters in the volume, by Catherine Cole and Mick Broderick, are concerned with the testimonial function of audiovisually documented public proceedings including hearings, commissions of inquiry, and legal trials. When they are available (Cole reminds us that public availability is not something we may take for granted) as "raw material" or edited works (or both, as in the case of the Eichmann trial of 1961),[50] these institutionally generated artifacts constitute a modality of "documentary testimony" helpful for the elasticization of the rubric. Instead of two people sequestered in a room, we encounter here panels of official auditors and galleries of spectators, often with personal involvement in the events under testimony by the speaker—who may him/herself be alleged to have engaged in criminal and/or sociopathic acts. The camera may be set off a ways, forced to zoom in for closer shots, observed or unobserved, and, as the case may be, party or not to the ricocheting play of looks.

A scholar of theater and performance concentrating on contemporaneous media coverage of South Africa's Truth and Reconciliation process, Cole reveals how "[t]he mediated and theatrical dimensions," of both hearings and broadcasts, "allowed for multiple renderings and interpretations of the truths, lies, and everything in between which spilled forth." Comparing footage of the Commission hearings themselves with the selective use of this footage in the 87-episode *TRC Special Report* by the South African Broadcasting Corporation, she finds salient differences in the physical and filmic *mise-en-scène* of staging, camera placement, and shot selection, differences that greatly affect the implication of audiences—that is, the public—in this historical state occasion.[51]

Mick Broderick's chapter examines the culturally specific and internationally significant process of generating and archiving orchestrated public testimony about the Rwandan genocide. Yves Kamuronsi, a digital producer and online archivist at the Kigali Memorial Centre, and independent filmmaker Gilbert Ndahayo both work with audiovisual records from community "gacaca," or local truth and reconciliation tribunals where tormented individuals and perpetrators meet face to face. "It is harrowing to watch," attests Broderick, when Ndahayo, as director of and gacaca participant in *Behind this Convent*, "confronts the murderers of his parents and sister in this public space." Keenly aware of the tensions between "a 'memory industry' dominated by characteristically Western official practices" and the local digital initiatives he describes—the makers of which are themselves cognizant of the wider import of their efforts—Broderick analyzes how a "new generation of Rwandans" is attempting to use innovative testimonial practices to achieve lasting impact.

The volume concludes with a chapter on a newly emerging form of witnessing, one that, in Lisa Parks' astute analysis, calls into question the very definition and function of media testimony. The Google Earth "Global Awareness" layer, including its central component "Crisis in Darfur" developed in partnership with the United States Holocaust Memorial Museum, is a geo-referenced humanitarian interface that invites users to "fly" to troubled areas of the globe that are represented on the site through satellite images, photographs, data frames, and graphics. But what happens to testimony and its attendant questions, Parks queries, when a set of non-anthropomorphic representations, technologies, networks, and practices—commercially driven and purporting to be a transparent window on the world—not only figures in (as always) but in this case actually marginalizes and in some respects even replaces diverse knowledge sources and personal accounts? What happens to the testimonial scene, we may ask, when its surveillance is expanded from a camera in a room to a camera mounted on a satellite in geostationary orbit 36,000 kilometers from earth? With this volume, cognizant of the balancing act it entails, we celebrate both the humanity inherent in the concept of the talking head and the criticality inherent in the concept of the testimonial apparatus.

II. bodies of evidence

The testimonial impulse is nurtured by and, in turn, feeds into proliferating archives of suffering. Many of these contemporary archives congeal around audiovisual testimonies. The contributions to this volume explore a fair range: the Kigali Memorial Centre in Rwanda ("12,700 audio cassette tapes, 3,300 DVCAM tapes, 3,300 VHS tapes and 7,700 DCs");[52] South Africa's Truth and Reconciliation Commission (thousands of testimonies videotaped and broadcast via television and radio);[53] and the US Holocaust Memorial Museum's holdings. But there are many others, some in novel sites and formats, which continue to expand in scope, size, and influence. For instance, in Japan, "Voice of Hibakusha" eyewitness accounts of the bombing of Hiroshima were filmed for the program *Hiroshima Witness* produced by the Hiroshima Peace Cultural Center and NHK, the public broadcasting company of Japan. In the 1990s the individual accounts were translated into English and digitized by college students for a web-based archive.[54] In conjunction with his documentary film *Sicko* (US, 2007), Michael Moore has established a website and portal entitled "SICKO: What Can I Do" as an organizing tool for the advocacy of healthcare reform in the United States.[55] In a direct address video posted to the site, Moore invites people to videotape their own "healthcare horror stories" and post them to the companion YouTube site "SICKO: Share Your Healthcare Horror Stories." The 98 videos posted at the time of writing, many of which are testimonial in style and all but one of which have garnered hundreds or thousands of hits, constitute a substantial, issue-driven video testimonial archive of an interactive, innovative nature.[56]

Clearly, testimonial holdings have emerged as a key and favored institution for coping with collective suffering across disparate geographical locations. What might these bodies of evidence teach us about the nature of the contemporary archive? What networked tendencies, ideologies, and regimes contribute to the translocal authority of these institutions? While the first question is the focus of this section, the second query is explored in the next.

Generally speaking, an archive is no mere aggregation of documents: it is driven by its internal logics of selection, classification and organization, orchestrated to produce a single and cogent corpus. That is to say, a set of regulatory concerns, aimed at achieving a measure of cognitive, ideological, and affective commensurability, comes into play in the creation of every collection. In this volume, our primary interest is in archives that are constituted through the very production of the audiovisual documents that the archive appears merely to assemble. In a fundamental sense, it is the act of archiving that designates the testimonies as such. Perhaps the sheer scale of social traumas and the resource needs of testimonial holdings demand that the creation of such documents be closely aligned with some archival formation: for instance, the recordings of eyewitness accounts for the *Hiroshima Witness* program broadcast by the NHK, or the 2,000 victim statements recorded at TRC hearings for public broadcasting in South Africa. So far as a testimony is being solicited for a particular collection (Shenker's account of the audiovisual depositions housed in the Holocaust Museum of Washington DC, whose definitive scope is articulated in its mission statement), or feeding into an emergent archive (Ghosh's analysis of an ecologic in the growing mass of activist documentaries featuring "drowned out" subalterns of the Narmada valley), considerations of integration with the entire collection will inform individual acts of witnessing on camera.

How does the archive present itself to its public as an institution with a certain social authority? Derrida proposes a reflexive logic that governs the institutionalization of a body of evidence, its consolidation into an *archive*. As he points out, the archive rests on two distinct but reciprocally enforcing principles: an ontological principle, invoking the primary or originary status of assembled documents (*commencement*), and a nomological principle, harnessing order and authenticity (*commandment*).[57] The archive is the place where we return to trace the beginning of things; it is also the site where authority inheres, which confers legitimacy. The mutuality of the two principles—the manner in which each fortifies the other—indexes the performativity of the archive as a social institution. In short, the archive is the name of a social performance that is both its subject and object: in that sense, it *nominates itself*.

The location and organization of the archive as a physical institution add to its social aura. The architectonics of the archive comprise not only a cognitive grid and a hermeneutic framework, entailing the classification of artifacts and interpretive schemata, but also a set of material features: the concrete form of its holdings, its actual spatial layout, and its technological and infrastructural support. With respect to audiovisual documents, considerations of format (16 mm film or super 8? analog or digital video?), source and copyright (newsreel or home movies? classified or public domain footage? industrial or non-profit?), editing and transfer parameters (linear or non-linear editing? commensurate formats, or requiring complicated transfer software?) become crucial to the questions of storage, access, and future use.

The chapters in this volume examine archives whose materiality and organization cover quite a range. The contributors' fieldwork and research objects present a similar diversity: Boyle, Chung, and Ghosh consider films; Broderick, Cole, and Walker visit actual sites of suffering; Shenker reads behind-the-scene memos to supplement his exploration of the USHMM; Sørenssen attends to radio; Cole examines television current affairs programming; Parks considers websites and satellite images; Broderick looks at grisly skull displays (his field trip and the resultant film provides the image on the volume's cover). This variety complicates the stereotype of the archive—the dank and dusty rooms, the ill-lit aisles and freezing vaults. With digitalization, the archive increasingly exists on microchips; networks turn topological assumptions on their head, making access potentially instantaneous. In short, the audiovisual archive is becoming more plastic, porous, and portable. Nevertheless, tangible constraints to technological development, access, and use remain. Switching to new formats requires not only the significant overhaul of equipment, but also the intensive retraining of personnel. Questions about the lifespan and reliability of digital formats persist, and are exacerbated by the drive toward cheap, soon-to-be-obsolete modes of data storage at the cost of quality and stability. It is not some arcane conservatism that induces many audiovisual archivists to prefer film to digital formats. Furthermore, archival resources continue to be sadly limited, funding being especially scarce in societies of the Global South.

The question of display is central to the architectonics of both the archive and the museum. Developments in museological practices in the past two decades have profoundly transformed the modalities of exhibition; emerging media forms compound these shifts by restructuring propinquity and immersion. Intermedial formats and displays now interact with the structure and space of the museum to generate novel contexts of exhibition. These transformations have implications for the public life of archives. Innovative spatial configurations and multiple scalar levels shape the ways in which we approach and experience archival holdings. Shenker, for instance, relates the visitors' perambulatory experience of the archive/museum to the sensory apprehension of its overall layout and its multimedia displays as they walk/work through it. He examines the specific ways in which testimonial recordings are incorporated into the USHMM in relation to its other exhibits. Broderick's chapter maps out an emerging archive, which began as a terrifying exhibition of skeletons from the Rwanda killings, was extended to the Internet as a photographic site, and is now augmented by the actual massacre sites (e.g., a church) being turned into nodes of commemoration. These contributions draw attention to the embodied learning facilitated by the topological and material dimensions of the archive.

The pedagogical intent is only one of many intersecting, and at times conflicting, objectives behind testimonial archives. Cole reminds us that it would be a mistake to reduce any such collection "simply to the level of utility": TRC public hearings, for instance, "were a complex 'rainbow' genre that mixed ritual, law, media event, religious ceremony, confessional, theater, therapy, storytelling, and politics." Let us explore some of these functions in more detail.

Survivors and witnesses provide testimonies to record their experiences, to generate empathy in their audiences, and to produce secondary witnessing on the part of other social groups. These recordings bring forth uncharted or overlooked dimensions of suffering, and help elicit recognition from broader publics. As Shenker shows, while the USHMM—"America's national institution for the documentation, study, and interpretation of Holocaust history"[58]—is deeply committed to historical education, it is also at pains to produce an "affective community." The very act of bearing witness in front of a camera helps politicize consciousness, stirring members of affected communities toward acts of resistance. Their testimonies mobilize collateral groups, producing empathic—and possibly activist—coalitions from below. As Ghosh demonstrates, the testimonies of tribals displaced by the construction of dams serve as charged evidentiary nodes around which peasants, workers, NGOs, and intellectuals come together to resist an impassive state wedded to an instrumentalist and opportunistic paradigm of development. As in Rabasa's chapter, testimony in this instance emerges as a conduit to radical participatory politics, instigating lateral networks of activism. Sørenssen records the transformation of public attitudes toward the Lebensborn women and children after the broadcast of radio and television documentaries about a few of them. Walker discusses Spike Lee's orchestration of standard and in-situ testimonies, which produces a trenchant critique of the ruling bloc's criminal neglect of disadvantaged communities of New Orleans, raising public awareness about policies that appear to rest on unstated presumptions about the relative disposability of entire groups.

As we noted in the previous section, providing testimonies allows survivors to narrativize their traumas, begin to find meaning in incomprehensible experiences, and realize a modicum of voice, perhaps even an attenuated sense of agency. This is why testimonies are intimately linked in the popular imagination to the possibility of healing. Two related impulses propel testimonials: the need to wrest a form of immortality, and the need to record one's experiences for posterity. In a sense, both are transgenerational imperatives: not only does the speaking subject hope to subvert the inevitability of her/his passing, but s/he also seeks to leave for succeeding generations a sense of history. Teleporting oneself from the other side of the grave, as it were, the witness strives for some manner of historical continuity. When the testimony is played back after the death of the witness, this spectral trace bridges various times. What begins as an eschatological impulse, as a reckoning of one's mortal life, ends up proffering an unbounded opening onto the future.

Testimonies do not aspire only to psychic and existential recompense: various injured communities, once exploited and marginalized (indigenous populations, descendants of slaves, minority groups), have based their claims to material reparations on archives of oral, written, and, now, audiovisual testimony. The testimonial situation enables feuding communities to confront each other in a civil manner and force perpetrators to encounter their own brutalities; it presents an opportunity to move beyond murderous conflicts and work toward social reconciliation. The significance of such a shift for the future of community life cannot be underestimated in societies torn asunder by rancor and violence. The Truth and Reconciliation Commission of South Africa remains by far the most noteworthy attempt at achieving such settlements. The TRC's ambitions are not limited to collective healing: it purports to nothing short of state formation in the post-apartheid era.

Testimonies recorded today give rise to an archive that will constitute a body of evidence in the future; in that respect, witnessing proceeds from what Shoshana Felman has called the "juridical unconscious."[59] Indeed, testimonies have a long history of performing quasi-legal functions in various war tribunals and judicial courts adjudicating crimes against humanity, from the Eichmann trials of the early 1960s to the World Court hearings on Central European pogroms in the past decade.[60] The significance of these trials for backstage diplomacy and international relations, while somewhat opaque, is undeniable. Contemporary media assemblages only intensify their impact, as seen with the trial of Saddam Hussein, widely covered by international media, and the subsequent Internet broadcast of the unsanctioned cellphone recording of his execution. Was this simply an opportunistic act feeding into a global voyeurism, or did it also mark a populist attempt at witnessing history? In the context of emergent telecommunication networks, transnational fora, and a post-state global system, such peripatetic and viral archives will play an increasingly crucial role in shaping public opinion, forging political alignments, and recalibrating ethical standards.

There is no guarantee that the complex attempts to achieve reconciliation and justice will work according to plan, or produce the intended effects: given the volatility of populations strained by violence and agony, the odds stack up against such initiatives. Documented public responses to well-intentioned media engagements with social conflicts underscore the endemic uncertainties of traumatized polities.[61] The persistent and extensive popular support for Central European leaders pronounced war criminals by international tribunals (e.g., Radovan Karadžić, who has been dubbed the "Butcher of Bosnia" for his alleged role in atrocities such as the 1995 Srebrenica massacre, and the late Slobodan Milošević, whose policies in Kosovo made the term "ethnic cleansing" a part of common parlance), indexes deeply engrained regional sentiments that fly in the face of global opinion.[62] More significantly, attempts at public resolution have contradictions built into them. For some perpetrators, the confessional mode of TRC hearings offers a royal road to impunity, shielding them from prosecution and denying survivors what they might consider proper justice. Official interventions, notwithstanding their aura of rationality and fairness, routinely lead to a gendered silence. Urvashi Butalia documents the erasure of agency on the part of women kidnapped during the 1947 Partition of South Asia, when the governments of India and Pakistan decided, without consulting these women, to return them to their families. Many of these "sullied" women became victims of honor killings at the hands of their family members; others were consigned to a kind of social death, spending the rest of their lives in shelters.[63] Alexis Dudden has shown that the Japanese government's gesture of apology to South Korea for the former's use of Korean "comfort women" during World War II effectively deprives these women of a voice.[64] Chung's contribution to this volume explores the increasingly collaborative labor to wrest a kind of public understanding for these women that official diplomatic maneuvers could never achieve.

There is a common, ingrained assumption that testimonies invariably contribute to social good and democratization, helping to make the world a better place. In practice, testimonies frequently get folded into archival formations with established command structures and entrenched social interests; at other points, they become the basis for emerging sites of power. And as Rabasa reminds us, perpetrators also testify and shape social truths. More importantly, why an individual testifies may have very little to do with how or why her testimony gets included—and in what manner—in an archive. The intricacies of the dyadic relation between individual testimonies and the overall archive, and their multifarious impacts in the public sphere, are the focus of several contributions. Cole comments on the continuing difficulties of not only accessing but also taking cognizance of the entire TRC archives; Parks interrogates Google Earth's use of a variety of assembled images to shape global opinion on Darfur and to promote intervention in the name of humanitarianism. What is insidious about archives in general is that their knowledge function, with its aura of authenticity, immediacy, and spontaneity, masks their cognate social role as institutions of power.

Nevertheless, testimonial archives hold great promise for participatory politics and the promotion of social justice. The institutional performativity of the archive (its self-nomination as a reserve of collective wisdom) also opens up the possibility for all kinds of contradictions and collaborations. The chapters here index many such moments: in Chung's chapter, the ageing "comfort woman" who takes over some of the interviewing in the testimonial trilogy; the reunion on camera of a man from the GDR with his Norwegian half-sisters, analyzed by Sørenssen; Broderick's account of Gilbert Ndahayo's realization while watching his footage in the editing room that the woman crying at the gacaca court while listening to graphic descriptions of the slaughter and incineration of nearly two hundred villagers is the daughter of one of the perpetrators rather than a relative of a survivor. Such unwitting and unanticipated potentialities constantly challenge the regulatory grasp of the testimonial apparatus; due to the stretched temporalities of testimonies, all such documents remain particularly amenable to interpretation and appropriation.

Keeping in mind the significance of such critical hermeneutical gestures in coping with archives of suffering, we must also recognize the limits of their utopian promises. While more affordable and fungible technologies have, undoubtedly, produced a democratization of the capacity to archive, we take note of the persistent global disjunctures and inequities (in culture, climate, resource, institutional networking) that impose very real constraints on archives in diverse locales. In short, the world of testimonial holdings is anything but "flat."[65] It remains essential to analyze how these assemblages not only help integrate stupefying experiences into collective knowledge, but also draw on—even as they inflect—global practices, institutions, and values. In the final section, we examine testimony's role in the instantiation of planetary civil society at a time when, as Mark Philip Bradley and Patrice Petro point out, "the sovereignty of the nation" is less determinate than the changing boundaries "among the rights of individuals, states, and the international community."[66]

III. ethical communities

As local testimonial archives are assembled into global networks, two countervailing processes unfold. On the one hand, archives adopt broader languages and frameworks to address translocal publics, undergoing a certain standardization through institutional forms of translation. On the other hand, these universal concerns—routine or inordinate violence, social justice, human rights—keep getting recalibrated in their encounter with local contexts. This mutuality points to the constant negotiations entailed in the global extension of a testimonial apparatus. What are the terms on which various communities will relate to each other and to the evolving universal norms? How do these global publics conceive of fundamental categories such as the human, or community? What are the ramifications of turning a singular experience such as the Holocaust into a test case for these queries? What happens when various injured populations recast their sufferings as "our Holocausts"? What coalitions and power blocs might these networks of empathy and affiliation congeal into? At stake is the production of a global civil society with its attendant values, institutions, and politics.

In theory, global civil society sounds like an attractive ideal, especially in the context of a world beset with seemingly obdurate conflicts: perhaps that is why the concept has achieved the broad support of scholars across the political spectrum.[67] However, the ideal comes with its own problems, not the least of which is the challenge of making it a reality. What kind of global institutions are required to facilitate its operation? How to devise universally acceptable principles and standards that might form its basis? Are such benchmarks possible at all? Who gets to adjudicate and settle disputes that arise from incommensurable outlooks and values? It is in the context of this indeterminacy that the testimonial form becomes significant, as its power derives more from a pledge of truthfulness and a performance of good faith than from a strict, conclusive evidentiary reliability.[68] But one's pledge of good faith is another's duplicitous intent to dominate. Even as we write this introduction, Radovan Karadžić has refused to enter any plea (either 'guilty' or 'not guilty') in front of the International War Crimes Tribunal, denouncing the tribunal as a western conspiracy to kill him.[69] The UN-sponsored International Criminal Tribunal for Rwanda, meeting in 2008 in Tanzania, raises similar charges from its defendants. Thus the question of a global civil society, with its ancillary testimonial archives, truth commissions, and justice tribunals, remains open-ended and subject to continual ethical evaluation.

That lessons from a local experience of social suffering have the potential to help prevent future atrocities all over the world has become something of a contemporary cliché. But how precisely such learning might be operationalized globally remains a largely unanswered question; indeed, even as this concern animates our volume, its intractability marks a limitation of our comparatist approach. How do people imagine and understand their overlaps and disjunctions with global principles and paradigms? How much of this relationality remains an opportunistic positioning, a mere pretense? What insights are more deeply absorbed, holding the promise of actual transformation?

The political efficacy of a testimonial apparatus is determined in the constant negotiation between universalizing norms and local imperatives: on the one hand, overarching and somewhat rarefied ideals of fairness, equality, and humanity continue to shape collective aspirations; on the other hand, there is the ground-level necessity of getting back to a semblance of normalcy in everyday interactions, for which the implications of translocal standards are not always clear. In her chapter, Boyle points out that local testimonial modalities may or may not translate to a distant audience. While Panh's films have "helped catalyze" in 2007 a UN-sponsored tribunal to investigate the Khmer Rouge's crimes against humanity, she reports, Indonesian filmmaker Garin Nugroho's adaptation of the musical form of the *didong*, with its innate circular structure and charged performative register, has been dismissed by a Ford Foundation spokesperson as producing, at best, "quasi-history." While Walker is critical of the claim that genuine fairness after Katrina may be achieved by invoking a generalized "right of return," she simultaneously appreciates the strong sense of community articulated by displaced residents of New Orleans' Lower Ninth Ward and the need for the allocation of federal resources to the region. The chapters by Ghosh and Broderick highlight the quandary of universal(izing) values and local practices, interrogating the notion that cultural modalities can and should circulate unproblematically. Their analyses bring out somewhat unanticipated nuances: Ghosh identifies the limited benefits that have accrued to local initiatives from global networks when demands have been couched in universalizing terms, and Broderick registers the eagerness of local filmmakers both to create their own commemorative works and to communicate to an international audience.

The globalization of a testimonial apparatus is aided by certain techno-economic developments since the late twentieth century. Rapid progress in telecommunication has had a profound and palpable impact on planetary networks and paradigms of knowledge. What John Tomlinson calls "telemediatization" has contributed to "shifts in our emotional sensibilities" and "the extension of our ethical horizons."[70] We take note of critical interrogations of media's fascination with suffering: the reification of suffering as prime-time spectacle, the desensitization induced by the excessive exposure to morbid imagery, the self-valorizing aspects of projective identification, and the specious nature of remote charity work.[71] Nevertheless, the extensive impact of the televisual coverage of devastations wrought by the South-East Asian Tsunami, Hurricane Katrina, or the earthquake in China, beamed into people's homes with a new immediacy and urgency, certainly cannot be dismissed. In early 2008 mobile phone recordings of official atrocities in Myanmar, posted on the Internet, mustered strong global opinion and led to talk of armed intervention on humanitarian grounds in the UN Security Council. And in July 2009, extensive audiovisual postings by people on the streets of Iran—on YouTube, Tweeter, and Facebook—covering the pro-democratic protests in the wake of an allegedly rigged presidential election culminated in an unprecedented "Global Day of Action on Iran" in cities across the planet. Clearly, contemporary technologies engender a more intense impression of proximity and engagement. This sense of involvement is part of a larger culture of intimacy, whose most patently populist expressions include reality/tabloid television, viewer participation through telephone calls and text messaging, and a ubiquitous confessional mode in the public sphere.

A series of cognate philosophical shifts have contributed to the cultural and political purchase of the testimonial apparatus. The so-called post-structuralist turn—privileging difference and heterogeneity, subjectivity and intimacy, the contingent and the everyday—encapsulates many of these shifts. The transformations in the discipline of history include a new attention accorded to memory;[72] appreciation of the phenomenological dimensions of experience inflects a modernist obsession with facticity.[73] In particular, the notion of "public history," with its expressive blending of fact and fiction, its affective punch, and its broad address, signals a sea change in historiographic standards.[74] The traumatic event, which poses challenges for referentiality, representation and knowledge, and brings embodied aspects of experience to the foreground, has emerged as a pivotal node for these transformations in critical thinking.

These disciplinary initiatives partake in a more general trend—what Charles Taylor has called a "politics of recognition"—through which heretofore marginalized groups come to constitute themselves as political subjects, and to wrest agency within mainstream political processes.[75] Not surprisingly, the empowering function of documentary testimonies and archives in the face of state brutality, negligence, and/or silence is a recurring point throughout this volume. The participation of minority groups in identity politics, or multiculturalism, and the formation of transnational coalitions among the dispossessed, comprise important steps toward the global democratization of politics. But multiculturalism gets all too easily folded into strategies of the hegemonic state: in western liberal democracies such as the US, France, and Australia, multiculturalism becomes more an instrument of managing difference than a means of promoting a radically pluralist society.[76] In the presence of significant, frequently insurmountable differences in resources, attitudes and institutions, the translocal extension of either a multiculturalist system or a liberal testimonial apparatus cannot be taken for granted.

Contemporary neo-liberalism speaks a language that, in many ways, expropriates minority and subaltern discourses, but to very different purposes. Ultimately, the vaunted ideals of freedom and democracy are made subservient to the consolidation of capitalist markets in all parts of the world. When political freedom and market calculations come into conflict, the latter take precedence; choice is reduced primarily to a consumerist preference among commodities. While the neo-liberal emphasis on the globalization of human rights and social justice has facilitated the dissemination of testimonial initiatives, it remains a vexed alignment, for market and humanitarian concerns are not easily reconciled. The non-profit nature of most testimonial collections, as well as their cultural-political significance, shield these initiatives against a strictly pecuniary calculus. Nevertheless, demand and supply—shaped by psychosocial and demographic determinants such as the clout of a community, the number of survivors, a persistent sense of threat—remain important factors. The archives generate not only cultural capital, but also employment for videographers, interviewers, and researchers, not to mention archivists. Large-scale private or corporate efforts—most notably Spielberg's Shoah Foundation and Google Earth's Darfur initiative—raise charges of the privatization and corporate branding of human misery. Thus testimonial assemblages, aimed at commemoration, education, and working towards a better future, carry within them the spectral trace of exchange value. One might even say that there is now a global testimonial industry with its own market specifications.[77]

The geopolitical implications of this confluence of neo-liberalism and a global testimonial imperative are even more noteworthy: the former harnesses the latter to shore up a neo-colonial world order. What guarantees the legitimacy of a planetary testimonial apparatus in a unipolar world? Even the past is not immune to forms of colonization: as Shenker points out, the aspirations of the US Holocaust Memorial Museum in providing ethical leadership, not to mention its geographical location, place it "squarely in the heart of an official American commemorative landscape." Even if we take a more pluralist view of the world, a few powerful states (the G8, the nuclear club) appear to exercise an inordinate amount of influence on the institutions of global governance (notably the WTO, the UN, and the World Court). In this post-Westphalian era, when the sovereignty of most nation-states stands eclipsed by these global bodies, societies of the Global South understandably blanch at any suggestion of a unitary globality—even a global responsibility to alleviate human suffering. If testimonial assemblages foster global civil society by promoting constructive human interaction and collective working through, they also instigate interventionist policies, the operative sentiment being: if we are all part of a global family, how can we remain silent and sedentary witnesses to human suffering? Humanitarian intervention is predicated on a discourse of rights steeped in long-standing prejudice: the link can be traced back to John Stuart Mill's 1859 essay "A Few Words on Non-intervention," in which he basically argued that not all populations were worthy of or ready for the same set of human rights. (For Mill, the principle of international reciprocity could not hold for "barbarians," who stood to benefit from civilized intervention.)[78] Not only are the arrangements achieved through international intercession usually short-term, as a rule they also are discriminatory, serving particular interests and reiterating the transnational authority of the armed arbiters. The trouble spots of our world, from Africa to Central Europe, from the Middle East to South Asia, stand as legacies of past meddling, their histories cautionary tales of externally imposed solutions. Even in the most egregious cases of communal violence—whether in Bosnia, Somalia, or Rwanda—the urgency to take action to save human lives is set in balance against local concerns, including fractious social stratification, resource distribution, and national sovereignty.

Nevertheless, the current trend is toward greater interventionism, as evidenced by the new approach outlined in the "Responsibility to Protect" or R2P Report of 2001, and the adoption of this doctrine by the UN in 2005, mandating armed action on humanitarian grounds (including genocide, war crimes, ethnic cleansing and crimes against humanity, but excluding natural disasters and health crises).[79] The collaboration between Google Earth and the United States Holocaust Memorial Museum (the topic of Parks' chapter, also alluded to by Shenker—thus effectively bookending this volume), touted as a means of raising consciousness, is clearly part of a global civil society initiative to bring a just solution to the Darfur imbroglio. At the heart of such endeavors is a strong testimonial impulse, now pressed into service of a universal community with all its attendant contradictions.

The truck between a globalized testimonial apparatus and hegemonic geopolitical structures comes under critical scrutiny in several chapters of this volume. Analyzing the formal, institutional, and political aspects of testimonial assemblages and exploring the furtive workings of power in them, the contributors collectively underscore the constitutive presence of suffering in contemporary experiences of globality. In that sense, our volume participates in a recent analytical move that comes to regard loss not as a simple waning of possibilities, but as a generative experience: the focus now shifts to the multifaceted fallouts of loss. As David Eng and David Kazanjian have argued so eloquently, such a move—from "what is lost" to "what remains," even if what remains is only the indelible sense of loss—restitutes a sense of agency even to melancholy subjects and enables a politics of mourning.[80] Hence our move from victimhood to survival within a framework of social suffering, a framework marked by a greater attention to collective mechanisms of working through and learning to live with loss. It is in terms of such maneuvers of analytical space-clearing that this volume seeks to make a modest intervention in thinking about, archiving, and instrumentalizing testimonies.

Assembling critical ruminations on documentary testimony from various geographical locations, our volume in effect puts forward a meta-archive of suffering. While we are clear about our objective of promoting social justice, our approaches and methodologies are far from sanguine. Nor are we always certain about the precise nature of our investments and positions: hence the worry about the portability of testimonial practices and forms across cultures, or the tension of wanting to hold onto a sense of ethical globality while being critical of it. The contributors share a set of core assumptions, central amongst which is a faith in the mobilizing potential of testimonies; but their engagements with particular instances of social suffering index a range of positions with regard to underlying concerns. The point is not to produce a definitive set of answers, but to mobilize the complexities of testimonial assemblages through this gathering of authors, and to instigate further research opening onto more hospitable futures.

notes

1. See Annette Wieviorka, *The Era of the Witness*, trans. Jared Stark (Ithaca, NY: Cornell University Press, 2006; originally published as *L'ère du témoin*, 1998).
2. For instance, the direct address interviews in Edgar Anstey's and Arthur Elton's influential *Housing Problems* (1935).
3. For example, the "Virtual Museum" site's posted video recordings of atomic bomb survivors. Virtual Museum, www.pcf.city.hiroshima.jp/virtual/VirtualMuseum_e/visit_e/testimony_e/testimo01.html (accessed 3 July 2008).
4. By "direct cinema" we mean a mode of documentary filmmaking that was developed in the late 1950s and early 1960s in Canada and the United States. This mode is characterized by a lack of extra-diegetic elements such as music or narration and the concentration on the filming of real people and events in uncontrolled situations. See Stephen Mamber, *Cinema Verite in America: Studies in Uncontrolled Documentary* (Cambridge, MA: MIT Press, 1974) and Thomas Sobchack and Vivian Sobchack, "The Documentary Film," in *An Introduction to Film* (Boston: Little, Brown & Company, 1980), 351–4. It is important to note, however, that while Mamber uses the terms cinema verité and direct cinema synonymously, Sobchack and Sobchack find it useful to distinguish the two modes on the basis of cinema verité's use and direct cinema's philosophical rejection of subject interviews (talking heads) by filmmakers (356).
5. Bill Nichols, *Representing Reality: Issues and Concepts in Documentary* (Bloomington: Indiana University Press, 1991), 5.
6. Shoshana Felman, "Education and Crisis, or the Vicissitudes of Teaching," in *Testimony: Crises of Witnessing in Literature, Psychoanalysis, and History*, Shoshana Felman and Dori Laub (New York: Routledge, 1992), 42, emphasis original. Discussing her choice to draw on materials from the repository now named the Fortunoff Video Archive, Shoshana Felman writes that she decided "to move on, as it were, from poetry into reality and to study in a literary class something which is *a priori* not defined as literary, but is rather of the order [of] raw documents—historical and autobiographical," to "shift in medium from text to video—from the literary to the real" (42). Likewise, Lawrence Langer, while emphasizing the textuality of video testimonial accounts in his path-breaking *Holocaust Testimonies: The Ruins of Memory*, nevertheless distinguishes videotaped interviews from written memoirs in part by characterizing the former as being "shorn of literary ornaments" such as the "lyrical subtexts" or "allusions" of the latter. Lawrence Langer, *Holocaust Testimonies: The Ruins of Memory* (New Haven, CT: Yale University Press, 1991), 57.
7. These quick characterizations, we believe, whether literal, as in the case of the WITNESS organization's mottos "see it, film it, change it" and "WITNESS uses video and online technologies to open the eyes of the world to human rights violations" (www.witness.org; accessed 18 July 2008), or assumed, are extremely effective in articulating for participants and announcing for supporters the organization's goals and commitment to the struggle for a just society. We wish only to draw attention to the enormous difficulty and uncertain trajectories of testimony-based political advocacy.
8. In the literature of documentary studies, Brian Winston and Calvin Pryluck offered seminal critiques of the tendency in socially conscious documentaries to patronize working class subjects as less educated, less able to look after their own lives. See Brian Winston, "The Tradition of the Victim in Griersonian Documentary," and Calvin Pryluck, "Ultimately We Are

All Outsiders: The Ethics of Documentary Filming," in *New Challenges for Documentary*, ed. Alan Rosenthal (Berkeley: University of California Press, 1988). See also Maurice Stevens, *Troubling Beginnings: Trans(per)forming African-American History and Identity* (New York: Routledge, 2003), and Laura Jeffery and Matei Candea, "The Politics of Victimhood," *History and Anthropology* 17, no. 4 (December 2006): 287–96.

9. Susannah Radstone, "Trauma Theory: Contexts, Politics, Ethics," *Paragraph* 30, no. 1 (2007). Here we are referencing Radstone's call for trauma theory "to act as a check against, rather than a vehicle of the Manichean tendencies currently dominant within western politics and culture" (26). However, in using that formation to support our understanding of the socio-cultural and subjective co-constitution of trauma, in fact we may be departing from Radstone's commitment to see trauma as an unconscious process located within the psyche.
10. Arthur Kleinman, Veena Das, and Margaret Lock, eds., *Social Suffering* (Berkeley: University of California Press, 1997), x. See also Veena Das, Arthur Kleinman, Mamphela Ramphele, and Pamela Reynolds, eds., *Violence and Subjectivity* (Berkeley: University of California Press, 2000) and Veena Das, Arthur Kleinman, Margaret Lock, Mamphela Ramphele, and Pamela Reynolds, eds., *Remaking a World: Violence, Social Suffering, and Recovery* (Berkeley: University of California Press, 2001). Proffering a constructivist model, Jeffrey C. Alexander ("Toward a Theory of Cultural Trauma," in *Cultural Trauma and Collective Identity*, eds. Jeffrey C. Alexander, Ron Eyerman, Bernard Giesen, Neil J. Smelser, and Piotr Sztompka [Berkeley: University of California Press, 2004]) writes that trauma is a "socially mediated attribution" (8) whereby a "claim" is made about "some fundamental injury, an exclamation of the terrifying profanation of some sacred value, a narrative about a horribly destructive social process, and a demand for emotional, institutional, and symbolic reparation and reconstitution" (11). With more space to devote to the subject, we would discuss the extent to which Alexander's model, though seemingly designed to link psychic and social subjectivity, in fact loses hold of valuable psychoanalytic insights.
11. Bhaskar Sarkar, *Mourning the Nation: Indian Cinema in the Wake of Partition* (Durham, NC: Duke University Press, 2009); Janet Walker, *Trauma Cinema* (Berkeley: University of California Press, 2005).
12. Michael Chanan, "Rediscovering Documentary: Cultural Context and Intentionality," in *The Social Documentary in Latin America*, ed. Julianne Burton (Pittsburgh, PA: University of Pittsburgh Press, 1990), 40.
13. Roxana Waterson, "Trajectories of Memory: Documentary Film and the Transmission of Testimony," *History and Anthropology* 18, no. 1 (2007): 52.
14. "Witness Workshop—WSIS Parallel Event; Video as a Tool for Human Rights Advocacy," handout for a workshop event held on 14 November 2005, Tunis, Tunisia, www.witness.org/index.php?option=com_content&task=view&id=26&Itemid=78 (accessed 30 June 2008).
15. Shoshana Felman, "Education and Crisis," 5. Citing Elie Wiesel, Felman states: "It has been suggested that testimony is the literary—or discursive—mode par excellence of our times, and that our era can precisely be defined as the age of testimony" (5). For Wiesel's original statement, see Elie Wiesel, "The Holocaust as Literary Inspiration," in *Dimensions of the Holocaust*, eds. Elie Wiesel, Lucy Dawidowicz, Dorothy Rabinowicz, and Robert McAfee Brown (Evanston, IL: Northwestern University Press, 1977), 9. Annette Wieviorka identifies the Eichmann trial in 1961 as

"a pivotal moment in the history of the memory of the genocide [the Holocaust], in France and the United States as well as Israel" and describes the end of the 1970s as "the era of the witness" when "the systematic collection of audiovisual testimonies began." *The Era of the Witness*, 56.

16. The phrase comes from the American Friends Service Committee's 71-page pamphlet *Speak Truth to Power: A Quaker Search for an Alternative to Violence; A Study of International Conflict* (Philadelphia, PA: American Friends Service, 1955). More recently it has been adopted by the following among other publications: Darlene Clark Hine, *Speak Truth to Power: Black Professional Class in United States History* (Brooklyn, NY: Carlson Pub., 1996); Anita Hill, *Speaking Truth to Power* (New York: Doubleday, 1997); Ariel Dorfman, *Speak Truth to Power: Voices from Beyond the Dark* (London: Index on Censorship, 2001); Kerry Kennedy, *Speak Truth to Power: Human Rights Defenders Who Are Changing Our World*, photographs by Eddie Adams, ed. Nan Richardson (New York: Umbrage Editions, 2005); and "Speak Truth to Power," an online human rights forum based on the Kennedy book, www.speaktruth.org/ (accessed 18 July 2008).
17. This definition of Julia Kristeva's notion of "abjection" as developed in her book *Powers of Horror: An Essay on Abjection*, trans. Leon S. Roudiez (New York: Columbia University Press, 1982) is drawn from the *Columbia Dictionary of Modern Literary References*, eds. Joseph Childers and Gary Hentzi (New York: Columbia University Press, 1995), 1. Ana Douglass states that Shoshana Felman, in discussing the problems of testimony, witnessing, and truth, "shows that the witness speaks from and about her own abjection." Ana Douglass, "The Menchú Effect: Strategic Lies and Approximate Truths in Texts of Witness," in *Witness and Memory: The Discourse of Trauma*, eds. Ana Douglass and Thomas A. Vogler (New York: Routledge, 2003), 83.
18. See Wei Shi, "What Do the Chinese Know about Tiananmen Square?" The Observers: Your Eyes across the Globe, 6 May 2008, observers.france24.com/en/content/20080605-tiananmen-square-china-censorship-media, (accessed 18 July 2008). See also "Censorship in the People's Republic of China," Wikipedia, en.wikipedia.org/wiki/Censorship_in_china (accessed 18 July 2008); and Pankaj Mishra, "Tiananmen's Wake: A Novel of Hope and Cynicism," review of *Beijing Coma* by Ma Jian, *The New Yorker*, 30 June 2008, 74–7.
19. James Conachy, "Victims' Families Campaign for Reassessment of Tiananmen Square Massacre," World Socialist Web Site, www.wsws.org/articles/1999/jul1999/Jun4-j14.shtml, 14 July 1999 (accessed 30 June 2008).
20. "Voices from the Dark: A Story of a North Korean Camp Survivor," dramatic reading by Courtney Ryan and Jason Narvy and interview of Yong Kim by Suk-Young Kim moderated by Hye Jean Chung, Interdisciplinary Humanities Center, University of California, Santa Barbara, 19 May 2008. See Yong Kim and Suk-Young Kim, *The Long Road Home: Testimony of a North Korean Camp Survivor* (New York: Columbia University Press, 2009).
21. Audiovisual and written testimonies by Holocaust survivors very often include the given speaker's explicit remembrance that her or his will to survive was strengthened by the hope of living to tell the stories of those who perished. See, for example, the testimony of Judith Meisel in the documentary film *Tak for Alt: Survival of a Human Spirit* (dir. Laura Bialis, Broderick Fox, and Sarah Levy, US, 1999). Janet Walker along with Kwame Braun and Dr. Elizabeth Wolfson, the latter with Jewish Federation of Santa Barbara, has been honored to videotape interviews with sixteen residents of the area who are survivors and refugees of the Holocaust, many of whom expressed

a desire to testify on behalf of others who did not live for the sake of current and future generations. DVD copies of these interviews are available in the media library of Jewish Federation of Greater Santa Barbara, 524 Chapala Street, Santa Barbara, California, 93101; 805-957-1115; www.jewishsantabarbara.org. *Video Portraits of Survival, Volume One* (2006) and *Volume Two* (2007)—compilations of short, expressive videos about Holocaust survivors and refugees created collaboratively by Walker, Braun, students of the Department of Film Studies (now Film and Media Studies) at the University of California, Santa Barbara, Wolfson, and the subjects themselves—are available for purchase through Jewish Federation; ordering instructions are available online at www.jewishsantabarbara.org/page.aspx?id=120323.

22. Felman, "Education and Crisis," 3, emphasis original.
23. Dori Laub, "An Event without a Witness: Truth, Testimony and Survival," in *Testimony*, 79–80.
24. Felman and Laub, foreword to *Testimony*, xvii, xv.
25. Felman, "Education and Crisis," 6.
26. See Noah Shenker, "Embodied Memory: The Institutional Mediation of Survivor Testimony in the United States Holocaust Memorial Museum," in this volume.
27. Bill Nichols, *Representing Reality*, 3–4.
28. James Young, "Holocaust Video and Cinemagraphic Testimony," in *Writing and Rewriting the Holocaust: Narrative and the Consequences of Interpretation* (Bloomington: Indiana University Press, 1990), 158.
29. Frances Guerin and Roger Hallas, Introduction to *The Image and the Witness: Trauma, Memory and Visual Culture*, eds. Frances Guerin and Roger Hallas (London: Wallflower Press, 2007), 1–22. See also Susan Sontag's *On Photography* (New York: Farrar, Straus, Giroux, 1977) for one among many discussions of the inevitably interpretive nature of the photograph. On visuality and iconoclasm, see Martin Jay, *Downcast Eyes: The Denigration of Vision in Twentieth-Century French Thought* (Berkeley: University of California Press, 1993).
30. Guerin and Hallas, introduction to *The Image and the Witness*, 5.
31. Ibid. What surprises us, though, about Guerin and Hallas's volume is the extent to which the materiality of the image is explored and in fact rhetorically secured, apart from, and, in places, in contradistinction to, an understanding of "the word" that seems to presume the latter's immediacy. Although a few chapters do raise the image/word relationship as a productive problematic (for example, Stephanie Marlin-Curiel's insightful analysis of the interaction of "media images and testimonial excerpts" in South African artist Sue Williamson's interactive panels and CD-ROM installation and Hallas's own chapter about a film of witnessing in light of its deliberate exclusion of the body from the frame), the majority focus on (silent) photography, sculpture, fiction films, and/or works in and around but determinedly other than those where direct address testimony is figured.
32. Veena Das and Arthur Kleinman, introduction to *Remaking a World*, 22.
33. John Beverley, *Testimonio: On the Politics of Truth* (Minneapolis: Minnesota University Press, 2004), 34.
34. We adapt the notion of film midwifery from Patricia Zimmermann, "Flaherty's Midwives," in *Feminism and Documentary*, eds. Diane Waldman and Janet Walker (Minneapolis: Minnesota University Press, 1999).
35. Beverley writes that "[i]n oral history it is the intentionality of the recorder—usually a social scientist—that is dominant, and the resulting text is in

some sense 'data.' In testimonio, by contrast, it is the intentionality of the narrator that is paramount" (*Testimonio*, 32). We would suggest that both of these statements apply to audiovisual testimony, since there is the triangular scene of narrator, listener, and camera that constitutes what we are calling the "testimonial apparatus."

36. Chon Noriega, "Talking Heads, Body Politic: The Plural Self of Chicano Experimental Video," in *Resolutions: Contemporary Video Practices*, eds. Michael Renov and Erika Suderberg (Minneapolis: Minnesota University Press, 1996), 211.
37. Literary *testimonio*, according to Beverley, "coalesced as a new narrative genre in the 1960s and further developed in close relation to the movements for national liberation and the generalized cultural radicalism of that decade," especially those of Cuba and Nicaragua. It "implies a challenge to the loss of the authority of orality in the context of processes of cultural modernization that privilege literacy and literature as norms of expression" and "represents an affirmation of the individual subject, even of individual growth and transformation, but in connection with a group or class situation marked by marginalization, oppression, and struggle." He draws on the work of Raymond Williams to develop the question of whether, or rather how, "social struggles give rise to new forms of literature." *Testimonio*, 31, 35, 41, and 29. See Raymond Williams, "The Writer: Commitment and Alignment," *Marxism Today* 24 (June 1980): 25.
38. See Chanan, "Rediscovering Documentary," and Julianne Burton's own "Toward a History of the Social Documentary" and "Democratizing Documentary: Modes of Address in the New Latin American Cinema," in *The Social Documentary in Latin America*.
39. Noriega, "Talking Heads, Body Politic," 210.
40. See, for example, the entry for "apparatus" in Susan Hayward, *Key Concepts in Cinema Studies* (London: Routledge, 1996), 7–8, and the discussion of the term in Pamela Robertson Wojcik, "Spectatorship and Audience Research," in *The Cinema Book*, ed. Pam Cook, 3rd edition (London: British Film Institute, 2007 [1985]), 538–9.
41. *I, Rigoberta Menchú: An Indian Woman in Guatemala*, ed. Elizabeth Burgos-Debray, trans. Ann Wright (London: Verso, 1984), originally published in Spanish in 1982 as *Me llamo Rigoberta Menchú y así me nació la conciencia* (*My Name is Rigoberta Menchú and This Is How My Consciousness Was Born*). David Stoll has identified factual inaccuracies in the account presented by Menchú, who survived massive human rights violations by the Guatemalan armed forces during the country's civil war (1960–96). See David Stoll, *Menchú and the Story of All Poor Guatemalans* (Boulder, CO: Westview Press, 1999). Defenders of the text's value tend to make their cases out of respect for both the culturally specific practices of oral testimony (here, the acceptability of narrating as one's own "the story of all poor Guatemalans") and the pressure exerted by the western valuation of eyewitnessing. The debate is the jumping off point for Beverley's *Testimonio*.
42. Douglass, "The Menchú Effect," 84. Douglass termed the book "the single most celebrated text of witness of the last two decades" (55). She makes her case with reference to Felman and Laub's *Testimony*.
43. Laub, "An Event without a Witness," 62. See Walker, "Testimony in the Umbra of Trauma: Film and Video Portraits of Survival," *Studies in Documentary Film* 1, no. 2 (October 2007); "The Vicissitudes of Traumatic Memory and the Postmodern History Film," in *Trauma and Cinema: Cross-Cultural Explorations*,

eds. E. Ann Kaplan and Ban Wang (Hong Kong University Press, 2004); "The Traumatic Paradox: Autobiographical Documentary and the Psychology of Memory," in *Contested Pasts*, eds. Katharine Hodgkin and Susannah Radstone (London: Routledge, 2003). See also a recent contribution to the debate on Laub's discussion of truth and testimony: Thomas Trezise, "Between History and Psychoanalysis: A Case Study in the Reception of Holocaust Survivor Testimony," *History and Memory* 20, no. 1 (Spring/Summer 2008): 7–47.

44. Christopher Browning, *Collected Memories: Holocaust History and Postwar Testimony* (Madison: University of Wisconsin Press, 2003), 39. Interestingly, Browning makes the point that perpetrator testimony is often used with appropriate historical skepticism in courts of law and historical accounts, whereas there has been more hesitancy to incorporate survivor accounts into the writing of history.
45. Interestingly, Browning located videotape from two different sessions of a single woman's testimony about the liquidation of a Polish labor camp. In the first interview, "barely audible" on a "technically flawed" tape, the woman stated, almost as an aside, that fellow Jews killed members of a labor camp elite on the train bound for Auschwitz. In a later retaping, to replace the cassette with technical problems, "she did not repeat the story" (presumably since it could be regarded as reflecting badly on Jewish survivors), Browning reports (79).
46. Linda Williams, "Mirrors with Memories: Truth, History, and the New Documentary," *Film Quarterly* 46, no. 3 (Spring 1993): 11.
47. We adapt this phrase from Kalí Tal, *Worlds of Hurt: Reading the Literatures of Trauma* (Cambridge: Cambridge University Press, 1996).
48. Barbara Halpern Martineau, "Talking about Our Lives and Experiences: Some Thoughts about Feminism, Documentary and 'Talking Heads'," in *"Show Us Life": Toward a History and Aesthetics of the Committed Documentary*, ed. Thomas Waugh (Metuchen, NJ: The Scarecrow Press, 1984), 259.
49. The "committed documentary" (as per Waugh's subtitle: *Toward a History and Aesthetics of the Committed Documentary*) may be seen as analogous in its oppositional or counterhistorical aims and attitudes to what we are describing here as alternative testimonial practice.
50. Wierviorka, *Era of the Witness*, 56–83.
51. Subsequent to Cole's three-year effort to obtain videotapes of the series, *Special Report* was digitized by the Yale Law School Goldman Library and made available via streaming video on the Internet as the South African Truth & Reconciliation Commission Videotape Collection, 84 episodes assembled by journalist Max du Preez, www.law.yale.edu/trc/. As such it constitutes another highly significant example of the documentary testimonial archive that is the subject of this volume.
52. See the United Nations Educational, Scientific and Cultural Organization (UNESCO) International Criminal Tribunal for Rwanda (ICTR) website, www.ictr.org. Quoted figures are from a summary of the ICTR judicial archives available at www.google.com/search?client=safari&rls=en&q=ictr+publications+and+materials+tanzania&ie=UTF-8&oe=UTF-8 (accessed 21 July 2008). See also the Kigali Memorial Centre website, www.kigalimemorialcentre.org.
53. Cole, "Mediating Testimony: Broadcasting South Africa's Truth and Reconciliation Commission" in this volume.

54. See "The Voice of Hibakusha," Atomic Archive, www.atomicarchive.com/Docs/Hibakusha/index.shtml. See also Mick Broderick, ed., *Hibakusha Cinema: Hiroshima, Nagasaki and the Nuclear Images in Japanese Film* (London: Kegan Paul, 1996).
55. Michael Moore, "SICKO: What Can I Do," www.michaelmoore.com/sicko/what-can-i-do/ (accessed 24 October 2008). Thanks are due to Bishnupriya Ghosh and Lucia Ricciardelli for drawing our attention to this site.
56. "SICKO: Share Your Healthcare Horror Stories," YouTube, www.youtube.com/groups_videos?name=SiCKOthemovie (accessed 24 October 2008). Additional video testimonial projects of note include the ACT UP Oral History Project (http://www.actuporalhistory.org/ [accessed 13 July 2009]) and the Nakba Archive (http://www.nakba-archive.org/ [accessed 13 July 2009]).
57. Jacques Derrida, *Archive Fever: A Freudian Impression* (Chicago, IL: University of Chicago Press, 1995), 1–2.
58. Mission statement, United States Holocaust Memorial Museum, www.ushmm.org/museum/press/kits/details.php?content=99-general&page=05-mission (accessed 5 January 2008).
59. See Shoshana Felman, *The Juridical Unconscious: Trials and Traumas in the Twentieth Century* (Cambridge, MA: Harvard University Press, 2002).
60. For a comparative evaluation of truth commissions and judicial trials, see Donald Shriver, "Truth Commissions and Judicial Trials: Complementary or Antagonistic Servants of Public Justice?" *Journal of Law and Religion* 16, no. 1 (2001): 1–33.
61. For instance, the 1987 broadcast of a fictional television mini-series about the Partition riots of 1947 led to the ransacking and burning of several television stations in India and a legal contest that went all the way up to the Supreme Court. Sarkar, *Mourning the Nation*, 230–58.
62. Indeed, many—not all of whom are Serbians—now consider such "global opinion" to be hopelessly lopsided and intent on demonizing Serbia. For some, the realpolitik of the Central European crisis has to do less with a virulent Serbian nationalism and more with the dissolution of Yugoslavia, which serves the interests of Germany, a key player in the EU. See, for instance, Ron Fraser, "The Demonizing of a Nation," *Trumpet*, www.thetrumpet.com/index.php?q=5466.0.108.0 (accessed 27 August 2008).
63. Butalia and other feminist scholars finally gathered their oral testimonies in the 1990s, crucially supplementing official history. Urvashi Butalia, *The Other Side of Silence: Voices from the Partition of India* (Durham, NC: Duke University Press, 2000). Ritu Menon and Kamla Bhasin, *Borders and Boundaries: Women in India's Partition* (New Brunswick, NJ: Rutgers University Press, 1998).
64. Alexis Dudden, "The Politics of Apology between Japan and Korea," in *Truth Claims: Representation and Human Rights*, eds. Mark Philip Bradley and Patrice Petro (New Brunswick, NJ: Rutgers University Press, 2002), 73–91.
65. We are in emphatic disagreement with the view, propounded most famously by Thomas Friedman, that globalization has led to a flattening of opportunities and aspirations across the planet, notwithstanding the very real differences in resources and institutional structures. Friedman, *The World Is Flat: A Brief History of the Twenty-First Century* (New York: Picador, 2005).
66. Mark Philip Bradley and Patrice Petro, introduction to *Truth Claims: Representation and Human Rights*, 1.

67. Mary Kaldor, *Global Civil Society: An Answer to War* (Cambridge: Polity Press, 2003). See also the *Global Civil Society Year Book* series published by Sage.
68. Derrida makes a sharper distinction between testimony and evidence: "It is possible for testimony to be corroborated by evidence, but the process of evidence is absolutely heterogeneous to that of testimony, which implies faith, belief, sworn faith, the pledge to tell the truth, the 'I swear to tell the truth, the whole truth, and nothing but the truth.' Consequently, where there is evidence, there is no testimony." Jacques Derrida and Bernard Stiegler, *Echographies of Television* (Cambridge: Polity Press, 2002), 94.
69. Bruno Waterfield, "Radovan Karadžić Refuses to Enter Genocide Plea," *Telegraph*, 30 August 2008, www.telegraph.co.uk/news/worldnews/europe/serbia/2645213/Radovan-Karadzic-refuses-to-enter-genocide-plea.html (accessed 29 August 2008).
70. John Tomlinson, "Globalization and Cultural Analysis," in *Globalization Theory: Approaches and Controversies*, eds. David Held and Anthony McGrew (Malden, MA: Polity Press, 2007), 157.
71. For a deeply felt and far-reaching rumination on these issues, see Susan Sontag, *Regarding the Pain of Others* (New York: Picador, 2004).
72. For Marita Sturken, history and memory are inextricably entangled. Sturken, *Tangled Memories: The Vietnam War, the AIDS Epidemic, and the Politics of Remembering* (Berkeley: University of California Press, 1997).
73. See the essays in Vivian Sobchack, ed., *The Persistence of History: Cinema, Television and the Modern Event* (New York: Routledge, 1996).
74. A critical view of memory's insurgence is provided by Kerwin Lee Klein, "On the Emergence of Memory in Historical Discourse," *Representations* 68 (Autumn 1999): 127–50. A more receptive engagement with cultural memory is to be found in Robert Rosenstone, *Visions of the Past: The Challenge of Film to Our Idea of History* (Cambridge, MA: Harvard University Press, 1998); and Sturken, *Tangled Memories*. See also the essays in the special journal issue "The Public Life of History," *Public Culture* 20, no. 1 (Winter 2008).
75. Charles Taylor, *Multiculturalism and "the Politics of Recognition"* (Princeton, NJ: Princeton University Press, 1992).
76. Elizabeth Povinelli, *The Cunning of Recognition: Indigenous Alterities and the Making of Australian Multiculturalism* (Durham, NC: Duke University Press, 2002).
77. Various commentators have noted the sprouting of entire industries of commemoration around instances of social suffering, including the Holocaust and the South Asian Partition. Perhaps the most famous of these is Norman Finkelstein, *The Holocaust Industry: Reflections on the Exploitation of Jewish Suffering* (London: Verso, 2000).
78. Mill categorically wrote that it would be "a grave error" to "suppose" that the "rules of international morality" that "obtain between one civilized nation and another" also hold "between civilized nations and barbarians." Further, barbarians (his examples included Gaul and Spain in Roman antiquity, and Algeria and India in the modern era) "have no rights as a nation, except *a right to such treatment as may, at the earliest possible period, fit them for becoming one*." Mill, "A Few Words on Non-intervention," *Online Library of Liberty*, oll.libertyfund.org/index.php?option=com_staticxt&staticfile=show.php&title=255&search=%22A+Few+Words+On+Non-intervention%22&chapter=21666&layout=html#a_809352 (emphasis added).
79. This doctrine was invoked unsuccessfully by Bernard Kouchner, a co-founder of the much-feted Doctors without Borders and the current French Foreign Minister, to argue for military intervention in the wake of

the government crackdown on Myanmar dissidents, and the subsequent devastation wrought by Hurricane Nargis in early 2008. Opinion on the matter was far from unified: the French argument prompted a Chinese diplomat at the UN to observe acerbically that the principle of "responsibility to protect" had not been invoked to sanction external relief action during the fatal French heatwave of 2003. *Economist*, "The UN and Humanitarian Intervention: To Protect Sovereignty, or to Protect Lives?," 15 May 2008, www.economist.com/world/international/display story.cfm?story_id=11376531 (accessed 25 August 2008).

80. David Eng and David Kazanjian, introduction to *Loss: The Politics of Mourning*, eds. Eng and Kazanjian (Berkeley: University of California Press, 2002), 1–25.

one

embodied memory

the institutional mediation of survivor testimony in the united states holocaust memorial museum

noah shenker

Although an extensive range of scholarship addresses archived Holocaust testimony, particularly in terms of its ethical, narrative, and psychoanalytic dimensions, considerably less work examines how the interrelationship between institutional and individual practices mediates the process of witnessing.[1] Furthermore, most of the critical inquiry on the subject focuses on the one-to-one transferential dynamic between the interviewer and the interviewee. It rarely extends to an analysis of how formal practices and institutional infrastructures shape not only the process of testimonial production but also dissemination and reception. This area of examination is particularly pressing, considering how Holocaust testimony archives have expanded in recent years in anticipation of the passing of the survivor community and the epistemological and ethical transition from living memory to postmemory.[2] This begs examination of how experientially charged testimonies of the Holocaust will be resuscitated in the absence of living witnesses, and how their pedagogical and commemorative potentiality will be activated beyond the boundaries of the archive and the museum. Rather than suggesting that the testimonies of living survivors delivered in person at museums and other spaces are somehow raw accounts in contrast to their framed audiovisual renderings, this chapter underscores how both forms of witnessing are subject to interrelated mediating forces in an effort by archives and museums to channel the immediate, embodied resonances of traumatic memory.[3]

With that concern at the foreground, this chapter examines how the institutional histories and practices of commemorative sites shape the conditions of possibility for channeling audiovisual Holocaust testimonies. How do the charters, structures, and policies of specific institutions establish parameters for debates on ethics, morality, and history? In what ways do recordings of Holocaust survivors become intertwined with testimonies from other extremities, thereby raising issues of the comparative and interventionist aspects of genocide studies more broadly? Although my larger research project examines the three most prominent sites of Holocaust testimony in the United States—the US Holocaust Memorial Museum, the Fortunoff Video Archive for Holocaust Testimonies at Yale, and the USC Shoah Foundation Institute—this chapter addresses the above questions as they apply solely to the practices of testimony within the US Holocaust Memorial Museum. While it possesses neither the oldest nor the largest collection of testimonies among the three sites in question, it is the most centralized and institutionally established among them, bearing the imprimatur of the United States federal government. In addition, its capacity not only as an archive, but also as a memorial site, exhibition space, and educational center, positions it as an illuminating case for examining testimony across phases of collection and transmission. What follows is not a comprehensive history of the development of the US Holocaust Memorial Museum, but rather a focused examination of how testimonial authority and authenticity are channeled by and through that institution.[4]

The mandate for the Holocaust Memorial Museum was officially authorized through a unanimous act of Congress in 1980, with a stated mission to serve as an interventionist, "living memorial" to the Holocaust that could attend not only to that past genocide but also to the emergence of contemporary atrocities.[5] At the core of the museum's charter was a tripartite function to commemorate, document, and activate the memory of the Holocaust in the face of current events, with its federal authorization solidifying its political and symbolic currency in pursuit of that aim. On the one hand, its location on the National Mall, adjacent to the museums of the Smithsonian and within close proximity to the Jefferson Memorial and Washington Monument, placed it squarely in the heart of an official American commemorative landscape.[6] Yet, at the same time, the museum's planners had to explore ways of importing the historical, evidentiary authority from the European topography of events. As expressed by Michael Berenbaum, the first Project Director for the Holocaust Memorial Museum and a principal figure in its development, the task was nothing short of Americanizing the Holocaust by bridging the historical, cultural, and spatial distance from the events for the visitors: "To move them back fifty years in time, transport them a continent away ... in 90 to 120 minutes, we must discharge them into the streets of Washington with a changed understanding of human potential and commitment."[7]

Central to establishing the foundations for that experiential encounter were a series of official visits by the museum's planners, staff, and chief donors to the European sites of destruction. The first visit was made in 1979 by the Presidential Commission on the Holocaust, the predecessor to the United States Holocaust Memorial Council, the governing body of the museum.[8] It organized a group trip to Poland that year, intended to provide museum dignitaries with an opportunity to stand in closer proximity to the physical evidence of the crimes and to absorb the moral implications and visceral charge of the Shoah. In the assessment of then Commission Chairman Elie Wiesel, by visiting the places of destruction and then returning to the United States, the museum backers and planners would be better able to "touch" and sense the "feel" of the events, and in turn deliver that experience to the American context (32). There would be subsequent trips to Europe made by museum staff, particularly in efforts to secure access to original artifacts and forge institutional arrangements with Holocaust museums, memorials, and historical sites. During one such trip, members of the Council formulated an arrangement with the museum at the former death camp of Majdanek in Poland. More specifically, this agreement called for providing the camp museum with video equipment for conducting testimonies with survivors and other witnesses in exchange for securing shoes and personal effects that could be placed on display in Washington (152–4). This represented a form of mutual authorization between the two institutions, whereby the Holocaust Memorial Museum provided its institutional capital and technological infrastructure in return for the much needed evidentiary and moral weight bestowed by original artifacts from Majdanek.

An equally essential source of historical authority and authenticity already resided within the United States in the form of a culturally and politically active Holocaust survivor community. A central aim of the Holocaust Memorial Museum was to anchor its institutional emergence on the still living authority of those survivors. The museum pursued this aim on a series of fronts, including its official merger with the National Registry of Holocaust Survivors, which had been established by Benjamin and Vladka Meed to collect the names, locations, and other details of Jewish survivors living in North America.[9] For Benjamin Meed, who later assumed a pivotal role in the museum as chairman of its Content Committee, the alliance enabled the registry and the survivor community at large to link their ephemeral legacies to a concrete national memorial. In addition to the museum providing institutional legitimacy to survivors, it was also to serve as an affective community for fostering networks between the survivor population and the general public, creating a space where survivors could make their stories known, including in the form of audiovisual histories collected by the museum's oral history department.

Originally intended to house the central national archive of Holocaust testimonies, the museum's oral history department has to date collected over six thousand interviews, mostly in English, in both audio and video formats.[10] However, one of the central priorities of the museum, and in turn a driving impetus for making the department of oral history operational, was a mandate from the main planners that the "soul" of the Holocaust Memorial Museum would be its Permanent Exhibition and that all other development, including that regarding testimony, was to be secondary to formulating that core space.[11] In service of the Holocaust Memorial Museum's deliberate conceptualization as a storytelling site, the Permanent Exhibition, or PE, provided the axis point through which oral histories, written narratives, authentic objects, and still and moving images guide the visitor through an emotionally driven narrative staged in three acts: "Nazi Assault/1933–1939," "The Final Solution/1940–1945," and the "Last Chapter—The Immediate Postwar Years."

For the first museum director, Jeshajahu "Shaike" Weinberg, the investment in moving patrons on an affective and visceral level is what distinguished the Holocaust Memorial Museum from what he referred to as its "traditional" and "cold" counterparts:

> Whereas the traditional, cold museum conveys impressions and a measure of information, it does not raise the blood pressure of its visitors ... The USHMM [United States Holocaust Memorial Museum], on the other hand, definitely intends to make not only an intellectual, but also an emotional, impact. It will be a hot museum, emotionally loaded, upsetting, disturbing.[12]

Within this conception of the Holocaust Memorial Museum, original and replicated artifacts were assembled to provide both moral authority and historical authenticity to the exhibition, lending a "perceptual advantage" to visitors by bestowing both an evidentiary and moral charge to the storyline.[13] In the assessment of Content Committee Chairman Benjamin Meed, the PE had to function as a site not only of information but also of moral understanding. Rather than offering a "textbook on the walls," it was to present "authentic, accurate history to create a compelling narrative, a visual epic of the Holocaust."[14] The exhibition's display of artifacts, including shoes, glasses, prayer shawls, brushes, and other personal effects, was to serve as material anchorage for the museum as it confronted both the opening of its doors and the fading of the Holocaust survivor community. As I have already pointed out, survivors played an instrumental role in granting moral authority and authenticity to the Holocaust Memorial

Museum, and anxiety mounted within the institution that the impending absence of living witnesses necessitated urgent efforts to secure not only their testimonies, but also their personal effects and documents before they passed away. This campaign to collect survivors' testimonies and their material artifacts went hand in hand at the Holocaust Memorial Museum with the oral history department's development of a protocol for soliciting items—often designated as "object survivors"—for donation from witnesses during the pre-interview process.[15]

In this sense, the Holocaust Memorial Museum developed as a site not only of historical preservation but also of communal and individual surrogacy. It archived the stories and physical artifacts of the victims and survivors, all the while positioning itself as a proxy, living body in its own right—an organic commemorative structure that would both house and activate the living resonances of history.[16] Shaike Weinberg articulated these imperatives just prior to the opening of the museum:

> The soul of the United States Holocaust Memorial Museum will be its permanent exhibition ... Through oral recollections, written narratives, authentic objects and still and moving images, the story of the Holocaust will unfold for the visitor ... Serving as guides will be the people who lived the story—victims, bystanders, public officials, liberators, rescuers, and perhaps even perpetrators—creating an intimate dialogue between the visitor and the dramatic historical events of the Holocaust through personal narrative and memorabilia.[17]

Despite this conceptual discourse of intimacy and embodiment, however, notions of what constituted the body and soul of the Holocaust Memorial Museum were often deeply contested. On the one hand, the museum relied upon authenticating objects and firsthand accounts—documents, photographs, torture implements, testimonies—to advance its storyline by fostering identification with its victims. At the same time, however, limits were placed on the types of artifacts and bodies put on display. Evoking authenticity was carefully calibrated to balance the cognitive and visceral aspects of commemoration and to attend to the sensitivities of the survivor community. Central to the debate was the question: for whom was the Holocaust Memorial Museum being constructed—for the survivors or for future generations with limited exposure to the histories and the material artifacts? The museum tried to balance the needs of both interests by providing access to images of death and destruction while it placed the most gruesome representations behind privacy walls or displayed the more highly charged objects by rendering them as castings or photomurals.

This tension became particularly evident during debates within the Content Committee on issues of displaying human hair shorn from concentration camp inmates. The museum had secured a sizable collection of that hair from Poland and had initially planned on exhibiting it in a large bin on the third floor of the PE.[18] Advocates for its inclusion stressed its strong visual and analytical impact—its ability to encapsulate without words what the renowned Holocaust scholar Raul Hilberg, a former member of the Content Committee, had called the "ultimate rationality of the destruction process."[19] Hilberg, who had previously expressed his concern that the museum would be an "empty" space devoid of sufficient material evidence, viewed the acquisition of hair as a major step in constructing a "full museum."[20] The majority of the Content Committee initially determined that the material would serve a compelling visceral and didactic function by instilling a sense of fear in the visitor while simultaneously encapsulating the genocidal teleology of the Nazi regime.

However, there was intense resistance to the display, particularly by survivor members of the committee who feared that the sanctity of the victims' bodies would be compromised. One such member, Helen Fagin, expressed concern that the hair of her deceased relatives might be included in the pile.[21] Although the museum's project director, Michael Berenbaum, assured her and the rest of the committee that human hair does not in fact hold sacred, bodily value in Jewish religious practice, many members remained firm in their opposition. In the end, only a photomural of the hair was put on display, with the original material being placed in storage in a warehouse outside of Baltimore.[22]

This process of regulating and segmenting the living memory of the Holocaust within the Permanent Exhibition was also crucial in shaping the development of the museum's collection of testimonies. The recognition that the living authority of survivors was dwindling provided the initial push for instituting the oral history department, with the aim to record those remaining voices that would advance development of the Permanent Exhibition in time for the Holocaust Memorial Museum's opening. As written in a memorandum detailing the role of the oral history department: "Because of the schedule for opening the museum and the aging of survivors, it is imperative that the interviewing process begin as soon as possible."[23] This particular preservational impulse linked the impending institutional birth of the Holocaust Memorial Museum with the fading life of survivors.

At the same time, the museum did not consider all testimonies to have equivalent exhibition value. A screening process was enacted, with certain witnesses designated as priorities, and not all those who applied were accepted to give their testimony (ibid.). As has been pointed out, the initial plans for the oral history department served the immediate needs of the Permanent Exhibition, so much so that Weinberg mandated that the exhibition director, Martin Smith, be granted the authority to supervise the selection and methodology for interviews rather than leaving that to the oral history director, Linda Kuzmack. Smith used that authority to develop a standardized framework for tracing the trajectory of the interviews, recommending that, with certain exceptions, testimonies should last no longer than two hours. That broke down into fifteen minutes for events before Hitler came to power, ninety minutes on events during the war, and fifteen minutes on life after the Holocaust—in short, a three-act structure consistent with the tripartite format of the Permanent Exhibition.

Smith also insisted that, in order for the recordings to be useful as raw footage for future exhibition, the interviewer should pose the fewest questions possible and withhold expressions of sympathy. Silence was deemed to be the operative term for the testimonies. In Smith's assessment: "Quiet empathy yields better results than repeated questioning since interviewers will be neither seen nor heard in edited video."[24] This was particularly crucial in order to produce concise, emotionally charged two to four minute long video clips that could be used for museum display. In light of this specific exhibition imperative, internal reviews were conducted of existing Holocaust testimony, cataloging interviewees according to their "key segments," or those moments deemed to constitute the core of their Holocaust experience. These included catalogue terms such as "selection by Mengele" or "escaping from a train," all designated with ratings indicating their exhibition quality. Grades ranged from "excellent," for "technically, emotionally and historically outstanding," to "fair," indicating that "tapes should be used to fill in details of life during the Holocaust, but may not provide outstanding drama." This fixation on the usability of testimony necessitated the "silent" approach to conducting oral histories at the museum—minimizing the voice of the interviewer and withholding the more dialogical aspects in order to facilitate editing and dissemination and to locate what the institution perceived to be the most dramatically compelling segments of testimony.

Initially, Smith hoped that this process of segmentation could enable a more complex representational structure to be adopted for a testimony media installation he was developing as one of the concluding areas of the Permanent Exhibition.[25] The space, officially designated as the Testimony Amphitheater, had initially been conceived and proposed by Smith as a display of video excerpts extracted from the museum's oral history archive. Although the individual segments of testimony were to be pre-edited into two to three minute long bites, they would be randomly selected and displayed through a central computer server onto a multiple screen installation. According to Smith's plan, the blocks of footage were to be pulled from a minimum of twenty-four hours of testimonies in the museum's oral history collection but would ultimately be enlarged to keep pace with the burgeoning holdings of the archive.[26] Smith envisioned the expanding and randomized format as a deliberate antidote to the more structured and redemptive strains of the Permanent Exhibition and as a means of bypassing what he characterized as the "artificial linkages" of conventional film editing. While Smith perhaps idealized the possibility of extracting pure, unadorned testimonies from this process, his vision for the installation nonetheless represented an attempt to introduce some semblance of spontaneity into the display of testimony. He thought of the format as a way of engendering more associative interpretations of the segments and capturing a sense of the vast yet ephemeral quality of archived testimony. However, with Smith's departure from the Holocaust Memorial Museum and with a push among its planners to strengthen the thematic coherence of the exhibition, the original vision for the Testimony Amphitheater installation was jettisoned.

Instead, the museum proposed a new concept to develop a single film entitled *Testimony*, composed of three fixed ten to fifteen minute long modules featuring twenty-four survivor and liberator interviews edited around a linear, three-part structure according to the themes of resistance, rescue, and defiance.[27] Although the work was inspired by testimonies originally submitted to the archive, the contracted filmmaker Sandy Bradley rerecorded each of those interviews, giving them more thematically grounded itineraries and higher production values. This included the use of film stock instead of the original video format, as well as the placement of subjects against domestic, rather than more neutral institutional, backdrops.

In the official proposal seeking federal authorization for *Testimony*, museum planners laid out their vision for how the film would integrate individual, eyewitness accounts into an exhibition space that had largely relegated testimonial material to its periphery.[28] The majority of the PE placed an emphasis on official documents and histories, coupled with original or replicated personal objects and other material artifacts ranging from concentration camp uniforms and confiscated eyeglasses, to castings of a gas chamber door and reconstructed barracks from Birkenau. Therefore, *Testimony* was intended to supplement that display strategy by giving "voice to individual witnesses of the Holocaust." Explicit in the proposal for the film was the notion that it would facilitate the convergence of both the cognitive and visceral impulses of the museum. Through its screening: "Museum visitors will have the opportunity to come closer to the events of the Holocaust as they see the faces of survivors and listen to accounts of a world full of contradiction, confusion, and choices." Planners hoped that the film could be used to both literally and figuratively flesh out the subjects of history by concluding the exhibition with a more living, albeit highly mediated, presence of survivors, giving faces and voices to otherwise less embodied history.

Although the museum planners conceived of the film as a means of reflecting the diversity and complexity of Holocaust experience, they also designed it to ground its representations in direct and unified moral lessons. The development of *Testimony* thus illustrated a larger set of tensions concerning the epistemological contours of the museum's exhibition space. The new, thematically grounded proposal for the film was implemented as a corrective to the more fragmented elements of Martin Smith's first design. At the same time, planners attempted to preserve some less traditional vestiges of that earlier concept, particularly by running the film on a continuous loop, withholding any explicitly clear markers of a beginning, middle, and end, and allowing visitors to enter and leave the space at their own whim. Ultimately, however, those attempts to incorporate some of Smith's suggestions were largely cosmetic. Any efforts at creating an open format with the film were illusory, considering the thematic and linear trajectory of the work, coupled with its use of voice-over narration to highlight thematic transitions and provide the personal backgrounds of the witnesses.

For the film's director, Sandy Bradley, the interview process that generated the footage presented an opportunity to forge a direct connection with her subjects and to shed light on what she considered to be the unadorned truths of their experiences. She elaborated in her treatment for the film: "It is to have no formal structure or storyline ... allow[ing] essentially no visual, no sound effects, no music, in short, nothing to aid the raw content of what is said other than the careful weaving of film editing."[29] Bradley was invested in uncovering the "deeper reflections" that emerge through testimony, while at the same time constrained by a temporal and thematic format that limited her ability to capture the messier, less overt processes that drive the work of traumatic memory. She deliberately chose to shoot her subjects in their own domestic settings, hoping that the more familiar, intimate locations would put them at ease. At the same time, she elected to frame the witnesses in tight close-ups with soft backgrounds to ensure that spectators would focus on the faces of the subjects. As Bradley explained in her film treatment: "I think most people in the audience will only see and hear the survivor him/herself. The film will seem to be purely: people."

Despite this rhetoric of pure, direct access to testimonial truths, it was a highly mediated process in which the framing, questioning, and thematic structuring of witnesses all had profound consequences for shaping the parameters of traumatic memory. While I will focus on the formal elements in more detail later on in this chapter, at this juncture I want to concentrate on the nature of the dynamic forged between the questioner and the subject. I will explore one particular archived video interview, and its subsequent filmed iteration in *Testimony*, in order to discuss how the labor of the interview process was often obscured if not suppressed in the course of channeling its pedagogical utility.

The interview in question is that of Agnes Mandl Adachi, recorded at the Holocaust Memorial Museum in 1990. A Hungarian Jew born in 1918, Adachi survived the war living in Budapest and worked closely with the famous Swedish diplomat and rescuer Raoul Wallenberg. She is a particularly compelling witness. Extremely sharp and articulate, she speaks in the interview with a Hungarian accent at once thick and yet easily comprehensible. Adachi exudes an urbane and cosmopolitan air, delivering her testimony with an upright manner and evident confidence, enacting a mode of testimonial performance and repetition that seemingly enables her to derive some comfort and mastery from her story. Throughout most of Adachi's interview, she appears to inhabit the realm of what both Charlotte Delbo and Lawrence Langer characterize as common memory, as she charts from a distance the linear accounts of her experiences while rarely triggering the more rupturing and immersive onset of deep memory.[30] Only near the very end of her archived testimony is there a small glimpse into the labored interaction between those two streams of memory, and of the tensions that often emerge between the voice of the Holocaust Memorial Museum and that of the individual witness. Adachi concludes her testimony by reflecting on an encounter she had many years after the war with a man whom she had saved from the Danube in Budapest after he and a group of other Jews had been tied together and thrown into that icy river by members of the fascist Arrow Cross. She expresses amazement not only that she survived the incident but also that she encountered one of the rescued Jews during a chance meeting much later in life: "Because you know, after a while, you don't believe it yourself because years going by and I was sick and it [the river] was frozen. But I was the only woman. So, and that is a life. And I thought it was a wonderful life and I am glad I lived through it."[31]

This marks the conclusion of the testimony as it is officially conducted on tape. However, there is an exchange caught on the camera directly afterwards but which remains absent from the typed, catalogued transcript for the interview, marked only as "technical conversation."[32] In that moment, Adachi turns her attention directly to the interviewer, Oral History Director Linda Kuzmack, to look for some expression of affirmation:

ADACHI: Well, how was it?
KUZMACK: Fine. [Delayed pause followed by a sigh.] Never before have I ... Bonnie [addressing her assistant], I hope we are off tape. I have never felt so much like screaming.
ADACHI: Well, why didn't you?[33]

The videotape then abruptly cuts away from this "off-the-record" exchange to the "official" photo and document-sharing segment of the testimony. It is a striking moment on many levels, but most relevant here is how it reveals the Holocaust Memorial Museum's approach to representing the mediations of memory. The closing exchange appears as a self-reflexive breach in the testimony, laying bare for one brief moment the performed, dialogical underpinnings of the interview. Furthermore, it evidences how the Holocaust Memorial Museum, while relying on the testimonies of Adachi and others to provide an embodied, visceral charge to its history, nonetheless attempts to ground that valence in more sober, analytically centered modes of address. In its efforts to stem the tides of traumatic memory, the museum often sequesters emotive expressions from cognitive inquiry, rather than displaying their entangled interactions. It searches out the deep reflections of Holocaust memory, all the while effacing the processes of testimonial production and reception that mark their transmission. As is evident in the initial testimony of Adachi, interviewer Kuzmack withholds and then keeps off the official record any trace of her own emotional investment in the process. Analytical sobriety rather than a mutual exchange of pathos takes precedence, and thus one of the most riveting and revealing aspects of Adachi's testimony is placed at the periphery. The moment that documents not only *what* Adachi recalls but *how* she recalls it in the presence of Kuzmack, representing what James Young refers to as "received history," is relegated to the realm of "technical conversation" in the museum's library transcript and later to the cutting room floor during the production of *Testimony*.[34] The historical exceptionality of Adachi's heroic work for Wallenberg is given precedence during her interview and in the final version of *Testimony* included in the exhibition, keeping at the margins the traces of the emotional and psychological labor shared between interviewer and interviewee. However, in her dogged insistence on keeping her visceral reactions off the official record of the testimony, Kuzmack ultimately brings to light the tensions that can emerge between the agency of the individual witness and the preferences of an archival institution.

This process of rechanneling Holocaust testimony extends beyond the Permanent Exhibition, however, and shapes how living Holocaust survivors, and not only their audiovisual incarnations, continue to circulate throughout the museum in ways that reflect that institution's epistemological parameters. To take the case of one Holocaust survivor, Nesse Godin, she has been positioned as an exemplary witness of the Holocaust Memorial Museum—a living embodiment of how it attempts to calibrate the sober and emotive dimensions of testimony. Godin is one of the most active Jewish survivor volunteers working within the museum, delivering talks to a diverse range of visitors including student groups, foreign dignitaries, and military personnel. And as I will examine near the conclusion of this chapter, the museum recently featured her as the keynote Holocaust survivor in an official museum ceremony to call attention to the ongoing genocide in Darfur.

However, before I analyze how Godin's living presence was disseminated, I want to first consider how her video testimony was recorded by the Holocaust Memorial Museum oral history department in 1989, four years prior to the public opening of the museum. Her performance of memory in that interview, I will argue, served to establish her appeal as a witness for the museum by representing an approach to testimony that could facilitate its larger pedagogical and commemorative aims. In that sense, the case of Nesse Godin provides a compelling example of how survivors, as they are both archived and presented "in the flesh," are intertwined with and subjected to overlapping mediating forces.

A Lithuanian Jew born in 1928, Godin survived the Holocaust, having gone through life in a ghetto, the horrors of the concentration camp Stutthof, and the unfathomable hardship of a death march before being liberated. Her archived testimony from 1989 was one of the interviews that had been internally reviewed by the Holocaust Memorial Museum in the course of determining how best to develop the oral history program in anticipation of the museum's opening. The museum assessed the interview as having "good" exhibition quality, particularly in terms of the "key segment" annotated: "Death March—eating undigested grain from dried cow manure," referring to how Godin was able to survive the march.[35]

Despite the dramatic quality of Godin's story, her testimony for the archive and her subsequent appearances in person at the museum are noteworthy for her poised and measured way of address. This is underscored in one particular moment during her video interview, in the course of recalling how a Jewish man living in her ghetto was scheduled to be hanged by the Nazis in 1942 after having been accused of smuggling bread:

> Well this man was marched in like this. He walked over to the table. He said to the two men "Thou shalt not kill," you know in Yiddish, "I will do it myself." He hopped on the table, on the chair, they did not even have a chance like you know in some places they tie their hands back or they put a cover on their face. Nothing. He hopped, he put a string of his own, the loop you know over his, the noose, whatever it's called, over his neck, and to the assassin, the Gestapo, he said, "You are not going to win a war by killing me." And somebody pushed or he pushed a chair from under his feet, and I remember his body dangling like this. I remember it so. Linda, it was terrible times. You know, I always try to control myself, not to be too emotional because otherwise if I get too emotional, I cannot bring the message. You know, you know, this [is] what people have to think about.[36]

Absent from the transcription are the intensely visual and aural dimensions of the videotaped recollection. Throughout her description of the hanging, Godin is extremely gestural, using her hands to mimic the motions of the condemned man, tying an imaginary noose around her neck, and speaking with intense defiance in repeating the words: "Thou shalt not kill ... I will do it myself." And then, as she begins to absorb and reflect on the tragic nature of this memory, she shakes her head from side to side in a struggle to remain composed. She teeters on the edge of despair, almost succumbing to her emotions, but ultimately she presses ahead with her story without breaking down. She speaks with plaintiveness in her voice, but also with the fluency of someone who, as she informs us, has told her story several times before and has grown accustomed to negotiating its terrain.

Her remark "I always try to compose myself, not to be too emotional ... this [is] what people have to think about" speaks directly to one of my primary arguments in this chapter—that the Holocaust Memorial Museum weds the emotive, viscerally charged authority of survivor testimonies with a more sober approach to storytelling. The museum's audiovisual pedagogy is developed to evoke and yet contain the excesses of traumatic memory, enhancing the pathos of its holdings, while ultimately preventing its overflow for the sake of narrative coherence and educational transmission. Godin displays a keen awareness of this need to regulate affective and analytic impulses, and that is precisely the basis of her utility as a historical interlocutor and exemplary witness for the museum. In contrast to Adachi, who in her testimony questions the interviewer about having withheld her screams and her emotional investment in the process, Godin seems to embrace the sequestering of pathos, realizing that doing so serves a particular pedagogical aim.

Godin's testimony also underscores the interpretative consequences of the way in which interviews of the Holocaust Memorial Museum are formally framed. Exhibition Director Martin Smith and Oral History Director Linda Kuzmack engaged in rather heated debates concerning the techniques for shooting video testimony. Smith expressed his displeasure with Kuzmack for having standardized a medium close-up approach to composition, rather than adopting his preferred tight close-up format. Smith noted in one memorandum regarding the use of the medium close-up: "There was too much shirt/blouse and not enough human face for the impact I would like." For Smith, the face was to be the primary screen for representing the emotional textures of Holocaust testimony. Yet, in one of the few victories for Kuzmack in her debates with Smith, she preserved the medium close-up as the standard framing method. In her assessment, moving in any closer with the camera was "too tight and too close to the neck, giving me a bit of a choked feeling."[37]

However, in the case of Godin's testimony, the wider framing is precisely what animates that "choked feeling" by capturing her gestures reenacting the hanging of the condemned man. In that sense, the use of the medium close-up provides some limited range of representation for her gestured, viscerally charged performance of memory. If Smith's position on the matter had ultimately prevailed, our encounter with Godin's testimony would be quite different, most certainly muting the physically intense nature of her recollection. That is not to suggest that the medium close-up utilized here and across the other Holocaust testimony archives examined in my research somehow provides extensive coverage of a witness's physical expressions. Rather, it is a narrow format that often conceals the "business" of performing memory—the workings of the arms and feet in expressing the labor of remembrance and the corporeal traces of trauma (often in the cases of tattooed arms mentioned by survivors but left out of the frame). Yet in Godin's testimony those movements captured on camera—including markers beyond her face—provide revealing glimpses into the emotional and physical labor of her testimonial reenactment. Her gestures lend an intense immediacy to her story and position her as a proxy of sorts, giving voice and living presence not only to her own experience but also to that of the hanged victim unable to tell his story.

The internal assessment and categorization of the video testimony of Godin and other witnesses in terms of their "key segments" is consistent with the Holocaust Memorial Museum's larger approach to utilizing testimony, whether in archived, exhibited, or living forms, for the purposes of capturing the core elements of Holocaust experience and making them accessible to the general public. In February of 1989, at a time when the oral history department was in its early development, planners working on the creation of the museum's Learning Center (eventually placed nearby the Permanent Exhibition) debated the pedagogical uses of testimony. In one memorandum, the Learning Center Advisory Committee gave explicit consideration to the interactive potential or "convertibility" of testimony. There is one particular passage concerning the criteria for judging a "good" testimony from an educational point of view. More specifically, planners pressed for the acquisition of dense segments filled with an avalanche of terms, concepts, and ideas presented very rapidly. Referred to in a Learning Center memo as the "Peanut Butter Theory," it posited:

> What are the qualities that constitute good oral history from an interactive point of view? They are the same qualities that make good peanut butter. It should be thick, chunky, and easy to spread. Smooth peanut butter is amorphous stuff ... what you need are chunks. In video, these are small identifiable segments that have clean beginnings and endings and which can serve some purpose out of context ... Is the oral history thick? Is it chunky? Is it easy to spread? Three "yes" responses lend a very powerful endorsement to conversion.[38]

It could be argued that this means of converting and instrumentalizing traumatic memory might potentially reduce survivors to exemplars of suffering mobilized in the service of a particular institutional narrative. Nonetheless, this process of mediation also enables greater access to archival holdings and thus may constitute its transformative social potential.

I want to further explore this point by examining two relatively recent events that highlight the challenges of recasting Holocaust testimony beyond the confines of the Holocaust Memorial Museum in ways that address contemporary issues. The first relates to a Holocaust denial conference held in Iran in December of 2006. The program, entitled "Holocaust: A World Prospect," included seventy participants made up of Holocaust deniers, discredited scholars, white supremacists, and a few members of ultra-Orthodox Jewish fringe groups—all gathered in Tehran under the guise of "debating" the Holocaust. One of the more striking dimensions of the ensuing public controversy was the response launched by the North American survivor community. The Simon Wiesenthal Center convened a counter-program called "Witness to the Truth," a videoconference of seventy Holocaust survivors, each giving brief testimony to challenge the seventy deniers attending the conference in Tehran—a body for a body, if you will.[39] The Holocaust Memorial Museum launched its own response to the Tehran conference by hosting a visit of local Muslim leaders, each of whom lit memorial candles in the museum's Hall of Remembrance after taking a tour of the Permanent Exhibition. With three Holocaust survivors at their side, the Muslim clergy invoked the moral lessons of the Holocaust, calling for tolerance, understanding, and the need for relating to the suffering of others. Sara Bloomfield, the executive director of the Holocaust Memorial Museum, also gave an address, invoking three primary forms of evidence granting her institution the authority to confront the dubious conference in Iran:

> We stand here in this Hall of Remembrance, America's national memorial to the victims of the Holocaust ... And right behind us, under this eternal flame, we have the ashes from the camps, the ghettos, and from American military cemeteries for those soldiers who died in the fight against Nazi tyranny. We stand here in this building that houses millions of pieces of evidence of this crime, perhaps the most well documented crime in human history ... We stand here with three survivors of the Holocaust, and with our great Muslim friends, to condemn this outrage in Iran.[40]

This response underscored how the physical remains of the Shoah, the federal mandate of the institution, and the living, verifying power of the survivors converged to situate the Holocaust Memorial Museum as a public sphere for addressing intolerance and Holocaust denial. However, these very discourses also revealed the underlying anxiety marking the transition to postmemory, when survivors of the Holocaust can no longer attest in person to having "been there." While their accounts will be preserved in recorded testimonies, their presence will inevitably be transferred onto archival and commemorative institutions, no longer able to match one living body for another in the cause of remembrance. The physical traces of the Shoah—the shorn hair, the human ashes, and the Polish cattle-car—are becoming increasingly animated to serve the cause of giving witness in the growing absence of living subjects.

The other event in question emerged out of the planning of the Committee on Conscience, or COC, an official department within the Holocaust Memorial Museum charged with activating the institution as a "living memorial" to confront contemporary genocides.[41] The COC was mandated to employ a wide range of actions, including public programs, temporary exhibitions, and public and private communications with policy makers to address contemporary crises. During the Thanksgiving week of 2006, the COC sponsored the projected photo installation entitled "Our Walls Bear Witness: Darfur, Who Will Survive Today?" and curated by Chicago architect Leslie Thomas, with photographs taken from her traveling exhibit "Darfur/Darfur." The event featured rotating images of the genocide projected onto three, forty-square-foot panels on the exterior

Figure 1.1

Spectators viewing "Our Walls Bear Witness—Darfur: Who Will Survive Today?"—a display of photographs projected on the exterior walls of the United States Holocaust Memorial Museum building during the week of Thanksgiving 2006 (photo by Max Reid, copyright USHMM)

walls of the museum. Accompanied by mournful Sudanese music, the photographs presented images ranging from malnourished bodies to burning villages and heavily armed child soldiers.[42]

The large-scale projection raised a series of concerns for the COC relating to the delicate balance between representational sanitization and humanization. A handful of the exhibit's more graphic images, particularly a photograph of a murdered three-year-old boy with a crushed face, were withheld from the display for fear of offending passersby. This approach was consistent with museum display policies to either exclude or otherwise conceal excessively graphic images, particularly those of non-decomposed corpses, behind privacy walls. It also reflected the mandated parameters for the architectural design of the museum, which stated that the structure should be prominent but nonthreatening, imposing but not too disorienting. It should evoke the Holocaust but not at the expense of compromising the American narrative of the National Mall. Rather than frightening people away from the horrors housed either on or inside its walls, the museum should inspire a sense of awe and sanctity.[43]

The opening night of the installation was launched with a public address within the museum's Hall of Remembrance, with speeches from Andrew Natsios, a member of the US special envoy mission to Sudan, as well as the before-mentioned Holocaust survivor Nesse Godin, Rwandan genocide survivor Clemantine Wamariya, and Darfurian refugee Omer Ismail, each there to give accounts of their respective experiences of genocide. As with the museum's response to the Iran conference, Holocaust survivors played a pivotal role in anchoring the "Our Walls Bear Witness" event. Before the opening address began, organizers asked survivors within the general audience to stand and be recognized, provoking a steady stream of applause. And the presence of Godin, an exemplary survivor of the Holocaust Memorial Museum, provided the crucial, authorizing link in the chain of other genocide survivors on the dais.

One of the more striking aspects of the "Our Walls Bear Witness" installation was the absence of descriptive captions accompanying the photographs projected on the walls. The members of the COC concurred that the large-scale, viscerally charged projections would speak for themselves.[44] But who are the children carrying guns in the photos? Which village is being destroyed and by whom? These and other questions remained largely unanswered by the installation, which appeared to be more heavily invested in drawing attention to the intensity of the suffering represented in the images than in providing historical or political exposition. This particular approach to visual pedagogy underscores the dilemma of how extreme images can be presented in ways that not only spark an affective response but also make legible potential forms of analysis and action.

Furthermore, in terms of the role played by the Holocaust survivors at the event, the specificity of their individual experiences was not at the foreground. Neither Godin nor any of the Holocaust survivors in the general audience went into much detail about their stories. Rather, they primarily served as personal markers of historical trauma, attesting to the paradigmatic status of the Holocaust and authorizing engagement with more recent genocides. Their symbolic presence was in keeping with the Committee on Conscience's overall approach to evoking the Holocaust. Instead of drawing a direct line from the Shoah to events in Bosnia, Rwanda, or Darfur, it channeled the moral authority of Holocaust experiences through the more general rubric of genocide awareness.[45] In that sense, the COC filtered the ethical imperative of the Holocaust in ways that evaded comparisons of suffering yet still structured the moral imagination for encountering other atrocities. Within this framework, the Holocaust was categorized as the paradigmatic genocide and yet remained on a separate register of experience. As Hyman Bookbinder, one of the central supporters behind the formation of the Committee on Conscience, remarked during debates concerning its creation: "When we identify something as genocide, we are not saying it is a Holocaust. Holocaust is still another one ... it is another kind of destruction."[46]

While survivors' embodied authority is primary to the museum's mission as a living memorial, I have emphasized how the institution has carefully and precisely managed the ways in which living and dead bodies are presented both within and outside its walls. Whether by withholding the more graphic photographs from "Darfur/Darfur," shielding certain representations of destruction within the Permanent Exhibition, or isolating the overflow of emotion to the realm of "technical conversation" in its video testimonies, the Holocaust Memorial Museum has constantly negotiated the delicate balance between analytic and visceral forms of address. Repeating the words of Godin: "You know, I always try to control myself, not to be too emotional because otherwise if I get too emotional, I cannot bring the message. You know ... this [is] what people have to think about."

Alison Landsberg has argued that "piles not people are the legacy of the Holocaust."[47] In other words, the artifacts left behind, charged with the resonance of once living subjects, will constitute the primary materials through which we engage with Holocaust memory. I would expand on that claim by arguing that the institutional structures and practices of memorials, museums, and archives are also positioned as the new bodies of memory in a postmemory landscape. At the same time as we must attend to this process of institutional reconstruction, however, we must also remember and be attentive to the traumatic referents involved, the individual experiences that anchor the mediations of testimony.

As film and media scholar Janet Walker has reminded us, there is also the frailty of traumatic memory to consider—the unavoidable gaps in recollection that require us to work in reconstructing the past, rather than assuming an immediate, unvarnished performance of memory.[48] In the case of the culture of the Holocaust Memorial Museum, it continues to register profound anxiety towards the vicissitudes of testimony. Ellen Blalock, the director of the museum's Office of Survivor Affairs, remarked to me in an interview that she is increasingly concerned about the failing memories of certain witnesses who have been enlisted to tell their stories to visitors. In response, Blalock has considered pulling those speakers from circulation, fearing that their faltering delivery will undermine their historical credibility.[49]

That is where Lawrence Langer's perspectives on testimony prove to be so instructive. He eloquently describes the painstaking processes and labor of Holocaust testimony, underscoring that it is a matter not only of retrieving the past but also of recording the ways one retrieves that past. It is crucial for interviewers and future generations who will inherit these resources to acknowledge that testimony is generated as part of a mutual, contingent process, rather than strictly privileging a static or infallible notion of memory. That seems to be the foundation for constructing testimonial projects as sites for cultivating what Langer has referred to as an "intuitive shared intimacy" between survivors and those who receive their memories.[50] In April of 1991, in his capacity as an outside consultant on issues of oral history at the Holocaust Memorial Museum, Langer wrote in a letter to Berenbaum: "The importance of these testimonies is that if we watch enough of them, we become part of this intuitively understanding audience, not perhaps in the same way as authentic former victims, but close enough to move into the subtext of their narratives" (ibid.).

Just as the Holocaust Memorial Museum has struggled to preserve the original condition of its disintegrating collection of shoes and other artifacts, it also faces the daunting task of embalming the living traces of trauma. To compensate for this challenge, the museum has placed an even greater emphasis on its holdings of material artifacts and documents to lend authenticity to survivor recordings. This marks a major reversal in the flow of testimonial authority. Whereas in its early development period, the Holocaust Memorial Museum had turned to survivors as the source for authorizing its collections, the material artifacts have now increasingly assumed that role, lending both institutional and evidentiary legitimacy to testimonies.

I want to conclude by arguing that, in anticipation of the paradigmatic shift from living memory to postmemory, it is essential to cultivate infrastructures and approaches to collecting and transmitting testimony that train our sensitivity to their lived, physical origins. Fundamental to inheriting Holocaust survivor memory is the recognition that the face, body, and voice of the subject provide a necessary interpersonal and ethical groundwork for social responsibility. However, testimony cannot be reduced to empirical historical content or raw visceral impact. Rather, it is an individually and institutionally embedded and embodied practice framed by a diverse range of aims and preferences. In that sense, we are not inheriting testimonies as fixed capsules of memory but as constantly contested, evolving, and living memorials. It is that dynamic nature of testimony that presents both the limits and the possibilities of confronting contemporary extremities through the lens of the Holocaust.

notes

1. There is a wealth of scholarship dealing directly with issues of archived Holocaust testimony. A few noteworthy examples include: Lawrence Langer, *Holocaust Testimonies: The Ruins of Memory* (New Haven, CT: Yale University Press, 1991); Henry Greenspan, *On Listening to Holocaust Survivors: Recounting and Life History* (Westport, CT: Praeger, 1998); Shoshana Felman and Dori Laub, *Testimony: Crises of Witnessing in Literature, Psychoanalysis and History* (New York: Routledge, 1992); and Geoffrey Hartman, *The Longest Shadow: In the Aftermath of the Holocaust* (New York: Palgrave Macmillan, 1996). These are formative works on the subject, but are nonetheless focused primarily on the testimonial exchange between interviewer and interviewee and rarely explore the manner in which testimonies are framed by institutional, cultural, and formal practices.
2. For a discussion of postmemory, see Marianne Hirsch, "Surviving Images: Holocaust Photographs and the Work of Postmemory," in *Visual Culture and the Holocaust*, ed. Barbie Zelizer (New Brunswick, NJ: Rutgers University Press, 2000). I am using the term postmemory here to distinguish between a moment of living memory, in which physically present witnesses, however small in number, exist to attest to experiences of the Holocaust, and an impending moment when only recorded traces of those witnesses will remain.
3. I am grateful to Michael Renov for his discussion of "embodied memory," which I incorporate into the title and body of this chapter. I first came across his engagement with that term in the following conference paper: Michael Renov, "The Work of Memory in the Age of Digital Reproduction" (paper presented at the Visible Evidence XI Conference, Bristol, UK, 17 December 2003). Renov utilizes it as a compelling term for describing the individual texture of testimonial subjects that can often work against the more universalizing dimensions of an interview protocol.
4. Edward Linenthal, *Preserving Memory: The Struggle to Create America's Holocaust Museum* (New York: Columbia University Press, 2001) provides the definitive, truly comprehensive history of the United States Holocaust Memorial Museum and served as an invaluable reference in helping me to navigate the vast institutional archives of the museum during my 2006–7 term as a Charles H. Revson Fellow in Archival Research at the Center for Advanced Holocaust Studies at the United States Holocaust Memorial Museum. It was during that fellowship that I compiled the research for this chapter. While Linenthal's work in *Preserving Memory* provides a wide-ranging chronicle of the development of the Holocaust Memorial Museum, issues relating to collecting testimony are of secondary concern in the book and there is little analysis of individual interviews, nor an in-depth discussion of interview protocols, preferences, and methodologies.

5. Jeshajahu Weinberg, Memorandum to Museum Staff. 6 February 1990. US Holocaust Memorial Museum; Institutional Archives; Director's Office; Records of the Museum Director—Jeshajahu "Shaike" Weinberg; 1979–1994; 1997–014; Box 22; Committee: Conscience. (This and further citations of material from the USHMM Institutional Archives conform to the museum's cataloging format.)
6. For a detailed examination of how the US Holocaust Memorial Museum is integrated into the landscape of American commemorative culture, see Linenthal, *Preserving Memory*.
7. Michael Berenbaum, Remarks to Joint Meeting of the Museum Development Committee and the Content Committee. 20 January 1988. US Holocaust Memorial Museum; Institutional Archives; Exhibitions; Permanent Exhibition—Development Files; 1990–1994; 1998–038; Box 13; Oral History.
8. Linenthal, *Preserving Memory*, 28.
9. Benjamin Meed, Internal Notes Regarding the National Registry. 3 January 1991. US Holocaust Memorial Museum; Institutional Archives; Director's Office; Records of the Museum Director—Jeshajahu "Shaike" Weinberg; 1979–1994; 1997–014; Box 5; American Gathering/Federation of Jewish Holocaust Survivors: Letters from Benjamin Meed to German Leaders 9/6/90.
10. US Holocaust Memorial Museum Department of Oral History, Oral History Interview Guidelines (Washington, DC: 1998), ii.
11. Author Unlisted, Press Release, "The Assault (1933–1939), The Holocaust (1939–1945), and Bearing Witness (1945–): The Permanent Exhibition of the United States Holocaust Memorial Museum." Undated (Prior to Opening of Museum). US Holocaust Memorial Museum; Institutional Archives; Research Institute; Records of the Director—Michael Berenbaum; 1986–1994; 1997–006; Box 26; Oral History (1 of 1).
12. Jeshajahu Weinberg, Memorandum to Museum Staff. 13 July 1991. US Holocaust Memorial Museum; Institutional Archives; Research Institute; Records of the Director—Michael Berenbaum; 1986–1994; 1997–006; Box 23; Concept Outline—Weinberg.
13. Levine Hillel, Remembering and Memorializing the Holocaust: Psychological and Educational Dimensions Report. US Holocaust Memorial Museum; Institutional Archives; Research Institute; Records of the Director—Michael Berenbaum; 1986–1994; 1997–006; Box 93.
14. Benjamin Meed quoted in the digested minutes from the Museum's Content Committee Meeting. 21 October 1987. US Holocaust Memorial Museum; Institutional Archives; Research Institute; Records of the Director—Michael Berenbaum; 1986–1994; 1997–006; Box 27.
15. Anita Kassof, Letter to Martin Smith. 29 November 1989. US Holocaust Memorial Museum; Institutional Archives; Research Institute; Records of the Director—Michael Berenbaum; 1986–1994; 1997–006; Box 21; Collections and Acquisitions Committee.
16. For further discussion of the Holocaust Memorial Museum as a site of organic memory, see Alison Landsberg, *Prosthetic Memory: The Transformation of American Remembrance in the Age of Mass Culture* (New York: Columbia University Press, 2004), 112. Although her chapter on the Holocaust Memorial Museum is extensive on issues of what she calls "living" and "prosthetic" memory, and provides rich analysis of the Holocaust Memorial Museum's

Permanent Exhibition, it only marginally focuses on matters of testimony. My research in this chapter is intended to fill in that gap by examining testimonies as highly mediated, calibrated, and often contested sources of what I am referring to here as "embodied memory." That is to say, while the Holocaust Memorial Museum is invested in capturing the embodied immediacy and urgency of witnesses' experiences, that embodiment is subject to the intertwined mediations of both the institution and the individual subject.

17. Author Unlisted, Quoting Jeshajahu Weinberg, Press Release, "The Assault (1933–1939), The Holocaust (1939–1945), and Bearing Witness (1945–): The Permanent Exhibition of the United States Holocaust Memorial Museum." Undated.
18. Content Committee Meeting Transcript. 13 February 1990. US Holocaust Memorial Museum; Institutional Archives; Research Institute; Records of the Director—Michael Berenbaum; 1986–1994; 1997–006; Box 27.
19. Linenthal, *Preserving Memory*, 214.
20. Hilberg quoted in Content Committee Meeting Transcript. 13 February 1990.
21. Fagin paraphrased from Content Committee Meeting Minutes. 13 February 1990.
22. The debate concerning the display of hair is extensively chronicled in Linenthal, *Preserving Memory*, 210–16, where I first learned of this controversy and where I was directed toward institutional files, including Content Committee meeting transcripts documenting the process.
23. Author Unlisted, Oral History Report: An Overview of the Process and Initial Steps. 20 September 1988. US Holocaust Memorial Museum; Institutional Archives; Exhibitions; Permanent Exhibition—Development Files; 1990–1994; 1998–038; Box 13; Oral History.
24. Martin Smith cited in Linda Gordon Kuzmack, Memorandum to Martin Smith. 18 October 1989. US Holocaust Memorial Museum; Institutional Archives; Research Institute; Records of the Director—Michael Berenbaum; 1986–1994; 1997–006; Box 26; Oral History (1 of 1).
25. Martin Smith, Memorandum to Jeshajahu Weinberg. 7 May 1990. US Holocaust Memorial Museum; Institutional Archives; Exhibitions; Permanent Exhibition—Development Files; 1990–1994; 1998–038; Box 8; Film Treatment.
26. Smith, Memorandum to Weinberg. 7 May 1990.
27. Author Unlisted, Request for Proposal No. CX-1100-RFP-1020-Title: Motion Picture on Testimony. 20 June 1991. US Holocaust Memorial Museum; Institutional Archives; Director's Office; Records of the Museum Director—Jeshajahu "Shaike" Weinberg; 1979–1994; 1997–014; Box 120; Permanent Exhibition Segments.
28. Author Unlisted, Request for Proposal No. CX-1100-RFP-1020-Title: Motion Picture on Testimony. 20 June 1991.
29. Sandy Bradley, Amendment to the Work Plan for Testimony Film. 21 October 1991. US Holocaust Memorial Museum; Institutional Archives; Director's Office; Records of the Museum Director—Jeshajahu "Shaike" Weinberg; 1979–1994; 1997–014; Box 120; Permanent Exhibition Segments.
30. Lawrence Langer, *Holocaust Testimonies*, 3; Charlotte Delbo, *Days and Memory*, trans. Rosette Lamont (Evanston, IL: Northwestern University Press, 2001), 3–4.

31. Testimony of Agnes Mandl Adachi. 29 November 1990. Videotape RG-50.030*0003, Collections Department, US Holocaust Memorial Museum, Washington, DC.
32. Transcript of Adachi testimony (videotape RG-50.030*0003), Collections Department, US Holocaust Memorial Museum, Washington, DC, 33.
33. Testimony of Adachi.
34. James Young, "Toward a Received History of the Holocaust," *History and Theory* 36, no. 4 (1997): 40.
35. Author Unlisted, Summaries of Completed USHMM Oral Histories. Undated. US Holocaust Memorial Museum; Institutional Archives; Research Institute; Records of the Director—Michael Berenbaum; 1986–1994; 1997–006; Box 26; Oral History (1 of 1).
36. Testimony of Nesse Godin. 8 May 1989. Videotape RG-50.030*0080, Collections Department, US Holocaust Memorial Museum, Washington, DC.
37. Linda Gordon Kuzmack, Memorandum to Martin Smith. 18 October 1989.
38. Steven Koppel, Memorandum to Learning Center Advisory Committee Regarding "The Peanut Butter Theory": Evaluating the Potential of Existing Video Testimonies for Conversion to Interactive Delivery. 9 February 1989. US Holocaust Memorial Museum; Institutional Archives; Director's Office; Records of the Museum Director—Jeshajahu "Shaike" Weinberg; 1979–1994; 1997–014; Box 22; Committee: Learning Center.
39. Simon Wiesenthal Center, "Holocaust Survivors in Three Cities across North America Join Together to Confront Iran's Conference of Holocaust Deniers and Revisionists," Simon Wiesenthal Center press release, 11 December 2006, http://www.wiesenthal.com/site/apps/nlnet/content2.aspx?c=fwLYKnN8LzH&b=4423617&ct=3287257 (accessed 15 December 2006).
40. United States Holocaust Memorial Museum, "United States Holocaust Memorial Museum Denounces Iranian Conference on the Holocaust," United States Holocaust Memorial Museum press release, 11 December 2006, ushmm.org/museum/press/archives/detail.php?category=07-general&content=2006-12-11 (accessed 15 December 2006).
41. Minutes of the United States Holocaust Memorial Council Ad Hoc Exploratory Group for a Committee on Conscience. 25 October 1994. US Holocaust Memorial Museum; Institutional Archives; Director's Office; Records of the Museum Director—Jeshajahu "Shaike" Weinberg; 1979–1994; 1997–014; Box 22; Committee: Conscience.
42. "Our Walls Bear Witness," US Holocaust Memorial Museum, Washington, DC, 20 November 2006. Personal observation.
43. Museum Concept Planning Committee Minutes. 6 November 1985. US Holocaust Memorial Museum; Institutional Archives; Records of the Chairman—Elie Wiesel; Box 21.
44. Bridget Conley-Zilkic, Project Director US Holocaust Memorial Museum Committee on Conscience, interview with the author, Washington, DC, 23 February 2007.
45. Interview with Conley-Zilkic.
46. Minutes of the United States Holocaust Memorial Council Ad Hoc Exploratory Group for a Committee on Conscience. 25 October 1994.
47. Landsberg, *Prosthetic Memory*, 118.
48. I am referring to Janet Walker, *Trauma Cinema: Documenting Incest and the Holocaust* (Berkeley: University of California Press, 2005), particularly her

compelling argument for a mode of engaging with representations of traumatic memory, including testimonies, in ways that can account for their subjective and rhetorical dimensions.

49. Ellen Blalock, Director Survivors Affairs and Speakers Bureau US Holocaust Memorial Museum, interview with the author, Washington, DC, 26 March 2007.
50. Lawrence Langer letter to Michael Berenbaum. 4 April 1991. US Holocaust Memorial Museum; Institutional Archives; Research Institute; Records of the Director—Michael Berenbaum; 1986–1994; 1997–006; Box 26; Oral History (1 of 1).

"we shall drown, but we shall not move"

the ecologics of testimony in nba documentaries

two

bishnupriya ghosh

> *We have lived here for twenty generations. The land is not only for us but for ants and insects and cattle and birds and trees and gods and demons—for all of us together.*[1]

The anonymous speaker iterates a mantra against the Indian postcolonial state. He lives in Domkhedi, one of the many villages slated for submergence by the coming of large dams. He represents the countless dam-affected—the relocated, the displaced, and the drowned out—in India's Narmada river valley for the past three decades. He speaks of an "ecologic," the logic of *oikos* (or the household),[2] of dwelling in an interconnected system (*oikonomia* or economy) of human and nonhuman relations. He offers such logic as a polemic against developmental projects undertaken by the state that provide compensation only for the loss of property—if that. The speaker intimates the losses go further, deeper. Some may be tabulated (land, home, cattle, crops), but others remain incalculable (forest, water, community, generational memory, religious practice). Together they provide the basis for the testimonies that I scrutinize here.

These testimonies materialize in multiple media, but I shall focus on a particularly *moving* instance: their audiovisual capture in a series of documentaries made in solidarity with the Narmada Bachao Andolan (NBA, Save the Narmada Struggle), a thirty year social movement launched against the Indian state (the federal government), regional governments (of Gujarat, Madhya Pradesh, Maharashtra, and Rajasthan), corporations (the German Siemens, the American Ogden Energy Group, and the Japanese ODA, to name a few), and institutions of global governance (such as the World Bank).[3] The movement seeks to curtail the single largest river valley hydro-irrigation project in India, involving the building of 30 major dams, 135 medium, and 3000 minor dams along the 820-mile Narmada River in western India, which spans four states. Construction on one of the largest dams, the Sardar Sarovar Project (SSP) that has evoked virulent opposition, began as early as 1961, but the project gathered speed as late as 1985 when the World Bank agreed to fund it. Proponents of the project argue the dams would bring irrigation, electricity, and drinking water to vast populations. According to government estimates 152,000 people would be affected by the project, 37,000 of them indigenous peoples or *adivasis*;[4] most other agencies, together with NBA documentarians, put the count of the dam-affected closer to 400,000.

The "NBA docs" (as I shall call them) shot on film and video have played a robust role in garnering global legibility for a series of heterogeneous struggles in the river valley involving heterogeneous actors with multiple grievances, demands, and agendas: K.P. Sashi and Ratna Mathur's *A Valley Refuses to Die* (India, 1988), Ali Kazimi's *Narmada: A Valley Rises* (Canada, 1994), Simantini Dhuru and Anant Patwardhan's *The Narmada Diary* (India, 1995), Jharna Jhaveri and Anurag Singh's *Kaise Jeebo Re!* (*How Shall We Survive*, India, 1997), Sanjay Kak's *Words on Water* (India, 2002), and Franny Armstrong's *Drowned Out* (Britain, 2002), along with two shorter videos, Aravinda Pillamarri's *I Will Report Honestly* (India, 1999) and Leena Pendharkar's autobiographical foray *My Narmada Diary* (US, 2002).[5] The documentaries range in their focus from preoccupations with deep ecology (in the Sashi/Mathur film) to shooting one long encounter between the NBA and the state (Kazimi's footage of an early face-off, December to January 1990). Despite the range, however, they share a significant political aesthetic that I shall develop in this chapter.

Deeply archival, the NBA docs assemble institutional archives (government-sponsored newsreels, engineering plans, budgets, public policy documents) as a spectral backcloth to testimonies from dam-affected indigenous communities; overtly activist, they seek to represent "public interest" against the state, echoing the NBA's challenge to national and regional governing bodies.[6] Their solidarity with the NBA is evident in the collaborative nature of these productions. One notices the *same* filmmakers, crew, and consultants cropping up in several documentaries: for example, Ali Kazimi (*Narmada: A Valley Rises*) is a consultant on Dhuru/Patwardhan's *Narmada Diary*, Jharna Javeri (*Kaise Jeebo Re!*) on Sanjay Kak's *Words on Water* and Kazimi's *Narmada*, Simantini Dhuru on the Jhaveri/Singh, Sashi/Mathur, and Kazimi films; Patwardhan's cameraperson Ranjan Palit is the photographer for Kak's documentary.[7] Other journalists, activists, and scholars who have documented the movement in print media (Chittaroopa Palit, Amita Baviskar, and Sanjay Sangvai) also variously appear in the credit sequences, testifying to a large informal network of collaborators engaged in a common project.[8]

A second collaboration between the documentarians and those who testify in the films tells us something more about the nature of this archive. The longest testimonials are garnered from established *adivasi* witnesses *and* activists such as Bhola Mundiya, Dedlibai, and Luhariya Sankariya. The most eloquent local spokespeople are repeatedly chosen to convey the "public interest" of disenfranchised populations. Their agenda is to *affect* audiences, to move them to solidarity. So the best translators in the business—those who, politicized by loss, can tell stories well, those who argue well—are employed to take on this Herculean task. Clearly the gathering of testimony here is not intended as a legal archive where numbers matter; rather, the testimonials work alongside voice-over narration to translate degrees and modalities of loss for target audiences in India and abroad.[9]

Figure 2.1

Luhariya Sankariya testing Franny Armstrong's camera (photo by Franny Armstrong, courtesy of www.spannerfilms.net)

But who are these translators? How are they framed as interlocutors of state violence? How do they move audiences distant from the Narmada Valley? One eloquent translator of the ecologic of subalterns with rare access to the media, one who crops up in several documentaries and essays,[10] is Luhariya Sankariya. (The protagonist of Franny Armstrong's *Drowned Out* (2002), he reappears in the other NBA docs as well.) A denizen of Jalsindhi village, Luhariya's house lies low on the embankment; yet he (along with his wife, Bulgi) has consistently refused to relocate. Luhariya has been pressing for *adivasi* rights since the 1980s, but still awaits rehabilitation.[11] With the documentaries opening channels of communication to greater national and international publics, on more than one occasion he argues the state does not "see" *adivasis* as citizens proper who stand to lose river, trees, belongings, crops, and home—they continue to live outside the fold of the state.[12] In Sanjay Kak's *Words on Water* (2002), he appears in medium close-up, sitting legs drawn to chest, black umbrella slung across his lap, facing the camera as he speaks; within the frame we see a lush verdant green landscape that is soon to disappear with the coming of the Sardar Sarovar dam. The shot is simply constructed, Luhariya plum in the center, the camera unobtrusive. So it is when we consider the narrative location of such a shot—shots that precede or succeed it—the interview gathers force of testimony. I shall argue such "force" is carefully cultivated in these documentaries. They forge a political aesthetic emplacing the spectator, often removed from the unfamiliar sites of struggle, within the world soon to be lost so that "we," too, might *inhabit* the loss of the dam-affected. Such an aesthetic turns fragmentary interviews speaking of rivers, trees, and homes into public testimony.

The documentaries gather all evidence of struggle as signs of democracy, a liberal consensus quite strongly criticized by many. Yet despite this pitfall, their ecologic indicates the degree to which they participate in what Partha Chatterjee has famously called "the politics of the governed"[13]—an argument I shall return to more substantially later in the chapter. Here my claims generate pressing questions. Who are the target audiences the NBA docs seek to move? What kind of solidarity between speaker and witness do the NBA docs forge and how? They direct us to look closer at the NBA as a social movement that motivates the will to testimony and archive.

"they have drowned our gods"[14]

If mobility conjures perhaps the most significant feature of contemporary globalization, Gayatri Spivak cautions us to remember "people who have not moved"—Fourth World or indigenous peoples—whose lives are nevertheless radically disrupted by their insertion into systems of transnational exchange.[15] The story of big dams is one story of the global South in which indigenous communities become central protagonists: key to large-scale developmental projects, big dams in India, Ghana, Kenya, China, and Brazil have now displaced millions who have lost their homes and livelihoods to rising waters bearing promise of irrigation, drinking water, and electricity. Large dams in India have displaced 16–38 million, while the Three Gorges project in the Yangtze River Valley has uprooted 10 million.[16] In the past three decades, 1554 dams have been built in India alone.[17] Hence these decades have seen strong responses from both those who govern (institutions and leaders) and those who are governed (dam-affected populations). The World Commission on Dams now encourages dam construction as the last alternative, and only when it is "economically viable, socially equitable, and environmentally sustainable," while popular opposition has come from "people who have not moved"—who vow "never to move."[18]

Not all these environmental justice struggles signify as "green." In the Indian case scholars have shown how the state responds to similar incidents of police brutality against environmental activists depending on the degree to which a struggle is globally legible.[19] An encounter[20] between activists and the police in the Maheswar anti-dam struggle of the NBA in 1998, Amita Baviskar writes, received a very different response from the Indian state than the one involving the Adivasi Mukti Sangathan (AMS)[21] mobilized around ethnicity, distributive justice, and local commons in the Nimar plains of Madhya Pradesh. Not only were the perpetrators of police violence *not* held accountable in the AMS incident, but also the state resorted to different tactics in each case. To the NBA they offered redress in the name of *saama* (equal and respectful treatment), while in the Nimar plains area they engaged in *daama* (buying out) and *bhed* (inciting differences) among indigenous populations. The different responses reveal the kind of social capital garnered by these different environmentalisms, a capital garnered, as scholars such as social historian Ramachandra Guha have argued, by the NBA's success in linking local actors to North-based environmental networks for advocacy, money, and media coverage.[22]

Yet the NBA's legibility has dismayed many. The presence of NGO benevolence prompts new suspicions of dependency: organizing resistance to dams, activists worry, can serve to defuse political anger turning folks into dependent victims. NGOs are not, after all, wholly free from governmental processes and procedures of governance, Upendra Baxi reminds us;[23] they therefore transform the modes of social action undertaken by those who stand to lose most and pass organizational power into the hands of intermediaries. Others criticize the mythopoetic capture in national and global media of a rapidly morphing movement—for example, the eternal dyad of activist Medha Patkar and "her" *adivasis*. The NBA has changed immensely since its first local stance—"the dam will not be built." From local resistance it has moved to a formal critique of large dams, to a broader inquiry into accepted models of development and, more recently, multiple engagements against privatization. But the cost of global legibility has been the fixing of the first moment in the public imagination, now a static iconic image of the movement.

These are but a few of the litany of criticisms leveled against the NBA. No doubt they cast a shadow on the cultural work of the NBA docs, key media for forging global linkages. So how may we understand the NBA docs' political agendas in the face of such criticism? After all, the NBA docs *are* in the business of making the NBA legible: that is, both recognizable and legitimate.[24] But legibility leads us into a more complex consideration of the question.

Legibility immediately invokes the materiality of documentary practice—those institutions, practices, and networks constitutive of documentary as activism. We might consider production values, formats (film, video, and digital), media technologies, and exhibition venues (audiences ranging from small-town India to international film festivals) to parse the garnering of legibility. Some of the NBA documentarians have strong allegiances to flourishing collectives (such as Media Storm, the Janamayam Cieds Collective, the Raqs Media Collective), participating in a "parallel and secondary structure" for production, distribution, and exhibition of the sort Charles Wolfe describes in the case of the American documentary collectives.[25] NGOs, foundations, social interest groups, and privately raised monies fund many of the NBA docs,[26] not the state-run Films Division that had long sponsored information and propaganda films; many of the filmmakers work on a flexible small scale, doing most of the camerawork and editing themselves;[27] debates erupt over subtitling, screening venues, and the packages of traveling film shorts; and the filmmakers often travel to local (village or small-town) venues to translate (sometimes literally) their films for local audiences. More significantly, the NBA docs directly target heterogeneous "global audiences" consisting of both lay audiences who may be self-conscious viewers of "global cinemas" (screened at film festivals, art cinema, or small screen local theaters) and self-reflexive documentary publics with some exposure to social change documentaries (screened at festivals and conferences). The subtitles and intertitles are telling in this regard: local measures such as quintals or *sher*, for example, are translated into kilograms or liters, while monetary transactions are transcribed to dollar amounts. Clearly transnational (English-speaking, literate) audiences are crucial for funds and advocacy, and the NBA docs undoubtedly seek to "sell" the movement to transnational audiences.[28]

While these questions of circulation, exhibition, and distribution are central to any consideration of the NBA's politics, in looking at testimony, my primary emphasis in this chapter falls on legibility in its second resonance: a cognitive framework. Many of the NBA documentarians, most famously Anant Patwardhan, who claims, "my style of documentary filming is simple—you just film the truth,"[29] self-consciously position their utterances as transparent captures of events. History happens; the camera snaps it up. Yet, these are finely crafted, even poetic, texts positioning the people who will not move as heroic figures who make good the promise of democracy. So we are tempted to ask: what kind of frameworks do we find in these documentaries? How do they encourage us to read testimony in specific ways?

"you have come to take our pictures? what will you do for us?"[30]

The famous words from an irritated interviewee in Anant Patwardhan's early film on Mumbai *Bombay, Our City* (1985) highlights the documentary problematic: to what extent do documents such as these bring about social change? *Do* they in fact, as Jane Gaines has asked, spur audiences to action? If they do, the answer seems to lie in the NBA docs' generation of spectatorial empathy for the losses encountered by the dam-affected. Despite their self-proclaimed straightforward style, these documentaries deploy the veiling effects of voice-over expositions, of high contrast editing, of distinctive camera movements and angles, and of post-production sound.

To a large extent, the filmmaker remains at a pedagogic distance from the indigenous subject—evident in Sanjay Kak's expository invocation to his *adivasi* subjects to take back "*your* land, *your* forests, *your* river" (my emphasis)—aligning these films and videos with the *oeuvres* of documentary collectives who saw their productions as part of a larger social movement. Most notable among eco-docs of this kind is the work of the Ogawa Pro, a group of filmmakers (led by Ogawa Shinsuke) formed in 1968 to document the long struggle of Sanrizuka farmers against the building of Narita airport in Sanrizuka; by 1970 the Sanrizuka struggle had become a magnet for anti-war and student movements.[31] Taking the environment as the catalyst for critiques of the state, the work of the collective was inspired by the famous Sanrizuka documentaries (beginning in 1966), whose aesthetics of direct cinema (the handheld shots, the loud jumble of noise, shaky close-ups, and disrupted frames) resonate with the NBA documentaries. We see this on several occasions: for example, in Dhuru/Patwardhan, when the NBA activists attempt to speak to World Bank representatives (Mumbai, 1993), as the filmmaker engages in a fracas the handheld camera slides, we lose both focus and frame, and our only guide becomes the noise of a scuffle and loud argument on the audio-track along with an explanation in post-production voice-over; just after, intertitles tell us that while the film crew were engaged with NBA leaders demanding entry, the police were beating up the NBA activists outside in the absence of the camera. At such moments, the making of the film becomes an event in the NBA mobilization.

Further, the NBA docs have an episodic structure, those famous "mosaics" of direct cinema. The narrative moves from crisis to crisis: Dhuru, Patwardhan, Kazimi, and Kak, in particular, present encounter after encounter in a loose episodic telling of NBA resistance to multiple actors. Where the episodes in the Sanrizuka documentaries are held together by a musicality, as Abé Mark Nornes has suggested, the NBA docs suture the episodes—the countless protests and numerous testimonials—slightly differently, through a poetic cartography. Throughout the documentaries we *return* to the river Narmada as a continuous stabilizing arena: sequences shot on the river consolidate the disparate settings of the narrative action (the villages of Manibeli, Domkhehi, Jasindhi, Mokhdi, Bargi, and so forth), while the voice-over narration spatially organizes these shooting locations as "further up along the Narmada," "on its west bank," or "where the Narmada enters Gujarat." In some of the NBA docs (notably, the Sashi/Mathur film, but also in Jhaveri/Singh), the cartography, history, and mythologies of the river cast *adivasi* losses in a historical frame.

More importantly, the insertion of an idyllic "unbound" river at regular narrative intervals heightens the spectator's sense of loss. The composition of episodes taking place at the resettlement camps are in stark contrast to the lush views of the river; close-ups of rusting machinery (partially obscuring the frame of a shot), the cluttered *mise-en-scène* of ramshackle huts, the pans over an arid parched earth are juxtaposed with the panoramic shots of the Narmada, which have considerable depth of field and are habitually interspersed with medium close-ups of trickling/lapping water or verdant foliage (reminiscent of nature docs). The audio-track for the river shots largely offers diegetic sound—lapping, trickling, quiet sounds of human activity on the river, the rustle of leaves as the filmmaker (with a handheld camera) makes his or her way around the banks; in contrast, the track for the resettlement camps registers camera static (unedited in post-production) combined with a pedantic voice-over on where we are or whom we shall meet.

Such careful aesthetics not only heighten the spectatorial affect suturing the spectator to the river as a place of repose, but also crystallize "our" relation to river ecology (humans, plants, water). Like the haptic cinema of the Sanrizuka documentaries, where the camera was sometimes "planted" in the mud to immerse us in the earth tilled by the insurgent farmers, the NBA docs work at emplacing us "in" the river, "in" the forest. The handheld camera rushing close to plants and the water, often in extreme close-ups, already offers pleasures beyond the cognitive—kinesthetic pleasures of moving in this landscape. We spend much time moving on the river from village to village, the rocking motion becoming haptic grammar as we progress. The filmmakers facilitate further immersion by turning up the volume of the natural world: a lapping becomes louder until it surrounds us. If we remember sound requires matter to make its way to its destination (our bodies), then such audio supplements the visual perspective in sensate ways. The combination of the cognitive, kinesthetic, and sensate, as Laura Marks has argued,[32] renders the river intimate, a living breathing organism coextensive with us, a system whose logic, constantly explained in the testimonials, begins to govern our grasp of the political matters at hand.

Several sequences illustrate this haptic dimension, an exemplary instance occurring thirty minutes into Sanjay Kak's *Words on Water* where we come upon two men winnowing grain in the middle of a soon-to-be-submerged field. The sequence is shot at low angle, with a full shot of both men at a diagonal (with one closer to us than the other) swinging a cloth filled with grain between them. The edge of the cloth reaches right up to the camera, out-of-focus as a blur of showering grain hits the lens. Lulled by the swinging motions of the rich harvest, we are caught in motion and lulled by the repetitive *chik-chik* of falling grain as the figure closest to us fades into rack focus before the dissolve. A similar sequence in Jhaveri/Singh's *Kaise Jeebo Re!* plunges us into the rhythms of the *adivasi* world, only this time with fishermen caught in silhouette as they fling their nets onto the river (the shimmer of net, like the grain, shot in close-up) and with ferrymen whose oars we habitually follow into the river. In such immersive cinema, the spectator "shares" the consciousness of the *adivasis* whose story of social, economic, ecological loss and consequent politicization the documentaries attempt to tell. The documentaries ensure political mimesis by spectatorial sensuous *dwelling* (*oikos*) within an ecosystem (*oikonomia*).

"we will die and live on this land"[33]

But who are these subjects we glimpse, who stand to lose this world? More importantly, *how* do they speak to us in these documentaries? The memorable concluding shot to the sequence I have analyzed in Dhuru/Patwardhan's *Narmada Diary* provides a point of departure. The bucolic sequence closes with a full shot of a ferryman (an envoy of the downstream dam-affected) silhouetted against the river. A romanticized, indeterminate cutout against the sky, he visually straddles river and sky, embedded in the ecological world the film discloses to us. Such a figure, a heroic visual figuration representative of those "who will not move," often concludes a litany of other subjects engaged in various social and economic activities on the river—a child playing in the mud, a farmer, a woman washing clothes, women bathing, and so forth. The romanticized subaltern who "dwells" on the Narmada is the ecologically lodged subject par excellence, recoded in populist vein, one who "stands in for" various others who testify to a disrupted ecology (the relations between humans and other living organisms) along the river with the coming of the dams. In the age of constant motility, evident in the geography of camps visualized in these documents (arid land, ramshackle tin huts, close-ups of rusted pumps, tractors, or hoses), the ecologically lodged subjects living on the banks of the great river seem utterly "placed" in the documentary imagination recuperating the logic of dwelling in this balanced economy of organisms. Such immersion in the *adivasi* world turns subaltern object into homely *paisan*, one whose losses move us in this populist cinema.

Figure 2.2

Satyagrahis, Domkhedi 1999 (photo by Harikrishna Katragadda and Deepa Jani, courtesy of Friends of the River Narmada, www.narmada.org)

Yet such a romantic figure is a far cry from the *heterogeneous* dam-affected whose *testimonies* we hear throughout the documentaries. Official estimates of PAP ("project affected peoples") are 245 villages or 40,000 families numbering 85,000; the NBA puts it at 60,000 families numbering 400,000, including downstream dam-affected communities.[34] The dam-affected range from farmers (both rich *patidar* crop farmers to *adivasi* subsistence farmers) who have not been compensated or have been inadequately compensated for their land; to downstream communities (fisherfolk, ferrymen, healers, sand quarry workers, among others, dependent on the Narmada embankment forests for their livelihood); to those who acquiesced to resettlement but find themselves in resettlement camps for 10–20 years (the earliest camps were set up in 1982); to others who move *back* to their drowned out lands to escape slow decline at the camps. Many of the dam-affected hardly fit the category of the subaltern visible to the state only when violently insurgent; many are highly articulate in their testimony. Several *adivasi* actors are visible to the state, registering discontent and demands in a litany of lawsuits and petitions; their exchanges with state representatives (politicians, bureaucrats, and the police) are often mediated via a network of activist leaders, translators, media representatives, lawyers, students, and NGO members.[35] More truly subaltern are two other groups: one comprises the disaffected camp-dwellers whose testimonials are carefully collected as primary documents, the other those who have not moved away but relocated to higher ground, eking out a living on scant means, whose daily brutalization fuels insurgency. It is their testimony—loss and subsequent dehumanization—that gathers moral force in these works of solidarity.

Scholars explain that a large percentage of the subalterns in the NBA docs are *adivasis*. In Amita Bavishkar's excellent scholarly study of resistance to the NBA, *In the Belly of the River: Tribal Conflicts over Development in the Narmada Valley*, the history of the NBA becomes part of a larger struggle for "tribal rights," which has now culminated in the passing of the Scheduled Tribes and Other Traditional Forest Dwellers' Act in the Indian Parliament, 2006.[36] The NBA docs carefully document the different communities (the Bhils, Gonds, Bhilalas, and Baigyas) that are officially ethnicized, the Jhaveri/Singh film interviewing locals who explicitly refer to resettled *adivasis* as "savages" (who only know how to eat and drink and who barely cover their bodies). If Bavishkar's NBA history renders subalterns legible by framing them as ethnically defined subjects, Arun Agarwal's *Environmentality: Technologies of Government and the Making of Subjects* (2005) makes legible a more heterogeneous conglomerate of actors—political ecologists who work on the commons, environmental justice advocates, and deep ecologists—for whom the environment is "a domain in conscious relation to which they organize their actions."[37]

The NBA documentaries also present the *adivasis* as "environmental subjects," but rather differently from these scholarly works. The *adivasi* becomes *representative* spokesperson, victim politicized into activism; all the documentaries introduce the *adivasis* as those who have *lost* the most. Several *adivasis* speak of a harmonious economy (the production of pulses, sorghum, millet, maize, oilseed, lemons, *tendu* leaves, gums, fruits, and *mahua* flowers; of folk medicines; of fish harvesting) "before" the dams; others insist on an ethics of compensation, angered at being offered land wrested from other *adivasi* communities; and still others intimate a desire for a commons.[38] Besides these aspirations, the dam-affected record grievances: not only failed legal entitlements, but failed rehabilitation (e.g. bad water at the camps destroying cattle, goats, and sheep) and unacceptable compensation (e.g. rocky land with silt poured over it). Most often the documentaries focus on loss—the full calculus of goats, cattle, yields, forests, crops, acres, household goods lost to rising waters—alongside documenting *adivasi* social ecology (dances, myths, stories, and poems) and the popular artwork of the NBA (songs, posters, and effigies). Ceremonies, family histories,[39] and rituals (such as the funeral of an activist to which all those in solidarity are invited) also become events in the life of the NBA. So, though initially the camera eye lingering on face decoration or folk dances, or intruding upon grief, may appear quasi-anthropological, we begin to realize the documentaries choose their subjects *only if* they have some connection to the NBA. For example, at the close of the *Narmada Diary*, after a year of *satyagraha* ("civil disobedience"), we see why the documentary began with a traditional Holi dance spectacle; by 1994 the traditional event had been transformed into a political one, the dance now interspersed with the burning of effigies.

The record of everyday rhythms only intensifies our sense of the losses accruing to the dam-affected. The documentaries meticulously catalog the everyday intimacies of the river world that the abstract dream of development will disrupt. The river bank sequences are replete with everyday activity: *parikrama* (praying at the river), washing dishes or clothes, carrying drinking water, bathing, sand quarrying, ferrying boats, sweeping huts, making *chapatis*, milking cows, tilling fields, brushing teeth from toothbrushes fashioned from branches, splicing tree-trunks for medicine ... the list is endless. The litany underscores the *extent* of the losses the *adivasis* will undergo, given their use of common space, forest, and water resources. As the ever articulate Luhariya Sankariya insists:

> Here we get things without money—fodder, fuel, wood for housing. In resettlement everything needs money, therefore we must make loans and we are trapped in a cash economy. We have never had to migrate for work—everything we need is here.[40]

But with the coming of dams, those *adivasis* who are *least* integrated into systems of exchange stand to lose "everything." The descriptive axis of the documentary supports the stature of their loss by recording a vital relationship with the river world, a relation with its own logic. Such an emphasis on the relations between human and nonhuman worlds moves beyond the otherwise mythic claims of origin—"we have a right to dwell *here*" or "the forest belonged to *our* forefathers." Ecology offers a grammar of collective ownership parallel to that of individual property rights.

"i have nothing more to say"[41]

The documentaries make it clear that despite mobilization, despite dying for a cause, those who have lost most by the coming of the dams remain subaltern, since their "speech" is lost in bureaucratic white noise or amid the din of state-sponsored pro-dam protests. And when *adivasi* demands *are* audible (writs filed, petitions submitted) they fade into obscurity with the passing of years. The highest court in the land fails to uphold the right to moral dwelling (implicit in the ecologic) as a juridical right (the Supreme Court lifted the ban on dam-building in 2000). Such suggestion intimates that subalternity *persists*—hence the right to disruption persists. The narrative logic of the documentaries leads us to frame insurgency as set in motion by the state, the fitting response to dehumanization.

Scholars, activists, and observers often suggest the root of the problem lies not only with the ideologies of development and an unwieldy bureaucracy, but with the languages of legal entitlements, rehabilitation and resettlement, and compensation. Neera Chandhoke, a long-time associate of the NBA, explains that it is not that the *adivasis* are incapable of self-representation, but that they do not have access to these specialized languages, illustrating her observation with an evocative story:

> [A] revenue official surveying land holdings in the valley for the purposes of assessing the amount of compensation asked a tribal about his land holdings. The tribal pointing towards an area of land claimed proprietorship of that land. Expectedly he was asked to show the relevant papers that establish land ownership—the *patta* [deed]. Equally expectedly, the tribal did not possess any such *patta*. "How do you know in this case that the land is yours?" asked the revenue official. "The bones of my forefathers are buried along the boundaries of the land," answered the tribal.[42]

Since such evidence cannot count toward a legal claim, the revenue official leaves without a record of the *adivasi* as deserving of resettlement. And one could multiply these examples. Another observer, Clifton Rozario, reiterates the dissonance of translating the *adivasi* view of loss (alighting once more on Luhariya Sankariya's case) in his careful parsing of the various bodies through which each voice travels: voiced grievances (sometimes directly tabulated, and sometimes in songs and myths) are transcribed into writ petitions and affidavits, then framed by a court case letter (with advocates selecting appropriate "facts") before submission to a judge who, in turn, will choose to hear only what is relevant.

It is in this context of failed transmission that the interviews of the dam-affected in the documentaries assume the force of testimony. All of the documentaries deliberately juxtapose the official record of the Narmada Valley Project with the popular view consolidated through testimony. Official views range from news excerpts from Doordarshan (the state-run television network),[43] government-funded advertisements for the dam (on television and in posters or banners), interviews with pro-dam activists, party workers, and state officials, to close-ups of documents and reports; Sanjay Kak films a museum dedicated to "tribal life" and the river ecology that has *already* frozen what will soon become historical artifact with the coming of the dams.

Clearly the NBA documentaries seek to create an audiovisual record as public archive against possible erasure. Within the documentaries, this agenda is most evident in the documentarians' self-styling as witnesses who compensate for the severe lack of coverage of *adivasi* grievances and aspirations in mainstream media. Kak self-reflexively underscores the participation of the filmmaker as an appropriate response to the "time-scale that the crises of the environment seem to demand";[44] Dhuru and Patwardhan acknowledge their participatory role in naming their documentary a "video diary." At several points in the documentaries, if unobtrusively, we are made aware of the presence of the filmmakers by their voice dimly caught on the camera's mike, or by the gesture of the interviewee left unedited in the documentary. In *The Narmada Diary*, a man who speaks of his drowned home brusquely turns away from the camera, suddenly impatient, muttering "I have nothing more to say"; at a later point, just as the camera focuses on a group of women laughing at someone who had slipped on the muddy riverbank, one woman humorously *performs* her activism for the filmmaker by the words, "We will slip, but we won't shift." Such self-reflexive moments position the documentarian as witness caught in complex social relations, and not as an objective reporter. Some of the interviewees demand such witnessing: "You listen to our voice," insists Baba Bhai early in the Sashi/Mathur film, "we will die and live on this land," while *Kaise Jeebo Re!* closes with people standing chest deep in water, insisting the educated remain attentive to "our plight" so it may not be that of others.

"i know how my heart feels"[45]

Although the primary imperative of the NBA docs is to capture the anti-dam mobilization, they are clearly interested in recording and figuring loss. Even apart from fragmentary snatches speaking of loss, all the documentaries consolidate several full-fledged testimonies, numbering anywhere from 7-8 (in Dhuru/Patwardhan and Kak) to as many as 15 (in Jhaveri/Singh). Testimonies are taken at village meetings which inform and mobilize; at rallies and protests; at the resettlement camps; on drowned out riverbanks (most commonly); and, occasionally, to record physical death (in the voices of the bereaved) or injury. Sashi/Mathur dedicate their film to Gangaram Keludia, who lost his life to the Subarnarekha Dam Project, while the Jhaveri/Singh film closes dramatically with *adivasis* chest deep in water who speak of their "exit" from the world, their fragile presence in the now as ghosts.[46] The tenor of the testimonies varies according to their site. For example, Dhuru/Patwardhan begin *The Narmada Diary* with the testimony of a woman, hands tied by Gandhian veteran Baba Amte to signal nonviolence, at the center of a crowd of protesters and police. Angrily she exhorts the police "to fire on us now," and not "drown us later," moving on to assert her right to dwell in the Satpura range that belonged to "our forefathers." Assuming a collective voice, this trenchant, fiery declaration is fairly representative of testimonies gathered at protests, a sharp contrast to the more emotional testimonials of loss at the riverbank. I will focus on the latter at some length because they are the most affective, intended as they are to move us; but let me pause briefly on the two other genres before I do.

Establishing shots of the camp, with close-ups of dry arid land and rusting machinery, often frame testimonies taken at the resettlement camps.

Interviewees are mostly placed inside their temporary dwellings, sometimes caught in humdrum activities (eating dinner or preparing food) and sometimes more formally facing the camera as the filmmakers trot out questions. Many such testimonies carefully and intricately tabulate grievances: a man from Mokhdi village who lives in a camp recounts the five acres of unusable land he received from the government, before taking Kak on a tour of the camp where others speak of the lack of fodder, contaminated groundwater, dry wells, the death of cattle, and lack of food. Armstrong's film captures Bhugabai Thakys' nine-member family displaced by the Bargi dam living in a slum, who have used up the meager cash compensation they were given for their 14-acre farm; once subsistence farmers, her daughter and son-in-law now join the millions of manual laborers in the cities who work as bricklayers or rickshaw-pullers. "I know how my heart feels," says Bhugabai to Armstrong. "And I don't even die!"

The third variant comprises testimonies at meetings where politicized *adivasis* speak to their comrades about their loss. Armstrong shoots Luhariya from his left, flanked by other activists, as he speaks of his losses but also his targets, goals, and plans at a meeting before the Jalsindhi *satyagraha* of 2000: "The country does not belong to the government exclusively," Armstrong's subtitles of Luhariya's speech tell us. "It also belongs to the *adivasis*, it belongs to everyone." A sequence of shots clearly frames Luhariya's testimony as democracy in action, as his speech is crosscut with three to four zooms to demonstrators in procession while police wait, batons in hand. Such testimonies at meetings are shot at medium range, with signature unobtrusive camerawork; perhaps the testimonies at the protests most reveal the presence of the camera as the handheld device is jostled in the crowd, sometimes sliding away from the interviewee as the filmmaker seeks to regain his or her balance. Together these testimonies, full of myriad detail, have a *cumulative* effect on the spectator overcome by a general sense of loss.

The sense of loss is keenest in the river testimonies that claim the lion's share of screen time in the documentaries (even as they vary in frequency and duration). They are often anticipated by the kind of immersive takes I have discussed already. About twenty-eight minutes into the Dhuru/Patwardhan film, there is a three-minute testimony from a woman whose land has been drowned out when the dammed waters rise at Manibeli village during the monsoons. Just before we get to the testimony, there is an extreme close-up of an oar in the river as the filmmakers appear by boat; as the boat arrives, a naked child stares at the camera. The camera slowly takes in the mud and moves close up to a destroyed hut, as the roar of the wind fills the soundtrack. This spectatorial emplacing is followed by a cut to a medium close-up of the woman, with a naked child peeping into the frame of her hut on the right. Sounds of everyday activity—voices far down the bank, a broom brushing leaves, the clink of pails—register on the soundtrack as the woman bewails their decision to stay despite government warnings.

"We have lost everything," she says, pointing to the river before looking away and wiping away a tear with the *pallu* of her sari. The camera modestly focuses on the child staring at the mother, before cutting to the river as its roar is amplified on the soundtrack.

Armstrong's documentary abounds in voiced testimony overlaying shots of the river, bank, fields, and homes. Forty-two minutes into the film, a voice bewails the drowning of gods as the camera pans over the bank and cuts briefly to a woman framed by the river behind her; as she continues to speak, we are in motion through high green stalks that rustle on the soundtrack until we are down to the river and the camera focuses on the muddy bank. Then we cut to extreme close-ups of the river, water splashing against the shore as the woman's voice continues to "narrate" losses. The voices link the spectator immersed in the river world to the speaker, establishing a sound bridge between images of the nonhuman (river, forest, and embankment) and human (activities on the river) worlds. The testimonies that follow describe losses that have become embodied knowledge for the spectator *already* immersed in the river world—a double wound heightening the pathos of the river testimonies.

Such an emphasis on voice is furthered by the NBA docs' critique of the visual apparatus. The filmmakers reiterate the state's blind hubris—a list of miscalculations, oversight, and mismanagement—in staging *invisible* losses in a distinctive audiovisual language. On several occasions, when a subject points to drowned out homes or property, the camera (zooming in, zooming out, panning or tilting) focuses on the rising waters but appears unable to capture or locate what lies beneath, what has been lost. Rather, we depend on the testimonial voice to replace in imagination what is now invisible. Twenty-seven minutes into Dhuru/Patwardhan's film, a man testifies to the loss of his home, land, and cattle to the rising waters during the 1993 monsoons. Once more in medium close-up, he is on higher ground with the great Sardar Sarovar Dam lying in full view behind him. "See that land jutting out," he says. "There ... there," he reiterates with frustration, pointing his finger beyond the dam. The camera follows the indexical gesture, zooming in to where his home *once had been*—but of course the zoom helplessly falters, it pans and tilts in an effort to locate the exact spot amid a great swathe of water. But what is indexed is lost, and the gesture only gives the loss the charge of the phantom real. The helpless slow zoom at such moments contrasts sharply with the fast zoom out (iteratively used by Dhuru/Patwardhan, Kak, and Armstrong) to capture the magnificence of the dam: a close-up of gushing waters at the dam is often followed by an abrupt zoom out that reveals the width of the monster as a shock. But in the river testimonies, the zoom fails. Giving up, the camera moves back to the subject's face that speaks of "my home, my belongings, fields, cattle ... these are the only clothes I have," before turning away with irritation ("that's all I have to say"). The testimony ends here with a cut to an extreme close-up of an oar dipping in the river.

Figure 2.3
What the camera cannot find. A still from *Narmada Diary* (courtesy of Anant Patwardhan)

Such disjuncture where the zoom fails to follow the indexical gesture is repeated in the river testimonies of the other documentaries. The disjuncture between what we see and what we are told, between the visual and the audio, opens up the gap between a before and after of development, reiterated at other points by the omniscient voice-over narration. "By the time you see this film," we hear Patwardhan expostulate, "these villages will be gone." The spectator will have arrived too late. Now immersed in this ecology, he or she will experience the losses suffered by the subaltern subject. The disavowal of the visual reverberates as a critique of the state: one village, for instance, refused to let the state government "survey" the land, map and document it, since this act usually began the processes of land acquisition. The oral testimonial assumes primacy in an audiovisual text whose visual style unabashedly seeks to garner empathy.

"here we get things without money"[47]

The dams disrupt the *adivasis*' homeliness. The river turns into a commodity, redistributed to metropolitan and richer rural grounds; now de-naturalized, the Narmada confronts the subaltern in alien, even threatening, form. An "old friend turns foe," recounts Armstrong, while Kak ruminates in a melancholic vein on how "something familiar turns against you."[48] The melancholia is deeper in these later documentaries (both made in 2002) in the aftermath of the submerging of many villages by then. The loss of the river moves centrifugally to finally represent the loss of life itself.

Figure 2.4

Bap Dedya from Anjanwada in a field of *bajri* (photo by Neeta Deshpande, courtesy of www.narmada.org)

The majority of *adivasis* insist they might as well have died (drowned, shot, or starved to death), since the state obviously perceives them as sacrificial objects. Disposable peoples, these are dehumanized unhomely subjects of the nation; in protest they disrupt the time and space of the nation-state.

How do the NBA docs frame these disruptions of the state's designs? What are their political potentials, given their goal of garnering global legibility? Here political scientist Partha Chatterjee's reflections on the politics of the governed are extremely instructive. Chatterjee has long argued a will to governance marks those who are privileged members of civil society, given to regulating state power. If, as I have intimated, these documentaries play a key role as linking mechanisms that render local struggles globally legible as "liberal green," in Lawrence Buell's words,[49] they clearly call for proper governance. To a large extent, the NBA docs recognize forms of struggle that fit the idea of a liberal democracy made good by civil encounters, including nonviolent "civil disobedience" (*satyagraha*). All actions by subalterns against the Narmada Valley Project—be they part of the movement or not—are consolidated in the NBA docs as signs of democracy, with nonviolent *satyagraha* commanding most screen time. The icons of the movement (most centrally Medha Patkar and Baba Amte)[50] speak of the vitality of Indian democracy, while an army of translators submits writs and petitions; anger only erupts as vocal protest amid meetings or demonstrations. Kazimi's voice-over shots of NBA marchers' dusty feet tells us they are "following in the footsteps of Mahatma Gandhi," historical civil disobedience instantly consolidating heterogeneous protests, marches, and demonstrations under the rubric of a *national* movement. The *naras* (slogans) and speeches—such as Patkar insisting the entire country would back the dam-affected if only they knew their water had the blood of the dam-affected in it (*Narmada Diary*, 1995)—streamline the struggle into a national popular movement, smoothing over differences within the movement (different degrees of loss, different idioms of representation).

For those populations that have historically never participated in the modern associational forms constitutive of civil society, but who nevertheless have a *political* relationship with the state (the "governed," in Chatterjee's terms, "looked after and controlled by various government agencies" [38]), responses to the state might be quite differently conceived. They may not be nonviolent; they may consist of contingent negotiations on behalf of small groups not working in solidarity; and they may consist of demands for temporary relief or recompense based on *moral*, and not civil, rights. While the documentaries no doubt participate in the liberal dream of a revitalized state kept in check by a global civil society, it would be a mistake to undercut their solidarity with the "governed" daily engaged in a political society. The constant shifting compromise between the normative values of modernity (democracy gained through civil actions) and the "moral assertion of popular demands" in these documentaries testifies to such solidarity. Kazimi's documentary explicitly underscores such labor, the initial exposition framing what we see not just as mobilization for civil rights, but further as a "moral struggle at the heart of the valley." This moral right to dwelling is most evident in the documentaries' ability to *move* the spectator into an ecologic where the *adivasis'* relation to land, trees, river, gods, and demons is not just the mythic imagination of the noble savage. Rather, the political aesthetic of the documentaries works to emplace *the spectator* as ecological subject, one who begins to dwell in the world to be lost captured on camera and therefore inhabits the *ecologic* governing subaltern action. Such moral solidarity productively complicates the work of cultural translation these documentaries undertake as they participate in the NBA; they attempt to move the spectator to the political mimesis Jane Gaines has theorized in social change documentaries.[51] Following Tom Waugh, we might read these texts as utopian practice instead of instrumental projects;[52] social change documentaries such as these not only move audiences to read resistance (violent and nonviolent) as the logical and legitimate response to a violent state, but they further impart the moral attributes of community to hitherto amorphous "populations" not legible as publics.

Most importantly perhaps, the documentaries disclose the *plans* of the dam-affected. They remain heterogeneous hopes, targets, and goals; they speak of microclimates, local demands, and contingent solutions. They are in fact the uneven negotiations of the governed, now turning their sudden access to media technologies into tactical encounters with the state.

Documentary becomes solidarity with a "political society" that does not square with the overarching "civil" consensus the NBA exemplifies. Rather direct, even angry, outbursts from the dam-affected chafe against the (often) poetic melancholia of the voice-over narration. Some interviewees present well-calibrated tabulations of costs (exact yields from mango trees to sorghum), others offer pragmatic schemes the state might have adopted in lieu of this grandiose design;[53] still others demonstrate how older irrigation systems (like the *pat* method) had been a model of sustainable development. The initiatives testify to what Arjun Appadurai has named "the capacity to aspire" seen everywhere in the activism of the poor.[54] Such "wants, preferences, choices, and calculations" embedded in cultural and social life reveal the *adivasi* as an *economic* actor oriented to the future,[55] adept at navigating a real world of conjectures and refutations, and not simply a person of the past bound by unchanging culture (habit, custom, heritage, tradition).

The words of the governed speak to the future. They *aspire*. The documentaries foreground an ecologically harmonious (and economically viable) "before" to development in their poetic capture of loss. They *move*. Together testimony and framing text transmit knowledge in embodied form so that we may engage in sensuous struggle with those who refuse to move.

acknowledgments

My thanks to both Janet Walker and Bhaskar Sarkar for their insightful and perspicacious commentaries on the text; Stephanie Lemenager for her generous advice on fine-tuning my conception of "ecologics" and ecological citizenship; and Andrea Fontenot for her editorial suggestions.

notes

1. Anonymous testimonial from Domkhedi, 2000. Cited in Paul Routledge, "Voices of the Damned: Discursive Resistance against Erasure in the Narmada Valley," *Political Geography* 22, no. 3 (2003): 243–70.
2. *Oecologie* was one of the neologisms coined by Ernst Haeckel, a disciple of Darwin, in 1866. A term derived from the Greek *oikos*, referring originally to family household and its operations, for Haeckel *oecologie* referred to "living organisms of the earth [that] constitute a single economic unit resembling a household or family dwelling" (Donald Worster, *Nature's Economy: A History of Ecological Ideas*, Cambridge: Cambridge University Press, 1994). Such a conception moves against more romantic separations of dwelling from property, as William Cronon's breakaway short book *Changes in the Land* (New York: Hill and Wang, 1983) insisted.
3. The first stirrings of active struggle began in 1978, but these turned into a palpable social movement in 1985 when the charismatic Medha Patkar, a social scientist from Tata Institute of Studies in Bombay, started working for mobilization against the submergence zone in the villages of Maharashtra.

Patkar's urban contacts drew media attention first, and then the participation of city-based nongovernmental organizations, which began disseminating news of the struggle in briefings, newsletters, and films, lobbying legislators, collecting funds, and organizing solidarity events to keep the NBA in the news. The efforts on the part of North-based NGOs pressuring international funding agencies to withdraw aid met with substantial success in 1992, when the World Bank withdrew its support for the SSP in 1993.

4. The term means "original inhabitants," etymologically quite different from the official categories that register these indigenous groups as Scheduled Tribes. One of the best elaborations on the term can be found in David Hardiman's *The Coming of the Devi: Adivasi Assertion in Western India* (Delhi: Oxford University Press, 1987).
5. The states attached to each title (for instance, "India" or "Canada") only document the source of financing; the film crews, however, are almost always drawn from multiple locations.
6. The NBA challenged the Indian state's aggrandizing of land under the 1894 Land Acquisitions Act (which allows the state to annex land based on "public interest") on the grounds that the latter had failed to act in the "public interest."
7. A note on my shorthand for these documentaries: I transcribe collaborations as "Dhuru/Patwardhan" to intimate a joint enterprise rather than either/or; the placing of the names is alphabetically arranged, except in the Sashi/Mathur case, where Sashi is listed as director and Mathur as editor (yet the documentary is often classified under both names: see www.narmada.org, accessed 15 June 2008).
8. The footage of May 1993 protests (in which several NBA activists sustained injuries, and one youth was shot) in Patwardhan's documentary recurs in Armstrong's text, while Sanjay Kak's footage of a dispute at the Maheswar dam site (2000) is later recycled as a video installation in an exhibit, "Building Sight," on urban space hosted by the Raqs Media Collective ("India Now" festival, London, June 2007). The documentaries therefore become one public archive of popular resistance to large developmental projects (dams, "clean city" drives, real estate schemes).
9. These are not legal documents necessarily, although some of the filmed grievances have been subsequently used as archival records: in 2000 the NBA included eyewitness accounts in their report to the International Labour Organization.
10. In Franny Armstrong and Sanjay Kak's NBA docs, but also Clifton Rozario's "... Bolti Band" ["... Silenced"], *Sarai Reader 2005: Bare Acts* (www.sarai.net/readers/05-bare-acts, accessed 15 June 2008), 18–25.
11. Angana Chatterjee tracks the writs he has filed as a petitioner in the NBA (1994 and 2002) to bring this case before the courts. See "India Together: A Contradictory Post-colonialism," 9 February 2008 (www.indiatogether.org/campaigns/narmada/whither.html, accessed 15 June 2008).
12. In Luhariya's allegations against the state, he echoes what Andrew Dobson has recently described as "ecological citizenship," where the "footprint," rather than contiguous territory, should determine obligations and duties. Andrew Dobson, *Citizenship and the Environment* (London: Oxford University Press, 2003).
13. Partha Chatterjee, *Politics of the Governed: Reflections on Popular Politics in Most of the World* (New York: Columbia University Press, 2004).

14. Statement by Bawabhai of Jalsindhi, 2000. See www.narmada.org (accessed 15 June 2008).
15. Gayatri Spivak, "Diasporas Old and New: Women in the Transnational World," *Textual Practice* 10, no. 2 (1996): 245–69.
16. Vandana Shiva, *Water Wars: Privatization, Pollution, Profit* (Cambridge: South End Press, 2002), 67. See also Dzodzi Tsikata's analysis of the Akosombo Dam on the Volta, Ghana, in *Living in the Shadow of Large Dams* (London: Brill, 2006). The Three Gorges project has recently prompted filmmaker Jia Zangke to make a film, *Sanxia Haoren* (*Still Life*, 2006), that won the Golden Lion at Venice in 2007.
17. Before this period, the government had spent $1.5 billion on large and medium-sized irrigation dams between 1951 and 1980; yet, as Shiva catalogs, the yield of water (1.27 tons per hectare) has been pretty low (Shiva, *Water Wars*, 62–3).
18. World Commission on Dams, *Dams and Development: A New Framework for Decision Making*, 16 November 2000, dams.org (accessed 15 June 2008).
19. Amita Baviskar, *In the Belly of the River: Tribal Conflicts over Development in the Narmada Valley* (Delhi: Oxford University Press, 1997).
20. In India, the "encounter" is common parlance for police brutality with intent to eradicate.
21. The AMS (or the Organization for Tribal Liberation) is a grassroots conglomerate of activists and *adivasis*.
22. Ramachandra Guha develops his elaboration of "the environmentalisms of the poor" in *The Unquiet Woods: Ecological Change and Peasant Resistance in the Himalayas* (Berkeley: University of California Press, 1989).
23. Upendra Baxi, *The Future of Human Rights* (London: Oxford University Press, 2005).
24. "Legible," in the strictest lexical sense, denotes a composition "plain enough to read." From the Latin root, *legere*, the word migrated to Middle English to imply two different modalities relevant to our conversation here. First, the materiality of signification: that is, to be legible requires decipherment, requires accessibility. This may be narrowly construed as technological: to hear or see something, with the primary emphasis falling on vision. The second involves cognition.
25. Charles Wolfe, "The Poetics and Politics of Non-fiction: Documentary Film," in *Grand Design: Hollywood as a Modern Business Enterprise, 1930–9*, ed. Tino Balio (Berkeley: University of California Press, 1996), 351–86.
26. Most of the NBA docs are funded by individuals, environmental groups, or independent media organizations from India; a few are funded or co-funded by agencies in Britain, Canada, and the United States.
27. For instance, Anurag Singh does camera for *Kaise Jeebo Re!*, while further editing, and directing, the film with collaborator Jharna Jhaveri; Ali Kazimi is cinematographer, writer, director, and narrator on *Narmada*.
28. Franny Armstrong's concluding shot juxtaposes intertitles, updating her global audiences about recent turns in the NBA's fortunes, with full shots of happy children singing one of the NBA's songs in a *jeevan shala* (the schools set up as part of the movement's agenda of local sustainability)—the children an obvious staple for marking the developing world.
29. Frances Bulathsinghala, "I Film the Truth—Patwardhan," *Sunday Observer* (Sri Lanka), 21 November 1999.
30. Woman interviewed in Anant Patwardhan's *Bombay, Our City* (1985). See Manjunath Pendakur's "Cinema of Resistance: Recent Trends in Indian

Documentary Film," *Documentary Box* (www.yidff.jp/docbox, accessed 18 June 2008).

31. See Mark Nornes' elaboration of the microstructures in the Sanrizuka documentaries in Abé Mark Nornes, *Forest of Pressure: Ogawa Shinsuke and the Postwar Japanese Documentary* (Minneapolis: University of Minnesota Press, 2007).
32. Laura Marks, *Touch: Sensuous Theory and Multisensory Media* (Minneapolis: University of Minnesota Press, 2002).
33. Baba Bhai's testimonial in the Sashi/Mathur film.
34. See estimates from Sanjay Sangvai, *The River and Life* (Mumbai: Earthcare, 2002) and Patrick McCully, *Silenced Rivers: The Ecology and Politics of Large Dams* (London: Zed Books, 2001).
35. For a description of the NBA's organizational structure, see R. Dwivedi, "Resisting Dams and Development: The Contemporary Significance of the Campaign against the Narmada Projects in India," *European Journal of Development Research* 10, no. 2 (1998): 135–83.
36. The draft bill aims to compensate the "historical injustice" done to forest-dwelling tribes that were denied their traditional rights to forestlands and resources in the last couple of hundred years. See Ashish Kothari and Neema Pathak, "Forest and Tribal Rights," *Frontline*, 21 May–3 June 2007.
37. Arun Agarwal, *Environmentality: Technologies of Government and the Making of Subjects* (Durham: Duke University Press, 2005), 165.
38. The claims to the commons are variously stated, the forests appearing as both regular resource and backup for hard times: one woman in the Jhaveri/Singh film tells us that in times of drought the forests still yield nutritious sweetened roots that can sustain *adivasi* families whose crops fail.
39. Bhola, interviewed in Armstrong's *Drowned Out*, tabulates twelve generations from memory to illustrate the centrality of social ecology to family genealogies in the village of Jalsindhi.
40. Luhariya's testimony cited in Paul Routledge, "Voices of the Damned," 243.
41. Testimonial in Simantini Dhuru and Anant Patwardhan's *The Narmada Diary* (1995).
42. Neera Chandhoke, an activist in the NBA, writes "The conceits of representation," in the Opinion section, *The Hindu*, 7 February 2001, 2.
43. Dhuru and Patwardhan further juxtapose a 1993 news segment with a segment from a 1950s newsreel ("A Village Smiles"), where the voice of God narration actually quotes Jawharlal Nehru's famous view that "dams are the temples of modern India."
44. Sanjay Kak, "Politics in the Picture: Witnessing Environmental Crises in the Media," *Sarai Reader 4: Crisis/Media*, 325–9 (http://www.sarai.net/publications/readers/04-crisis-media).
45. Bughabai to Franny Armstrong in *Drowned Out*.
46. Before this sequence, we focus on Rahman's parents who are still building a hut for him even after his death with the coming of the Bargi dam.
47. Luhariya's testimonial, cited in Paul Routledge, "Voices of the Damned," 243.
48. These notations foreground the unhomeliness as the structure of feeling, as Spivak maintains, of planetarity—an invisible system of relations deeply other to human exchange. Gayatri Spivak, *Death of a Discipline* (New York: Columbia University Press, 2003).
49. Buell poses liberal green against the more radical propensities of ecofeminism or deep ecology as the philosophical framework for thinking environmental justice. See Lawrence Buell, *The Future of Environmental Criticism:*

Environmental Crises and the Literary Imagination (Boston, MA: Wiley-Blackwell, 2005).

50. Baba Amte, the *satyagrahi* known for his work with leprosy, gave the NBA instant national visibility when he joined the protests in 1989–90, despite his failing health; but it is Patkar who is largely seen as responsible for the grassroots mobilizing from 1985 until today.
51. Jane Gaines, "Political Mimesis," in *Collecting Visible Evidence*, eds. Jane Gaines and Michael Renov (Minneapolis: University of Minnesota Press, 1999), 84–102.
52. Thomas Waugh, "Introduction: Why Documentaries Keep Trying to Change the World, *or* Why People Changing the World Keep Making Documentaries," in *Show Us Life: Toward a History and Aesthetics of the Committed Documentary*, ed. Thomas Waugh (Metuchen, NJ: Scarecrow Press, 1984), xi–xxvii.
53. For example, a localized small-scale water harvesting plan costing 90 million rupees which would bring water to 900 water-scarce villages in Gujarat, a state which stands to spend 200 million rupees for its dam-related costs.
54. Appadurai's case in point is the Shackdwellers International (SDI) in Africa and Asia (but also Japan, Latin America, and the United Kingdom). Arjun Appadurai, "The Capacity to Aspire: Culture and the Terms of Recognition," in *Culture and Public Action*, eds. Vijayendra Rao and Michael Walton (Palo Alto, CA: Stanford University Press, 2004), 59–84.
55. Appadurai, "The Capacity to Aspire," 67.

three

rights and return

perils and fantasies of situated testimony after katrina

janet walker

"After the storm, I came back. Things were so ... turned over that ... I actually got disoriented in the neighborhood that I grew up in."

James Gibson, III, *Right to Return: New Home Movies from the Lower 9th Ward*[1]

The object *of knowledge is, precisely, the fragmented and uncertain connection between elaborated representations of space on the one hand and representational spaces (along with their underpinnings) on the other; and this "object" implies (and explains) a* subject*—that subject in whom lived, perceived and conceived (known) come together within a spatial practice.*

Henri Lefebvre, *The Production of Space*[2]

[T]he lived body is coterminous with place because it is by bodily movement that I find my way in place and take up habitation there.

Edward S. Casey, *Remembering*[3]

Judith Morgan and a friend command the space of Morgan's demolished home, its raised foundation a haunting platform for their gestural and verbal descriptions of its former state. Now the debris has been removed, the premises cleaned and painted, and a small camping tent pitched in what was once the interior space of the home. The women, at first in front of the structure and then within its footprint, trace with physical movements the rooms and features that were washed away when the levees breached in the wake of Hurricane Katrina. "Duck your head," reminds her friend, with conscious irony, as Morgan mounts the three short steps-to-nowhere—all that remains of a staircase that once led to a second story supported by a low beam.

This walking testimonial is one of many heart-rending on-site interviews that comprise the video footage and finished documentaries shot in New Orleans in the months and years after Hurricanes Katrina and Rita and the flood control system failures that put 80 percent of the city under water. The cameras captured a devastated landscape in which everything had shifted: houses lifted off foundations, or reduced to jutting piles of rubble; cars climbing the walls or weirdly conjoined, chassis to chassis; people wandering displaced, lost in the once-familiar neighborhoods where they had been born and raised. "That china closet doesn't have no business being over here," exclaims a grief-stricken Wilhelmina Blanchard, inspecting her destroyed home for the first time since having evacuated. As director Spike Lee comments on the documentary's commentary track, "The foundation is not there. Your feet are not on solid ground." The geography of the terrain—from its furnishings to its urban architecture to its ecology to its economic and racial relations—was massively altered such that the ways and means of rehabilitation and bioremediation are an open question. And yet the bodily presence of returning residents describes a strong and tangible connection to place, community, neighborhood, and home, an affective geography that is established and transitory, solid and imaginative.

The current chapter focuses on the potentialities and limitations of filmed or videotaped testimony delivered *in situ*, from the place where catastrophic past events—that generate the subject and the subject matter both—occurred. This is a form of *situated* direct address simultaneously to filmmaker, camera, and spectator. It is elicited for the purposes of retrospective documentary works, where typically it is intercut with other direct address interviews conducted with the same and different individuals in their homes, offices, by-ways, or against a neutral background arranged by

Figure 3.1
New Orleans under water (*When the Levees Broke*)

the filmmaker. By figuring the relationship among the body of the individual, the ground from which s/he speaks, and the past events that transpired of a time but are, at the same time, brought into being by the testimonial act,[4] situated testimony realizes the materiality of testimony in the power of place.

As a type of filmed interview, an audiovisual testimony is always in some sense "staged"; staged in that the interviewee would not be speaking if not for the occurrence of the filming, and staged in the sense of being put into a scene, a *mise-en-scène* in fact, that can be as simple as a black background or as complicated as a churchyard of Polish villagers surrounding a child survivor returned years later to the site of a genocide (as in Claude Lanzmann's *Shoah* [France, 1985]).[5] Situated testimony, then, not only staged but also localized to certain haunts, may be said to found a geography of return.

But what of reminiscence and the psychic aspects of testimonial reflection? Psychoanalytically informed trauma studies has drawn on the concept of temporal "belatedness" to theorize trauma as a psychic structure of experience for which violent acts and physical settings are of passing importance. As Cathy Caruth has written: "The impact of a traumatic event lies precisely in its belatedness, in its refusal to be simply located, in its insistent appearance outside the boundaries of any single place or time," or, putting it differently, "in connection with another place and time."[6] Indeed Caruth's influential work has inspired a rich debate about the historical truths and enigmas that traumatic experience arguably renders—but significantly less attention has been paid to its spatial aspects.

Focusing here as much on place as time, I want first to relate this notion of trauma's distanced, other place to the apparently self-same geography of situated testimony. What of those occasions when testimony is given from the very spot, and not "another" spot, where catastrophic events transpired? What about the Rwandans who speak from the grounds of the Kigali Memorial Centre, built on the site of the graves of more than 250,000 Tutsi and moderate Hutu massacred during a one hundred day period, or from a school classroom near to where neighbors set against neighbors? What about the indigenous activists who edge as close as possible to land their families farmed for generations prior to its inundation by the construction of massive dams for hydroelectric power?[7] It may be that the prominence of Holocaust subject matter in testimony studies, the prominence, that is, of a major diasporic testimonial paradigm in which the overwhelming majority of testimonies have been delivered at a temporal and geographic distance from the events they invoke, has obscured our view of the other distinctive testimonial paradigm: that of situated testimony as a kind of post-traumatic reassertion of physical belonging and right of return. Tens of thousands of people around the world have presented their audiovisual testimonies through the pain of disastrous propinquity: because they have chosen—or because they have no choice but—to reregister their presence in a place from which they (temporarily) and loved ones and/or neighbors (permanently) have been wiped out.

I wish, therefore, to examine rooted testimony, to take it seriously, that is, while still recognizing that the presence of returnees to a "fatal environment" does not by any means obviate the need to comprehend the psychic dimensions and the unassimilability of place and occurrence that make up the traumatic experience of which they speak.[8] The ground of testimony *sur place*—like exilic space—is always, already "other." Here, the insights of critical human geography are crucial, for in this post-positivist subdiscipline a materialist critical spatial perspective is reasserted (against what Edward Soja, for example, sees as "despatializing historicism"[9]) such that location matters, but place is not essentialized or reified as a truth-telling topography. The stones don't speak except through a kind of critical ventriloquism, yet they are more than mere inert features of a fixed terrain.

Inspired by Henri Lefebvre's concept of social space, art historian Irit Rogoff celebrates critical human geography's "situated knowledge" as enabling a "shift from a moralizing discourse of geography and location, in which we are told what ought to be, who has the right to be where, and how it ought to be so, to a contingent ethics of geographical emplacement in which we might jointly puzzle out the perils of the fantasms of belonging as well as the tragedies of not belonging."[10] Contemporary works of art engage with the "problematic of geography," she proposes, by arraying the "alternative strategies available to review our relationship with the spaces we inhabit" (frontispiece). And indeed, film and media studies—as a field that studies nothing if not the constitution of subjectivity within and through what Lefebvre has termed the "representation of space" (found, constructed, or both) and "representational spaces" (media aesthetics, institutions, and practices)—is benefiting from scholars' increasing attention to the mutually formative aspects of spatial topography and being-in-the-world.[11]

Zooming in on several documentary works about people in a disaster landscape in the United States, this chapter studies how situated testimony as a performance of return materializes as both an expression of social suffering and a spatial practice that transforms the social ecology of place. Here in the United States, as elsewhere, "natural disasters" or sudden "acts of god"—wind, earthquake, fire, drought, flood—are inextricably entwined with public policy and private sector decisions that exacerbate or alleviate pollution, erosion, famine, displacement, and inter-group strife; here, as elsewhere, place is "space invested with meaning in the context of power."[12] In the case of "Katrina," social justice was usurped by an aggressive discriminatory husbanding of resources, disguised as passive neglect, and I use the moniker in its popular sense to evoke the constellation of meteorological and man-made forces that wreaked havoc on the Gulf Coast and beyond.

The situated testimonies this chapter seeks to witness are protests delivered after (and sometimes before and during) Hurricane Katrina: what people say or do not, or cannot, say from their silted streets and water-ransacked homes; the meanings imported and exported with the cameras and crews who also "return" to the scene. From the vast and growing archive of online and physically distributed testimonial works about suffering and survival after Katrina,[13] I will look at Spike Lee's *When the Levees Broke: A Requiem in Four Acts* (US, HBO, 2006); Tia Lessen and Carl Deal's *Trouble the Water* (US, 2008); and a video short, *New Orleans for Sale!* (US), by Brandan Odums and Nik Richard, with the group 2-cent;[14] for how these works, each in its way, help us envision new and promising modes of "practicing space."[15]

showing, telling, and missing new orleans

Spike Lee's Emmy Award-winning four hour and fifteen minute documentary[16] premiered at the New Orleans Arena on August 16, 2006 and aired on the HBO cable network in its entirety on August 29, 2006, the first anniversary of Katrina's landfall. Described as "one of the most important films HBO has ever made,"[17] the magisterial work stands as a passionate critique of the profound *unnaturalness* and ongoing negative effects of Katrina.

In documentary studies terms, the film may be categorized as an analysis documentary of the compilation type for its assemblage of archival footage drawn mainly from television news sources, on- and off-site interviews conducted for the purposes of the film, and original sequences in which peoples' actions are facilitated and captured by the cameras of Lee and his crew.[18] Broadly chronological, the film's four acts carry us through from immediately before to after the hurricanes (Katrina and Rita) and flood.[19]

But a finer vernier reveals a "sort of overture" to each act,[20] comprised in most cases of an achronological, associational montage set to music that includes at least one, usually more than one, aerial shot of New Orleans amongst images on the ground including a signature shot along a road narrowed by the heaped timbers and shingles of ruined homes. Each act or "movement" (to invoke the film's rich soundtrack as well as its own titular musical reference) ends with a departure of sorts: Act II's montage of dead and bloated bodies, left floating or breached by the receding waters, is followed by a low-angle long take of poet Shelton Shakespear Alexander delivering his piercing recitation against the high arched gate of a cemetery with the sky behind. Then comes a repetition of the roadway tracking shot, and finally, over the destroyed rooftops, an indelible image of the giant barge that allegedly (court cases are still pending) broke through the Industrial Canal Floodwall into a residential neighborhood in the Lower Ninth Ward causing massive physical destruction and contributing indirectly and directly to Katrina's total death toll of over 1,800 people. A model of its kind for epic complexity as well as sweep, the film spirals down into the maelstrom of the flooded city and yet resuscitates the bodies, voices, and ideas of people on the ground.

Although they are not as numerous, nor do they command as much screen time as the interviews conducted against artificial backdrops, the film's interviews on site are crucial to its geopolitical claims.[21] Their spare but increasing inclusion as the film advances—as people *can* get back to their neighborhoods to be interviewed there—adds weight and rhythmic momentum as the subjects seem, in Edward Casey's phrase, to "find [their] way in place and take up habitation there." Bodily, gesturally, as well as vocally, the subjects of these grounded interviews comprise the connective tissue between the city's ruined landscapes and the interviews in the indeterminate space (of which more later). Situated testimonies do not just state but also *incarnate* the film's core problems and critique—that people were stranded, evacuation impaired, help and rescue grievously delayed; that the government was and is at fault, racial and economic discrimination a factor, insurance companies corrupt, developers poised to profit from desperate homeowners forced to sell out cheaply, the act of return immeasurably difficult or impossible for the poor, of which most, in New Orleans, are black; that white gentrification is occurring; that many subsequent deaths should rightly be ascribed to the traumas of Katrina; that suffering is extending, hyperbolically, into the post-evacuation phase (as one protest sign puts it, "Katrina Survivor, FEMA victim," referring to the Federal Emergency Management Agency); and that the reengineering of the levees was not achieved in the nearly 40 years after Hurricane Betsy and was by no means achieved to date of filming (or writing).

One of the film's most memorable speakers is Phyllis Montana LeBlanc, a woman of great charisma whose emotional range from ironic humor to deep despair is matched by her ability to assess the complicated issues at hand, and whose interviews in two locations (and against the neutral background) anchor the film. We see her first—and this is also the first situated testimony of the film—at the Louis Armstrong New Orleans International Airport. In that emphatic interview, distributed across the length of the film, she describes her call for rescue by a helicopter pilot: "I mean, I'm standing there with a mop on a stick with a towel that I found somewhere, a white towel, with SOS and on the back of it 'help me please.' And I'm waving this thing like I'm going crazy, and he looks at me and he does this [index finger pointing and spiraling up into the air], like 'get up and go.' And he left us!" Right there in the airport where people were marooned, and intercut with a walking tour by airport director Roy Williams, LeBlanc tells how special details were brought in to "keep order" because "we were getting 'out of order' because people were yelling 'my child is dying,' 'my mother is dying,' we were getting 'out of order.'"

In addition to the sequences featuring LeBlanc's testimony, substantial on-site interviews conducted with Joyce Moses and Anthony Dunn; Gralen Banks; and Tanya Harris, Josephine Butler, and Chirrie Harris (three generations of women), also segmented and distributed throughout the film, make up some of its most physically explicit and affecting moments. Following news footage of men wading chest deep in water to the soundtrack's solo trumpet rendition of the "St. James Infirmary" blues, a new sequence begins with the camera picking out a red "Danger" sign and panning right, across where the flood waters invaded, to the landlocked barge. "This is the barge, and when it came ... we thought we were going to die," we hear Moses recall in anguished voice-over. Then a close-up of the barge's alphanumeric marking accompanied by Moses' voice-over testimony: "and I remember the number ING 4727." The camera cuts to her: a slender African American woman, perhaps in late middle age, with yellow hair, and bracelets on her wrists. Now we are on the ground in proximity to this iconic image of upheaval (around the other side of it, I believe). "If they would've took this away I would've remembered the number, 'cause I wrote it down and put it in my pocketbook."

The camera follows Moses' gesturing arm and pointing finger to the settled barge, and the houses crushed beneath and in front of it. "And the couple that live there, they couldn't get—afford to get—out either. They're still in there if they're still there."[22] The camera continues right to reveal a different house that withstood the inundation, its spray-painted marking including a "0" to denote no dead bodies found within. But we know from media reports that two children and a man were sucked off a rooftop and drowned as the floodwaters in this vicinity rose and surged through the floodwall breach.[23] With a downed roof as backdrop, Moses turns around nearly one hundred and eighty degrees and stretches out her other arm. Again the camera follows. We see houses and their contents

Figure 3.2

Situated testimony by Joyce Moses (*When the Levees Broke*)

smashed to smithereens, a white appliance, and something yellow—perhaps a child's ride-along toy—pop against the grey driftwood of peoples' former lives. These objects are generative of narrative rather than mere vessels for symbolic meaning. Her companion attends quietly as Moses speaks: "They have a man that living here. He tied hisself to beer kegs. They may still be in the yard. And he floated in the water just for three days and I just kept talking to him, telling him God gonna make a way, God gonna make a way. You goin' a make it. And he was saying, I'm so tired. I know you're tired." Now Moses looks straight into the lens as the sequence ends with her remembered helplessness. All she could do was observe, record what she could, and, later, tell what she witnessed and felt: "And I wanted to feed him what I had, but I couldn't get to him 'cause I didn't know how to swim." It is possible to question whether the choice to open the sequence with a danger sign might not be overly melodramatic, too on the nose. But the sentiment is more than balanced by the resonance of human feeling in Moses' voice and body. "Object survivors"[24]—physical reminders of what was—stop and start Moses' memories of prior habitation as they unfold vacantly in the crook of her extended arm. Riffing on the connotations of the camera "viewfinder," Martin Lefebvre points out that views are as much framed as they are found, and, concomitantly, that "the view itself cannot be divorced from the other experiential aspects that accompany it."[25] Turning as the camera pans, Moses delivers a kinesthetic testimony that is a matter of sensory and cinematic movement both.

Against the backdrop of the city, Gralen Bryant Banks celebrates the life-giving smell and taste and sight of New Orleans that residents imbibe:

> When you are born in this, and your first breath when the doctor slapped you was tinted with magnolia blossoms,

> and you drink Mississippi tap water in your first formula, it's a thing you won't find anywhere else. And folks who had to evacuate know. You might go somewhere and you might have a good time. But it's nothing like home. And when you can call New Orleans, Louisiana home, *baby, you know what it means to miss New Orleans.* Trust me.

Elsewhere a printed sign with the bold announcement "I am coming home/I will rebuild/I am New Orleans" makes explicit the felt connection: people and their city inhabit a single body.

belonging

It is against this painful reality of displacement that the film makes its case for return. "New Orleanians and Louisianians are a resilient people," states New Orleans City Council Member Cynthia Hedge-Morrell, as the film cuts from a sequence in which the Harris-Butler family describe the wreck of their maternal home to a formal (unsituated) interview with her, "they will rebuild their lives." But weak as it is today, recovery in New Orleans was still weaker—and certainly a struggle—during the film's shooting and post-production phases and at the time of the film's release one year after Katrina.[26] Civic groups such as ACORN (the Association of Community Organizations for Reform Now) were fighting for the resources and the right to rebuild African American neighborhoods against pressure from certain quarters, including the Urban Land Institute, to rebuild only on high ground, i.e., in the wealthier, whiter areas of the city.[27] Basic public services and infrastructure, including public schools, child care, mail delivery, garbage pick-up, restaurants, bus and streetcar routes, and so on, took months or even years to resume in various parts of the city.[28] There is no definitive "after" to the brief before and extended during that are the time frame of this film.

But the film has adopted a number of strategies to do its part to secure New Orleanians', and especially African American New Orleanians', staked claims to the territory and right of return, with situated testimony, both encountered (as when the crew comes upon a person who consents to be interviewed) and enacted (as with Wilhelmina Blanchard), prominent among them. Blanchard presumably would have inspected her home around this same time in any event, but this particular visit—accompanied by her son, musician Terence Blanchard, his aunt, and also, off camera, by cinematographer Cliff Charles and Spike Lee who had asked to be present for the occasion—was made in partnership with the film project. The light illuminating the interior space of the home was likely shone from a portable spotlight provided by Charles. On the commentary track, Lee expresses gratitude to Blanchard for allowing the visit to be filmed, as well as uncharacteristic tentativeness about the breach of privacy: "Now the camera follows Terence, his mother, and his aunt into the house, but I stayed outside ... I mean she, Terence's mom, was breaking down even before she went into her house and I just did not want to be in there. So I stayed outside."

Be it ethically sound or not, the film relies on this instance of enacted return to develop the relationship between indigenous belonging and shocking dispossession.[29] As Blanchard says, tearing up, when interviewed later on the neutral set, "Today when we went to the house; that was really hard because, you know, you can't go home." In several other instances, edited sequences are used to construct the impression of what we are hearing from an interview subject, an impression, that is, of the audience's situated witnessing. Off-site, in the formal setting, actor Wendell Pierce describes the visit of an insurance adjustor to the damaged home of his octogenarian father. Pierce's father had purchased the home after World War II by putting down $10 to hold the contract—rushing home to tell Pierce's mother the news—and he had paid off the 30-year loan and laid out 50 years of homeowners insurance premiums. Meeting at the house, he asked the adjustor to be fair: "Just be fair, be fair," Pierce quotes his father as having said. But what his father didn't know, Pierce tells us, is that the adjustor had already taken Pierce aside to tell him that the company would not pay out more than 40 or 50 percent of the value of the home. Intercut with Pierce's verbal account of that visit to the home is another visit in which hand-held footage of the ruined house personifies the particularly traumatic return with the adjustor through its bobbing motion, as if Lee and his crew had been there with Pierce and his father to witness this draining away of the social contract through the loopholes of the literal one.[30]

In its production history as well, Lee's filmmaking process constitutes a kind of (home)coming to New Orleans. The disaster hit while Lee was in post-production on the thriller *Inside Man* (US, 2006). He knew he wanted to make the film but was unable initially to leave the New York area. So he sent a crew to Louisiana to conduct research and do some preliminary shooting while he himself followed the news, read voraciously, and began interviewing evacuees who had ended up in New York,[31] against backdrops that betray no hint that a given interview was not taking place in New Orleans. Gina Montana was an early New York interview subject and it was she who led Lee to her sister Phyllis, already back in New Orleans. As soon as possible, Lee made it to New Orleans, and we hear his voice from time to time on the dialogue tracks of situated interviews (with Judith Morgan, for example) and sense his directorial presence, as when he returns to Gentilly Woods with Terence Blanchard, who is after all a long-time collaborator having scored a number of Lee's films, including *Inside Man*.[32]

Quite beautiful to look at for their warm ochres and siennas, luminous blues and greens, and various subtle textures, the geographically neutral interview backdrops are another important aspect of the film's signature aesthetic and ultimately much more than a choice for expediency's sake: this visual (dis)location of more than half of the interview subjects, their interviews set in no place at all rather than in New Orleans—and rather than someplace else in particular—underlines the massive, continuing displacement of people that the film works to overcome in its depiction and advocacy of the right of return. When Phyllis Montana LeBlanc explains from her FEMA trailer (finally delivered four months after she put in for it and eight months after landfall) that although she and her husband are in the city they love, her mother, sisters, niece, and nephew are dispersed and unable to return because, for one thing, appropriate support services for LeBlanc's autistic nephew no longer exist in the city, her words are affirmed by the fact of Gina Montana's interview, out of place against its neutral background. Montana's pained reflection on the lack of physical options and autonomy serves as an apt and moving summary: "With the evacuation scattering my family all over the United States, I felt like it was an ancient memory; as if we had been up on the auction block."[33] The use of the neutral backgrounds also levels the playing field for interview subjects, since "ordinary people," public officials, and experts receive the same graphic treatment; and furthermore, floating free of the city's recognizable landmarks, the neutral space of the interviews encourages the realization that the concerns of the monologists extend beyond the local arena.

Oscillating as it does, therefore, between situated testimony as an expression of territorial belonging and geographically neutral testimony as a controlled expression of outrageous dispossession, the film pauses pregnantly at the words of FEMA chief Michael Brown. Caught in news footage from the time, struggling to explain his lack of response to the tens of thousands stranded without food, water, tampons, or diapers, Brown stated: "There are people that are beginning to manifest themselves out in the community that *we didn't know were there*." Just so.

The famous split-screen CNN interview by Soledad O'Brien juxtaposing Brown's professed unawareness with Louisiana Superdome and Morial Convention Center footage the whole world was watching is included in *Levees*, along with the film's own interview with O'Brien expressing her bafflement that the FEMA chief could have less "intelligence" than that contained in a research file prepared by her 23-year-old production assistant. This interview-about-an-interview is itself embedded in a larger sequence that combines retrospective assessments of the situation by scholars[34] and public officials[35] with localized footage of people "we didn't know were there" to rebut the murderous irresponsibility of Brown's pronouncement and government inaction. In news and archival footage of those who rode out the storm we see: a woman in a life vest stepping out of a boat, the Coach purse she grips a wordless testimony to safer times; adults importuning the media to give or seek aid; and kids taking up the chant, some seemingly more able than the adults to maintain high spirits, perhaps confident of the shelter of their parents or, naively, the government. Gathered in as well are situated testimonies, including Judith Morgan's, about how the evacuation was grievously mishandled given peoples' lack of means of evacuation: "They don't have the funds, they don't have the place to go, they don't have the vehicles." All of these filmicly coordinated claims are juxtaposed, in best Michael Moore fashion, with archival footage of public figures making empty protestations that all is in hand, or callously going about their privileged lives—among these President George W. Bush, Vice President Dick Cheney, Secretary of Homeland Security Michael Chertoff, Deputy Chief of Staff Karl Rove, and, memorably, Secretary of State Condoleezza Rice shoe shopping and playing tennis.[36]

The film directs the attention of viewers—returns it in a way—not only to physical presence in this city but also to people's neglect when public transportation out of the city was not arranged, to their confinement (as when some were turned back by armed police as they tried to self-evacuate by walking across the Crescent City connection into the demographically white city on the other side[37]) and, most of all, to their apparently *alienable* belonging that the film itself undertakes to rectify through enacted return, cinematographic return, and the exposure of impossible return.

social ecology of a documentary

Disenfranchisement as a kind of distancing of certain residents from their home city was already a problem of enormous historical, economic, social, *and environmental* consequence *before* Katrina struck. Key premises of social ecology, according to Yoosun Park and Joshua Miller, are that "[t]he most disadvantaged members of the most disadvantaged communities suffer the greatest losses when disaster strikes," and that, according to the demographics of disadvantage, "[t]he ongoing environmental risks for poor people and people of color are consistently higher than for white people and those who are economically privileged."[38] Specifically in New Orleans, "[s]ome of the most historic Black neighborhoods ... were on the lowest ground and sustained some of the most severe damage."[39]

Certainly I agree with the Internet Movie Database's description of the film as being about "the gross incompetence of the various governments and the powerful from the local to the federal level" and "how the poor and underprivileged of New Orleans were mistreated in this grand calamity and [are] still ignored today."[40] But I believe the film's even greater impetus is to represent the calamity as social ecological in nature.[41] Park and Miller's social ecological analysis of urban landscapes reads like a location breakdown of this documentary project:

> The socially disadvantaged are more likely to live near chemical plants, landfills, and other contaminated lands.

> There is a greater likelihood that they will be living in more vulnerable, substandard dwellings served by older, less well-maintained infrastructures, for example, roads, sewers. They are more likely to be living in overcrowded, environmentally risky areas. Much of public housing, built during the 1950s and 1960s, tend to cluster in areas that are along major transportation routes, reclaimed land, or adjacent to industrial facilities.[42]

In *Levees*, location shooting in the devastated Ninth Ward, combined with archival footage of the stranded inhabitants, reveals a city noticeably segregated by race and income where middle and upper-middle class white residents of New Orleans' "outlying (and ... literally higher) suburban communities" are nowhere to be seen, while poor blacks wade through the toxic ooze in "low-lying flood-prone areas."[43] Although some people in post-Katrina New Orleans continue to regard Katrina as a colorblind or "equal opportunity" natural disaster,[44] the film for its part portrays the unevenness of risk factors in the face of calamity and the "malign intersection of weather and water with a man-made social and racial topography."[45]

Moreover, the film's character and narrative trajectories correspond with a social ecological analysis of institutional life. The frustrated inability of so many of *Levees*' interviewees to rectify the problems that they so eloquently describe pertains to a larger context in which the people who are the most dependent on governmental support of major flood-prevention projects (the building and maintenance of levees; the preservation and restoration of protective wetlands) lack money, education, and political clout for mobilizing to demand change.

Throughout the film we see and hear many individuals decrying the neglect of the disadvantaged: Kanye West's impromptu statement to Mike Myers that "George Bush doesn't care about black people" and the film's own interview with West; Mayor Nagin's query after noting that people were dispersed with one-way tickets: "Why don't you give them a ticket home?"; Al Sharpton addressing the Congressional Black Caucus and importuning the media "Stop calling them refugees. These are American citizens that in most cases were very viable taxpayers and ... the connotation of refugees is like they are others from somewhere else needing charity" [and if they were from elsewhere??].[46] A woman holds up her mortgage statement before the Bring New Orleans Back Commission meeting as proof of paid-up property taxes earmarked for police and school services while protesting that she "can't get a school open" in her neighborhood. As Florence Jackson asks: "Where is my government?" All of these are passionate speakers with legitimate claims. But we see little or no evidence of responsive action.

In fact, the film's vision of the future is dire, especially given its concentration in the penultimate segment on the interruption of the intergenerational transfer of wealth (this section is where Pierce's story of his father's loss comes in) and the continuing inadequacy of the flood protection.[47] Professors Robert Bea and Calvin Mackie, and Louisiana State Representative Arthur Morrell, among others, describe the history, politics, and engineering of New Orleans' flood control system: in certain places there was an I-wall but no actual levee (created from a dirt berm) because the necessary land was deemed too costly to purchase and because revenue from oil and natural gas leases in the Gulf of Mexico was appropriated by the federal government instead of flowing to Louisiana. The breaches represent the "most tragic failure for a civil engineering system in the history of the US" and yet the Army Corps is immune to lawsuits. To Lee's audible question "Is it safe [to return]?," Bea responds "The answer is no, it's not safe." It would be difficult in this context not to give credence to Hot 8 Brass Band leader Benny Pete's comment: "They been knowing this thing could happen ... if they knew it *could* have happened, it's almost like they *let* it happen."

Two interviews in contradistinction with one another exemplify the film's expressivity: Dr. Ivor van Heerden of Louisiana State University Hurricane Center discusses his trip to the Netherlands and the film cuts to footage of the extensive flood control installation there. "I was actually embarrassed to talk about ours," he says.[48] Back in the US, Colonel Lewis Setliff, Commander of Taskforce Guardian, US Army Corps of Engineers, has been photographed and interviewed inspecting the sheet pile and I-wall levees. At the beginning of Act III we saw him in close-up turning his face to the sheeting. Now, almost at the end of Act IV, he walks away from the camera. The film then dissolves to his further receding form, until, in an optical effect, his body fades away completely as if absorbed in a cinematographic/atmospheric heat mirage. The disappearance of this would-be guardian of the disadvantaged connotes another kind of vanishing: structural failure in a geopolitical environment lacking accountability and economic justice. The end comes with LeBlanc in her FEMA trailer (before the formaldehyde contamination problem was widely known) reading for the camera a poem of her own composition that I quote in part: "My being together broke when I fell apart. My smell broke away from my skin."

evacuating agency

When the Levees Broke: A Requiem in Four Acts is a commanding work on Katrina by virtue of its visual and analytic power as the creation of a cinema auteur and authoritative commentator on race relations in America for whom the regional tragedy of Katrina bespeaks the national shame of ongoing, widespread, institutionalized racism. Its images and sounds were in my eye and ear when I undertook my own small trip to this environment out of which people were blown, flown, bused, flooded, rescued, evacuated, and disappeared, about which they speak with such dignity, and to which they struggle to return, both literally and in terms of a return to structural integrity.[49] The disposition of areas of the city in April 2008 was very much in line with what Lee and those who appeared before his cameras had predicted two years before.

Pictured overleaf (figures 3.3a, 3.3b, and 3.3c) is the Lafitte Avenue public housing complex on the verge of demolition, the last of the ambitious projects built in post-World War II New Orleans by President Roosevelt's Works Progress Administration to be demolished against public protest. The Lafitte had become notorious for criminal, especially drug-related, activity. But, scaled to fit the surrounding neighborhood and designed with wrought iron balustrades and communal courtyards, the red brick housing blocks were also home to working poor: the maids and other service workers of the city's tourism industry. Tenants were given a window of opportunity to return to New Orleans from Houston, Memphis, Atlanta, or Chicago to collect their belongings. But when that metaphorical window closed, so did the *actual* doors and windows of their homes, sealed up at considerable expense by the installation of metal plates before being opened for clearing. Latino workers, possibly recent arrivals, bagged up and threw away the worldly possessions of displaced African American families, in preparation for demolition.[50] All but one block of the complex is gone now and as I write this the residences of some of New Orleans' working poor, with the destruction of public housing, the end of federal rental subsidies, and the recall of temporary trailers, are tents under the I-10.[51]

This condemning and razing of the houses of the poor in the aftermath of Katrina is an effect of the phenomenon Naomi Klein has described as "disaster capitalism": a form of opportunistic corporatism that capitalizes on sudden catastrophic events to "rai[d] the public sphere" by suspending governmental checks and balances in favor of high stakes insider business dealings, privatization, deregulation, and drastic reduction of social spending, all of which adversely affect poor and middle-class people and any others who dissent.[52] Disaster capitalism is "fundamentalist," Klein explains, invoking the supremacist ideology of its advocates as well as its historical and philosophical affinities with religious extremism. Within the first three paragraphs of her book *Shock Doctrine*, Klein quotes Congressman Richard Baker's chilling post-Katrina statement (also included in *Levees*): "We finally cleaned up public housing in New Orleans. We couldn't do it, but God did."[53] As of March 2008, two and a half years after Katrina, the city had reached only 71.8 percent of its pre-Katrina population of about half a million people, with African Americans, those living in poverty, and registered Democrats as significantly overlapping demographic categories in which the rate of return is dramatically lower.[54] The city of NOLA (New Orleans, Louisiana), it could be said, is under the kind of occupation known as gentrification.

And so I've been praising *Levees*' use of the various forms of testimony to stake an ongoing claim to New Orleans' contested landscape. However, it seems important simultaneously to recognize the nostalgic aspect of *Levees*,

Figures 3.3a, 3.3b, and 3.3c

Lafitte Avenue public housing complex on the verge of demolition (photos by Janet Walker)

a "longing for a home that no longer exists or has never existed."[55] In its occupation with the "tragedies of not belonging," the film may lose its chance to "puzzle out" Rogoff's aforementioned "perils of the fantasms of belonging." Relatedly, while *Levees* includes frequent references to (lost) home ownership by African Americans in New Orleans, it contains few references to the long-term, intransigent problems of poverty even though—as outside statistics reveal—prior to Katrina 91.2 percent of the city's poor families of all races were African American and 35 percent of African Americans (compared with 11 percent of whites) were living below the poverty line.[56] By concentrating on immediate contingency, idealizing home and community, and embracing identity politics, *Levees* may actually inhibit to a certain extent the "working through" of a long-standing social malaise at the very moment when exposed racism demands a new order.

Likewise, the film's investment in the human rights discourse of "right of return" may be a political, interpersonal, and geographic dead end. I hazard this claim while acknowledging monumental negligence by the federal government and private insurance companies; disproportional capital in the hands of residential, commercial, and industrial developers; and the fact that rational people may find quite a bit of traction invoking the right of return from the standpoint of ethical commitment. The deepest problem of right of return, I submit, is not that people are not back, but rather that the geography this discourse tends to imagine lacks potential. In a petrified topography, return may serve no purpose more fully, as Wendy Brown has argued, than to further "reify and regulate the subject produced by social powers."[57] It is not safe to return to former conditions in which subjects were constrained by the economies of structural engineering and engineered race- and class-based segregation. Interviewee Herbert Freeman represents a possible, albeit sad, exception to *Levees*' and the speakers' advocacy of the right of return. Telling with great self-possession the story of how his mother died in her wheelchair while waiting for the buses to come outside the Morial Convention Center—the buses came four days later—Freeman concludes: "I don't ever want to be under their jurisdiction. I don't want to be under the leadership of no one in New Orleans or Louisiana or nothing."[58]

trouble the water

Kimberly and Scott Roberts, protagonists of *Trouble the Water*, do return to New Orleans, initially to survey the destruction of their neighborhood (like Wilhelmina Blanchard, Joyce Moses, Wendell Pierce, and others in *Levees*) and eventually to take up residence once again. But the film is less idealizing with regard to return, more open than *Levees* to airing the dirty laundry of monoeconomic and monoracial community, and thus more resistant to a separatist geography that "bind[s] us all together under the aegis of the dominant."[59]

In terms of testimonial time, person, and place, *Trouble the Water* could be viewed as *Levees* inside out. With its complicated temporal structure that begins in the middle and flashes back and forward, *Trouble* encompasses distinct "before" and "after" Katrina time frames in which the Lower Ninth Ward neighborhood is depicted warts and all; there is an active agent in the person of Kimberly Rivers Roberts who not only self-evacuates with her husband, taking along children and others who cannot help themselves, but also plans and shoots the cinema verité-style home movie footage that anchors this autobiographical documentary (a model of *its* kind).[60] As we hear her say to neighbors from behind the video camera she happened to pick up just prior to the storm,[61] "If I get some exciting shit, maybe I can sell it to the white folks"; and, more than a situated testimony here and there, the film includes an extended return trajectory in which the Robertses retrace their evacuation route, reencountering along the way objects, obstacles, and those who would also testify.

"I'm on my way to New Orleans," Kimberly Roberts says into her cellphone as she and her husband return with their friend Brian two weeks after the storm (although released after *Levees*, *Trouble* began its post-Katrina location shooting earlier). "Some people I met are doing a documentary; a real documentary." And through the windows of the car, the lens of the camera these protagonists hold, and the lens of this "real documentary," we see the muddied streets and downed buildings, the unfortunate iconography of the Katrina cycle: "I didn't expect to see this. This is like a movie. This can't be real." And once she arrives, we see Kimberly and company walking and gesturing and speaking of what was: "Everybody! This is my neighborhood ... I miss those days and it's hurt me to know that it's not going to be the same no more."

Roberts is not only viewing the devastation but actually reconnoitering, performing inspections that had not yet been carried out: "keeping it real," as Hot 8 band member Dinerral Shavers put it in *Levees*, gesturing toward homes bearing spray-painted marks of inspection but also barred windows and locked doors belying the graphic claim that anyone had entered ("They didn't go into none of these houses!").[62] We are with Roberts on the street when the group discovers her uncle, dead in the front room of a house where he had sought shelter, and pulls in National Guardsmen to handle the body; the odor of death suffuses the scene throughout their efforts to show respect while bearing the stench. And we are with Roberts inside her own former house when she reclaims from its wall hook the framed photograph of her mother who died of AIDS when Roberts was a girl of 13.

Nor do the proactivity of the group's situated testimony and the critical acuity of the film's compound testimony stop there. The next "return" installment is constituted from Kimberly and Scott Roberts and company's retracing of the path they had followed during their self-evacuation, returning, that is, to the stations of their self-help and mutual cooperation in the face of abandonment by the government. Like Joyce Moses in *Levees*, the group members narrate the steps they took, perhaps tamping down some of the same mud molecules that had swirled around their legs upon evacuation. But in comparison with *Levees*, here the territory is not inertly deserted but rather occupied by personnel of the powers that be and reanimated by the group's perambulatory dialogues with these squads. Outside the US Naval Support Activity, ten blocks from his former house, Scott Roberts explains that the Coast Guard had directed the band to this naval base that was being decommissioned so that they could take advantage of the potential resource of its two hundred empty family housing units and five hundred evacuated barracks. Not only was the group denied entrance, he reports, but twenty troops came out to the gate with M-16s cocked and aimed to disperse the crowd. His testimony is disputed, however, by a military authority who states that there was "never any hint of us using any type of force," yet continues, somewhat self-contradictorily, "we had to do our job and protect the interest of the government." Another example of conflicting perceptions of a single situation follows when Scott Roberts pushes student desks together at Frederick Douglass High School to show how they improvised to avoid sleeping on the floor, while young white Guardsmen describe in disgust how "they," the evacuees, "trashed" the high school and how lacking they are in survival skills. Although *Trouble* shares the Robertses' perspective by presenting a trajectory strewn with landmarks of the group's resourcefulness and generosity (the dogs that greeted them with wagging tails upon their first return to their street; the boat they used to ferry the group to high ground; the spot where Scott and Brian felt around with their feet under standing water to find the keys to the truck owned by a local business that they used to evacuate thirty people to Alexandria, Louisiana), it also enhances the possibilities of testimony as a truth-seeking mode by acknowledging the existence of conflicting testimony.

I would compare these sequences in *Trouble*, in which the face value of individual testimony is superseded by a more complex testimonial regime, to an exceptional sequence in *Levees* that complicates the film's generally straightforward acceptance of the evidential status of testimony. In Act I half-a-dozen people talk about having heard an explosion. Some ascribe it to an engineered bombing of the levees to prevent the waters from flooding into wealthy areas. Michael Knight describes the sound: "At first I heard one boom. I thought it was a big transformer. 'It's a transformer,' I say. But, we been sitting in the dark now for about two hours, three hours [so the transformer would have blown previously; this must be something else]." Sylvester Francis offers, "I think the levee cracked and they helped it the rest of the way. They had a bomb; they bombed that sucker." As the sequence proceeds, we are presented with black and white archival footage of damage wrought by Hurricane Betsy in 1965 and of the purposeful dynamiting of the levees during the 1927 Mississippi flood. We witness as well

Gina Montana's statement that "during Betsy ... they dynamited the levees and flooded the Lower Ninth Ward in order to save some of the more expensive property in the lakefront area." These claims are not so much confirmed as explained by Professor Mackie ("when the water gushed through a gaping hole ... you gonna hear some type of sound; the levees gave") and (former) Mayor Marc Morial who states that while the rumors of the dynamiting of the levees during Hurricane Betsy "became almost an article of faith with people," the situation has never to this day been investigated. Historian Douglas Brinkley calls the belief that the levees were dynamited during Katrina an "urban myth" but one that is understandable given that "these people have a long experience of being ripped off," thereby articulating what must be Lee's own view. On the commentary track, we hear Lee respond with some trepidation as this "dynamiting" sequence begins, saying, "Alright, here we go. I felt that it was my duty as a filmmaker to have this in the film." Proceeding with his commentary, he insists that there is "some legitimacy" to what people say, even though whether you want to believe it, "that's on you." Lee concludes with the explanation that many African Americans, he among them, "don't put anything past the United States government when it comes to black people." *Levees* and to some extent *Trouble* refuse the role of exposing falsehoods and adjudicating testimonial factuality in order to suggest, through the accumulation of information and opinion, that testimony is contingent on social ecological perspective, and knowledge on a relational reading of persons and places.[63]

Cinema verité lends immediacy to *Trouble*'s enunciative presence. In contradistinction to *When the Levees Broke*, where situated and geographically neutral testimonies hark back with feeling to a community we spectators know mainly through these elegiac means, *Trouble the Water* presents Roberts' own down-to-earth footage of "the before": "It's me, reporting live; Kold Medina," using her professional name as singer/songwriter.[64] This is no idyll of community. Through Roberts' eyes and our own saccadic vision we observe alcoholism, drug dealing, and combative behavior, as when the men at a corner store challenge Kimberly filming them and she snaps back, presumably alluding to the surveillance camera, "What you looking at? You got *me* on camera."[65] We see snippets of a car interior while on the soundtrack Roberts' voice is heard talking with the car's occupant who is looking to buy some weed (another type of "shit" for her to sell?); we see her uncle passed out on a well-trodden stoop in a drunken haze, prior to his death in the storm. "Don't do that when ya'll get big," Roberts warns children playing nearby.

The film is pragmatic in its assessment of the causes of the social problems we observe. In its orchestration of situated testimonial and cinema verité sequences, we hear the accusation of bias so loudly played in *Levees* as well as the tones of self-induced damage. Scott Roberts explains that he had previously turned to drug dealing because there were no good employment options for a person with limited education and yet, by the end of the

Figure 3.4
"Three cars of people pass and they all know me" (Kimberly Roberts in *Trouble the Water*)

film (perhaps eighteen months later), we see the results of his personal choice to take a carpenter job with his comment that it is good to "do something and come back and see it and say 'I did that.' ... Now I get to rebuild my city ... I love the smell of that sawdust."

Near the end of the film Roberts is back in her neighborhood, speaking warmly of the benefits of community:

> Three cars of people pass and they all know me ... If something happened to me right around here, right now, somebody's gonna do something for me 'cause they know me ... If I ain't got a ride, somebody's gonna give me a ride. And if I need some money ... they might not loan me no money, but they'll give me some conversation. So, you know, it feels good to be back home.

Yes, but. In her own footage at the beginning of the film, we had heard Roberts state that she had tried to rent a car but just "couldn't afford the luxury" of leaving. And as the film too informs us with a line of text subtitling the image of the bumper-to-bumper exodus, there was no public transportation provided for pre-storm evacuation. (Although Mayor Nagin did order traffic contraflow for those with wheels.) Perhaps Uncle Ned also lacked a neighborly ride out of town.

More than simply sharing *Levees*' longing for black community, *Trouble* suggests the perils of the fantasms of belonging to a racially and economically segregated geography where neighbors lack the resources to help neighbors, and interracial strife makes hotspots of the islands and perimeters that mark out difference. And yet, where *Levees*' mood is one of tragic dignity against outrageous injustice,[66] *Trouble* ends with an impression, however utopian, of integrated community. Scott's white boss is presented as a good person and mentor, and the "white folks" to whom Kimberly did sell her footage (or, presumably, reach some sort of positive financial arrangement) incorporated her music as Kold Medina amply into the film. Roberts' displacement by the storm and flood and, significantly, her co-authorship of a return narrative (living history that could be filmed and filming history that demanded to be lived) expanded Roberts' orbit beyond New Orleans: "I'm trying to do something different. I see it now. I couldn't see it before when I was inside."

conclusion

If at first I distinguished the spatial otherness through which Caruth defines traumatic experience (that it is only "fully evident in connection with another place and time") from testimony in *the same* place, in light of documentary uses of situated testimony I have also qualified that view. In a certain respect, the situation and even the place to which people return is always both an "other" spot and the same spot. Heraclitus' "continually flowing river" applies, as does Rogoff's insight that territories are always multiply inhabited—with an effect of strife or benefit as the case may be.[67]

Unprecedented upheaval on the Gulf Coast exposed the grotesqueries of a racially biased infrastructure and I share the outrage of residents and activists who are experiencing and protesting the disenfranchisement of African Americans from New Orleans by profiteering disaster capitalists. But it does not seem to me that the equitable solution lies in a return to pre-Katrina conditions.

In the context of Israel-Palestine, Eyal Weizman has suggested that how we "practice space" is important, especially when historical moments of evacuation offer new and humanizing possibilities for the reallocation of resources (that we would implement thoughtfully and in opposition to the "clean slate" fundamentalism of a Richard Baker). Importing Weizman's terms, the flooded city of New Orleans could be seen to represent a moment of "ungrounding"; undeniable disaster, yes, but, still, an opportunity to "disactivate" the ills of economic and racial segregation characteristic of the pre-Katrina environment.[68] Buildings can be repurposed, surface structures—such as roadways and green spaces—reorganized to connect formerly divided habitations, and the US infrastructure—including the levees—reengineered in the interest of human rights. I cannot but feel that such a *transformative* view of race and place—which could, arguably, include an economically, architecturally, and, where appropriate for the black community, a racially mixed housing plan along with a complete reworking of the system of resources distribution—would be a most desirable and ethical foundation for a rebuilt New Orleans.

Levees and *Trouble* are at their most interesting when they offer a critical sense of space, as they do when their situated testimonies expose the politicized granularity of the ground below our feet or the deceptiveness of landmarks. To take one final example, consider the sequence in *Levees* when Tanya Harris (an ACORN activist) tells how she misread the rubble in her grandmother's neighborhood and brought back incorrect information about the house her grandmother had built on property bought around 1949. "We were looking for the house. We were, like, 'Do you see it?' 'Did it move?'" To her grandmother she reported, "I think it's in Mr. Johnny's yard." Turns out she had been mistaken in a street where the landmarks themselves had shifted and it was not easy to be definite about anything in the wreckage.

In certain respects, if not to perfection, *When the Levees Broke* and *Trouble the Water* deploy situated testimonies of return to tap the potential Rogoff sees in contemporary artworks; they suggest how far we have come and how far we still must go to realize spatial transformation. So I want to end with a comment about a video piece that, while short in length (at a minute and a half), is long on commentary, as an explicitly activist art piece, about the complexities of shared space.

New Orleans for Sale! screened at the 2008 New Orleans International Human Rights Festival and is currently available for viewing on YouTube, as well as 2-cent.com. I saw it on my visit to the city several days after the desire to conduct ethnographic research on "disaster tourism" led me to take an official "Hurricane Katrina Tour" with the Gray Line bus company. To create the video, the group 2-cent performed and documented a special kind of "return" to the Ninth Ward, reoccupying the space from which many families have been expunged and registering (to disaster tourists such as myself and others) the gains of carpet-bagging entrepreneurs and outsiders.

But the video includes shots from the inside (Figure 3.5c) as well as from the outside of passing vehicles. The filmed performance succeeds, I contend (hoping this example amounts to considered opinion and not mere self-justification), because the tourists and 2-cent meet on common ground.[69] While the video polices the boundaries of the neighborhood, it also enacts an energetic encounter between those who have returned home and those who visit. In the spirit of engagement, I submit that we have an ethical imperative to come, to see, and to act together; to spend our dollars not only to visit but also to remake space as multiply inhabited community. And, indeed, the new and colorfully painted homes of Musicians' Village in the Upper Ninth Ward were jointly created by New Orleans Area Habitat for Humanity and the sweat equity of local homeowners. Moreover, although the Lafitte Avenue and other housing projects were torn down rather than remodeled,[70] the nonprofit developer has made a commitment to the "'one-to-one' replacement of public housing units" with a promising mix of new on-site housing and "'in-fill' development" in the surrounding neighborhood. Existing but dilapidated

Figures 3.5a, 3.5b, and 3.5c

Disaster tourism engaged (*New Orleans for Sale!*)

homes are now being stripped back to their cypress studs, remodeled, and prepared for subsidized ownership by low-income residents.[71]

Committed to physical propinquity, engaged with the affective lure of home, a given documentary of situated testimony may also describe an "*unheimlich*" or "unhomed geography" that is transformative with regard to rites/rights of return and porous in its ethnic, racial, generational, and economic contours.[72] Each of the three Katrina documentaries discussed here invites a particular form of the "site-seeing" Giuliana Bruno attributes to cinematic spectating in general,[73] a form that migrates through checkpoints and across geographical distance to contest a racially and topographically essentialized mapping of post-Katrina New Orleans. Each is an active interlocutor in a conversation about the geopolitics of our multiply inhabited planet at a time of increasing mobility, forced migration or forced repatriation, and intense struggle for places to call home.

acknowledgments

Thanks are due to Holly Willis for introducing me to *Trouble the Water* and for her insightful, informative review of the film on the occasion of its Sundance premiere (see note 61). I am also grateful to Dave Cash, a friend and now high school teacher of history and African American history in New Orleans, for teaching me about the city and sharing a trip to the Lafitte Avenue housing projects on the verge of demolition. Liz Dunnebacke, Royce Osborn, Jennifer Peterson, Tim Ryan, and Betsy Weiss also showed me generous hospitality in New Orleans. Finally, thank you Bhaskar for going it alone as editor of your co-editor's chapter; your astute comments and high standards are much appreciated!

notes

1. *Right to Return: New Home Movies of the Lower 9th Ward* (US, Jonathan Demme, 108 min.). The film was presented by Demme at the 5th Annual New Orleans International Human Rights Film Festival, 9 April 2008.
2. Henri Lefebvre, *The Production of Space*, trans. Donald Nicholson-Smith (original French language text 1971; Malden, MA: Blackwell, 1991), 230.
3. Edward S. Casey, *Remembering: A Phenomenological Study* (Bloomington: Indiana University Press, 1987), 180.
4. This concept of testimony or traumatic witnessing as a process not only of recording but actually of bringing the past into being is drawn from the work of Shoshana Felman, Dori Laub, and Cathy Caruth, prominent among other theorists of trauma and testimony. In particular, see Dori Laub, "Bearing Witness or the Vicissitudes of Listening," in *Testimony: Crises of Witnessing in Literature, Psychoanalysis, and History*, coauthored by Shoshana Felman and Laub (New York: Routledge, 1992), 57. See also Cathy Caruth, *Trauma: Explorations in Memory* (Baltimore, MD: Johns Hopkins University Press, 1995) and Cathy Caruth, *Unclaimed Experience: Trauma, Narrative, and History* (Baltimore, MD: Johns Hopkins University Press, 1996).

5. See my discussion of staging in Janet Walker, *Trauma Cinema: Documenting Incest and the Holocaust* (Berkeley: University of California Press, 2005), 26, 135–6.
6. Caruth, *Trauma*, 8–9.
7. These specific examples are drawn from other chapters in this volume: on Kigali, see Mick Broderick, "Mediating Genocide: Producing Digital Survivor Testimony in Rwanda," and on the *adivasi* of the Narmada river valley, see Bishnupriya Ghosh, "We Shall Drown, but We Shall Not Move: The Ecologics of Testimony in NBA Documentaries."
8. I adapt the term "fatal environment" from Richard Slotkin, *The Fatal Environment: The Frontier in the Age of Industrialization, 1800–1890* (New York: Atheneum, 1985).
9. Edward Soja, *Postmodern Geographies: The Reassertion of Space in Critical Social Theory* (London: Verso, 1989), 1–4.
10. Irit Rogoff, *Terra Infirma: Geography's Visual Culture* (London: Routledge, 2000), 25–8, 3.
11. For several superb film and media studies works that incorporate spatial studies, see Linda Krause and Patrice Petro, eds., *Global Cities: Cinema, Architecture, and Urbanism in a Digital Age* (New Brunswick, NJ: Rutgers University Press, 2003); Edward Dimendberg, *Film Noir and the Spaces of Modernity* (Cambridge: Harvard University Press, 2004); and Martin Lefebvre, ed., *Landscape and Film* (New York and London: Routledge, 2006). I wish also to mention here Maurice Stevens' valuable development of the concept of "traumatic iconography" in its particular relationship to the experiencing and representation of Hurricane Katrina. For Stevens, the mode of visual representation that traumatic iconography describes is simultaneously materially significant and profoundly inaccessible. Maurice Stevens, "From the Deluge: Traumatic Iconography and Emergent Visions of Nation in Katrina's Wake," *English Language Notes*, 44, no. 2 (Winter 2006), Forum on Photography and Race, eds. Leigh Raiford and Elizabeth Abel.
12. Tim Cresswell, *Place: A Short Introduction* (Malden, MA: Blackwell Publishing, 2004), 12.
13. In addition to the films discussed here, see *Right to Return: New Home Movies from the Lower 9th Ward, Still Waiting: Life after Katrina* (dir. Ginny Martin and Kate Browne, 2007, 58 min.); *The Drive: A Documentary Tour of Post-Katrina New Orleans*, Segment One: The Lower Ninth Ward (dir. Tim Ryan and Matt Wisdom, 2006, 75 min.); *Kamp Katrina* (dir. David Redmon and Ashley Sabin, 2007, 75 min.); *The Axe in the Attic* (dir. Ed Pincus and Lucia Small, 2007, 110 min.); *God Provides* (dir. Brian M. Cassidy and Melanie Shatzky, 2007, 9 min.); and *Faubourg Tremé: The Untold Story of Black New Orleans* (dir. Dawn Logsdon, 2008, 68 min.). See also online archives including: the Hurricane Digital Memory Bank, a project of George Mason University's Center for History and New Media and the University of New Orleans, in partnership with the Smithsonian Institution's National Museum of American History and other partners, www.hurricanearchive.org (accessed 15 August 2008); the New Orleans Video Access Center, which supported local film- and video-makers to create works about Katrina that were posted online and screened throughout the country, www.novacvideo.org (accessed 15 August 2008); Alive in Truth: The New Orleans Disaster Oral History and Memory Project, which collects and makes available transcripts of oral interviews, www.aliveintruth.org (accessed 15 August 2008). For a discussion of some of these and other Katrina archives, see Alan H. Stein and Gene B. Preuss, "Oral History, Folklore, and Katrina," in *There Is No Such Thing as a Natural Disaster*,

eds. Chester Hartman and Gregory D. Squires (New York: Routledge, 2006).

14. Available on 2-cent.com (accessed 4 October 2008). The piece was screened at the 5th Annual New Orleans International Human Rights Film Festival on 12 April 2008 under the title(s) *Truth*, or *This Is What You Paid to See* and won the Audience Award for Best Short.
15. Eyal Weizman used this term in "Conversations," a talk presented at the REDCAT, Walt Disney Concert Hall, Los Angeles, 6 May 2008. See also Weizman, *Hollow Land: Israel's Architecture of Occupation* (London: Verso, 2007).
16. The HBO mini-series won Emmy Awards in the categories of Exceptional Merit in Nonfiction Filmmaking (Spike Lee, Producer; Sheila Nevins, Executive Producer; Jacqueline Glover, Supervising Producer), Outstanding Directing (Spike Lee), and Outstanding Picture Editing for Nonfiction Programming (Sam Pollard, Supervising Editor; Geeta Gandbhir, Editor; Nancy Novack, Editor).
17. Wikipedia, "*When the Levees Broke*," en.wikipedia.org/wiki/When_the_Levees_Broke (accessed 14 August 2008).
18. Thomas Sobchack and Vivian Sobchack set out the categories of "observation," "analysis," "persuasion," and "aesthetic expression," as well as the three subcategories of the analysis documentary: epic, compilation, and cinema verité. Sobchack and Sobchack, "The Documentary Film," *An Introduction to Film* (Boston: Little, Brown & Co., 1980).
19. For the sake of accuracy, I would like to point out that the film does contain some sparing use of earlier images of life in New Orleans prior to the fateful storm season. These are drawn from archival and news sources and include, for example, black and white footage of the devastation caused by Hurricane Betsy in 1965, more recent footage of musicians playing and diners dining in New Orleans, and so on. Such sequences appear as relatively brief flashbacks in a temporal structure that concentrates, as I have indicated, on the Katrina period.
20. Ernest Callenbach, "*When the Levees Broke: A Requiem in Four Acts*," *Film Quarterly* 60, no. 2 (2006): 4–10.
21. The film includes more than three-dozen people interviewed in the local environment, many of whom are also within the group of nearly seven-dozen people interviewed against the neutral background. However, as indicated, the screen time of the on-site interviews is disproportionately less.
22. Having listened repeatedly to this passage, I think Moses' words are properly transcribed. But she may have stated that the couple "couldn't get aboard [a boat perhaps?] to get out either" rather than "couldn't get—afford to get—out either." Suffice it to say that financial wherewithal was an enormous factor in people's ability safely to evacuate.
23. Martin C. Evans, "Recalling Family Taken by Katrina," *Newsday*, 30 August 2006, newsday.com/topic/ny-usmom304870424aug30,0,6469431.story (accessed 15 August 2008).
24. The term "object survivors" is borrowed from its use in Holocaust museology. See Noah Shenker, "Embodied Memory: The Institutional Mediation of Survivor Testimony in the United States Holocaust Memorial Museum," in this volume.
25. Lefebvre, Introduction to *Landscape and Film*, xv.
26. One year after Katrina less than 50 percent of New Orleanians had returned, including substantially fewer African American than white former residents.

US Census Bureau, State & County QuickFacts, quickfacts.census.gov/qfd/states/22/22071.htm (accessed 15 August 2008); Adam Nossiter, "New Orleans Population Is Reduced Nearly 60%," *New York Times*, 7 October 2006; Wikipedia, "New Orleans, Louisiana: Demographics," en.wikipedia.org/wiki/New_orleans#Demographics (accessed 14 August 2008). Other major reports on post-Katrina recovery include Amy Liu, Matt Fellowes, and Mia Mabanta, "Special Edition of the Katrina Index: A One-Year Review of Key Indicators of Recovery in Post-Storm New Orleans," Brookings Institution Metropolitan Policy Program, August 2006, http://www.brookings.edu/metro/pubs/2006_KatrinaIndex.pdf (accessed 22 October 2008); and Amy Liu and Allison Plyer, "Executive Summary: State of Policy and Progress, April 2008: Two Years, Eight Months since Katrina Made Landfall," *The New Orleans Index* (Brookings Institution Metropolitan Policy Program and Greater New Orleans Community Data Center: April 2008), http://www.brookings.edu/reports/2007/~/media/Files/rc/reports/2007/08neworleansindex/200804_katrinaES.pdf (accessed 22 October 2008). An additional feature length segment of *Levees*, entitled "Next Movement: Act V," is included on the DVD box set (released 19 December 2006). However, it does not represent a later period of recovery, being comprised instead mainly (perhaps entirely) of interview material and other footage that was available for but not included in Acts I through IV.

27. See Sheila Crowley, "Where Is Home? Housing for Low-Income People after the 2005 Hurricanes," in *There Is No Such Thing as a Natural Disaster*, and Martha Carr, "Rebuilding Should Begin on Higher Ground, Group Says," *New Orleans-Picayune*, 19 November 2005.
28. See Liu, Fellowes, and Mabanta, "Special Edition of the Katrina Index," and Rick Jervis, "66% Are back in New Orleans, but Personal Services Still Lag," *USA Today*, 13 August 2007, usatoday.com/news/nation/2007-08-12-neworleans_N.htm (accessed 15 August 2008).
29. By "enacted" I mean real people in a real situation engaging in an activity for the purpose of its filming: see Walker, *Trauma Cinema*.
30. The film also documents Paris Ervin's search for his mother, whom he had assumed had escaped the flood. Instead her body was found under the refrigerator, where she had been dead for weeks.
31. Spike Lee, commentary track, *When the Levees Broke* DVD.
32. The score of *When the Levees Broke* borrows themes Blanchard composed for *Inside Man*. We also sense Lee's literal and orchestrating presence when the Hot 8 Brass Band reunites in New York and, subsequently, New Orleans after many had lost their instruments and more. Act IV opens with the band accompanying a horse-drawn hearse carrying a coffin labeled with a homemade sign, "Katrina," down the debris-straitened street we had seen several times previously, emptied of life, while playing a funeral dirge. About an hour later, the closing sequence of Act IV and the film itself features the band playing an upbeat "I'll Fly Away" ("hallelujah by and by …") as per the tradition to conclude funerals with a joyful sound.
33. An interview with public intellectual Michael Dyson is edited in here to take up Montana's reference to the history of slavery. He mocks those who would disclaim the validity of the reference: "Oh, no, you're being hyperbolic. You're just engaging in all forms of racially inflammatory rhetoric." And then concludes: "Well, the fact is they were treating them like slaves in the ship. Families were being separated. Children were being taken from their mothers and fathers. Those more weary and those who were more

likely to be vulnerable were separated from those who were stronger ... The separation of the evacuation where people lost sight and lost sound and lost sense of their loved ones."

34. These include Michael Dyson (*Come Hell or High Water: Hurricane Katrina and the Color of Disaster* [New York: Basic Civitas Books, 2005]); Douglas Brinkley (*The Great Deluge: Hurricane Katrina, New Orleans, and the Mississippi Gulf Coast* [New York: Harper Collins, 2006]); John Barry (*Rising Tide: The Great Mississippi Flood of 1927 and How It Changed America* [New York: Touchstone, 1997]); and Associate Professor of Mechanical Engineering at Tulane University Calvin Mackie.
35. These include Al Sharpton, Louisiana State Representative Karen Carter, and Mayor Ray Nagin.
36. With thanks to Bhaskar Sarkar, who pointed this out, I would say that, yes, the film could very well be construed as a documentary example of Fredric Jameson's "conspiratorial allegory": a new (from the 1970s) cognitive mapping realized in cultural productions as "heightened and spatialized perception" that "on some level, in the superstate, the conspiracies are real." Although the "object survivors" seen in *Levees* are not generally of a technological nature, Jameson's discussion of the "technological object" of the "conspiratorial text" gets at a generative quality of objects in certain narratives that those of *Levees* would seem to share. See Fredric Jameson, "Part One, Totality as Conspiracy," *The Geopolitical Aesthetic* (Bloomington: Indiana University Press, 1992), 31–3, 19.
37. While widely known and decried, *as an example of racial bias* this event has been denied by Gretna Mayor Ronnie Harris. A lawsuit was filed by State Senator Cleo Fields (D-Baton Rouge) and State Representative Cedric Richmond (D-New Orleans) against the city of Gretna and the Gretna Police Department. See Richard Webster, "Gretna Police Blocking Passage of New Orleanians Seeking Refuge," *New Orleans CityBusiness*, 9 October 2006, findarticles.com/p/articles/mi_qn4200/is_2006009/ai_n16769340 (accessed 4 August 2008).
38. Yoosun Park and Joshua Miller, "The Social Ecology of Hurricane Katrina: Re-Writing the Discourse of 'Natural' Disasters," *Smith College Studies in Social Work* 76, no. 3 (2006): 10.
39. Crowley, "Where Is Home?" 141.
40. Kenneth Chisholm, Plot Summary: *When the Levees Broke*, Internet Movie Database, imdb.com/title/tt0783612/plotsummary (accessed 15 August 2008).
41. One might also say, immediately to borrow the term defined by Bishnupriya Ghosh, that the film operates through an "ecologics," or "a logic of *oikos* (*house* in Greek), or dwelling in a system connecting human and nonhuman worlds," in its abutment of *situated testimonies* about the human effects of Katrina to *place-specific* images of people in a storm-churned landscape and to unsituated but deeply informed expert and eye-witness testimonies (Ghosh, "We Shall Drown," in this volume).
42. Cited in Park and Miller, "Social Ecology," 10. The authors for their part cite L. Cutter, "The Geography of Social Vulnerability: Race, Class and Catastrophe, 2005," http://understandingkatrina.ssrc.org/cutter/pf/.
43. Chester Hartman and Gregory D. Squires, "Pre-Katrina, Post-Katrina, Editors' Introduction," *There Is No Such Thing as a Natural Disaster*, 5.
44. Such a statement was made by the guide of the Gray Line "Hurricane Katrina Tour" in which I participated on 8 April 2008.

45. The Brookings Institution Metropolitan Policy Program, 2005, 17, quoted in Park and Miller, "Social Ecology," 15.
46. Viewed in a comparative context, including various occurrences of displacement around the world, Sharpton's and the other speakers' calls for this change in vocabulary might be seen as a jingoistic demand for special treatment for US citizens. A related, sore irony is seen in the efforts by various agencies to deny aid to people who were already homeless before Katrina in favor of the "homeless homeowners" (evacuees, that is) displaced by the storm and flood. The National Alliance to End Homelessness estimated that 6,000 to 10,000 people who were homeless before Katrina were ineligible for disaster aid. See "HUD Program May Strand Many Previously Homeless Katrina Victims," National Low Income Housing Coalition, 2005, endhomelessness.org/do/uncoveredhomelessdhap.pdf, discussed in Crowley, "Where Is Home?" 134. See also Avis A. Jones-Deweever and Heidi Hartmann, "Abandoned before the Storms: The Glaring Disaster of Gender, Race, and Class Disparities in the Gulf," in *There's No Such Thing as a Natural Disaster.*
47. Before Katrina, the Lower Ninth Ward was 98 percent African American, with approximately 60 percent of residents owning their own homes, many of them free and clear. See Wikipedia, "New Orleans."
48. Van Heerden participated in a study of the path of the floodwaters by plotting the location and times of stopped clocks. David Kestenbaum, "Stopped? Clocks Tell Tale of Katrina Flooding," NPR, 30 January 2006, npr.org/templates/story/storoy.php?storyld=5175772 (accessed 19 August 2008). He continued to act as a whistleblower in his role as deputy director of the Louisiana State University Hurricane Center, having indicated that the Army Corps of Engineers and FEMA knew the levees had breached and had flown over to take photos, but that the federal government chose not to alert the state or begin rescue operations. The reason for this inaction, according to Van Heerden, was fear of federal culpability in the event of a systems failure rather than a hurricane as an "act of god." See Greg Palast, "Hurricane George: How the White House Drowned New Orleans," 23 August 2007, gregpalast.com/hurricane-georgehow-the-white-house-drowned-new-orleans/ (accessed 19 August 2008).
49. My friend Dave Cash in the Fair Grounds Race Course area of New Orleans still does not have heat upstairs because water remains in his gas line and neither his homeowners insurance nor the city will take responsibility.
50. See Mandalit del Barco, "Katrina Cleanup Puts Focus on Latino Workers," an NPR story originally aired on 24 October 2005, for a report on the controversy over the arrival of Latino workers from Texas, Florida, and Mexico to undertake the strenuous cleanup work in post-Katrina New Orleans, in some cases over the protests of local residents concerned that they had been "replaced by lower-wage Spanish-speaking workers" (1 of 2), http://www.npr.org/templates/story/story.php?storyld=4972419 (accessed 28 December 2008). See also Tom Bearden, "New Orleans Sees Rise in Latino Population," Online NewsHour: Report, originally aired 28 August 2007, http://www.pbs.org/newshour/bb/social_issues/july-dec07/katrina_08-28.html (accessed 28 December 2008).
51. "Recently released estimates by Unity for the Homeless show that 150 people are living in tents under the I-10 overpass, 31 percent of whom are recently homeless because of the loss of federal rental assistance or their removal from temporary trailers," according to Amy Liu and Allison Plyer, "Executive Summary," 1.

52. Naomi Klein, *The Shock Doctrine: The Rise of Disaster Capitalism* (New York: Metropolitan Books, 2007), 6.
53. Klein, *Shock Doctrine*, 4.
54. Gordon Russell, "New Population Statistics Gloomy—Rate of Return to Area down Dramatically," *Times-Picayune*, 8 August 2006; William W. Falk, Matthew O. Hunt, and Larry L. Hunt, "Hurricane Katrina and New Orleanians' Sense of Place: Return and Reconstitution or 'Gone with the Wind'," *Du Bois Review* 3, no. 1 (2006): 115–28; William H. Frey, "Are We 'A Whole Other City'?" *Times-Picayune*, 28 August 2007. Frey indicates that "while 64 percent of the city's pre-Katrina white population returned by July 2006, only 43 percent of black residents—and just 22 percent of black residents age 25–34—did so." See also John A. Powell, Hasan Kwame Jeffries, Daniel W. Newhart, and Eric Stiens, "Towards a Transformative View of Race: The Crisis and Opportunity of Katrina," Crowley, "Where Is Home?" and Robert O. Zdenek, "Reclaiming New Orleans' Working-Class Communities," all in *There Is No Such Thing*.
55. Svetlana Boym, *The Future of Nostalgia* (New York: Basic Books, 2001), xiii.
56. Cited in Park and Miller, "Social Ecology," 13. There are some such references in *Levees*, as when Mackie refers to pre-Katrina social problems including New Orleans' high murder rate, high dropout rate, and low wages.
57. Wendy Brown, "Revaluing Critique: A Response to Kenneth Baynes," *Political Theory* 28, no. 4 (2000): 471. See also the chapter "Rights and Losses" in her book *States of Injury* (Princeton, NJ: Princeton University Press, 1995). Although space constraints preclude the development of this thought in the body of the chapter, I would like to mention here that reification of black subjectivity in the case of Katrina also consists in the tendency to attribute discriminatory actions, inactions, and practices on the part of public officials to the "fact" of blackness instead of to the failings of said officials. This point occurred to me while listening to Nessan McMillan's superb presentation "Bearing Witness: The Rwandan Genocide on the Global Stage" at the international conference entitled Interrogating Trauma: Arts & Media Responses to Collective Suffering, sponsored by Murdoch University and Curtin University of Technology, Perth, Western Australia, 3 December 2008. I would also like to acknowledge Claire Sisco King's response to my presentation of a shorter version of this chapter at that same conference. It's all too easy, she indicated, to bracket off New Orleans as an isolated place of trauma—a kind of "Global South" in the United States, I would add.
58. There is only one short sequence in which we see Freeman *in situ*: he lights a memorial candle at the crypt in New Orleans where his mother was laid to rest. His acts of defiance, as I see them, are to have told this story, to have stated clearly that he will not return to New Orleans, and, also, to have pursued a lawsuit against the state of Louisiana, city of New Orleans, and several public officials. On 2 April 2008, however, the 4th Circuit Court of Appeal in New Orleans upheld the decision by the Orleans Parish Civil District judge to toss out Freeman's case on the basis that the government is entitled to immunity. Michael Kunzelman, "Appeals Court Denies Katrina 'Wrongful Death' Lawsuit," Associated Press, http://www.wwltv.com/local/stories/wwl040408tpwrongful.30516b44.html (accessed 15 August 2008).
59. Rogoff, *Terra Infirma*, 110–11.
60. The film won the Grand Jury Prize in the Documentary category at the 2008 Sundance Film Festival among other awards, and received an Academy Award nomination for Best Documentary.

61. Holly Willis, "The Political Becomes Personal: Docs Use Real People to Make Big Issues Easier to Tackle," Sundance Film Festival, Focus on Film, 22 January 2008. sundance.org/festival/insider/2008-01-22-FOF-political-personal.asp (accessed 23 January 2008).
62. A prominent New Orleans musician, Shavers was shot dead while driving in a car with his wife and two children on 28 December 2006. He was 25 years old. See Gwen Filosa, "Two Die in New Orleans Shootings," *Times-Picayune*, 29 December 2006.
63. This sequence, like quite a few in the film, possesses a similar construction to that of *Shoah*, as described by Patricia Erens, where the process of testimonial evidence gathering is cumulative and open. "*Shoah*," *Film Quarterly*, 39, no. 4 (Summer 1986): 28–31. See Walker, *Trauma Cinema*, especially "Catastrophe, Representation, and the Vicissitudes of Memory" and "Disremembering the Holocaust: *Everything's for You, Second Generation Video*, and *Mr. Death*," for extended discussions of the uneven relationship among testimony, factual accuracy, and truth.
64. The songs of Kold Medina (Kimberly Rivers Roberts)—included in the film—are autobiographical and recursive; testimonial in a way.
65. I use the term saccadic vision with all due caution against overinvestment in the democratizing capabilities André Bazin attributed to long takes composed with multiple planes in sharp focus such that the spectator's eye, in theory, may rove at will. See André Bazin, "The Evolution of the Language of Cinema," in *What Is Cinema?*, trans. Hugh Gray (Berkeley: University of California Press, 1967).
66. This affective meaning with which *Levees* leaves us is consolidated in the ending coda; the film's credit sequence is presented as successive images of the people who have appeared, stating their names and identifying information while holding in front of their faces, or being digitally framed by, empty picture frames.
67. Rogoff, *Terra Infirma*, 23.
68. Weizman, "Conversations."
69. Reference here is to Common Ground Collective, founded seven days after Katrina struck by Sharon Johnson, Malik Rahim, and Brandon Darby to "rebuild the spirit of Southern Louisiana." See commongroundrelief.org.
70. The sole remaining block, mentioned above, has been left standing to serve as temporary housing while the new buildings are under construction.
71. Katy Rechdahl and Leslie Williams, "Lafitte Revival to Encompass Neighborhood," *Times-Picayune*, 21 August 2008, posted on nola.com, nola.com/news/index.ssf/2008/08/meeting_tonight_on_lafitte_off.html (accessed 21 September 2008).
72. Rogoff, *Terra Infirma*, "Introduction: This Is Not ... Unhomed Geographies."
73. Giuliana Bruno, "Site-Seeing: The Cine City," in *Atlas of Emotion: Journeys in Art, Architecture, and Film* (New York: Verso, 2002).

four

from "super babies" and "nazi bastards" to victims finding a voice

the memory trajectory of the norwegian lebensborn children

bjørn sørenssen

I

A spread of nine photos taken by Robert Capa dominates page 37 of the August 13, 1945 edition of *LIFE Magazine*. The images are of toddlers looking at the camera, six of them more or less preoccupied with food or with eating. Under these photos we find the following caption: "The Hohenhorst [*sic*] bastards of Himmler's men are blue-eyed, flaxen and pig fat. They must eat porridge whether they want or not." This leads into a short comment:

> **"SUPER BABIES" Illegitimate children of SS men are housed in a German chateau**
> Last fortnight *LIFE* photographer Robert Capa visited a German chateau which housed a Nazi establishment known as *Lebensborn*, or "Well-of-Life," home. At the Hohenhorst *Lebensborn* home, as in many such institutions in Germany, live dozens of illegitimate babies who have no father or mother but the now-defunct Nazi state. They are the products of an official government policy of encouraging

> illegitimacy to keep up the country's birth rate. Soldiers going off to war were urged to do their bit, whether married or not. The government promised to care for the illegitimate offspring, to honor and respect unwed mothers.
>
> The Nazi bastards at Hohenhorst, aged 2 to 5, are the children of SS men encouraged by Heinrich Himmler to father "super babies." Grown pig-fat under care and overstuffing of Nazi nurses, they now pose for the Allies a problem yet to be solved.[1]

The photo-feature then goes on for another two pages, with six more photos underscoring how the children lead a pampered and luxurious life in the chateau and its "immense playgrounds and formal gardens," as stated in one of the photo captions. Other captions follow the same trend: "This Hohenhorst nurse replaces both mother and father in raising this illegitimate child. The baby's parents willingly gave up to the Nazi state all claims on him," and under an image of an especially fat baby: "Too much porridge, plenty of sunlight has made this Nazi baby ... so fat and healthy that he completely fills his over-sized carriage." The scorn heaped upon these toddlers must be understood in the light of the harrowing experiences Capa must have had, having witnessed the opening of the Nazi concentration camps

Figure 4.1

Lebensborn children at the Hohehorst home (photo by Robert Capa, courtesy of Magnum Photos)

and the dire needs of the civilian German population in contrast to this seemingly idyllic place.

Capa's presentation of the Lebensborn children was to have a lasting impact on public opinion, contributing to the view that the Lebensborn homes were specialized "breeding institutions" (*Zuchtanstalten*) for the SS, where all moral and ethical considerations were cast aside in order to provide racially pure citizens for the Reich.

But the children at Hohehorst (the correct spelling of the place name), stigmatized as "Nazi bastards," "illegitimate offspring," and "SS super babies" in this feature, were, in spite of their obvious well-being, victims themselves and would soon be sent out on a journey with traumatic consequences. At the same time Robert Capa was taking his photos at the children's home, a captain in the Norwegian army, Einar H. Sørensen, was visiting the premises with a mandate from the Norwegian government to localize and return Norwegian war children. Contrary to Capa's assumption, the majority of the children at Hohehorst were not the result of the planned breeding of "SS super babies," but of encounters between average Wehrmacht soldiers and Norwegian women.

The present chapter aims to recount the fate of the Norwegian Lebensborn children and discuss how radio and television documentaries in the decade between 1986 and 1996 were instrumental in bringing about a change in the Norwegian opinion of the so-called "war children" by literally giving voice to this stigmatized group through their testimonies. It will also serve as a reminder that the documentary format traverses audiovisual, verbal, and literary genres, and may in cases like the present one be extremely effective when used across media platforms. The documentaries under analysis here deal with the sensitive issue of womanhood and nation during war and warlike conditions—where the female body is regarded as a crucial field of contention between occupier and occupied and where a strong nationalist rhetoric comes into play—and will be considered in that regard.

II

The SS organization Lebensborn e.V. (e.V. for *eingetragener Verein* meaning "registered association") was established in 1935. As Capa noted in 1945, "Lebensborn" means "Spring of Life," and the main objective of the organization was to strengthen the Aryan race and raise the racial standard of the German population.[2] In the prewar years this included programs to increase the birth rate by giving help and support to children born out of wedlock. According to its statutes, the primary functions of Lebensborn were:

1. to support racially and biologically valuable families with many children;
2. to accommodate and take responsibility for racially and biologically valuable expecting mothers and secure, after thorough examination of

their family and the family of the caretaker by the Race and Settlement Office of the SS, that equally valuable children may be brought into the world;
3. to provide for these children;
4. to provide for the mothers.[3]

As Georg Lilienthal has shown, the establishment of this organization was deeply rooted in the worldview of Adolf Hitler, the German National Socialist Party (NSDAP), and its race theorist Alfred Rosenberg. What set the Lebensborn organization apart was its place in the SS organization of Heinrich Himmler, who had his own personal agenda when it came to racial policy in the Third Reich (24–5). According to Himmler's view, the purity of the "Nordic blood" of the German people was at stake, as it was being undermined by a lowering of the birth rate and by the acceptance of abortion and homosexual practice. The Lebensborn racial policy of the SS was the inverse of its propaganda for genocidal tactics against "unwanted" groups of the population: the improvement of the quality of the population by strengthening the Aryan and Nordic component in the nation.[4] It was necessary, therefore, to counteract the rejection of pregnancies, a goal addressed by the strengthening of the already restrictive laws on abortion and, at the insistence of Himmler and the SS organization, by the creation of a supportive environment for unwed mothers.

However, these ideas were controversial within the Nazi hierarchy. There were strong objections from those who wanted to stress the importance of the family as the cornerstone of a racially "sound" society. For their part, Himmler and the SS made the claim that, in terms of ideology, the ideas behind Lebensborn were in close accordance with the ideas of the Führer. This difference of opinion within the NSDAP meant that the Lebensborn organization had to make certain compromises with the competing social and medical organization of the NSDAP, the Nationalsozialistische Volkswohlfart (NSV). The competition between these two organizations would resurface in the countries occupied by the Germans during the war.[5] In any case, the Lebensborn in Germany in the years leading up to the war did establish a number of maternity homes and children's homes throughout Germany and initiate an adoption program to ensure that "racially and biologically valuable" children would grow up in a racially "sound" environment.

During 1940 and 1941 the extent of the German Reich expanded dramatically and at the same time one of the main concerns of the SS program became crucial: how to secure a new generation of the highest racial quality soldiers to make up for the losses in war. Implementing a program for the care of offspring from German soldiers in the occupied countries was seen as a natural extension of the work of Lebensborn in Germany and both Lebensborn and the NSV were established in these countries. In accordance with the racial theories of the Nazi state, there were significant differences in how these policies were implemented in the various occupied countries. The populations of northern countries or areas such as the Netherlands, Flanders, Denmark, and Norway were considered as Aryan, and should be treated as parts of the Germanic "racial community." As millions of German soldiers now were stationed in various European countries, the question of offspring from sexual encounters between German men and "foreign women" became a matter of concern not only for the Nazi ideologues, but also for the administrative apparatus of the Wehrmacht. In 1941 the High Command of the Wehrmacht suggested that the financial obligations towards children born out of wedlock to German soldiers in Belgium, France, the British Channel Islands, the Netherlands, and Norway be resolved by a separate court administered by the Wehrmacht. At this point, the Führer himself intervened, making it clear that German obligations could only be expected to apply according to racial politics. On this basis, it was decided that the policy proposed by the Wehrmacht High Command should only apply to Norway and the Netherlands. As for obligations towards Belgian and French mothers, Hitler stated that "We want to protect and support extramarital *Germanic* children; in the French we have no interest in terms of racial policy."[6]

One of the results of this policy was that the most successful Lebensborn operation in occupied countries was the one in Norway. The Norwegian Lebensborn organization was established in February 1941 and the first maternity institution was opened at Hurdal Verk in August 1941. This was also the first Lebensborn institution to be established outside Germany and Austria. As a result of the increased number of war children born during the following years, around ten more homes were established in Norway during the war, equaling the number of similar homes in Germany. According to the archives of Lebensborn Norway, between nine and ten thousand children were registered as having a German father and Norwegian mother, and were thus entitled to the protection of the Lebensborn organization. However, the actual number of Norwegian children with a German father must have been higher, since there were obviously cases of births not being reported to Lebensborn. Kåre Olsen suggests a number between ten and twenty thousand and puts the number of Norwegian women involved with German soldiers at between thirty and fifty thousand—i.e., up to 10 percent of all Norwegian women between the ages of fifteen and thirty. These figures, Olsen suggests, are important for understanding why the war children, their mothers, and other women who had relations with German men became a central topic in a heated public debate in Norway at the end of the war.[7]

According to Georg Lilienthal, Norway represented an "ideal case for Lebensborn" in terms of "racial purity"; Himmler himself had declared that "he was overjoyed for every child we get from there,"[8] and the

Lebensborn organization was given a much freer rein in Norway than in other occupied countries in a similar situation, such as the Netherlands and Denmark. In the Netherlands the "competing" NSV organization seems to have had greater influence, while in Denmark the matter was dealt with under Danish law because of the special situation allowing Danish authorities to run civil society until 1943. A Lebensborn home in Copenhagen was planned, but it did not open until May 1945, just as the Germans surrendered. Thus, Norway was left as the prime field for the Lebensborn organization in occupied territories.[9]

The fate of the women and children involved with German fathers varied. In some cases the relationships ended in marriage (Kåre Olsen suggests that 400–500 Norwegian/German marriages of this kind took place during the war), a process that, in spite of the fact that from 1942 German soldiers were permitted to marry "racially valuable" women in the Netherlands, Denmark, Norway, and Sweden, could take a long time, since strict proof of "pure Aryan blood" had to be procured.[10] The majority of the children born under Lebensborn auspices did stay with their mothers, but there were also a considerable number of children who were "left behind" at the maternity homes. To solve this problem, three of the Lebensborn homes were organized as orphanages, and the children from these orphanages were considered for adoption by German families. During the war some 250–300 Norwegian children were airlifted to the German Lebensborn orphanages of Kohren-Salis, Bad Polzin, and Hohehorst.

III

As noted above, the end of the German occupation left between thirty and fifty thousand women considered collaborators with the German occupiers, and around ten thousand children with German fathers. For the majority of these children, the stigma of fraternizing with the enemy was added to the stigma of having been born out of wedlock. In Norway, as in the other newly liberated countries of Europe, the joy of liberation went hand in hand with vengeful actions against those who had betrayed their country, and, as usual, a large part of this fury was directed against women who had consorted with the enemy. Danish historian Anette Warring writes in connection with the treatment of Danish women who had fraternized with the Germans:

> The female body and sexuality was a question of honour and a combat zone between the occupier and the occupied. National and individual honour was related to sexuality, but in different ways according to the gender in question. Gender and sexuality played a distinct role in the identity process of inclusion and exclusion, both as cultural discourse and as social practice.[11]

The female body is seen as the embodiment of nationhood—a fact that has been duly noted in literature[12]—and forges an unlikely bond between occupier and occupied. This complex concept serves as a background for understanding the treatment received by the female collaborators in liberated Europe immediately after the war. The women in question might not have been accomplices in treason in the legal sense of the word, but their behavior—offering their bodies, and thus their nationhood, to the enemy—was seen as tantamount to treason.

With victory and liberation came reckoning and retribution. Looking back at some of the documentation of that immediate fury, in the form of official Norwegian documents, one is struck by the vindictive and harsh words used to describe a group that in reality may be characterized as the innocent victims of these years: the war children. The discussion about "what to do" with the offspring of German soldiers and Norwegian women started before the war had ended among Norwegian politicians in exile in Sweden and Great Britain, supplemented by a document written by Norwegian clergy interned by the Germans. Under consideration was the possibility of deporting children with German fathers, and in fact a report from Stockholm in July 1944 concluded: "Current opinion in Norway is that, after the war, both mothers and children should be deported."[13] After liberation in May 1945, a committee was formed to deal with the problem and, as discussed at length in a monograph by Lars Borgersrud, the question of deportation was again brought up, supported by a minority of the committee. While the committee debated, actual steps were taken to act on the possibility of deportation of the Lebensborn children, as both Swedish and Australian (!) authorities were contacted to this end. When the committee finally gave its recommendation, deportation was ruled out. Furthermore, it was decided to repatriate the children already sent to Germany (139–57). This was already too late for the group of Norwegian children who were localized at the Hohehorst Lebensborn home in June 1945. Captain Sørensen was told by the British Army that the home was needed as a headquarters for the British occupying forces and that it was necessary to move the children immediately. Sørensen contacted the Norwegian administration, assuming that the children would be returned to Norway. But in Norway the authorities were expecting the committee to support the deportation of Lebensborn children, and looked for other solutions. One such solution was to contact the Swedish authorities to find out if the children could be placed there. The Swedish Red Cross agreed to take in the children at a home in Fiskeboda outside of Malmö in southern Sweden, and a convoy was arranged to transport the children from Bremen (where they had been sent first from Hohehorst) to Lübeck, from where they were shipped to Sweden in late July 1945.

The children were held there while the Swedish authorities sought adoptive parents. For some reason, possibly to take away something of the stigma that surrounded the children, it was announced that the children were orphans whose parents had died in concentration camps. Consequently, the children from the Fiskeboda transit camp were regarded as Swedish citizens and issued Swedish passports with names and dates of birth found in the information from Hohehorst. In the Swedish passport registers the space for "Name of parents" was filled in with "Unknown to Swedish Authorities." The identity cards that had followed the children from Hohehorst "disappeared," thus robbing the Fiskeboda children of their real identities. Borgersrud gives several examples of how these children later would struggle in vain to have their real identities documented, concluding that they were subjected to a falsification of history by the Swedish state in order to secure adoption on false premises as Swedish citizens and thus deprived of their rightful Norwegian citizenship. The Norwegian authorities knew about this and let it happen (123), thinking an official recommendation to deport was in the offing.

As it turned out, however, the commission's report in October did not propose deportation, due in part to pressure from the Allied Forces in Germany and the realization that deportation would amount to an unconstitutional act. Instead it was decided to bring home all of the Norwegian children still in Germany, whether they were living in orphanages or had been adopted. As will be documented below, this heavy-handed decision also resulted in many personal tragedies.

The Lebensborn protocols were used to find parents or relatives willing to take the children once they had been returned to Norway. They were housed in a temporary orphanage and representatives of the Norwegian government actively tried to track down the mothers of the children, in many cases managing to reunite mother and child. However, in other cases the economic and social situation was too much for the mothers, and the fate of the children left behind varied from instances where children found good adoptive families to instances of outright mistreatment, as in a case where children from the orphanage were placed in an institution for "retarded children" (as children with mental disabilities were called at the time; 260–81). For the children who stayed or were reunited with their mothers, life would also be difficult. In addition to the social stigma attached to being a *tyskerunge* ("German brat") came the many indignities and obstructions the Norwegian authorities inflicted on the war children and their mothers. Criminologist Kjersti Ericsson and historian Dag Ellingsen cite several examples of how the attribution of "unsatisfactory national stance" during the war was used as a pretext to make this group exempt from several of the social benefits that were introduced in the postwar Norwegian welfare state.[14] As the war experience faded, so did the heated debate around the *tyskertøser* ("German tarts") and *tyskerunger*, and the active attempts at letting the state decide the fate of those unhappy human beings lapsed into an embarrassed silence. This silence continued for almost 40 years.

IV

The silence surrounding the Norwegian war children was broken in 1985 and 1986 with a series of radio documentaries by Veslemøy Kjendsli, a journalist with the Norwegian broadcasting corporation, NRK. The radio documentary is, as Paddy Scannell has pointed out, an almost invisible form of documentary, although the format, often under the "Radio feature" tag, has had an almost parallel history with that of the Griersonian film documentary.[15] Following the fall of the Berlin Wall and the events of 1989–90 in Europe, Kjendsli was able to access more material on this topic and produced three documentaries for NRK Television. Here follows a description of these radio and television documentaries, along with a discussion of their institutional and genre-related framework as well as their larger historical and theoretical context.

In the spring of 1985 Kjendsli had made a radio documentary with the title *Island of the Damned Women* (*De fortapte pikers øy*) about the fate of some of the women who were accused of being *tyskertøser* in the Oslo area during the liberation days. Despite the fact that there was no law against fraternizing, several hundred women were interned on an island in the Oslo fjord during that period. In Ålesund in western Norway, Turid, a 43-year-old woman, listened intently to the radio broadcast, sensing that this story would have a bearing on the 20 years she had been struggling to learn about her own identity.[16] When she was 13 years old, she had learned that she was adopted and that her father was German; eight years later she had started her own research into her background. But the trail had ended at a now defunct orphanage outside Oslo from which, according to her adoptive parents, she had been transferred to their care in 1948 at six years old. Of these first six years of her life, Turid has absolutely no memory. She contacted Kjendsli, told her story, and asked for the journalist's assistance in looking into her background. The cooperation between Turid and Kjendsli did not yield the wanted results, but Turid's situation and the search for her origins did result in another radio documentary, *Jeg vil vite hvem jeg er!* (I want to know who I am!) aired on December 26, 1985.[17]

This radio documentary led to a rush of reactions from people all over Norway in a similar situation to that of Turid—war children who had been searching for their background without finding it. Most of the grown children, unlike Turid, knew their mothers but were searching for information about their German fathers. However, there were also individuals, like Turid, for whom the years prior to their adoption represented a blank space. Motivated by this gap, Kjendsli and Turid continued their quest and finally found the lead they were looking for in the vaults of the Norwegian National Archive, where the protocols of the Norwegian Lebensborn organization, kept with German thoroughness, were stored. Here Turid learned that although Turid is the name she was given at birth, for four years of her early life her name was Elke Schneider and she had lived in Germany.

The radio documentary *Veien fram går langt tilbake* (The road ahead goes a long way back), aired on March 23, 1986, follows Turid and Kjendsli as they unravel the story of Turid's past.[18] She learns that she was born in the Lebensborn maternity home of Klekken on August 16, 1942 and registered as "Lebensborn child No. 2022 in Norway." Later that year, after her mother had signed an affidavit affirming that she had no intention of keeping her child, she was put on one of the transports to Germany, in this case to the Lebensborn orphanage at Kohren-Salis near Dresden. In 1944 she was adopted by the Schneider family in Munich and stayed with them until February 1948, when a car with two men and a woman arrived in front of the Schneider home. They picked up the girl, who was playing with her brother in front of the house, carried her to the car, explaining to her shocked foster parents that they had to take her in for a medical examination. They then drove off, and that is the last the Schneider family saw of Turid, or Elke as she was known to them. Kjendsli managed to locate the Schneider family in 1986, now living in the vicinity of Hamburg, and brings Turid to meet "Mutti" and "Vati" as she used to call them when German was her only language. The documentary ends with that reunion, although Kjendsli will stay with Turid and her quest for several more years, as covered in the two editions of her book *Skammens barn* (Children of shame), culminating with Turid meeting her biological mother.

With the two radio documentaries about Turid, Kjendsli had managed to pry loose the lid that was put on the fate of the Norwegian Lebensborn children in the years following World War II. Kjendsli made two more radio documentaries in 1986, one of which was a re-edited version of the two stories about Turid. The focus of the other, *Krigsbarn i fredstid* (War children in peace time), was the general fate of children fathered by German soldiers during the war and the stigma applied to the "German children" in postwar Norway.[19] Kjendsli interviewed a number of people, now in their early forties, who for the first time were able publicly to vent their anger and frustration over having grown up as pariahs in the postwar society.

The fall of the Berlin Wall in 1989 opened up another chapter in the story of the Norwegian Lebensborn children. Most of the 250–300 Norwegian Lebensborn children transported to Germany during the war ended up in the Kohren-Salis orphanage outside Dresden in East Germany, which would become the Soviet Zone of occupation and then, from 1949, the German Democratic Republic, a country closed to the outside world after the erection of the Berlin Wall in 1961. In 1991 Veslemøy Kjendsli returned to Germany, this time to meet some of the Norwegian children who were not brought back to Norway because of the Iron Curtain. In the vicinity of Kohren-Salis, she found several people in their late forties who knew that their background was Norwegian, and who were then featured in the television documentary *Tapt fortid gjenfunnet* (Lost past, refound), aired on Norwegian television on April 18, 1991.[20]

The documentary is introduced with the image of a woman in Norwegian national costume standing beside a German soldier. Between them, they are holding a little child. A caption in Gothic letters is superimposed over the image and the words are read in German: "Heilig soll uns sein jeder Mutter guten Blutes" ("Sacred is to us every mother of pure blood"). These words dissolve into the runic symbol of the SS, while the faces of mother and child dissolve into different faces. The soldier remains the same. On the soundtrack a children's choir sings the German children's song "Hat ein Vogel geflogen." After a montage of newsreel shots from occupied Norway and reconstructed sequences relating to the courtships and plight of unwed mothers, a middle-aged woman is shown stating in German: "My name is Anita Bertram, born Andersen. I was born on January 7, 1943 in Bø in Vesterålen (northern Norway)."[21] This leads into a sequence where a number of people in the former GDR relate how they learned about their Norwegian parentage and how, following the events of December 1989, they have been able to look into their own background.

This is done against an exposition of the Lebensborn organization in Norway consisting of off-screen commentary over archival footage, images from the vaults of the Norwegian National Archive, and interviews with the archivist in charge of the Lebensborn archives. During this presentation, the faces and voices of the seven former Lebensborn children are presented, accompanied, where possible, by photos of them as children and pictures from the Lebensborn home Godthåp (Good Hope) outside Oslo. Over an animated map of northern Europe an off-screen commentator states: "And from 1943 hundreds of children were sent on a long journey ... where they lost their past. The journey led them to the heart of what was to become the GDR." A rather crudely reconstructed scene of a car approaching a stately building ends up with a reporter standing in front of the building: "And this was their final destination—the SS Orphanage Sonnenwiese (Sunny field) in Kohren-Salis outside Leipzig ... A highly rated orphanage for the cream of the Aryan race." The Norwegian TV team has organized a meeting between some of the surviving nurses at the Sonnenwiese home who remember how the Norwegian children arrived around 1943, and we are told how some of the children were given away for adoption, while others stayed until the end of the war ("They were all beautiful, blue-eyed children with blond hair").

The final part of the documentary is mainly about rediscovery and attempted reunification. As a girl, Aud Rigmor Grafe was adopted by a farmer in the vicinity of Sonnenwiese and managed as early as 1977 to find the identity of her mother. But all attempts at getting in touch with her were hindered by the GDR authorities. Then, in 1991, with the camera team present, she manages to get a phone call through on her mother's birthday.

In nearby Espenhain, coal mineworkers Werner von Ries and Arno Kaube have discovered that they share a background as Norwegian Lebensborn children. Arno has located his mother in Norway, but she does not want any further contact, while Werner has been more successful. After gaining information from the Lebensborn archives, he has been reunited with his biological father, who lives in Dresden. The story then returns to Anita, the first of the Lebensborn children to be introduced in the documentary, as she states: "I would like to meet my mother and sister." Cut to a car emerging from a tunnel in Vesterålen, Norway. Anita and her husband have come to visit the place she left as a one-year-old. Her mother has died, but she still has a sister there. They meet with warm embraces and tears. Anita also meets her aunt, who was the last person to see her before she left Norway. In the final image we find the newly united sisters at their mother's grave in a graveyard overlooking the Arctic Sea.

Five years later Kjendsli presented another aspect of the Lebensborn experience in Norway. The documentary *Okkuperte hjerter* (Occupied hearts)[22] was aired on April 9, 1996, the anniversary of the date German troops entered Norway in 1940; it tells a piece of the story of the war children from the mothers' points of view. The documentary opens with 1940s tango music on the soundtrack, accompanied by archival footage of occupying soldiers in the streets of Oslo. This leads into the off-screen commentary: "Today it is exactly 56 years since the German soldiers conquered Norway as well as the hearts of some Norwegian girls. But isn't that forgotten by now?" Cut to the silhouette of a woman with the caption "Anna," sitting in front of a window overlooking a hillside in Bergen and speaking in what can easily be identified as an upper-middle-class Bergen accent: "To say it is forgiven is one thing, but to use it against you on every occasion is something else," which introduces Anna and her story about occupation, love, childbirth, shame, and retribution.

Using Anna as the focal point of the story, the film becomes a retelling of how the Lebensborn organization functioned for the around ten thousand Norwegian women who found themselves in situations where they were pregnant by men who represented repression and fear to the majority of Norwegians. Compared to the previous television documentary on the Lebensborn children, *Okkuperte hjerter* represents considerably higher production values. The filmmakers have found highly relevant archival footage of German soldiers, mainly officers, enjoying the night life of Norwegian cities in the company of young girls, and they present this footage intercut with a commentary by historian Dag Ellingsen, who in 1991 was conducting a study of Norwegian wartime collaborators and their fate. Ellingsen points out in the film that the treatment of the "German tarts" after the war is an area of recent Norwegian history that has been neglected: "It is as if we have never closed this chapter, nor have we studied it thoroughly. It has become a taboo."[23]

This is supported by Anna, who, as the off-screen commentary informs us,

> does not want to show her face, since she, and other women in her situation, are still at risk of being confronted with the past, as in the case of the woman who, after the war, married a Norwegian war hero who was not bothered by her past. However, when he died, she was denied a war widow's pension, since her past was "sullied."

There follows an interview with a female bureaucrat in the state pension department about this and similar cases. She lists the criteria for being denied a pension—the number of Germans the person has been in contact with and the time they were together. The question of "worthy national attitude" during the war seems to have functioned as a criterion used in the Norwegian social bureaucracy without any legal precedent. The story moves back to Anna, who speaks about how she, to the horror of her family and friends, met and fell in love with a German soldier, and as a result of this found herself pregnant. She speaks about the contempt she was met with and how her parents tried, in vain, to keep her away from her boyfriend: "They tried to keep me from meeting him—but it was no use. It was how it was." She then talks about her decision to contact Lebensborn in Bergen. This is illustrated by a reconstruction where a girl in the clothes and hairdo of the war period sits on a bench outside the building housing the Gestapo headquarters in Bergen. "We knew it was called the Gestapo House and that there were interrogations and, possibly, torture there." The girl walks hesitantly toward the main door and there is a cut to Anna with her back to the camera in front of the door. "I felt terrible, humiliated, but I knew that if I were to go through with this, I had to ask the help of the Lebensborn. There was a nice young man in SS uniform. I was well treated and I felt respected."

Anna was sent to the Lebensborn maternity home at Klekken, a fashionable hotel in the countryside of eastern Norway. The camera team follows Anna and Kjendsli as she revisits Klekken 48 years after she went there to give birth. She talks about how the hotel was organized in the Lebensborn days, points to the garden where she and the other girls pinched apples ("You see, we were pregnant, we had the munchies"), but when she enters the room where she actually gave birth, she breaks down in tears and runs away from the camera. Afterward she informs us that she was given the option of leaving her boy for adoption, but that she refused. She also tells Kjendsli that 28 years later she took her son to Klekken so he could see his birthplace.

Anna gives no information about what happened to her and the boy after the war. The final sequence of the documentary deals with the general aspects of the aftermath for the "German tarts," with archival shots of jubilant Norwegians running through the streets with national flags intercut with still images of a woman with shorn hair and a naked body painted with swastikas. Ellingsen comments on the rage vented on these women: "Because this had to do with sexuality, there were a lot of strong feelings. In many wars and conflicts, the sexuality of women is considered a national commodity." At the very end the off-screen commentary states: "For fifty years they have feared that the past would reach them. As late as this year, a woman was refused her husband's war pension because of an old document from 1945." This statement is confirmed by a female Social Department bureaucrat: "We still practice according to the rules of 1946."

The last in the series of Lebensborn documentaries produced by the Norwegian Broadcasting Corporation, *Den perfekte agenten* (The perfect agent), aired on June 16, 1997, was the most sensational, but brought little new general information about the Lebensborn organization.[24] It did, however, give an explanation as to why the Norwegian Lebensborn children in the former GDR were denied any contact with the country where they were entitled to citizenship. The story of Ludwig Bergmann started, like the life stories in *Tapt fortid gjenfunnet*, at the Lebensborn orphanage of Kohren-Salis in East Germany. But unlike his crib-mates at the orphanage, Ludwig Bergmann—born in 1941 in Haugesund, Norway—was allowed by the GDR authorities to apply for a Norwegian passport in 1967, an application that was granted by the Norwegian authorities. Bergmann left the GDR for Norway the same year and found work there. He also managed to get in contact with his lost family in Haugesund, where his mother still lived. Mother of three and married to a sailor in the Norwegian merchant fleet sailing for the Allies, she became pregnant by a German soldier during the first year of the war. The little boy, Ludwig, was sent to the Godthåp Lebensborn home in Oslo and from there, in 1944, to Kohren-Salis.

In 1967 he was welcomed into the family as a lost half-brother, and he later invited his mother and half-sister to his wedding in the German Federal Republic, where he had relocated after spending several years in Norway. In 1982 his mother died, and Ludwig went to Norway to obtain a portion of his inheritance. Later he moved to Vienna and became an Austrian citizen, leaving suddenly for the GDR in 1983, as he came under suspicion for industrial espionage. With the fall of the Berlin Wall and the reunification of Germany, the files of the Stasi, the feared German security police, were made available to the public. From these it became apparent that the Stasi had used the identity of several of the Norwegian children from the Kohren-Salis home as a cover for East German intelligence agents. Among the identities used was that of Ludwig Bergmann.

The Norwegian documentary of 1997 tracked the story of the false Ludwig Bergmann through interviews with his Norwegian family, before going to Falkenhorst in Saxony to locate the real Ludwig Bergmann, who had been informed by the GDR authorities in the late 1950s that both his parents in Norway had been killed in a bombing raid. In front of the camera he is informed about his real background, about the deception scam run by the Stasi, and about the fact that an impostor had taken over his identity and his place in his Norwegian family. The documentary ends with the real Ludwig Bergmann being reunited with his half-sisters in Haugesund.[25]

Den perfekte agenten functions as a sardonic last chapter in Kjendsli's documentary series about the Norwegian Lebensborn children, a saga that started as a quest for identity and ends in a story of stolen identity. The documentary also bears witness to a changed media landscape in Norway. The four radio documentaries of the 1980s and the first television documentary in 1991 were all made within the Norwegian one-channel noncommercial public broadcasting system. In 1992 broadcasting in Norway was deregulated, opening the way for an alternative commercial television broadcaster, TV2. The Norwegian public broadcaster NRK responded by competing for audience share with the new commercial channel. The marks of this development may be discerned in the differences in the production strategies between the first 1991 documentary about the children left behind in the GDR and the documentary about Ludwig Bergmann from 1997. The latter was made as an expensive co-production with the German television company Spiegel-TV and was duly advertised in the press before its release. The manipulation of the real Ludwig Bergmann was obviously a part of this strategy. Whereas the interview subjects in the 1991 documentary had been given information beforehand, the news that someone had been usurping his identity is sprung on Ludwig in front of the camera lens. To make sure the audience is aware of this, an off-screen commentary is added: "And now Ludwig, for the first time, learns that someone else has taken his identity, down to the point of attending his real mother's funeral." This voyeuristic streak, reminiscent of sensationalist talk shows and reality television, is inconsistent with the sobriety of the earlier documentaries.

V

The three television documentaries about Lebensborn in Norway are characterized by the relatively traditional expository documentary format typical of the in-house productions of the Norwegian Broadcasting Corporation in the 1980s and 1990s. The first of these films, *Tapt fortid gjenfunnet* (1991), was produced by what was then the section for social affairs (Samfunnsseksjonen) in the information department (Opplysningsavdelingen—literally the "Enlightenment Department") of the NRK and presented on the current affairs program *Sosialkanalen* (The social channel). True to convention for these current affairs programs, there were no credits for the director. Instead the credit of *programansvarlig* (responsible for the program) was shared between Sten-Rune Sterner and Veslemøy Kjendsli. Sterner was a veteran documentary filmmaker with close to 30 years of production experience within the NRK organization and a key figure in the *Sosialkanalen* program concept.[26]

The current affairs program *Brennpunkt* (Focal point) was introduced in 1996 with an emphasis on investigative journalism and inaugurated a more hard-hitting journalism, no doubt as a result of competition from the newly introduced Norwegian commercial public broadcaster TV2. The documentary produced for *Sosialkanalen* and the two items for *Brennpunkt* (where Kjendsli is credited as *programansvarlig*) share the same main structure, where the problem at hand is illustrated by a mix of archival material, interviews, and reconstructed and illustrative sections bound together with the help of an off-screen commentary. However, the narrative focal point of all three documentaries is the retrospective interview, or what might be characterized as the main agent of what David MacDougall calls "films of memory." MacDougall points out some of the problematic aspects of attempting to represent memory audiovisually:

> Films that focus on memory do not of course record memory itself, but its referents, its secondary representations (in speech for example) and its correlatives. In films, objects survive from the past, people reminisce, and certain objects evoke or resemble those of memory. We end by filming something far removed from memory as it is experienced, but instead a mixture of dubious testimony, flawed evidence, and invention.[27]

In an article in *History and Anthropology* (2007) Roxana Waterson takes issue with what she perceives as MacDougall's overly pessimistic view of the relationship between film and memory and his tendency to dismiss filmed testimonies as "unreliable as expressions of memory." She emphasizes the importance of the performative aspect of the filmed testimony and suggests three crucial dimensions of memory in this respect—as *trace*, as *event*, and as *trajectory*.[28]

Trace deals with memory as evidence: someone in front of the camera presents an oral testimony relating to the subject of the documentary in question. Waterson draws attention to the *materiality* of this situation, where the person in question represents to the audience, through his or her appearance, a direct link with the time and period in question. When, after having presented various sources of knowledge about the Lebensborn organization, Kjendsli then presents the middle-aged men and women who were, once, the Lebensborn children from Capa's *LIFE Magazine* feature, they become something more than an abstract historical concept. Through their appearance and through their words they forge an indexical link with the past in question.

The memory *event*, according to Waterson, is closely connected to the act of testifying, letting the audience witness the, often traumatic, act of reminiscence (66). Waterson uses the example of Marceline Loridan coming to terms with the trauma of childhood experiences in the Nazi concentration camps in Jean Rouch and Edgar Morin's *Chronique d'un été* (Chronicle of a summer, France, 1961). In Kjendsli's documentaries about the Lebensborn children, there are several events of this kind. For instance, consider the final sequence of the first film, *Tapt fortid gjenfunnet*, where Anita finally is unified with her family in northern Norway and meets her aunt, who was the last person to see her as she left for Germany as a baby. Here, the setting as well as the situation are just as important as, if not more important than, the information given. As an audience, we are given access to a private moment, and this access is meant as an invitation to participate in the knowledge given—for our own sake. As Waterson puts it: "There are moments in film when we sense that something transformative is happening, in which we as spectators become caught up ourselves; when we realize that the effort at transmission is changing us, as much as it may be changing things for the participants" (64–5).

In her book *Trauma Cinema*, Janet Walker introduces the concept of "documentary enactment" for these cases where the act of remembering is facilitated by organizing pro-filmic situations, such as family reunions and the like.[29] Another case of this kind of "memory event," although far more debatable on an ethical level, is the scene in *Den perfekte agenten* referred to above where Ludwig Bergman is confronted with the fact that another man has usurped his identity for more than a decade.

In her discussion of the memory event, Waterson emphasizes the social function these events play when presented in a documentary film. By presenting and sharing memories through the testimonies of the Lebensborn children and women, Kjendsli's radio and television documentaries are making the transition, from individual to social memory, that Waterson calls the "trajectory of memory." In this way they come to function as active agents, participating in a fundamental change in the perception of Norwegian history during and immediately after World War II.

VI

In a traditional televised New Year's address on January 1, 2000, Norwegian Prime Minister Kjell Magne Bondevik offered an apology to the Norwegian war children on behalf of the Norwegian people. This gesture was welcome but long overdue and, as it would turn out, too late. About the same time, the Norwegian Association for War Children (Norges krigsbarnforbund) initiated the equivalent of a class action in the Norwegian legal system to seek compensation for the hardships they had endured in the years after the war. The court case was deemed time-barred, that is, too much time had elapsed between the actual wrongdoing and the time of the claim. This decision was appealed through all the levels of the Norwegian court system, being turned away at every level, until the European Court of Human Rights in January 2008 finally came to the same conclusion—the case had its roots too far back for the present Norwegian government to take on economic responsibility.

However, in the 20 years that had passed since Kjendsli's first radio documentary about Turid and her search for the past, the documentaries and the articles and books that followed had given the Norwegian war children a collective identity and personal historical backgrounds. Founded in 1986, the Norges krigsbarnforbund organization had seen its membership grow from the original eight members to more than four hundred.

There is no doubt that Kjendsli's documentaries were influential in drawing new attention to the fate of the Norwegian war children, Lebensborn children especially. The act of presenting them as human faces and voices contributed to countering the myths surrounding the "German tarts," their children, and the public condemnation of both in the initial postwar years. The documentaries were also instrumental in debunking the myth about Lebensborn as an SS "stud farm," as suggested by Capa in the *LIFE* article and repeated in a book by French journalists Marc Hillel and Clarissa Henry in 1976.[30] In his thorough examination of the Lebensborn history, Lilienthal finds no support for this myth, but assumes that some of the documents of the SS Lebensborn leaders might couch a wish of that sort.

As mentioned above, the debate about the fate of the Lebensborn children has been revived in Norway, as the class action suit of the War Children Association has shown, and this time it is being met with support and understanding. The renewed debate has also shed light on the Norwegian authorities' treatment of the large number of Norwegian women who fraternized with the Germans. As late as August 2008, the major Norwegian newspaper *Adresseavisen* ran a feature series on the topic—63 years after the war. One of the questions that arise in this connection is that of "victimhood," as the children in these articles, as well as in the general public discourse on the subject in Norway, are referred to as *ofre* or victims.

In their introduction to an issue on "The Politics of Victimhood" of the journal *History and Anthropology*, editors Laura Jeffery and Matei Candea state that they intend to subject the interface between victimhood and politics to critical scrutiny.[31] In this introduction, as well as in several articles in the issue, the concept of the victim as a "pure" category is challenged, and cases where victimhood has been used actively in a political sense are discussed. The article also raises the question of *agency*: to what extent do the perceived victims represent more than passivity and suffering, and when do they cross the line between passive victims and active agents (291)? The journal issue in question is an example of how the concept of victimhood has been problematized in recent English language literature on the subject.

In Scandinavian languages, the word *offer* (in German: *Opfer*) is used for both *victim* and *sacrifice*, in contradistinction to a narrower definition of the word in English: "victim, *n* ... 2 d. In weaker sense: One who suffers some injury, hardship, or loss, is badly treated or taken advantage of, etc."[32] Thus, when the Norwegian war children were recently given the status of *offer*, this may be regarded as a first step on the way to justice. While the English words "victim" and "victimhood" would seem to exclude agency, the concept of victim as a solely negative and passive category does not apply to the same extent in the Norwegian context. Therefore, on a linguistic basis, as well as through this history of the Norwegian radio and television Lebensborn documentaries provided here, I argue that these successive documentaries realized a process whereby the Norwegian war children have been reconstituted as victims and, as a result of this process, agents. This process has made the Lebensborn children *visible* in Norwegian public discourse—and the victimhood conferred on this group has had a positive function: that of facilitating action in the form of demands for social exoneration and financial restitution.

The Kjendsli documentaries managed to present the voices and testimonies of individuals, and in so doing to offer the possibility of breaking through the myths and silences surrounding the difficult field of nation and female sexuality. We have therefore witnessed a process, introduced by the first radio documentary in 1986, that led eventually to a decisive shift in Norwegian public opinion. The war children of Norway, once vilified as "Nazi bastards," now are being reconstructed as victims, as a sacrifice made on the altar of national revenge.

notes

1. Anon, "Illegitimate Nazi 'Super Babies' Live in German Chateau," *LIFE Magazine*, 13 August 1945, 37.
2. The seminal work on the Lebensborn organization is Georg Lilienthal, *Der "Lebensborn e.V." Ein Instrument nationalsozialistischer Rassenpolitik. Erweiterte Neuausgabe* (Frankfurt am Main: Fischer Taschenbuchverlag, 2003), and the historical account here is based on this source.
3. Lilienthal, *Der "Lebensborn e.V.,"* 43, my translation.
4. Kåre Olsen, "Under the Care of Lebensborn: Norwegian War Children and Their Mothers," in *Children of World War II: The Hidden Enemy Legacy*, eds. Kjersti Ericsson and Eva Simonsen (Oxford: Berg, 2005), 16.
5. Lilienthal, *Der "Lebensborn e.V.,"* 14–39.
6. "Wir wollen uneheliche *germanische* Kinder schützen und betreuen; an Franzosen haben wir rassenpolitisch kein Interesse." Note from the "Reichskanzlei," 27 June 1941, quoted in Lilienthal, *Der "Lebensborn e.V.,"* 163.
7. Olsen, "Under the Care of Lebensborn," 24.
8. Lilienthal, *Der "Lebensborn e.V.,"* 168–70.
9. The Lebensborn activities in occupied "non-Aryan" countries will not be dealt with here, but in the eastern and southern European regions these activities were often tantamount to the kidnapping of children who were considered to be of "Volks" German extraction.

10. Olsen, "Under the Care of Lebensborn," 24.
11. Anette Warring, "War, Cultural Loyalty and Gender: Danish Women's Intimate Fraternization," in *Children of World War II*, eds. Ericsson and Simonsen, 43.
12. See, for example, Andrew Parker, Mary Russo, Doris Sommer, and Patricia Yaeger, "Introduction," in *Nationalisms and Sexualities* (New York: Routledge, 1992), 6.
13. Quoted in Lars Borgersrud, *Vi ville ikke ha dem: Statens behandling av de norske krigsbarna* (We did not want them: How the Norwegian state treated the war children) (Oslo: Scandinavian Academic Press/Spartacus Forlag, 2005), 43, my translation.
14. *Children of World War II*, eds. Ericsson and Simonsen.
15. Paddy Scannell, "The Stuff of Radio," in *Documentary and the Mass Media*, ed. John Corner (London: Arnold, 1986), 1.
16. Veslemøy Kjendsli, *Skammens barn* (Children of shame), revised edition (Oslo: Egmont Bøker Fredhøis, 2001), 31.
17. *Jeg vil vite hvem jeg er!* (I want to know who I am!), dir. Veslemøy Kjendsli, NRK Radio, Nasjonalbiblioteket Mo i Rana, Norway, 26 December 1985.
18. *Veien fram går langt tilbake* (The road ahead goes a long way back), dir. Veslemøy Kjendsli, NRK Radio, Nasjonalbiblioteket Mo i Rana, Norway, 23 March 1986.
19. *Krigsbarn i fredstid* (War children in peace time), dir. Veslemøy Kjendsli, NRK Radio, Nasjonalbiblioteket Mo i Rana, Norway, 31 March 1986.
20. *Tapt fortid gjenfunnet* (Lost past, refound), dir. Veslemøy Kjendsli and Sten-Rune Sterner, *Sosialkanalen* (The social channel, a current affairs series), NRK TV, Nasjonalbiblioteket Mo i Rana, Norway, 18 April 1991.
21. Translation of dialog here and throughout is mine, unless otherwise noted.
22. *Okkuperte hjerter* (Occupied hearts), dir. Veslemøy Kjendsli, Brennpunkt NRK TV, Nasjonalbiblioteket Mo i Rana, Norway, 9 April 1996.
23. All the quotations of Dag Ellingsen are from the documentary *Okkuperte hjerter*.
24. *Den perfekte agenten* (The perfect agent), dir. Veslemøy Kjendsli, Brennpunkt NRK TV, Nasjonalbiblioteket Mo i Rana, Norway, 16 June 1997.
25. Kjendsli also found out that the identity of Rigmor Aud Graefe, who was featured in *Tapt fortid gjenfunnet*, was stolen in a similar manner.
26. Jan Anders Diesen, *Fakta i forandring: Fjernsynsdokumentaren i NRK 1960–2000* (Changing facts: The television documentary in NRK 1960–2000) (Oslo: Universitetsforlaget, 2005), 175.
27. David MacDougall, *Transcultural Cinema* (Princeton, NJ: Princeton University Press, 1998), 232.
28. Roxana Waterson, "Trajectories of Memory: Documentary Film and the Transmission of Testimony," *History and Anthropology* 18, no. 1 (March 2007): 53.
29. Janet Walker, *Trauma Cinema: Documenting Incest and the Holocaust* (Berkeley: University of California Press, 2005), 135.
30. Clarissa Henry and Marc Hillel, *Children of the SS* (London: Hutchinson, 1976).
31. Laura Jeffery and Matei Candea, "The Politics of Victimhood," *History and Anthropology* 17, no. 4 (2007): 287.
32. *Oxford English Dictionary*, s.v. "Victim," dictionary.oed.com (accessed 20 October 2008).

five

reclamation of voice

the joint authorship of testimony in the *murmuring* trilogy

hye jean chung

What will die with me when I die?

Jorge Luis Borges, *The Witness*

In the documentary trilogy *The Murmuring* (1995), *Habitual Sadness* (1997), and *My Own Breathing* (1999),[1] Korean woman filmmaker Byun Young-joo deals with the long-neglected issue of "comfort women," a euphemistic term used by Japanese military forces during World War II to refer to the women they abducted and forced into sexual slavery. The use of the term "comfort women" is contested, and many activists and scholars suggest that we replace it with the more accurate expression "military sexual slaves." However, others knowingly use the term because they believe it conveys the irony of deploying the word "comfort" to veil the brutalities experienced by the women. It is in this vein that I use it here (always in quotes), as I believe the term is emblematic of the denial of the violence inflicted on survivors in the past and the present. In the three films, Byun presents the testimony of these hitherto silenced former "comfort women" and the documentation of their everyday lives, including their continued participation in the weekly protests that have taken place every Wednesday since 1992 in front of the Japanese Embassy in Seoul.

The trilogy raises such questions as: what does it mean to bear witness to a historically traumatic event through the medium of film (especially by subjects who have been silenced for decades)? What kinds of discursive strategies are deployed in the film to reclaim formerly silenced voices into official history, and how are they effective? As implied by the title of the first film, the trilogy is about the "murmurings" of the former "comfort women." The low voices of the women, subdued almost to the point of incomprehensibility, serve as a reminder of how their voices—or rather their very existence—have been devalued and ignored in the past. Watching the three films in succession, one is struck by the marked difference in the women's demeanor and interactions with the camera in each installment. As the trilogy progresses, the women noticeably acquire confidence and ease in front of the camera, and gradually demonstrate savviness of the power of the documentary medium. Through the developing process of joint authorship between filmmaker and subject, based on the telling and recording of testimony, the trilogy gives voice to these formerly silenced women. Through their collaboration, the filmmaker and the victims conjoin to interpellate the spectator to action by expanding the scope of relevancy from the personal to the collective. Thus the trilogy becomes political through its (subtle) invocation of the spectator to take action.

Historical documents and accounts from soldiers and victims have provided evidence that the Imperial Japanese Army systematically controlled the capture and enslavement of an estimated 200,000 women from Japan's colonies, predominantly Korea and China, and shipped them to "comfort stations" in various regions around Asia, including China, Singapore, Indonesia, Myanmar, and the Philippines, until the end of the war. Despite this evidence, the Japanese government has continuously refused to provide either an unqualified official apology or legal compensation to the survivors. In 1992 Yoshiaki Yoshimi, a Japanese historian, went to the Self-Defense Agency's library and discovered documents revealing military involvement in establishing brothels, including one entitled "Regarding the Recruitment of Women for Military Brothels." Faced with this evidence, the Japanese government acknowledged the military's role in forcing women into sexual slavery, and Yohei Kono, then chief cabinet secretary, issued an apology to former "comfort women." The survivors and their supporters did not accept this apology, however, protesting that the Japanese government was not fully acknowledging its responsibility because the declaration issued by Kono was not approved by Parliament. The fact that the Japanese government rejected most compensation claims made by the victims cast further doubt on the sincerity of the apology. Instead, Japan established a fund based on private donations in 1995 (this ended in March 2007). Because they believed that the Japanese government was evading accountability by offering unofficial private funds instead of using government money to compensate the survivors, many former "comfort women" refused to accept the money and demanded that the Japanese Diet issue an unequivocal official apology and offer formal reparations.[2]

The "comfort women" issue remains volatile and unresolved to this day, decades after the end of the war, as Japan's continuous denial of wartime crimes and refusal to compensate victims sustain deep-seated anti-Japanese sentiments in neighboring countries, and influence diplomatic relations among them.[3] The urgent need to publicize these women's stories increases each year, not only because of the imminent deaths of the elderly survivors, but also because certain Japanese right-wing politicians vehemently proclaim the women's accusations to be false in attempts to undermine their validity and accuracy. In March 2007 Japan's Prime Minister, Shinzo Abe, reignited the debate by stating that there was "no evidence to prove there was coercion" by Japan's military to force women into sexual servitude during the war.[4] His official statement reflects the recent efforts of a group of ruling Liberal Democratic Party lawmakers in Japan to rescind Kono's 1993 apology. At the time Abe made his controversial claim, the US Congress was debating a resolution calling upon Japan to issue an official apology for the military's role in sexual slavery, so Abe's

Figure 5.1

A former "comfort woman" speaks during a weekly protest in front of the Japanese Embassy in Seoul (*The Murmuring*)

statement was read as a pre-emptive declaration that his government would reject the call for an official apology.[5] Later that July a nonbinding resolution was passed in the House of Representatives that urged the Japanese government to "formally acknowledge, apologize and accept historical responsibility in a clear and unequivocal manner."[6] Japanese officials protested, asserting that the country's leaders, including Abe, had apologized repeatedly, but supporters of the resolution responded that Japan has never assumed full responsibility, as evidenced by the aforementioned comments made by Abe. On April 17, 2007, an advertisement was placed in the *Washington Post* to highlight and raise support for the "comfort women" issue.[7]

Against this background, the testimony of the survivors expands beyond its necessity in the healing process of personal trauma, and takes on added meaning as a collective *political* act. Indeed, it is difficult to separate the two, as the issue of military sexual slavery is a complex site in which national pride, international politics, sexual violence, and war trauma intersect. The feminist psychiatrist Judith Herman stresses the need to remember and to tell the truth about "unspeakable" psychological trauma from the past in order to heal individual victims and to restore social order. The path to recovery, however, is strewn with obstacles, as "the conflict between the will to *deny* horrible events and the will to *proclaim* them aloud is the central dialectic of psychological trauma."[8] This conflict is made evident in the films when the women express disappointment and weariness at the fact that their testimonies seem to make no difference in changing the Japanese official stance, and when they describe the shame and discomfort they feel during the weekly demonstrations in onscreen conversations with the filmmaker. Their initial unease is palpable in the way they evade the camera in the first installment, *The Murmuring*. At one point during an interview with Byun, one survivor remarks that she would be embarrassed if this scene were shown in theaters and abruptly ends the conversation by leaving the room. Despite their reluctance, the women continue to participate in the weekly protests and in the making of the film, as they are propelled by their sense of justice and responsibility to tell the truth, which are fueled by the Japanese government's continuous denials.

Herman further points out that the "will to deny" trauma functions on a social as well as an individual level. Thus the stakes of the issue are considerably raised, as the scope of recovery from trauma transcends the individual and moves toward the collective, particularly in the context of rediscovering knowledge of the past. In the case of the "comfort women," the will to forget operates in the double spheres of public and private. For almost five decades after the war, this willful forgetting has led to the suppression of the women's voices in order to shield individual, familial, and national dishonor. For these women, the original trauma of sexual assault was exacerbated by the additional trauma that came from the collective denial of their painful past and the erasure of their very existence. It was not until August 1991 that Kim Hak-soon became the first Korean woman to finally break this decades-long silence by publicly revealing her past as a "comfort woman," which prompted others to follow suit.

In the realm of the personal, the women survivors kept silent out of shame and fear of stigmatization for themselves and their family. In the films, a number of survivors relate how they were ostracized and chastised by their own families when they returned after the end of the war. (One woman recalls that her mother told her that she should have died rather than come back home in disgrace.) In the realm of the national, the two governments have ultimately colluded—whether intentionally or not—in their repression of this "shameful" past. The Japanese government has been adamant in its denials in order to protect its national honor and reputation, and has repeatedly rejected compensation claims on the grounds that postwar treaties had settled these issues. Meanwhile, the Korean government has shied away from confronting the issue due to national pride and shame that the Korean people were unable to protect not only their nation but also their young women from foreign invasion. In addition to the patriarchal traditions of a society founded on Confucian values, the identity of the modern Korean nation has been greatly influenced by the "emasculating" experiences of Japanese colonial rule (1910–45), the Korean War (1950–53), the national division of the two Koreas, and the oppressive military dictatorship (1962–87). It is often observed that colonized males assume the position of the colonizer toward colonized women as a means of recovering their masculinity. To overcome their emasculation as colonized subjects, Korean men have likewise "obsessively disciplined and regulated women's bodies as metaphors for their uncontaminated, uninterrupted homonational (or homosocial) identity, and imposed on women the ideology of chastity and self-censorship," which resulted in the engendering, or renewal, of a masculine nationalism.[9] Therefore Korean "comfort women" have been victimized not only by the Japanese government but also by their own country, whose efforts to reclaim patriarchal order as a nation and to allay threats to the unity of masculine national identity have resulted in the refusal to acknowledge the plight of these women.

In the trilogy, the tension between the will to deny and the will to proclaim emerges as both internal and external conflicts. The films portray the survivors' battle to break not only their own silence, but also the reticence of the two nations. We see the conflict within the subjects between wanting to speak and wanting to stay silent, between struggling to remember and longing to forget, and between the need to publicly claim victimhood in order to receive official reparation and the personal desire to cast off the victim mentality in order to heal their trauma. In their testimonies, the division between internal and external conflicts is further complicated by the fact that the national will to forget and to suppress the past is internalized by the women survivors themselves. Several women confess that they feel shame and embarrassment during the weekly demonstrations because they are worried that passersby might recognize, judge, or criticize them. Others describe the sense of despair they experience when fellow Koreans accuse them of needlessly digging up the past for personal gain.

It is revealed in the films that, while the survivors gradually overcome their anxiety and unwillingness to testify openly, their continued efforts to motivate both Korean and Japanese governments to action are less successful. This prompts us to recognize how these women's voices have been marginalized in the discourse of national identity. The erasure of female agency is embodied in the figure of the survivors, who have been forced to remain silent for decades—either for internal or external reasons. Throughout the trajectory of the trilogy, the women survivors endeavor to reclaim their voices—literally and figuratively. In the beginning, they do not address the camera directly, but with wary caution. The women look away and murmur in low voices, as though they are not used to receiving attention and encouragement to tell their stories. As the films progress, the women gradually grow more confident and, presumably, more comfortable before the camera. In stark contrast to their reluctant acquiescence to the making of the first installment (the filmmaker says that it took almost a year to persuade them), the women themselves actively suggested to the filmmaker that they make the second and third installments, in which they perform assertive roles as narrating subjects and as collaborators in the filmmaking process. In the Director's Statement from the pamphlet included in the DVD set, Byun writes that the women were quite vocal in expressing their own ideas and desires while filming the second installment, *Habitual Sadness*, thereby reclaiming agency over their images as well as their voices. This fact is emphasized in the film's original poster, which depicts three survivors surrounded by such film equipment as a camera and a boom microphone. Also, in the film, Byun asks a survivor how she would like to be portrayed, to which she promptly answers, "hardworking." Her wish is duly fulfilled in the numerous scenes depicting the women working on their farms and taking care of livestock.

The women's efforts to reclaim agency through their active participation in the making of the films are also manifested in the collaboration between filmmaker and subject that develops throughout the trajectory of the trilogy. In the first installment, the relationship, while friendly, is primarily that of interviewer and interviewee, and Byun's presence is signaled mostly through her voice as she questions the women about their past. In the second, the filmmaker expresses a closer affinity with her subjects, as she visually aligns herself with them through her frequent physical appearances in the frame: for instance, in the scenes where the filmmaker eats and converses with the women in an intimate setting. Finally, in the third,

Figure 5.2
Two survivors work on their farm (*Habitual Sadness*)

the demarcation between filmmaker and subject is blurred even further, as one of the survivors, Lee Young-soo, takes on the role of interviewer and replaces the filmmaker as the medium through which we hear the testimonies of the former "comfort women." Lee's conversations with the other women are better described as joint testimonies, as both interviewer and interviewee discuss their shared experiences in front of the camera. Lee draws upon her own past to pose such questions as: "I was dragged off to Taiwan ... Where were you taken to?" Thereby the hierarchical interview format between filmmaker and subject is substituted by a relationship between equals, which reveals Byun's philosophy on filmmaking, as well as her efforts to free the women from the tenacious burden of victimhood that has been doubly imposed upon them by others and by themselves. By thus participating in the filmmaking process, the women demonstrate their ability to exercise control over their images and to reclaim their voices. This assertion of authorial power is not only therapeutic for the women survivors, but it also serves to change our perception of the women from helpless victims of historical violence to participating agents in the telling of history.[10]

As the films progress, the relationship between filmmaker and subject develops into an intimate partnership. In the Director's Statement, Byun describes how she constantly visited the six former "comfort women" living together in the "Nanum" (Sharing) shelter in Seoul[11]—at first, to obtain their approval to make the film and, later, to make them feel comfortable during the filmmaking process and to capture their everyday lives. Byun subsequently likened the filmmaking process to a "love affair" between the survivors and herself in order to emphasize the collaborative nature of her filmmaking style. The filmmaker's affinity with the subjects is palpable in the films when the camera affectionately draws close, as if not to miss a single precious word, creating a blanket of intimacy that envelops not only the filmmaker and the subject but also the spectator. This closeness between filmmaker and subject is also made evident in the way Byun addresses the women as *halmoni*, an affectionate appellation in Korean for an elderly woman, and in the friendly tone in which the filmmaker addresses them (which unfortunately cannot be sufficiently translated in the subtitles), as well as the informal, sometimes playful, manner of their interactions, as in the scene where one *halmoni* demonstrates an effective maneuver to grab an attacker by the throat. In fact, the elderly survivors are often addressed in popular discourse as *halmoni*, a term that signifies both deference and closeness. The familial connotations associated with this word evoke the sense that the survivors are not distant strangers, but closely related to all Koreans; the personal and the national are conflated in this familiar term.

This pervading sense of intimacy elucidates the significant role of testimony in the three films. As an introduction to the issue of military sexual slavery and to the victims, the first installment includes several scenes that show the former "comfort women" attending public demonstrations and official meetings. For the most part, however, the testimonies are presented in intimate settings as private conversations between the filmmaker and the women. As such, they are imbued with a sense of intimacy generally lacking in the testimonies given on public platforms as a declaration or as evidential proof of the existence and experiences of "comfort women." In this way, the trilogy endeavors to overcome the inevitable distance that is created by the layers of mediation between filmmaker, subject, and spectator. Here the spectators are invited to participate in the experience of giving and receiving testimony, as the women in the films often acknowledge the presence of a listening audience that includes both filmmaker and spectator, and sometimes directly refer to the audience, as when the dying *halmoni* Kang Duk-kyung expresses her wish that many people would come to see the film. Along with the hierarchy between interviewer and interviewee, the demarcation between insider and outsider also gradually dissipates throughout the trilogy.

In light of this significance on a collective scale, what is striking about the films is a sense of *lack*—a lack of archival material, of interviews with Japanese officials or other authority figures, and of historical data, except those provided by the survivors themselves. This elision could invite criticism that the trilogy perpetuates the obscurity and ambiguity of a political issue that needs stronger clarification. As the first installment, *The Murmuring*, was begun in 1993 and released in 1995, not long after the issue of "comfort women" was first publicized, this lack of material was more or less expected.

The exclusion of documentary footage and historical documents from the film no doubt reflected the absence of official evidence in actuality, as many records were lost or deliberately destroyed after the war. Therefore this lack in the film is symptomatic of Japan's efforts to deny past incidents by obliterating material traces of Japanese wartime crimes. Furthermore, this very lack, in conjunction with the survivors' continuous efforts to make their story heard publicly, functions to accentuate the gap between the public and the private by underscoring the irony that what should have been made official has been relegated to the personal level, thereby amplifying the poignancy and the urgency of these testimonies. Because of the paucity of official records and the past suppression of the women's stories, the survivors' testimonies are necessitated by a very practical demand for substantial evidence. Also, due to the urgency of the issue, *The Murmuring* could not afford to dwell upon philosophical debates on the inadequacy of testimony and the impossibility of representation. But this need not imply that the film is based upon a simplistic belief in the power of media testimony.

I read the filmmaker's exclusion of historical facts not simply as a decision made by necessity or negligence, but as a political act. Instead of the past incident itself, the film focuses on its aftermath and the repercussions in the present lives of the survivors. Byun refuses to use historical facts and figures to objectify and depersonalize her subjects. In the films, the women's testimonies are prioritized over official documents, which implies that what is at stake in the writing of history is not simply reclaiming facts and figures, but rather identifying and recognizing the repercussions, the traces, and the scars extant in the present in order to reach a better-informed interpretation of the past. More importantly, the film avoids deploying such archival photographs as those you would find in a history textbook that confine the women in the distant past, as if they are perpetually frozen in time as "comfort women," to underscore their tragic, yet unknowable and unfathomable, quality.

Photographs often engage in a strange and ambivalent relationship with memory. They are indispensable as a visual record of the past. They function as evidence that "one was there" and as a material entity that informs one's sense of history. As a signifier of the real, a photograph can overpower our belief in our own memories by positing an undeniable, indisputable visual truth, and can even create "phantom," or virtual, memories. Noting that Holocaust photographs paradoxically suggest both the necessity and the impossibility of mourning, Marianne Hirsch writes that photography's relation to loss and death is "to bring the past back in the form of a ghostly revenant, emphasizing, at the same time, *its immutable and irreversible pastness and irretrievability*."[12] She asserts that, as a "medium connecting first- and second-generation remembrance, memory and postmemory," photographs simultaneously "affirm the past's existence" and "signal its unbridgeable distance" from the postwar generation who lack first-hand memories of the war (23). It is this inherent quality of the photograph to connote the finality of death and to imply an irretrievable past that becomes problematic in the context of documentary films that attempt to politicize past trauma. I argue that the lack of archival material in the three films—*The Murmuring*, *Habitual Sadness*, and *My Own Breathing*—signals an acknowledgment of the temporal and affective distance that a photograph evokes between the subjects trapped in the two-dimensional realm of the past and the second-generation viewers who gaze upon them in the present. As if to compensate for the sense of lack that comes from the absence of archival images, the filmmaker fills the frame with vivid images of the survivors in their everyday surroundings as contemporaneous subjects who laugh, cry, sing, dance, drink, and converse with the filmmaker and one another. Thus the sense of absence is mitigated through the creation of an intimate space shared by filmmaker, subject, and spectator. This accentuates the present-ness, not the past-ness, of their plight.

The pervasive sense of absence is reminiscent of the debate surrounding the documentary film *Shoah* (dir. Claude Lanzmann, 1985), which centered on the filmmaker's decision to exclude archival images and focus on present-day images. Many critics have commented upon the prominent sense of absence that haunts the film. As Lanzmann himself notes, the film is based on the "nothingness" that remained after the disappearance of traces of the past and the "impossibility" of recounting the history of the Holocaust.[13] In a letter sent to the French newspaper *Le Monde*, Lanzmann criticized Steven Spielberg's decision to reenact particular scenes imagined to have taken place in the gas chambers of Auschwitz in his film *Schindler's List* (1993), which has been accused of trivializing and sensationalizing the Holocaust.[14] Lanzmann went on to make the controversial claim that even if he had found archival footage of the killings, he would have destroyed it, because he believed showing this footage would transgress the ethical boundaries of representability.

Shoshana Felman sees *Shoah* as a valuable text that provides "a disorienting vision of the present" and "insight into the complexity of the relation between history and witnessing" due to its refusal to use archival footage.[15] Meanwhile, Dominick LaCapra problematizes this omission, noting that Lanzmann ironically ends up returning to what he denies, that is, "a tendency to sacralize the Holocaust and to surround it with taboos," namely, the "prohibition on images" and "a prohibition on the question *why*."[16] This raises the issue of the "unrepresentable" quality of a traumatic experience, which prompts some critics to admonish that this refusal of representation, based upon the belief that the past can never be recovered or that certain historical traumas are too horrifying to be reenacted, could ultimately lead to the silencing of trauma survivors. LaCapra asserts that it is the ghostly presence of the absent archival footage that renders effective the "traces of traces in a present that is marked by its relation to the past and future," and asks whether this meaning would be lost on viewers from a later generation who are unfamiliar with the images excluded by Lanzmann (104).

Through their films, Lanzmann and Byun demonstrate how the absence of archival images can in fact conjure the presence of the past, especially in collaboration with the evocative power of oral testimony. Lanzmann refused to use archival materials in *Shoah*, as he saw them as "images without imagination," and preferred to create "evocative and powerful" images that spring from the viewer's imagination.[17] In contrast to Spielberg, Lanzmann and Byun made similar decisions not to use archival footage or reenactments to evoke or re-envision the past. Their films, however, diverge in the way the subjects' oral testimonies interact with their surroundings. In *Shoah*, the survivors return to the sites of their traumatic past, and their testimonies are relayed over images of the contemporary landscape. This juxtaposition highlights the temporal distance and visual discrepancy between what they are describing and what we see onscreen, which generates a sense of ironic distance for the spectator. This disjunction reiterates the difficulty of representing historical trauma and the impossibility of witnessing, as well as the precarious nature of visual evidence. Meanwhile, instead of transporting the subjects to historical sites, the *Murmuring* trilogy situates the subjects in their everyday surroundings as they relate their testimonies, thereby focusing on the "traces of traces" of the past that are perceptible in their present lives. Gertrud Koch notes that, in *Shoah*, "the presence of an absence in the imagination of the past is bound up with the concreteness of images of present-day locations."[18] While this statement is also applicable to the *Murmuring* trilogy, I argue that the pervading sense of absence is lessened in the latter, as it lacks the ironic disjunction between past and present that is accentuated in *Shoah* when Lanzmann demonstrates how the past cannot be sufficiently retrieved or imagined by taking the survivors (and the spectators) back to the sites where extant traces of past trauma no longer remain. In the *Murmuring* trilogy, Byun does not highlight the invisibility of traces of the past, but rather focuses on disclosing the materiality of past traces in the women's present surroundings. Although their past experiences are constantly evoked aurally through their testimonies, the camera's visual focus is firmly fixed on their present situation, thereby revealing how the traumatic events of the past have left indelible marks, and how repercussions still persist in the present and could possibly be perpetuated into the future.

These "traces of traces" of the traumatic past are not only made evident in the present situation of the survivors, but are also physically embodied by the women themselves. Most of the women in the film suffer from various ailments, some of which are direct consequences of wartime physical and sexual assaults. For instance, Park Doori suffers from hearing loss

Figure 5.3

Kang Duk-kyung relates how she was forced into sexual servitude by the Japanese military (*Habitual Sadness*)

caused by the severe beatings she received at the "comfort station," and Kim Yun-shim has permanent scars on her body because she contracted various sexually transmitted diseases as a "comfort woman." Also, Kang Duk-kyung's battle with cancer is documented throughout the second installment, which follows her physical deterioration until her death, and several survivors interviewed in the films are bed-ridden due to a combination of illness and old age. The last sequence of the first installment most notably depicts how the harsh traces of war and ensuing hardship have been inscribed on the bare body of a survivor. As we see her aged frail body palpitate with breath, we realize the fragility of the women's situation through this manifest visualization of their advanced age and vulnerability. The visual impact of this scene becomes even more powerful when we remember the women's oral testimonies on the physical and sexual violence inflicted on their bodies by the Japanese soldiers earlier in the film, as in the scene where a survivor describes how a Japanese doctor cut her vagina to enlarge it because her body was not yet sexually mature.

As biological reproducers of national subjects, the female body has often been metaphorized as the nation in discourses on nationalism and colonialism. Although the bare body in the aforementioned sequence is revealed, bearing testimony to decades of hardship, the woman's face is shrouded in darkness. This act of respect to shield the woman's individual identity reminds us that this is not a personal, but a collective, matter, and her body represents the hardships endured by all former "comfort women." Although anonymous depictions of trauma victims are often prone to the risk of depersonalization and abstraction of personal experience and individual pain, this critique becomes irrelevant in this case because the scene immediately follows the very personal and intimate testimonies of the women, and it visually and thematically maintains the sense of closeness established throughout the film between filmmaker, subject, and spectator. The anonymity also underscores the allegorical power of the visual image, which takes on added meaning when one reads the woman's body as a metaphor for the geopolitical body of a nation that remains scarred by traces of war. Without showing historical evidence of violence-saturated warfare, the film conveys the brutality and inhumanity of war and the indelible traces that it leaves behind—both physically and mentally. Although we do not see actual acts of brutality reenacted onscreen, the presence of past violence permeates the films through signs of war-related trauma and internalized scars, such as the women's oral testimonies, averted gazes, faltering voices, and silent expressions of despair. This sequence illuminates the fact that history has left literal marks on their bodies—which are clearly visible as opposed to the *invisible*, yet no less indelible, marks on their psyches.

What is at stake, however, is not only reclaiming the (past) bodies of the former "comfort women," but also protecting the (present) bodies of contemporary Korean women. This is emphasized from the beginning of the first film, when Byun explains how she was initially drawn to this project. While making another film, *A Woman Being in Asia* (dir. Byun Young-joo, 1993), a documentary on sex tourism in Korea for Japanese tourists, Byun met a woman who had started prostituting her body to earn money to pay for her invalid mother's operation fees, and learned that her mother was a former "comfort woman." The *Murmuring* trilogy thus begins with the filmmaker's observation on the continuing colonial legacy of sexual violence inflicted on the bodies of Korean women by Japanese men. The indelible remnants of the past are also exemplified in the story of another survivor, Kim Yun-shim, whose testimony is presented in the third installment, *My Own Breathing*. Here we are told that the traces of war have been inscribed not only upon Kim's own body, but also upon the body of her daughter, who was born with cerebral palsy because Kim contracted syphilis during the war. These women's stories clearly draw attention to the visible, tangible, and physical present-ness of past acts of wartime violence.

Instead of interviewing other witnesses or perpetrators, the filmmaker steadfastly focuses on the survivors and their testimonies. Therefore, no tension exists in the films among different testimonial stances or heterogeneous points of view; no irony is created by the disparity of various viewpoints. Instead, the vital forces that coexist, closely intertwined, are the dynamic interactions among filmmaker, subject, and spectator, and also among past, present, and future. It is the vigorous energy brought forth by these tensions, rather than the conflict between victim and perpetrator,

Figure 5.4

Kim Yun-shim learns that her daughter, who was born with cerebral palsy because Kim contracted syphilis during the war, knows about her past as a "comfort woman" (*My Own Breathing*)

that propels the narrative of the *Murmuring* trilogy. Within the filmic realm, the women triumph over their perpetrators—it is the latter that are silenced, and it is their denials that are devalued.

Writing on the temporal dynamics of the documentary film *Who Killed Vincent Chin?* (dir. Renee Tajima-Peña and Christine Choy, US, 1987), which examines the circumstances of Vincent Chin's murder in 1982 by Ronald Ebens and his stepson, Michael Nitz, film scholar Bill Nichols explains how historical consciousness is created and sustained in the spectator through the "ceaseless dialectic of past, present, and future" that occurs within the viewing context.[19] He asserts that this film, which delves into the racial implications and social background of the murder of a Chinese-American man who was supposedly mistaken as Japanese, is the most important political documentary of the 1980s, because it "establishes a present moment of viewing in relation to what has already taken place in the film, such that we regard our own present as past, or more conventionally, as prologue to a future outside the film which, through the very process of viewing, we *may* bring into being" (160, emphasis added). The sense of urgency is heightened through the word "may," which indicates possibility but provides no guarantee of actualization.

A dynamic dialectic of past, present, and future similarly operates in the *Murmuring* trilogy. In the three films, the past is superimposed onto the present. Instead of trying to go back in time to explore the past through archival photos and official documents, the past is mediated through the present, as the women's present-day lives are still deeply infused with, and directly influenced by, their past trauma. Many of the former "comfort women" who came forth to testify in the films have no family, and live together in a shelter. Others live in exile, either unable or unwilling to return to Korea due to various restrictions, such as their ongoing sense of shame and lack of resources. Paradoxically, this focus on the present ultimately emphasizes the corporeal and material presence of the past, and consequently affirms the need to reevaluate the past, which affects not only the present but also the future. The superimposition of the three temporalities in the film is a defiant response to those who say that the past should be buried and forgotten in order to ameliorate relations between the two countries and to heal the wounds of the survivors.

The notion of temporality is further complicated by the inclusion of the *subjunctive*—that is, what the women's lives could have been if circumstances had been different (163). At the end of the second film, the women answer the question of what they would do with their lives if given another chance. The various answers they offer reveal both the personal and social scope of the matter. Some women wistfully reply that they would like to get married, have a family, and raise many children and grandchildren. In reality, many former "comfort women" refused to get married after the war because they could not overcome their aversion to men, while others did marry but were rejected by their families when their past lives were revealed, and still others were unable to bear children because of the physical abuse or sexually transmitted diseases that they suffered. One woman's response reflects the double burden she has borne as a colonized female subject, when she expresses the wish to be reborn as a man and become a soldier to protect the nation from invasion so that the tragedies of the colonial past would not be repeated. The subjunctive mood, invoked to show what the women wish would have been, or what they think could have been under different circumstances, does not simply reveal wishful thinking but underscores what actually did happen among many possible alternatives, which in turn emphasizes the historical conditions that brought forth this traumatic event in history. This question of "what if" is reinforced when one of the activists—an elderly woman professor who accompanies and supports the survivors during meetings and the weekly protests in front of the Japanese Embassy—presents herself as an embodiment of alternative possibilities, since she is roughly the same age as most of the women; she notes that she could easily have been taken away and thus deprived of the privileges she was able to enjoy because that did not happen.

But the important question is this: what lies ahead for the spectator after viewing the films? The trilogy utilizes the tension created by the dialectic between the two tenses—past and present—to motivate the spectator to action in the near future. In the first installment, *The Murmuring*, the voices of the rallying women are barely acknowledged by the passersby or by the Japanese Embassy officials. While the fact that their protests have been going on for fifteen years shows the tenacity and passion of the survivors, it also highlights the limited scope of their political influence. So what role is the spectator asked to fulfill? As the trilogy does not provide a litany of facts and figures, the audience members are prompted to take an active stance if they want to find out more after viewing the films. The trilogy does not offer ready answers to such questions as why the issue of "comfort women" has been ignored for so long in Japan *and* Korea—while watching the films one can only infer what happened through the limited amount of information provided by the survivors' testimonies. Therefore, it is through the spectator that the cycle of political action is completed; the unanswered questions raised by the trilogy interpellate the viewers, encouraging them to insert themselves into the space in which the personal becomes the political.[20]

Many, perhaps most, documentary films induce their viewers to take action—some in more overt ways than others. What is striking here is how the ostensible lack of archival material in the three films and their elliptical style are in fact particularly conducive to provoking an active engagement of the spectator by evoking what is absent. The productivity of absence is well expressed by documentary filmmaker Trinh T. Minh-ha when she writes: "On the one hand, we face the danger of inscribing femininity as absence, as lapse and blank in rejecting the importance of the act of enunciation. On the other hand, we understand the necessity to place women on the side of negativity (Kristeva) and to work in 'undertones' (Irigaray) in our attempts at undermining patriarchal systems of values."[21] In the *Murmuring* trilogy, the filmmaker invokes absence to encourage the spectator to actively participate in filling in the gaps in the historical and political discourse surrounding the "comfort women" issue by pondering on what happened, why it happened, what could or should have happened instead, and what we can do to influence what may happen in the future.

In the trilogy, this absence does not necessarily mean silence. Here silence is equated with death; both the second and the third installments conclude with scenes from a funeral. The second film, *Habitual Sadness*, documents Kang Duk-kyung's battle with terminal lung cancer. Kang, who also appears in the first film, was forced into sexual servitude for the Japanese military at the age of fifteen while working at a factory for military supplies. She kept her past as a "comfort woman" secret until 1992, when she joined the weekly protest against the Japanese government. Watching the film, we learn that the ailing Kang asked the filmmaker to document the final moments of her life because she was anxious that, after her death, no one would remember her personal experience or the collective plight of the "comfort women." Kang passed away in February 1997, six months before the film's release. At the end of the film, the screen turns to black as the filmmaker narrates the circumstances of Kang's death and mourns her passing. The black screen implies that no images could convey the sense of loss, and visualizes the state of nullification after death. The equation of death and silence is more evident in the third film, *My Own Breathing*. Here the sense of loss caused by the death of another survivor, Kang Myo-ran, is conveyed through the conspicuous absence of sound. Shots of the lifeless body lying in a coffin and the funeral rites are accompanied only by the subtle sound of rushing wind. Here the sense of bereavement is amplified through the lack of the diegetic sounds of mourning. Furthermore, the women's deaths underscore the urgency of settling this issue. Kang Duk-kyung's fervent wish to record the final moments of her life is particularly compelling, as it shows that her former unwillingness to remember has transformed during the filmmaking process into a strong compulsion to tell her story. Her final days are consumed by the desire to record everything, the fear that others might forget their testimonies, and the anxiety that, despite all their efforts, the "comfort women" would once more be relegated to the margins of history.

The *Murmuring* trilogy manifests the joint authorship of the filmmaker and the survivors in their collaborative efforts to fill in the fissures of official history through personal testimonies, and to reclaim the hitherto unheard voices, the low "murmurings," of former "comfort women." The telling and recording of their testimonies continue to be urgent and relevant today, especially in regard to the persistent denials of the Japanese government of its role in enforcing military sexual slavery, and also the large numbers of contemporary victims of sexual violence—the countless

Figure 5.5

During a memorial service, a survivor lights a candle for former "comfort women" who have passed away (*My Own Breathing*)

women in Korea who are sexually assaulted but cannot publicly condemn their attackers because of shame, guilt, or lack of sympathy and support. At the end of the second film, Byun provides statistical numbers of sexually assaulted Korean women alongside the estimated total of "comfort women" during World War II. The filmmaker thereby reinforces the urgent relevancy of the "comfort women" issue to contemporary society by highlighting the close relation between past and present victims of sexual violence. The scope of this issue expands on a global scale when we consider the cases of women who were sexually assaulted during recent wars in various parts of the world, for instance in Eastern Europe and Africa, as contemporary examples of the violation of social justice and human rights, and of the systemic violence that is perpetuated in the intersection of militarism, colonialism, and gender politics. Such connections emphasize once again why we cannot afford to repress past trauma through collective denial, as the importance of reassessing and rewriting history stretches beyond the reaches of the past into the realm of the present and, by close extension, the future.

notes

1. The trilogy has been well received by the public and critics in Korea and overseas, including in Japan. *The Murmuring* was the first documentary to be commercially released in Korean theaters, and was selected in 1999 by the New York Women in Film and Television as one of the twenty-three best International Women's Films (1979–98). *Habitual Sadness* was screened at various international film festivals, including Berlin International Film Festival, Montreal International Film Festival, and Hong Kong International Film Festival, and *My Own Breathing* won the Woonpa Award at Pusan International Film Festival. Docu-factory VISTA ("Boim" in Korean), the documentary film production company founded by Byun Young-joo in 1993, won the National Art Award of the Year from the Korean People Artist Federation in 1999 for the *Murmuring* trilogy. The films were released by Docu-factory VISTA as a three-disk DVD set in 2007, which includes a thick booklet that provides interviews with the filmmaker and, interestingly, a teacher's guide, among other things.
2. The seven demands to the Japanese government by the victims are: 1) Japan must admit that it forced women to serve as sexual slaves; 2) war crimes committed against "comfort women" must be investigated; 3) the Japanese Diet should issue an official apology; 4) restitution should be made to the survivors and their families; 5) Japanese textbooks should accurately reflect the history of Japanese military sexual slavery during World War II; 6) a memorial and museum should be built to commemorate the victims; and 7) all surviving perpetrators must be punished (Mission Statement for the World Conference on Japanese Military Sexual Slavery, convened on the UCLA campus in Los Angeles, California, 4–6 October 2007). This Mission Statement appeared in an official booklet distributed at the conference and is also available online at http://www.jmss.info/ (accessed 25 October 2008).
3. As further evidence of the current relevancy of the "comfort women" issue, an international conference was held from 4 to 6 October 2007 at

University of California, Los Angeles. Comprised of three parts—the NGO, academic, and law symposia—the conference drew NGO representatives, activists, scholars, filmmakers, lawyers, and political figures invested in the issue, including Patricia Sellers, special legal adviser for the UN High Commission for Human Rights and the former legal adviser for gender-related crimes in the Office of the Prosecutor for the International Criminal Tribunals for Rwanda and the former Yugoslavia.

4. I accessed this on the BBC News website (on 3 March 2007): http://news.bbc.co.uk/2/hi/asia-pacific/6411471.stm. It appears that Abe was at a press conference responding to a US Congressional resolution calling for Japan to resolve the "comfort woman" issue.
5. Three former "comfort women" testified in the US Congress during the hearing, saying that Japanese soldiers had kidnapped them and forced them to have sexual intercourse with dozens of soldiers a day. Also, historical documents from the US Office of War Information were released the same year. This report, based on information obtained from the interrogation of twenty Korean "comfort women" in 1944, reveals how the Japanese recruited the women and describes their living and working conditions at the time. Further proof resurfaced in May 2007, when documents were found in Dutch government archives, including the testimony of a 27-year-old Dutch woman from May 1946, which provided evidence that women were coerced into sexual servitude in Indonesia during World War II. I gathered this information from several Internet sources, including http://www.exordio.com/1939-1945/codex/Documentos/report-49-USA-orig.html (accessed 15 March 2007); and the BBC News website http://news.bbc.co.uk/2/hi/asia-pacific/6374961.stm (accessed 3 March 2007); and http://news.bbc.co.uk/2/hi/asia-pacific/6646297.stm (accessed 15 May 2007).
6. This is a quote from the resolution itself. Available on the website http://www.govtrack.us/congress/billtext.xpd?bill=hr110-121 (accessed 17 July 2008).
7. This advertisement can be recovered at forthenextgeneration.com/comfort/ (accessed 17 July 2008). The owner of the website is Kyoung-duk Seo, a doctoral candidate at Korea University who describes himself as a "Korean PR expert."
8. Judith Herman, *Trauma and Recovery* (New York: Basic, 1992), 1, emphasis added.
9. Chungmoo Choi, "Nationalism and Construction of Gender in Korea," in *Dangerous Women: Gender and Korean Nationalism*, eds. Elaine H. Kim and Chungmoo Choi (New York and London: Routledge, 1998), 13.
10. The survivors do not explicitly discuss the therapeutic effect of authorial power in the films, but it is implied through the women's vocal and willing participation, and through parallels drawn between the filmmaking process and other creative acts of expression, such as writing and drawing. A sequence in the first installment shows an art therapy session, during which the women explain what their paintings signify and how drawing helps them forget their pain; some paintings are expressions of the women's suffering and anger, while others are depictions of wish fulfillments. The third installment shows one survivor, Kim Yun-shim, receiving the Jeon Tae Il Award for her book of essays on her experiences as a "comfort woman," and provides excerpts from her book that describe how she was harassed by the soldiers.
11. In the second installment, we learn that the "Nanum" shelter has been relocated to the suburbs of Seoul.

12. Marianne Hirsch, *Family Frames: Photography, Narrative and Postmemory* (Cambridge, MA: Harvard University Press, 1997), 20, emphasis added.
13. Claude Lanzmann, interview by Marc Chevrie and Hervé Le Roux, "Site and Speech: An Interview with Claude Lanzmann about *Shoah*," in *Claude Lanzmann's* Shoah: *Key Essays*, ed. Stuart Liebman (Oxford and New York: Oxford University Press, 2007), 39.
14. Claude Lanzmann, letter to the editor, *Le Monde*, 3 March 1994, quoted in Miriam Bratu Hansen, "*Schindler's List* Is Not *Shoah*: Second Commandment, Popular Modernism, and Public Memory," in *Spielberg's Holocaust: Critical Perspectives on* Schindler's List, ed. Yosefa Loshitzky (Bloomington: Indiana University Press, 1997), 83.
15. Shoshana Felman, "The Return of the Voice: Claude Lanzmann's *Shoah*," in *Testimony: Crises of Witnessing in Literature, Psychoanalysis, and History*, eds. Shoshana Felman and Dori Laub (New York: Routledge, 1992), 205.
16. Dominick LaCapra, *History and Memory after Auschwitz* (Ithaca, NY: Cornell University Press, 1998), 100, original emphasis.
17. Lanzmann, interview by Chevrie and Le Roux in *Claude Lanzmann's* Shoah, 41.
18. Gertrud Koch, "The Aesthetic Transformation of the Image of the Unimaginable: Notes on Claude Lanzmann's *Shoah*," *October* 48 (Spring 1989): 22.
19. Bill Nichols, "Historical Consciousness and the Viewer: *Who Killed Vincent Chin?*" in *Screening Asian Americans*, ed. Peter X Feng (New Brunswick, NJ: Rutgers University Press, 2002), 160.
20. This call to action is repeated in the Teacher's Guide section in the booklet included in the DVD set. The section explains the importance of considering films as pedagogical texts, and provides possible questions to discuss before and after viewing the films, such as: "in your opinion, what is the reason the film is titled *The Murmuring*?" or "how is the relationship between the filmmaker and the subject different from other documentaries usually seen on television?" Hwabum Kim and Heimi Park, Teacher's Guide included with *Murmuring* trilogy, DVD (Seoul, Korea: Association of Korea Independent Film & Video, 2007).
21. Trinh T. Minh-ha, *When the Moon Waxes Red: Representation, Gender, and Cultural Politics* (New York and London: Routledge, 1991), 151.

six

trauma, memory, documentary

re-enactment in two films by rithy panh (cambodia) and garin nugroho (indonesia)

deirdre boyle

official silence … prevents public witnessing. It forges a secret history, an act of political resistance through keeping alive the memory of things denied. The totalitarian state rules by collective forgetting, by denying the collective experience of suffering, and thus creates a culture of terror.

Arthur and Joan Kleinman[1]

This chapter examines two films whose subjects are genocide and the official silence that followed in their wake—one concerns events during Pol Pot's regime in the mid-1970s when nearly two million people, roughly a quarter of the Cambodian population, were systematically destroyed by means of starvation, overwork, torture, and execution; the other occurred in Indonesia in the mid-1960s after the fall of the Sukarno regime when a new government under General Suharto ordered the military to execute as many as two million Indonesians suspected of being communists. I am deeply moved by both these works: *S-21: The Khmer Rouge Killing Machine* (*S-21: la machine de mort Khmère rouge*, dir. Rithy Panh, France/Cambodia, 2003, 101 min.) and *The Poet: Unconcealed Poetry* (*Puisi tak terkuburka*, dir. Garin Nugroho, Indonesia, 2001, 90 min.). They each recuperate memory using very different strategies of re-enactment and performance to utter speechless horror and shatter lingering silence.

In the minefield that is cultural politics today, I hesitate briefly at labeling these as films about genocide given the welter of legal terms that now apply.[2] I also hesitate to refer to both works as documentaries because of the long-standing debates among filmmakers, critics, and historians over the border dividing fiction and nonfiction in documentary cinema. Historical re-enactment was common in early documentary film, but with the development of cinema verité in the 1960s such performance became suspect. In today's cinema, however, strategies of staging and enactment have returned to documentary, especially works contesting official or hegemonic versions of history. The hybrid film—neither fiction nor fact but something in between—seems to be the most vital and innovative cinema being made around the world, most often by non-Western filmmakers who creatively mine the crack between one reality and the other. The films under discussion certainly fall into this category.

Andrei Tarkovsky, in *Sculpting in Time*, wrote that time gives every person the opportunity of knowing himself as a moral being engaged in the search for the truth. Tarkovsky believed that cinema was called to create "a vast edifice of memories."[3] Garin and Panh must agree since each forges an impressive "edifice of memories" in his film. With its unsettling re-enactments by former prison guards, *S-21* allows us to observe how memory and time can collapse to render the past as present and by doing so reveal the ordinary face of evil. With its structure rooted in *didong* (a form of Indonesian song and dance), *The Poet* evokes the way memory as story-in-song serves as a bulwark against dehumanization and a monument to those who have died. "When scholars and critics study time," wrote Tarkovsky, " they speak of the *methods* of recording it ... the way the individual who does the recollecting actually records his experience. They will study the forms used in art to fix time, whereas I am interested here in the inner, moral qualities essentially inherent in time itself" (57–9). I too am interested in the moral qualities of time conveyed in these films. But first, let's discuss the different methods used to record and fix time and memory.

Rithy Panh is considered by many to be the cinematic voice of Cambodia.[4] His feature films have been funded by the French-German television station Arte and by France's Canal Plus and awarded prizes at international film festivals like Cannes. In 2003 he launched Bophana, an Audiovisual Resource Center in Phnom Penh to archive the memory of Cambodia and train technicians in the skills needed to collect, preserve, and maintain that legacy. He has also begun the training of a new generation of documentary filmmakers. Panh has made several documentary and narrative films about the Cambodian genocide during the Pol Pot years (1975–9), but the best known is *S-21: The Khmer Rouge Killing Machine*, which was released in 2003.

Panh is himself a survivor. His family was deported from Phnom Penh to a rural village, where they died one-by-one of starvation, physical and psychological exhaustion, and disease. He was placed in a forced labor camp at age eleven and escaped at fourteen, eventually finding his way to a refugee camp in Thailand and then ultimately to France, where he studied cinematography at l'Institut des Hautes Etudes Cinématographiques (IDHEC), determined to make films about what happened.

S-21 was an obvious choice for a film. It was the code name for Tuol Sleng, the high school in Phnom Penh that was used as a prison and where it is estimated 17,000 Cambodians were interrogated, tortured, and executed—men, women, and children. Only seven people survived; three were alive when Panh began the film, and two agreed to participate.[5] Vann Nath is one and he credits his survival to the fact that his paintings of Pol Pot and other high ranking cadres were favored by the prison staff.[6] He functions as the film's conscience and the filmmaker's alter ego: "Calmly holding up a mirror to each of his ex-captor's acts of inhumanity ... [h]e seems the only man in full possession of his path," as one writer noted.[7] The other survivor is Chum Mey, an engineer, who plays a smaller role in the modern interrogation of the interrogators.

The film began when Panh, who was then shooting a documentary about a woman who died at Tuol Sleng, noticed Nath sitting silently during an interview with Him Houy, deputy head of prison security. Nath was smoking cigarettes and trembling. "I saw him rise, take Houy by the shoulder to see one of his canvases. He kept asking, 'Is this true or not?' And Houy would say, 'Yes, it's true. You haven't exaggerated.' Unfortunately," Panh notes, "we the victims also need the words of the perpetrators to tell their side of the story" (24).

It took Panh three years to locate and coax a handful of perpetrators to participate in the project. Their mission was to compare eyewitness accounts: "How do you survive absolute horror? How do you become a killer?"[8] Clearly, the hardest task was to build enough trust with the staff at Tuol Sleng: Panh ultimately persuaded former guards, interrogators, a clerk-typist, a photographer, and a "doctor" to return to S-21 for an inquiry into what happened there. "The idea of putting victims and executioners together is very seductive, but it's also very tricky," Panh has observed. "You don't want to be a voyeur. You have to develop a kind of ethic of the image."[9]

There were thousands of portrait photos of internees taken before, and sometimes after, execution and innumerable documents produced by the killing machine, including absurd confessions of improbable wrongdoings signed by prisoners who assented to them out of fear of undergoing further

Figure 6.1
Vann Nath, right, interrogates his interrogators in the film *S-21*

torture and starvation. Using many of these records as prompts, Panh encouraged his witnesses to tell their stories as a means of saving their essential memories, not just for themselves but for future generations.

As historians like Philip Short point up, S-21's role was not to kill but to extract confessions that offered "proof" of treason, which would then justify the purges that the Khmer Rouge leadership had already decided to carry out: "Death was the finality, but it was almost incidental."[10] The extensive confessions found at S-21, which Panh and Nath ask the interrogators to explain, were fabrications of acts of sabotage or membership in a phantom Kampuchean Workers Party as well as in the CIA and KGB. Part of Panh's goal was to rescue the truth denied by layers of falsehood in the voluminous written records of interrogations, and to restore the memory of the thousands who died as well as the memories of what happened to them from those who tortured and killed them.

What Panh does throughout the film is summon traumatic memory by repeatedly exposing both perpetrators and victims to the site of trauma. By placing them in the empty rooms of S-21 and amid its artifacts, he propels them to move beyond re-enactment to "re-live" the past. There are many scenes in which we see the prison staff re-creating their routines, walking past cells, and shouting threats through peepholes or sitting at a desk typing the "confessions" concocted by them for their victims. But there is one scene in the film that leaps out as something special. In this remarkable scene, the guard Khieu Ches slips out of the present into the past: he repeats his actions and verbal harangues as though time had reversed and the past was alive again. Like an insect preserved in amber, Ches, who began working as a guard at S-21 at the age of 12 or 13, embodies the boy he once was, *as he still is* in memory, a figure of terror and power and abuse, shackling and unshackling inmates, beating and humiliating them.

The camera is positioned outside the former classroom that served as a cell of mass detention, where internees were chained to the floor in rows, head to foot, subject to the scrutiny of a teenaged jailer upon whom they depended for all their needs. Ches parades up and down the corridor outside the cell, yelling at now invisible inmates, responding to remembered requests for water or a urinal, repeatedly locking and unlocking the cell door, all the while narrating his actions between his orders to the revenant inmates. Panh's camera observes all this from outside the room, following Ches patrolling back and forth in the corridor and entering and exiting the cell; the camera arcs from one end of the room to the other, pressing up against the barred windows. Wisely it never enters within. We remain on the outside with only Ches as intermediary between past and present. This scene is neither scripted nor directed and only minimally staged. I believe it transcends the other re-enacted scenes in the film and opens up the possibilities for re-enactment in documentary.

Panh remarked in an interview that, though Ches had great difficulty *speaking* of the past, "his gestures, the memory of his body, came flooding back. Because someone trained him to do this. And the memory of the body never lies."[11] The physicality of traumatic memory seems perfectly clear here, but not all viewers may see Ches's behavior so clearly. One writer, who likened the film in its austerity and reverence for personal memories to Claude Lanzmann's *Shoah* (France/Belgium, 1985), faulted Panh for this scene. Looking for the testimony of stories, which is the hallmark of Lanzmann's classic, he did not find stories here. Addressing

Figure 6.2
Guard Khieu Ches re-enacts his memories at S-21

Ches's unsettling behavior, the writer wondered why Ches was going through this re-enactment and asks why Panh did not explain this. "While the re-enactment is a useful window into the past, it encourages an *ill-informed judgment* [italics added] against this man based on how he acts today rather than what he did then ... it's hard to tell whether the behavior on display is natural or a response to the off-screen prompting from the director."[12]

I disagree. Although Ches's behavior may be difficult to understand, it fits well within the paradigm of traumatic memory. There's nothing new about this: the origins of modern psychiatry at the end of the nineteenth century arose from the study of consciousness and the disruptive impact of traumatic experiences. Jean Martin Charcot and Pierre Janet in France and William James in the United States devoted enormous attention to how the mind processes memories, exploring why certain memories become obstacles that keep people from going on with their lives. Janet believed that lack of proper integration of intense, emotionally arousing experiences into the memory system results in *dissociation*[13]—or *splitting*—and the formation of traumatic memory. The legacy of Janet, who was one of Freud's teachers, was crowded out by psychoanalysis, with its emphasis on the *repression*[14] of unacceptable wishes. It was not until the 1970s that Janet's ideas were revived, contributing to a better understanding of post-traumatic stress disorder in the wake of the Vietnam War.[15] Janet's ideas are particularly helpful when considering how dissociation of traumatic memories may render them virtually inaccessible through language until they can be translated into the symbolic language necessary for linguistic retrieval and thus brought into consciousness. This may explain why Ches's testimony is not provided in the form of verbal testimony, as a story of what it was to be a guard, but rather requires him to physically re-enact his experience in minute detail.

An example from Janet's work may help illustrate this behavior. Psychiatrist Bessel van der Kolk, who has applied Janet's ideas to modern trauma theory, differentiates between "traumatic memory" and ordinary or narrative memory. Narrative memory—which is a social act—takes only a few minutes to recount and is an aspect of ordinary life integrated with other experiences. Traumatic memory takes too long—in fact it demands re-enactment for its recall; it is inflexible and invariable, has no social component, is not addressed to anyone, and usually is a solitary activity. Van der Kolk discusses Janet's client Irène, who could not recall her mother's death even though she witnessed it, yet several times a week afterwards, when seated at a certain angle before an empty bed, Irène would quickly adopt a bizarre posture and begin elaborate mimetic activities—bringing a glass to the lips of an imaginary person, talking to that person, and cleaning that person's teeth. She would re-enact the scene over the span of three to four hours, meticulously reproducing in real time all the details of her actions on the night of her mother's death. On the one hand, she had no conscious memory of the death, and on the other she had what seemed to be an excess of dissociative memory. Under treatment, Irène consciously recovered her memory of the event, and she was then able to tell the memory in half a minute. Once this memory was accompanied by feelings, it became complete and she was "healed."[16]

Ches's re-enactment of his daily activities as a guard is not a social act. Although a camera is present observing him, Ches has his back to the camera and is instead facing a room of ghostly inmates; he repeats an inflexible routine. The otherwise silent Ches speaks nonstop, not to the camera but to himself, narrating his daily acts and performing them in detail, hitting revenants on the head, repeatedly opening and closing the padlock each time he enters or exits the cell, an action that disturbingly punctuates this scene.

Why is this sequence so significant, so powerful? Why do the hairs on one's neck stand up while viewing the transformation of the laconic Ches into a tyrannical guard before our eyes? As we watch Ches re-enact his experience, we witness the past become present. This scene was not written and directed by Panh; it is a moment of memory relived. Irène's case illustrated how traumatic memories may return as physical sensations, horrific images or nightmares, behavioral re-enactments, or a combination of these. Ches's re-enactment demonstrates how alive Cambodia's violent past is in the psyche of its survivors, both victims and perpetrators. Denial of that past has been the national pattern for dealing with the Cambodian genocide, and Panh quietly argues throughout his film—through these re-enactments—that his nation's split-off traumatic memories are the wellspring for its social pathology, violence, and corruption.

Panh relates the story of a Cambodian survivor of the killing fields living in France who was a model mother until she cut off her son's head just as her father had been decapitated before her by the Khmer Rouge. "If you can't grieve, the violence continues," Panh notes.[17] Janet would agree: if a person does not remember, he is likely to "act out"—i.e., to repeat the trauma. Freud added that repeating is the traumatized person's way of remembering.[18] The presence of mute, unsymbolized, and unintegrated experiences is the crucial factor in determining the repetition of trauma. Exposed to trauma, a person experiences "speechless terror." The experience typically cannot be readily organized on a linguistic level, and the failure to arrange memory in words and symbols leaves it to be organized on a somatosensory or iconic level: as somatic sensations, behavioral re-enactments, nightmares, and flashbacks.[19] This, I would argue, is what we observe as Khieu Ches re-enacts his memory.

We have no way of knowing whether Ches suffers because of his past, but Him Houy, who is briefly profiled at the beginning of the film, clearly suffers, and his headaches are only part of his trouble. Casually holding his newborn child, he is wooden when speaking with his parents about the past. His flat affect and strained expression, which is mirrored in the faces of many of the perpetrators interviewed in the film, bears witness to the lingering impact of the past. Houy cannot free himself from what he has done. His parents cannot understand what has happened to him, and they want an exorcism to restore him to health, to release him from his karma. Panh's film carefully brings Houy's memory—and the memories of each of the perpetrators—into consciousness, not as an exorcism or therapy for them as individuals but for all Cambodian society.

The film acknowledges the perpetrators were often young and indoctrinated, many of them abducted from their families and deprived of human contact, trained first to raise pigs, then kill "the enemy." "I had power over the enemy—I never thought of his life," one guard recounts in a monotone. Panh does not obviate their guilt, but he raises the difficult question of whether these teenaged guards were not themselves victims. Nath cannot forgive them, but he tries to understand them; there are no simple answers to difficult questions such as the one he asks a guard: "If you are victims, then what are we?"

One of the chief forms of storytelling in this film is nonverbal, expressed in the large-scale canvases painted by Nath that now hang on the walls of S-21, which became a genocide museum in 1980. For a genocide in a culture without religious proscriptions against graven images, without a history of widely seen images of dehumanization and death,[20] there is no need for the *bilderverbot* that has become the norm for representations of genocide since the Nazi Holocaust. So much of trauma theory in cinema has been predicated on the Shoah. But not every culture is the same: not all cultures reject the visible representation of trauma, valuing the spoken or written word above all other means of witnessing. The Cambodian genocide has relatively few documented images to persuade deniers of what happened. Vann Nath, a visual artist, survived because of his ability to paint. His way of bearing witness to trauma through the life-sized images he painted after he was released helped him to come to terms with his ordeal. But even more importantly, Nath's images fill in the missing pictures of what happened in S-21 and have become essential documents of genocide. What is appropriate in documenting trauma needs to be considered in terms of the specific cultural context in which it occurred.

Panh's film asks what is the future of a country that has denied its past. By reviving memory of this traumatic period, he makes that past present to engage public conscience about the evil done in the name of the state. When Panh released the film in 2003, he told journalists that he was convinced his country could not recover its identity unless it put the past on trial, but he doubted it would happen. After nearly thirty years of denying, ignoring, or selectively forgetting this history, in 2007 Cambodia finally convened a UN-sponsored special tribunal to investigate crimes against humanity

Figure 6.3
One of Vann Nath's paintings of S-21

committed by the Khmer Rouge. In 2009 Kaing Guek Eav, aka "Duch," the notorious head of S-21, was the first major figure to go on trial. Although he testified to his responsibility for torture and killings, he also asserted that he was just part of the chain of command. The outcome of the trial as of this writing is uncertain.[21] At his pre-trial hearing in November 2007, Khieu Samphan, confidant-successor to Pol Pot and the intellectual head of the Khmer Rouge, denied responsibility for any crimes, claiming he first learned of the atrocities committed by his regime when he saw Panh's documentary in 2003. Faced with the evidence in this film, Samphan could no longer assert, as he had in his memoir, that there was no direction for carrying out mass killings.[22]

Panh's films helped catalyze the tribunal that, however flawed it may prove to be, finally may enable Cambodia to confront its silence about the past, to pay a debt owed to the dead and an obligation to its children. Panh's perspective is clear: "We shan't be able to get rid of this 30-year culture of violence, cast out the monster that is fear, and put behind us the collective guilt we feel as survivors unless we manage to understand our history."[23]

Born into a family of artists, Indonesian producer, director, and screenwriter Garin Nugroho has made more than 15 award-winning films, including long- and short-form documentaries as well as feature-length dramas. *The Poet: Unconcealed Poetry* (*Puisi tak terkuburka*) is a work of mourning for the massacre of between 500,000 and 2 million people when Suharto's forces purged Indonesia of communists in 1965.[24] Released in 1999, it was the first Indonesian film to revisit the 1965 massacres. The story of this slaughter is told by Ibrahim Kadir, who was mistakenly detained for nearly a month at the height of the massacre; during those dreadful days his job was tying the hands of those being led off for execution. Kadir plays himself in the film,[25] and he is joined by other survivors from Takengon in central Aceh—rice farmers, fishermen, housewives, mothers. *The Poet* is a re-enactment of Kadir's captivity and revolves around the inmates of two cells—men on one side of a wall, women on the other—as they wait to hear their names called, struggling to comprehend what is happening and to hold onto their humanity. Kadir's story is told through *didong*, a culturally unique song style known for its emotional expressivity and incisive political critique. It is a combination of song, story, and movement popular among the Gayo of central Aceh; it consists of sung poetic duels that take place over several nights and is characterized by humor and word-play that use metaphor as a vehicle for political commentary and transmission of cultural history and values. Kadir is a *ceh*, a master of *didong*.

When the New Order came to power in Indonesia, it was recognized that a popular art form like *didong* could be a dangerous means of dissent, and so it was appropriated in the service of the government's agenda. In making this film, Garin and Kadir reclaim *didong* as a part of Acehnese culture and history and as the perfect vehicle for documenting the collective memory of this trauma. The video begins and ends with *didong* groups shot from above, the camera recording circles that often seem to breathe with one breath. Throughout the 90-minute work, men and women sing of their longing to be reunited with their families, their love for the homeland, their fear of the unknown that awaits them, their contempt for the sinister power that holds them captive. Now lively and flirtatious, now mournful or enraged, *didong* expresses the hopes and fears of the villagers, and alternately the sounds of authority and menace. The lines of Kadir's songs haunt one ("I looked at the moon and from it there came a cry/The moon and the stars were crying just like my own child"). The powerful clapping rhythms seem to hold the group together as one and give way to a single voice expressing his or her deepest feelings. With *didong* as the organizing principle of the video, Kadir—now in monologue, now in song—remembers what happened as Garin restores dignity to the dead and the dead to history, a goal apparent in another translation of the video's subtitle, "a poetry that cannot be buried," that has not been surrendered to the grave, as film scholar Ann Rutherford astutely observes.[26]

Garin's form of re-enactment is different from Panh's, yet it has many elements in common. Even more than *S-21*, this witnessing is problematic as documentary yet true to the recollection of traumatic memory. What we experience in *The Poet* is a dramatic performance of Kadir's memory of the massacres, enacted by Kadir, other survivors, and some professional actors. It involves the body of these survivors—dancing, swaying, clapping, and singing. The resonance of sound and movement along with story help to evoke memories and emotions. This is what happened to peasants seized without warning, who waited for death without reason. It is documentary as embodied memory, an idea that seems more acceptable to Asian documentary makers than to most Western audiences.

Garin spent two-and-a-half years researching and preparing for the film, going outside Indonesia to find information not available at home. Because the scale of the trauma was so large,[27] he decided in the end to concentrate on the raw experience of a few people. He focused on the memory of Ibrahim Kadir, and he rehearsed him with his fellow survivors, many of whom had no acting experience. "It was a very emotional experience. Ibrahim ... suffered from recurring nightmares and would wake up every night. It was very difficult for him to relive these events, but he said that it lifted a weight off his shoulders. It was also very important for others involved who began to realize how this history had been covered up."[28]

The staging of Kadir's memories might be considered a form of "acting out" of traumatic memories, a therapeutic effort to enable survivors to process their trauma.[29] But psychological healing was not Garin's intention. Garin, like Panh, was concerned about the welfare of his witnesses, but he had future generations in mind when he set in motion his cinematic work. The "others" who began to realize the vast cover up of these events were the young cast and crew who had never learned about what had happened in 1965. The retelling of Kadir's experiences was not merely an entertaining means of engaging an audience in a historical event. More than photos or literary memoirs or formal interviews, *didong* about genocide performed by a *ceh* provided unparalleled cultural authority for the denied history being re-enacted and remembered.

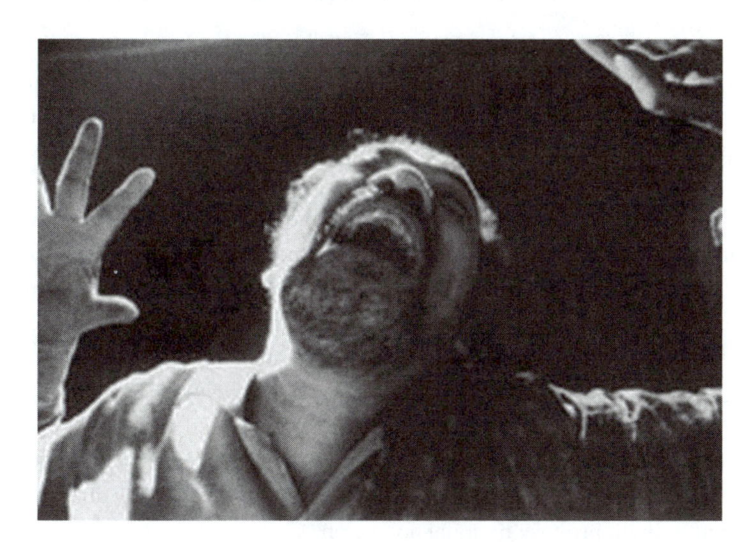

Figure 6.4
Ibrahim Kadir in *The Poet*

Garin adapts the traditional form of *didong* into a visual style that is highly cinematic; it begins and ends with two circles of men seen from overhead creating a full circle that inscribes the event. He alternates between close-ups of Kadir commenting often ironically on his memories and the linear narrative of the unfolding story. There are a series of vignettes of inmates in their cells where we see Kadir preparing prisoners for execution or singing to hearten the spirits of the remaining prisoners and their guards. With handheld camera movements that emphasize the claustrophobia of men huddled together in dwindling numbers for comfort and support, Garin's cinematic skills continually reinforce a sense of fear and anxiety as well as the circular structure of the *didong*. It is an imaginative and apt approach that breaks with conventional expectations about history, testimony, narrative, and documentary. One of the video's funders, a spokesperson for the Ford Foundation, referred to it as "quasi-history," failing to grasp the point that there is nothing "quasi" about this history. Shot in a week on a slim budget ($390,000),[30] *The Poet* does not provide the kind of visible evidence presented in *S-21*, the sort that can be catalogued, filed, and submitted in a court of law to prove the facts of genocide. But much as Vann Nath's paintings offer witness in *S-21*, the use of a cultural practice like *didong* enables Kadir's oral storytelling to present no less compelling evidence. Walter Benjamin offers one explanation for why this is so:

> It is not the object of the story to convey a happening *per se*, which is the purpose of information; rather, it embeds it in the life of the storyteller in order to pass it on as experience to those listening. It thus bears the marks of the storyteller much as the earthen vessel bears the marks of the potter's hand.[31]

As cultural critic Andreas Huyssen notes, we in the West are experiencing an anxiety of amnesia thanks to globalization, mass media, and a hypertrophy of emerging (and rapidly obsolescing) technologies which have aroused wide-scale cultural fear of oblivion as the relationships between past, present, and future are being transformed.[32] Yet our anxiety is nothing compared with the worries of Garin Nugroho and Rithy Panh, who live in countries that "lie in the shadow" of mass murder and crimes against humanity, where people still suffer from the official silence imposed about the past, dissociated from memories that hold them and their nation hostage. Just as Vann Nath and Ibrahim Kadir, artist-survivors and witnesses to genocide, used their art to testify to what they had seen and experienced, so too do filmmakers Panh and Garin use theirs to communicate not only the past but also the emotional effects of the past on individuals and through them provoke national discussion.

"I want to create a situation where people feel free to voice their opinions about this event," Garin says. What lay behind *The Poet* was his desire "to show that what happened [in 1965] was against all humanity. And if you don't try and understand what happened, then it is impossible to prepare a decent future for the next generation or the country as a whole." He decided to take on this highly dangerous project because he realized "that events in the Balkans could happen in Indonesia, which is also a multicultural society, and that there had to be a dialogue, without revenge, about our history."[33]

In conclusion, I want to recall the highly evocative final image of *S-21*. The large classroom that once housed prisoners awaiting torture and death is now vacant. The few props that had been assembled to help unlock memories from the staff of S-21 have been put away. Only the dust of decades remains in small piles in the corners of the room. The camera angle is low and close to the floor as we see a gust of wind disturb the stillness, raising an eddy of dust like the ashes of the dead. It is an image of the presence of absence. This haunting image of an abandoned room addresses the future, much as do the driving rhythms and nuanced chanting of *didong* at the conclusion of *The Poet*, much like the final words of Jean Cayrol's narration at the end of *Night and Fog* (*Nuit et Brouillard*, France, 1955). These memorable films, each in their different ways, address generations to come and urge them not to forget.

Memory discourses are critical if we are to regain strong temporal and spatial grounding in life and to be able to imagine a future. These documentaries use re-enactment to make time past visible and present. And they make palpable why memory—particularly traumatic memory—is essential to what makes us moral beings.[34]

acknowledgments

This essay was written for a panel on documentary re-enactment convened by Jonathan Kahana for the Visible Evidence XIV conference in Bochum, Germany, in December 2007. I am grateful to Jonathan for inviting me to participate in a wonderful panel and stimulating conference. It was there I met Bhaskar Sarkar, and I am delighted that he and co-editor Janet Walker were so enthusiastic about including my text in this book. I am particularly grateful to my friends at the Center for Religion and Media at New York University (NYU), who invited me to attend their conference entitled "Signs of Crisis: Religious Conflict, Human Rights and the New Documentary Film in Southern Asia" in May 2007. Here I was introduced to Garin Nugroho's *The Poet* and also heard him speak, which inspired my admiration for his work and desire to write this piece. Many thanks to Barbara Abrash and Faye Ginsberg at NYU and to the conference sponsors for including me in this eye-opening and sobering event. Thanks also to the Asian Cultural Council for a fellowship to attend the 2007 Yamagata International Documentary Film Festival in Japan, where I was able to view

Rithy Panh's recent work. A shorter version of this text was presented at "Is an Interdisciplinary Field of Memory Studies Possible?," a conference convened at The New School in New York in February 2008. This shorter version was later published under the title "Shattering Silence: Traumatic Memory and Re-enactment in Rithy Panh's *S-21: The Khmer Rouge Killing Machine*," in *Framework: The Journal of Cinema and Media* in 2009.

notes

1. Arthur and Joan Kleinman, "The Appeal of Experience; The Dismay of Images: Cultural Appropriations of Suffering in Our Times," in *Social Suffering*, eds. Arthur Kleinman, Veena Das, and Margaret Lock (Berkeley: University of California Press, 1997), 17.
2. Genocide is the term used by Rithy Panh in discussing the slaughter of Cambodians by the Khmer Rouge, and in this chapter the tragedies in Cambodia and Indonesia are both referred to as genocide. However, it is worth noting that some historians and political analysts prefer the broader term "crimes against humanity" to describe such events because, as Philip Short points out in *Pol Pot: Anatomy of a Nightmare*, the Khmer Rouge did not set out to exterminate a national, ethnic, racial, or religious group; they "conspired to enslave a people" and this is a crime against humanity (446). When General Suharto unleashed army-led massacres in Indonesia in 1965, they were directed at communists, trade unions, and other mass organizations. Most of these killings took place in rural areas, targeting peasants of Central and East Java, North Sumatra, and Bali—even the CIA ranked them among the worst mass murders of the twentieth century—but since the massacres were widespread and systematic government policy against civilians, they too can be defined as "crimes against humanity." I leave it to readers to navigate among concepts of *genocide*, *politicide* (killings of people in groups targeted because of organized political opposition), *democide* (state mass murder), and "crimes against humanity." These events entered popular consciousness in the 1980s largely through feature films like *The Year of Living Dangerously* (dir. Peter Weir, Australia, 1982), with Linda Hunt, Mel Gibson, and Sigourney Weaver in a story of an Australian journalist reporting the collapse of Sukarno's regime, torn between a career-making assignment and romance with a British embassy staffer; and *The Killing Fields* (dir. Roland Joffé, United Kingdom, 1984), which featured Sam Waterston and Haing S. Ngor playing real-life journalists Sydney Schanberg, a *New York Times* reporter covering the rise of Pol Pot, and Dith Pran, his imperiled translator. Apart from what we learned from dramatic films, most Americans knew little about genocides in Asia or the United States' role in facilitating them. A detailed discussion is not possible here. For readers interested in learning more about Indonesia and Cambodia in the 1960s and 1970s, you may wish to consult: Helen Fein, "Revolutionary and Antirevolutionary Genocides: A Comparison of State Murders in Democratic Kampuchea, 1975 to 1979, and in Indonesia, 1965 to 1966," *Comparative Studies in Society and History* 35, no. 4 (1998): 796–823; Robert Cribb, ed., *The Indonesian Killings 1965–1966: Studies from Java and Bali* (Centre of Southeast Asian Studies, Monash University, 1990); Israel W. Charney, William S. Parsons, and Samuel Totten, eds., *A Century of Genocide: Critical Essays and Eyewitness Accounts*, 2nd edition (London and New York: Routledge, 2004).

3. Andrei Tarkovsky, *Sculpting in Time: The Great Russian Filmmaker Discusses His Art* (Austin: University of Texas at Austin Press, 1986), 57–9.
4. Lekha Shankar, "Rewinding Memory," *Thai Day*, 3 February 2006. http://www.manager.co.th/IHT/ViewNews.aspx?NewsID=9490000 (accessed 19 September 2007). Panh's works include: *Site 2* (Germany/France, 1989, 92 min.), a documentary about a family of Cambodian refugees in a camp on the Thai–Cambodian border in the 1980s; *The People of the Rice Field* (*Neak Sre*, Cambodia/France, 1994, 125 min.), a lyrical narrative about a rural family struggling with life in post-Khmer Rouge Cambodia, which introduced Panh to international audiences at the Cannes Film Festival; *Bophana: A Cambodian Tragedy* (*Bophana, une tragédie cambodgienne*, France/Cambodia, 1996), a documentary about a young woman and a former Buddhist monk turned Khmer Rouge cadre; *The Burnt Theater* (*Les Artistes du Théâtre Brûlé*, Cambodia/France, 2005, 82 min.), a dramatic narrative based on the lives of actors and dancers trying to maintain their art in the burned-out shell of Cambodia's national theater. In 2006 Panh helped found Bophana, an audiovisual resource center in Phnom Penh dedicated to collecting and preserving Cambodia's audiovisual heritage and training a new generation of filmmakers. Panh's most recent works include: *Paper Can Not Wrap up Embers* (*Le papier ne peut pas envelopper la brais*, France, 2007, 90 min.), a documentary about the lives of Cambodian sex workers, and *The Sea Wall* (*Un barrage contre le pacifique*, France/Cambodia/ Belgium, 2009, 115 min.), a fiction film based on a novel by Marguerite Duras and starring Isabelle Huppert.
5. Reports vary, with some claiming that as many as twelve survived and that four are still alive: Vann Nath, Chum Mey, Bou Meng (another artist), and Chum Math, the only woman.
6. To view some of Vann Nath's canvases of S-21 on exhibit at Tuol Sleng Genocide Museum, see Human Rights Watch, hrw.org/photos/2007/cambodia0207. Nath also wrote a memoir about his experience, *A Cambodian Prison Portrait: One Year in the Khmer Rouge's S-21* (Bangkok: White Lotus Co. Ltd, 1998).
7. Leslie Camhi, "The Banal Faces of Khmer Rouge Evil: How Can Torturers Seem So Ordinary?" *New York Times*, 16 May 2004, 24.
8. First Run Features, *S-21: The Khmer Rouge Killing Machine*, press release, www.frif.com/new2003/s21.html (accessed 30 June 2007).
9. Panh quoted in Camhi, "The Banal Faces of Khmer Rouge Evil: How Can Torturers Seem So Ordinary?" 24.
10. Philip Short, *Pol Pot: Anatomy of a Nightmare* (New York: Henry Holt and Co., 2004), 359, 364.
11. Panh quoted in Camhi, "The Banal Faces of Khmer Rouge Evil," 24.
12. Robert Davis, "Review of *S21: The Khmer Rouge Killing Machine*," *Errata*, 29 March 2004, www.erratamag.com/archives/2004/03/s21_the_khmer_r.html (accessed 17 August 2007).
13. Dissociation is a defense mechanism in which certain thoughts, emotions, sensations, and/or memories are compartmentalized, often producing psychogenic amnesia. Dissociation is generally found in people with a history of trauma. As an isolated response, it is a form of protection, but when it becomes habitual, dissociation can become a marker of psychopathology.
14. Repression is an act of excluding unacceptable desires and impulses—wishes, fantasies, and feelings—from one's consciousness and holding or subduing them in the unconscious. It is a common defense mechanism that has no particular relationship to trauma.

15. E. Ann Kaplan, in tracing the origins of trauma studies, carefully differentiates two schools of thought on trauma. The Freudian psychoanalytic theorists found trauma to be no different from ordinary neurosis with its repression of the undesirable desire, memory, or fantasy, whereas the humanist trauma theorists, who came to prominence in the 1990s, viewed trauma as producing a special memory that was dissociated and not neurotically repressed. Neuroscientists' discoveries at the time seemed to support the humanists' claims, although recent research by experimental and cognitive psychologists further complicates the issue. Kaplan suggests that there is not just one set of brain processes relevant to everyone confronting a traumatic experience, but three possible processes, and none need be ruled out. She goes on to point out a major problem in trauma studies—"distinguishing different domains within which people work or relate to trauma." There is a distinction between the trauma victim and his work with a clinician and the work of scholars studying trauma. And there is also the distinction between the many scholarly discourses about trauma—psychological, psychoanalytic, political, philosophical, historical, or sociological—and images of trauma in film and popular culture studied by media scholars. E. Ann Kaplan, *Trauma Culture: The Politics of Terror and Loss in Media and Literature* (New Brunswick, NJ: Rutgers University Press, 2005), 39. As a media studies scholar and a practicing psychotherapist, I have attempted to bring both perspectives to bear, finding that some witnesses in *S-21* seem to strikingly illustrate dissociation, and that dissociated memory—when called into consciousness—opens up interesting possibilities for re-enactment in documentary.
16. Bessel A. van der Kolk and Onno van der Hart, "The Intrusive Past: The Flexibility of Memory and the Engraving of Trauma," in *Trauma: Explorations in Memory*, ed. Cathy Caruth (Baltimore, MD, and London: Johns Hopkins University Press, 1995), 158–82.
17. Rithy Panh, "Cambodia: A Wound That Will Not Heal," *UNESCO Courier*, December 1999, www.unesco.org/courier/1999_12/uk/dossier/intro07.htm (accessed 25 October 2008).
18. Pierre Janet, *L'Etat Mentales Hystériques* (1901) and Sigmund Freud *Inhibitions, Symptoms, and Anxiety* (1926), quoted in van der Kolk and van der Hart, "The Intrusive Past," 166–7.
19. Elizabeth A. Brett and Robert Ostroff, "Imagery and Posttraumatic Stress Disorder: An Overview," *American Journal of Psychiatry*, 142, 421–4, quoted in van der Kolk and van der Hart, "The Intrusive Past," 172.
20. Thousands of portraits of internees were taken at S-21. Most were detached from their dossiers when the Vietnamese entered Cambodia and discovered Tuol Sleng, and so the portraits that remain are largely anonymous today. Although photographs were taken documenting unknown internees who died of torture and abuse in detention and historical figures after their execution, what dominates the public consciousness are these passport-like photos of bewildered men, women, and children who had yet to meet their torturers and executioners. These images, which are displayed on the walls of S-21 and in the film, have been published in book form. As representations of the Cambodian genocide they seem mild when compared to the vast and horrific imagery of the dehumanized victims of the Nazi Holocaust. Nath's paintings, on the contrary, convey the surreal horror of the prison and its abuses.

21. In July 2007 the thirty international and Cambodian judges and prosecutors for the Khmer Rouge tribunal, which was established as an extraordinary chamber within the Cambodian court system, were sworn in and prosecution investigations began. Many of the Cambodian judicial officials had poor track records in terms of judicial independence and competence. The US$56 million tribunal commenced its trial phase in late 2007, with pre-trial hearings at a military base outside of Phnom Penh. Khmer Rouge leader Chit Choeun (Ta Mok), 82, died in July 2007. He had been detained without trial since 1999, along with Kaing Guek Eav (Duch), chief of the Khmer Rouge's S-21 prison, who in 2009 was the first figure to go on trial. Still in custody are the aging Khieu Samphan, Nuon Chean, Ieng Sary, and Ieng Thirith. Duch's trial has stirred much controversy, and it is unclear what the future holds for further trials. For more information, see: Seth Mydans, "Torture and Death Recounted in Cambodian Trial," *New York Times*, 14 July 2009, http://www.nytimes.com/2009/07/15/world/asia/15cambo.html?emc=eta1 (accessed 20 July 2009).
22. Seth Mydans, "Cambodia Arrests Former Khmer Rouge Head of State," *New York Times*, 20 November 2007, www.nytimes.com/2007/11/20/world/asia/20cambo.html?ref=asia&pagewanted=print (accessed 8 December 2007). Khieu Samphan, *L'histoire récente du Cambodge et mes prises de position* (Reflections on Cambodian history up to the era of democratic Kampuchea) (Paris: L'Harmattan, 2004).
23. Panh, "Cambodia: A Wound That Will Not Heal."
24. This also touched Nugroho's family. When the military came in 1965 demanding a list of communists in the area from his father, a writer and a publisher, he refused. This made him suspect, although his role as a national hero who had fought the Dutch for independence confused things considerably. For two months he was placed under house arrest, then the tension passed and the family escaped the bloodletting that followed Suharto's rise.
25. *The Poet* was shot on video, a decision dictated by the low budget for the production; it was later transferred to 35mm film for exhibition.
26. Anne Rutherford, "Poetics and Politics in Garin Nugroho's *The Poet*," *Senses of Cinema*, October 2001, www.sensesofcinema.com/contents/01/17/poet.html (accessed 15 August 2007).
27. In addition to those who were massacred at the outset of the violence, tens of thousands more were incarcerated and held for more than a decade without charge or trial. Thirteen thousand were banished to the remote island of Buru, where many died due to the harsh environment and forced labor. Hundreds of women political prisoners were also detained in a remote prison camp in Central Java. Carmel Budiardjo, "Suharto Dies without Ever Being Brought to Justice," *Tapol*, 27 January 2008, tapol.gn.apc.org/news/files/Suharto%20Statement.htm (accessed 2 August 2008).
28. Richard Phillips, "To Explore One of the Dark Episodes in Indonesian History: Interview with Garin Nugroho," *World Socialist Website*, 19 September 2001, www.wsws.org/articles/2001/sep2001/ganu-s19_prn.shtml (accessed 15 August 2007).
29. Consider, for example, how Dominick LaCapra approaches the subject of witness testimony in "Holocaust Testimonies: Attending to the Victim's Voice," in *Writing History, Writing Trauma* (Baltimore, MD, and London: Johns Hopkins Press, 2001).

30. Phillips, "To Explore One of the Dark Episodes in Indonesian History."
31. Walter Benjamin, "On Some Motifs in Baudelaire," in *Illuminations*, ed. Hannah Arendt, trans. Harry Zohn (New York: Harcourt, Brace, and World, Inc., 1968), 161, quoted in Rutherford, "Poetics and Politics in Garin Nugroho's *The Poet*."
32. Andreas Huyssen, *Twilight Memories: Marking Time in a Culture of Amnesia* (London: Routledge, 1995), 7.
33. Garin quoted in Phillips, "To Explore One of the Dark Episodes in Indonesian History."
34. Why am I called by this "edifice of memories" and particularly by these two genocides? I have arrived at one likely answer, quite apart from my admiration for these extraordinary films: the events they document were instigated, in large part, by my own government. Were it not for US bombing runs over Cambodia during the Vietnam War, one can argue the scourge of the Pol Pot regime might never have come to devastating power or lasted as long as it did. And in the 1960s, when Indonesia had the third largest communist party in the cold war world, it was not the communists who planned a coup to overthrow the Sukharno regime but factions of the army. According to CIA operatives in the 1990s, the United States, already involved in Vietnam, supported the Indonesian army's annihilation of the communist party (the PKI—Partai Komunis Indonesia) in 1965 by providing it with communications equipment and lists of names for execution. The United States was not alone in supporting these mass murders since there was also assistance from Muslim extremists and backing from British and Australian intelligence forces as well. Following these massacres, Suharto's New Order of authoritarian rule paved the way for globalization in the region. If contemplation of time yields moral understanding, then the United States is responsible, in large measure, for setting in motion circumstances that culminated in crimes against humanity in Indonesia and Cambodia, among other nations. I cannot shake off a sense of responsibility for the evil committed by my country.

seven

on documentary and testimony

the revisionists' history, the politics of truth, and the remembrance of the massacre at acteal, chiapas

josé rabasa

> *Nevertheless, the ideologues are at work. You can be confident of that. Certain ideologues conjure away the facts, in somewhat the same fashion that the Hitler genocide (to which I am in no way comparing the crimes of Sabra and Shatila) is made to vanish under the pens of the "revisionists." It wasn't a matter of massacres, you see, but of battles.*
>
> Pierre Vidal-Naquet[1]

On December 22, 2007, the community of Acteal, Chiapas, celebrated the tenth anniversary of the massacre of 45 defenseless, unarmed members of the pacifist civil organization Las Abejas ("The Bees"). For this occasion Las Abejas sponsored an *Encuentro Nacional Contra la Impunidad* (National encounter against impunity), in which two documentaries were screened: *A Massacre Foretold* (2007) by the Scottish filmmaker Nick Higgins, and *Acteal. 10 Años de impunidad, ¿y cuantos más ...?* (Acteal: 10 years of impunity, and how many more?, 2007) by the Tzotzil member of Las Abejas José Alfredo Jiménez. More than two thousand people participated in this encounter and celebration calling for a national mobilization against impunity and thus seeking to bring to justice the highest authorities responsible for rampant human rights abuses in Mexico, including, importantly, the case of the massacre of Acteal. The call for justice entails, beyond the trial of isolated individuals, an interrogation of the Mexican juridico-legal structures: the objective of the mobilization is to question the model of the nation, hence to dismantle state institutions that monopolize violence while claiming to be democratic. The victims of the massacre included 1 infant, 14 children, 21 women, and 9 men. Five of the women were pregnant, and one had the fetus pulled out of her womb with a machete. The attack was conducted by paramilitaries trained and armed by the Mexican army and the police force known as Seguridad Pública (Public Security). The monthly celebration of martyrdom re-creates a community committed to popular democracy: first by engaging in the Mesoamerican practice of consensus politics, and second by exposing the impunity of those in power.[2]

The tenth anniversary, however, has been haunted by a series of articles that have sought to undermine the community's remembrance of the massacre. My aim has less to do with disputing alternative claims than with offering a poetics of testimony that illuminates the force of the documentaries. These videos provide powerful pedagogical tools for complicating the revisionist appeal to so-called facts and for undoing the attempt to manufacture a historical framework that would generalize all discussions of the event in conformity with the revisionists' perspective.

Higgins' and Jimenez's documentaries have had ample circulation within the Tzotzil communities of Las Abejas and thus exemplify a noncommercial modality of producing popular history—that is, history that effectively counters the hegemony of state historiography. In Higgins' filming of the testimonies we can identify, in those giving testimony (in particular, the Tzotzil witnesses and victims of the massacre), an understanding of video technology—an awareness not only of the visual rhetoric of documentaries, but also of the haptic dimension of being touched by the camera as well as of touching the technology that makes the films possible. In Jimenez's documentary practice we find a young filmmaker who manifests the ability of a community member to produce a cinematic archive. To rephrase Gayatri Chakravorty Spivak, the subaltern can film.

In addition to these two retrospective documentaries screened at the *Encuentro*, we count three other documentaries that were produced in the months following the massacre: *Acteal. Estrategia de muerte* (Acteal. Death strategy, 1998) by the Mexican filmmaker Carlos Mendoza, *"Towards the Mountain": Chiapas: A Prayer for the Weavers* (1999) by anthropologist Judith Gleason, and *Alonso's Dream* (2000) by the French-Canadian filmmakers Danièle Lacourse and Yvan Patry. Mendoza is part of a team known as

"Canal 6 de julio" which organized after the fraudulent elections in 1988 with the objective of providing direct accounts of events that would otherwise be subjected to censorship by the official television channels. Mendoza started filming only hours after the massacre became known. He was there when the paramilitaries riding on military trucks were identified, pulled down, and arrested. He also recorded the return of the bodies in caskets to the community of Acteal for a collective burial.

Carlos Martínez's *Tierra sagrada en zona de conflicto* (Sacred land in the zone of conflict, 2000) is also important to mention. Although it addresses the massacre at Acteal only in passing, Martínez's archive provides footage to the other documentarists for creating a political context as well as a memory that enables them (particularly Higgins) to trace the origins of violence into a past time when the massacred could not foresee their fate and yet anticipated their own death. Thus the clips themselves take on a new life, become "actors" in the narration of the future.

I will first discuss the revisionists' history. This discussion will provide a background for understanding the political and aesthetic challenges the documentarists faced. I will then offer a theoretical discussion of the politics of truth that covers three questions: a) the epistemological limits of testimony; b) the fabricated and nonfabricated nature of truth; c) the phenomenology of the violation of the face and the assassination of memory. The respect accorded to the testimonial face offers a key element for examining the remembrance of the massacre of Acteal in the last section of this article. The question, then, would be in what ways do the documentaries deploy sound and image to resist the imposition of a historical framework that seeks to destroy the face of testimony and the iconicity of Las Abejas, who, since the massacre, have reconstituted themselves as a community of martyrs whose land was made sacred by the shedding of innocent blood? And in what ways do the documentaries participate in the creation and reproduction of the memory of "los martires de Acteal" (the martyrs of Acteal) and "la tierra sagrada de Acteal" (the sacred land of Acteal)? There is no hope of appealing to the state, even when there might be honorable persons working within its institutions, if structurally it is fraught with corrupt interests. Recourse resides, therefore, in bringing to light abuses by the state that may be cloaked by impunity but still recognized by most Mexicans who will find their experiences captured by the films on the massacre of Acteal. Beyond the certainties of science, the documentaries' appeal to the subjects' affect (made manifest through both expression and reception) instantiates such work as the ultimate arbiter of truth in testimony.

the revisionists' history

We must keep in mind that revisionist histories, as exemplified by Hector Aguilar Camín's series of articles "Regreso a Acteal," may also claim truth in testimony, in this case by validating the testimonies of police officers and those who protest imprisonment on false charges.[3] On the basis of Priístas' (after PRI, followers of the Partido Revolucionario Institucional [Institutional Revolutionary Party]) testimonies to the effect that a group of Abejas ambushed members of the police, Aguilar Camín discredits the Abejas' pacifist vocation: "hubo en Pechiquil un choque armado entre agentes de seguridad estatal y miembros no tan pacíficos del grupo Las Abejas" (there was in Pechiquil an armed confrontation between agents of the state's security forces and not so pacifist members of the group Las Abejas).[4] This statement strikes at the core of the Abejas' identity as a pacifist Roman Catholic organization.

The state and federal governments denied and continue to deny all responsibility for the paramilitaries and characterize them as spontaneous groups for self-defense that sprang up to resist the threats of the Ejercito Zapatista de Liberación Nacional (EZLN). They have proposed the scenario that the deaths were the result of a legitimate battle between equals, insurgents and self-defense groups—thereby undermining the testimony given by survivors and witnesses that the paramilitaries plotted and executed a massacre. Initially, the federal and state governments had tried to conceal the bodies, but after the event became public, those in power had only the consolation, indeed the expectation, of collective amnesia, or what Pierre Vidal-Naquet has observed as the logic of massacres, citing the examples of Sabra and Shatila: "For a few weeks, the massacre, followed by the Israeli reactions, the establishment of a commission of inquiry, and the first meetings of this commission were front-page news, before disappearing into the common grave of forgetfulness, where massacres are buried."[5] But the Mexican government's wager on forgetting backfired as the international press divulged the massacre and influential foreign states expressed outrage, embarrassing the government of Ernesto Zedillo Ponce de León.

The recent revisionist efforts have adopted to a great extent the perspective of federal and state authorities in which the official version of the events and those of the survivors are given equal weight. Thus Aguilar Camín characterizes the Acteal massacre as the collateral violence of a battle–45 people were killed but this was the consequence of getting caught in crossfire between Zapatistas and Priístas—and so undoes the claim of a perpetration of a crime against humanity. As such, Camín's is a textbook case of what Victoria Sandford has characterized as "the conflicting truths of those with power and those marginalized by it."[6] The work of Aguilar Camín and those following his "police" procedures, like the governmental denials, also matches Vidal-Naquet's exposé of the revisionist commonplace cited in the epigraph. Where Vidal-Naquet writes, "It wasn't a matter of massacres, you see, but of battles," Aguilar Camín coincides, "El tiempo ha sumado testimonio y evidencia que obligan a añadir trazos al cuadro. Uno de ellos es que la matanza de Acteal no fue sólo una matanza sino una batalla" (Time has added testimony and evidence that obligate us to add traces to the picture. One of them is that the massacre of Acteal was not only a massacre but a battle).[7] If the massacre cannot be denied, after all the police couldn't make the corpses disappear, the "evidence" now suggests that the victims got caught in the middle of a battle between Zapatistas and the so-called *grupos de autodefensa*, self-defense groups. Aguilar Camín wages his bet on "time" as a historical actor against the remembrance and celebration of Las Abejas who, having undergone a transformation into a community of martyrs in a sacred land, vow to reproduce their commitment to pacifism by celebrating the massacre every month on the twenty-second.[8]

However, as alluded to above, the revisionists' history also seeks to augment the official version with the pretence of objectivity and new factual evidence. Revisionists proceed as if they were just listing the facts. At one point in his revisionist account, Aguilar Camín questions the credibility of the testimonies in the following terms: "O mintieron los testimonios o mienten las autopsias" (Either the testimonies lie or the autopsies lie).[9] However, confronting survivor testimonies with police evidence in fact commits one to a revisionist attempt to silence the survivors. This cannot be done in all innocence. Nor is there room for emotion in this hammering away at the iconicity of Las Abejas' martyrdom and the conceptualization of Acteal as a sacred land. Aguilar Camín's ultimate objective is to muddle all the evidence that could link the massacre to ex-president Zedillo but also to the current administration which continues to arm and train paramilitaries. Since the massacre of Acteal, federal and state institutions have continued to fund paramilitary groups, paying no heed to the call for the disarmament of paramilitaries.

thesis

Testimonial documentaries, like all forms of collecting testimony, are by definition forms of engaged dissemination of truth. If testimony necessarily offers the account of a particular individual, its inclusion in a documentary necessarily involves recognition of its veracity. If one were to include a false testimony, one would mark it as such, as untrue. Given this definition, testimonial documentaries call forth an engaged observer: that is, an observer who is willing to believe. Testimonial documentaries are thus political interventions in the context of disputed truth. In analyzing the work of testimonial documentaries, or, for that matter, any collection, any argument based on testimony must be suspected of manipulation when claiming no other motivation than providing objective truth. This thesis holds as much for reports by human rights organizations that respond to and document atrocities in the immediate aftermath of events as for documentaries and other studies produced after some time has lapsed. One cannot but lend credence to the accounts of those one calls forth to give testimony. In analyzing the work of a testimonial documentary or collection, we must acknowledge that the search for wider truths on the basis of testimonial evidence must be leavened by a critical attitude toward the strongly seductive claims of individual testimonies purporting to be objective. There is one more modality of collecting testimonies that doesn't include the observer form (i.e. an external mediation): that would consist of witnesses creating their own documentaries. In this case the politics of truth stands in its most open nakedness.

the politics of truth

If I address the revisionist texts, it is not to debunk their versions of the events and thus contribute to the detailed responses that have already exposed these manipulations of truth. The goal is rather to shift to the level of the politics of truth, also veiled over in the revisionists' claims to be solely concerned with setting the record straight. Claiming the evidential status of their sources necessarily if unwittingly commits revisionists to a biased approximation to the events—not only because the biases of the sources go unacknowledged but also because the political motivation of bringing to light the culpability of former president Ernesto Zedillo Ponce de León, currently Professor of Globalization at Yale University, is obviated. For their part, the community of the Abejas, human rights organizations, engaged documentary filmmakers, and activists seek not only to expose and denounce Zedillo's culpability and the state's criminality, but also to uncover the impunity of the rich and powerful in Mexico. At least among some groups, this amounts to a call to dismantle the Mexican juridico-legal system as a whole.

In writing and reflecting on these documentaries as testimonies of truth, we face the situation that revisionist historians will simply call these testimonies partisan and characterize the tears of the testimonials as sham. They cite the falsity of Benjamin Wilkomirski's narrative of his childhood experience in a German concentration camp, as exposed by Stefan Mächler in *The Wilkomirski Affair: A Study in Autobiographical Truths*, to shore up their reminder to us that history shouldn't be subjected to emotional arguments and that the task of the historian is to tear through appearances in the pursuit of objective truth.[10] One can easily image a montage that would produce a comparable revisionist effect.

Here we might benefit from Beatriz Sarlo's interrogation of the epistemological limits of knowing the past in the context of the uses of testimony in the commissions for truth in Argentina. By systematically inquiring into the limits of experience, memory, and the transformation of "testimony into an icon of Truth or into the most important resource for the reconstruction of the past," Sarlo offers an iconoclastic undoing of the primacy of testimony.[11] But hers is not a revisionist text, nor do her political motivations have anything to do with the exculpation of military responsible for the regime of terror during the dictatorship. Rather she aims to expose the incapacity of testimony to do away with the theory of the two demons, that is, the narrative that proposes that both the left and the right were responsible for the violence. Sarlo's project elicited the indignation of those who experienced torture and the loss of family members. But her iconoclasm offends not only because she shows the testimonials to be subjective and constructed, but also because she defies the possibility of appealing to a historical logic in which testimony holds an unquestionable epistemological privilege. Her critique applies both to revisionist historians who question the evidence and to those who claim truth on the basis of testimony.

Notwithstanding the value of Sarlo's intervention, we may still question the iron-fisted critical stance that underlies her dismantling of testimony: that is, her appreciative acceptance that "Paul De Man's critique of autobiography is perhaps the highest point in literary deconstructivism, which today still is a hegemonic current."[12] Sarlo's is one of many possible takes on deconstructivism, and we need not accede to her demand to respond to its "radical critique" of the certainty of knowledge, at least not here. Instead, we may limit ourselves to the observation that testimony partakes of other forms of knowledge besides those based on fact and falsification, or even on experience, a point I will return to later on. For now I would refer to Janet Walker's discussion of deconstruction and history, which I take as an antidote to Sarlo's hegemonic deconstructivism (whatever that is) and in particular her location of problems of testimony under the deconstructivist umbrella. Walker adopts the concept of disremembering or remembering that does not bear an obviously indexical relationship to past events from Toni Morrison's *Beloved* and José Muñoz's description of a performance piece by Marga Gómez: "As both Morrison's story of slavery and Muñoz's examples of gay subjectivity suggest, disremembering is not a whimsical practice but a survival strategy for minoritarian subjects. Disremembering can become urgent when events are personally unfathomable or socially unacceptable."[13] In Walker's terms: "Disremembering is not the same as not remembering. It is remembering with a difference," and in fact one could argue that all remembering entails a form of disremembering (18). In any case, the point is that mistaken memories, amnesias, and other such aporia shouldn't entail the dismissal of testimony, but rather a redefinition of epistemological terms that would no longer call forth factuality as the ultimate criterion.

The testimonial film can sidestep the framework revisionists attempt to impose, therefore, not by an immediate, innocent, and iconoclastic expression of truth, but by taking full advantage of the fabric of the testimonial film. From Bruno Latour we learn how belief is bound to the iconoclastic destruction of the icon:

> "Fetish" and "fact" can be traced to the same root. The *fact* is that which is fabricated and not fabricated .... But the

> *fetish* too is that which is fabricated and not fabricated. There is nothing secret about this joint etymology. Everyone says it constantly, explicitly, obsessively: the scientists in their laboratory practice, the adepts of fetish cults in their rites. But we use these words *after* the hammer has broken them in two: The fetish has become nothing but empty stone onto which meaning is mistakenly projected; the fact has become absolute certainty which can be used as a hammer to break away all the delusions of belief.[14]

Bringing fact and fetish back together, Latour calls for an understanding that both are fabrications, historical artifacts that at once gain and lose the power of their claims in coming to be known as (artifactual) *factishes*. Therefore, although Latour has Pasteur's fabrication of bacteria in mind ("the scientists in their laboratory practice"), we may extend his notion of fabrication to the cinematographic act of recording moving images and sounds. We may cite Latour again: "I never act; I am slightly surprised by what I do. That which acts through me is also surprised by what I do .... Action is not about mastery. It is not a question of a hammer and shards, but one of bifurcations, events, circumstances" (281). Indeed, this applies to the filmmaker, the witness, the viewer, and also to the apparatus. The *artifactuality* of testimonial films will thus include both the human actors (the interaction of witness, filmmaker, cinematographer, etc.) and the agency of the technological innovations of video and film in general.

Rather than seeing these audiovisual texts as truthful representations of the community of martyrs (which they are), we ought to underscore that these documentaries, as Latour would put it, do *fabricate* and *not fabricate* the truth of Acteal, by strategically juxtaposing verbal testimony and visual information, providing close-ups of the faces of survivors and witnesses, inserting strident *concrete music* to the slow-motion images of tanks or of arrogant paramilitaries parading through towns, recording and profiling musicians playing traditional instruments and elders chanting prayers, and capturing the beauty of the highland landscape with views of immense mountain ranges and deep canyons. The truths produced in the documentaries should be understood as *factishes*, rather than just the facts.

Ultimately, we must ask ourselves in what consists the offense of revisionist histories, of their iconoclasm, of their destruction of the testimonial face? In drawing a phenomenological reflection on the injunction "Thou shall not kill," which implies a "me" addressing a "you," but also the "face" of another person, Jean-Luc Marion has extended the meaning of "to kill" beyond the act of putting to death: "To kill"—writes Marion—"thus indicates the destruction of the other person or thing, its objectivization into an insignificant term, entirely annulled, henceforth without force or value."[15] The assassination of memory in revisionist histories furthers the initial objectivization that led to murder. But in the end, the assassination of memory depends on, or, more precisely, responds to, the capacity of the face always to be caught up in an epistemological chain: "The possibility that this face lies to me or, as happens more often, first lies to itself results, as one of its possible consequences, in the irreducible gap between expression starting from infinite lived experience and conceptualizable, sayable, and always inadequate expression" (120). In giving us the testimonies, filmmakers ask viewers to respect the injunction "Thou shall not kill" and to understand that the group of those giving testimonials includes the "me," the face of my testimony, persistent beyond death. With full awareness that the face remains vulnerable, those giving testimony entrust themselves to the filmmakers' commitment to the veracity of their testimony. While remaining conscious of the impossibility of preventing their violation by viewers, they opt for forcefully acting on the potential objectification by camera.

the remembrance of the massacre at acteal

The documentaries I examine here approach Las Abejas and the massacre from different perspectives that include anthropological methodologies, political analysis, and the creation of audiovisual archives for countering official accounts that have distorted and continue to distort the nature of the massacre. These latter archival practices were begun only days after the president of Mexico, Ernesto Zedillo Ponce de León (1994–2000), addressed the nation on television to lament the events, calling the nation to mourn the dead. The creation of a visual archive of testimonies has been undertaken, incrementally over the years, to reveal the responsibility of Zedillo by underscoring that the massacre must be understood in the frame of a state crime. The more recent documentaries counter revisionist histories that have been written to safeguard Zedillo and the other officers from accountability in anticipation of the tenth anniversary of the mass murders.

If Mendoza's 1998 video offers vibrant immediate documentation of the events, fully conscious of deploying the aesthetics of "imperfect cinema," Higgins' offers an aesthetically accomplished yet politically forceful addition to earlier accounts. "To this day, the full story of the massacre of Acteal has never been told," Higgins tell us in his deep Scottish accent at the beginning of the film. Jiménez's video responds to the most recent revisionist efforts with testimonials by survivors of the massacre and by witnesses of the paramilitaries' plans to attack Acteal, but also with testimonials by the well-known journalist Carlos Rocha, Director of *Agencia Detrás de la Noticia* (Agency behind the News), and General José Francisco Gallardo, who was incarcerated for over a decade on false charges of corruption aimed at silencing his accusations of terrorism by the military. Rocha and Gallardo testify authoritatively that the massacre was indeed a state crime. Gallardo's testimony documents the training of the Mexican military and the constitution of paramilitary forces with the aid of Mexican training films on the subject of low-intensity warfare. These films, although produced by the Mexican army, were adapted from similar training films at Fort Bragg, North Carolina, a military base that bills itself on its website as "one of the United States' most combat ready and active military installations."[16] Moreover, in Mendoza's film we learn that Israeli experts in counterinsurgency have also participated in the training of the Mexican army on Mexican soil. In the footage compiled from the Mexican counterinsurgency films, we see and hear soldiers screaming slogans calling for death to the Zapatistas and claiming to be crazy and demented, "somos locos y dementes." In contrast to these more overtly political films, the documentaries by Lacourse and Patry and Gleason offer ethnographic documentation of Las Abejas' spirituality, which lies at the root of their definition as a pacifist indigenous organization committed to the exposure of state terrorism.

Both early and recent documentaries repeatedly project Zedillo's presidential address in montages that juxtapose his sorrowful expression with images of tanks, heavily armed police, and paramilitaries forcing thousands into refugee camps. His high-pitched voice and stiff posturing on television, calling the nation collectively to mourn the tragedy, have a false ring when editorially confronted with the state-sponsored military and police violence. These latter images are punctuated with avant-garde music, further exposing and intensifying the sordidness of the presidential address.

Given the limitations of the written form, I can only suggest the intensity of the soundtrack in these works by mentioning how, in Higgins' film, the vibrant strings of Nils Økland's experimental Norwegian folk sound alternate with the Montreal-based Set Fire to Flames' post-rock/math/noise sound to accentuate the menace already recorded in the slow-motion replay of film stock of tanks. The foreboding of terror one feels while "riding" in the passenger seat on dark roads is palpable. We hear the avant-garde sound of Set Fire to Flames' "Shit-heap-gloria of the new town planning," syncopating the march of the Zapatistas at the start of their travel across the nation to disseminate the ideals of the "other campaign," the *otra campaña* (the promotion of a popular democracy as an alternative to electoral politics during the 2006 presidential elections), flowing seamlessly into the traditional music played by Tzotzil Abejas at the end of a pilgrimage that had carried the virgin to several Abeja communities (for the promotion of Catholic-inspired radical pacifism).

Thus, the sequence opens with a speech by Comandante Tacho announcing the beginning of the *nueva campaña* in the context of the Zapatista uprising in 1994, moves to the Zapatistas' marching accompanied by Set Fire to Flames, and then cuts to the Abeja pilgrimage to end with an exposition of the history of the Abejas by a Tzotzil witness named Antonio. In this way, Higgins' brilliant montage conveys the shared nature of the struggle for democracy in Mexico. Not unlike the Abejas, who move with ease from traditional music to tropical *cumbia*, Higgins' play with the avant-garde Zapatista march and the Abeja traditional instruments conveys the Tzotzil ability to dwell in a plurality of worlds in which the multiple temporality of the modern and the nonmodern coexist without contradiction. As such the nonmodern does not refer to a premodern antechamber, but rather to an *elsewhere* from which the most modern technologies are observed and deployed.[17]

Across the documentary films, we find a broad range of approaches that include immediate documentation right after the massacre (Mendoza's *Acteal. Estrategia de muerte*), two documentaries that offer windows into Tzotzil life forms and practices of remembrance (Gleason's *A Prayer for the Weavers* and Lacourse and Patry's *Alonso's Dream*), and the two recent documentaries produced on the eve of the tenth anniversary (Higgins' *A Massacre Foretold* and Jiménez's *Acteal. 10 Años de impunidad, ¿y cuantos más ...?*) that counter the claims by revisionists. But in every case we must attend not only to the forceful testimony to the reality of the massacre but also to the cinematic rendition of the reenactment of martyrdom in ritual, the welcoming of the gift of death, and the grounding of the community in faith (reenactments which encompass testimony but are not limited to it). Faith here is not based on abidance to a creed but understood as inseparable from a state of grace. Gleason's *A Prayer for the Weavers* conveys the community of the faithful by organizing the narrative around the prayer chanted by an elder. As the prayer is chanted in Tzotzil, Gleason provides a translation but also interrupts the chant to give information on the Abejas and the massacre. Gleason requests what seems obvious but what we often forget: "We ask you to listen closely to the people. They are the experts here." Going beyond the intellectual hubris that insists on demonstrating the incompatibility of Mesoamerican life forms and Christianity, a position shared by both anthropologists and postcolonial critics eager to find proof of their theories of resistance, Gleason remains true to her subjects' spiritual expressions. (Nowhere does the interrogation, by our modern inquisitors, manifest a more insulting form than when revisionist historians denigrate the community of the faithful of Acteal by suggesting that Tzotzil modes of Christianity are flawed, as if the revisionists themselves could claim propriety over what it means to be a Christian, indeed a *católico*).

The prayer invokes the Holy Mother and the Holy Father and calls for the care of hearts, minds, and bodies. It calls for a gathering of the community, of the community of believers, of *creyentes de la religión católica*, as the Abejas refer to themselves. The remembrance of the dead is likened to a festival—it is indeed a marvelous day, in which they come to dwell among the living; in which the community of believers celebrates the massacre as giving rise to the sacred land of martyrs of Acteal. The Abejas see their speech as fighting words that, by manifesting their faith, sting those bent on destroying them. It is an apt metaphor for a militant pacifist organization willing to join forces with the Zapatistas and yet remain independent—the recurrent theme in all the Abejas documentaries. In the background of Gleason's film one hears the cries of the community of weavers who day and night weave in sorrow and sadness. The song ends by calling on the Creator, in the singular, who comes to resonate with the Holy Father, the Holy Mother, the plural "Oh Creators" of the opening lines. One mystery now resides within the other. The singer asks those present to excuse him for ending the oration.

Also in an ethnographic vein, Lacourse and Patry's *Alonso's Dream* organizes the account of the massacre around Tzotzil life forms, which in their case includes the significance of dreams in Tzotzil communities, the centrality of corn and the reverence of Mother Earth, and the tradition of weavers in which the women use waist looms and embroidery in the production of their clothing while the men work with large looms to produce the ubiquitous blue cloth used for skirts. The film punctuates the narrative of the massacre with scenes that document all the stages in the production of the cloth (the fabrication of cotton, spinning, dying, and weaving, traditions passing from fathers to sons) and different moments in the planting and sowing of corn. These latter practices are linked together by an elderly woman who chants a prayer to Mother Earth in scenes of tilling the earth and planting the corn, a chant that recurs and is only completed at the end of the documentary.

This last scene follows the refugee Alonso's narration of a dream believed to have been dreamt by the murdered catechist Alonso—whom the Abejas remember and constitute as an icon of martyrdom in their chants and prayers—a dream in which the land had become extremely fertile. Alonso the narrator also had a dream in which the land was on fire and he ran from the flames; after analysis within the community, it was concluded the dream meant that he and the Abejas were being accused of causing the conflict and that they would have to pay for it. Alonso's refusal to join the paramilitaries and his eventual naming of paramilitaries forced him and his family to abandon the village of Los Chorros and seek refuge in the city of San Cristobal de las Casas. Another reason Alonso cannot return to his community of Los Chorros is that some of the responsible paramilitaries that he named, instead of having been charged and jailed like the others, continue to this day to roam the highlands threatening to kill those who don't join their efforts to combat and destroy Zapatista sympathizers and EZLN bases of support.

In one of the most memorable moments in the film, we find Alonso sitting in his house in San Cristobal with his wife and children, watching edited footage of the town of Los Chorros by filmmakers Lacourse and Patry. What they (and we) are seeing is originally recorded archival evidence of paramilitaries patrolling the town and imposing their authority, replayed in slow motion and silence (the only sound we hear is the barely audible voice of a man questioning a woman, dialogue that was not completely filtered out in the editing process) so as to accentuate the force of what transpires: Alonso's sudden identification of the paramilitaries by name and his description of their sordid activities terrorizing the municipality of Chenalho. This sequence of a film within a film draws attention to the filmmaking process as it unfolds, since Lacourse and Patry—having shared their footage with Faustina, Alonso, and their children—went on to create this powerful, self-reflexive montage to propel their narrative.

Just prior to the sequence with Alonso and family, we had already been introduced to the same images of the paramilitaries Antonio Santis Vázquez and his brother, interrupted by a close-up of Vázquez. The close-up would seem properly to belong to another series of frames except that it is this very shot that enables Alonso, while he himself is on camera, to recognize and identify Vázquez. One wonders if the redundant inclusion of this whole first sequence of the brothers is a mistake. But the redundancy does after all have the doubly reflexive effect of reproducing the process through which the filmmakers shot and edited the video footage to create an archive, screened it for the family, and included the results in the film itself. We become witness, in this way, to the winding and rewinding of the identification process. The play between Alonso the catechist martyr, Alonso the witness, and Alonso the displaced subject living in the city sums up the collective experience of the Abejas. The segment certainly conveys the *factish* nature of the truth about the paramilitaries—here, a handsome, smiling man walking down the streets of his village turns into a paramilitary by means of Faustina's pointing finger and the eeriness of the slow motion footage—and the segment's status as both *fabrication* and *not fabrication*, as Latour would put it. (See Figures 7.1a and 7.1b).

I will now move on to a detailed discussion of Higgins' *A Massacre Foretold*. Beyond the proffered information (all those elements he might claim "have never been told before"), we must attend to the aesthetic form that lends force to the film. This should enable us to sidestep the revisionist framework that seeks to destroy the face of the Abejas, to hammer the iconicity of the testimonials to ruins.

We state unequivocally that *A Massacre Foretold* is a documentary film by Nick Higgins. But what does it mean to attribute authorship when the film is as much a product of the witnesses giving testimony, of anthropologists lending their expert opinion, of human rights activists documenting the events, of religious authorities laying down their moral authority, and of film stock from previous documentaries—most particularly from Carlos Martínez's archives, but also from news briefs taken from NBC and CNN?

Figures 7.1a and 7.1b

Juxtaposition of Faustina and paramilitary (from *Alonso's Dream*, courtesy of Danièle Lacourse and Atler-Ciné)

Note that the stock in Martínez's archive goes well beyond the materials he used in his own documentary, *Tierra sagrada en zona de conflicto*. Higgins draws from Martínez for his opening scene in which a member of Las Abejas, in his sixties, testifies to the oppression from the paramilitaries and the restrictions they face on carrying out their most basic everyday activities of tending the fields, collecting coffee beans, or even traveling to other communities. In a brilliant instance of *in medias res* a witness named Vicente speaks in voice-over the words "ayer empezo," it started yesterday that the paramilitaries were shooting their arms, "estaban sonando sus armas," before appearing in the frame, with just the mountains in the background. It is November 1997.

Figure 7.2
Scene from *A Massacre Foretold* (courtesy of Nick Higgins and Lansdowne Productions)

We see Alonso, who led the community in prayer on the day of his death in the massacre, and who has become an icon of martyrdom, standing quietly next to Vicente. This is the only image of Alonso, other than the family photographs. Soon after this scene from the past, recurrent throughout the film, Higgins informs us that most of the people depicted here were dead 28 days later. The film immediately cuts to Antonio, who reappears at strategic moments, providing the main narrative thread of the events. Later in the film, this opening scene recurs as a reminder of the victims of the massacre. We see children, young boys and girls grouped by gender, for the most part very young, just kids. One boy, no older than six, is particularly moving as he makes his way into the frame, with a toothless smile.

In Higgins' documentary, Martínez's film stock from November 1997 functions as an "actor" whose meaning exceeds the immediacy of the events, thus revealing the nature of temporality in film. It is not just a passage quoted but a voice and sequence of shots that bring the dead back to life and periodically anticipate the massacre. It is a fragment from the past, from a time in which the participants ignored their destiny, even if Vicente's speech conveys an uncanny prescience of death: hence the title of the documentary, *A Massacre Foretold.* Martínez has captured a time that becomes integral to the duration of the remembrance of massacre in Higgins' work. It is a time past, a time that ignored the future but that now functions as testimony of the group's vulnerability. But the sequence is invulnerable to revisionist iconoclasm that would seek to smash its iconicity by insisting that maybe Vicente is lying—since Vicente merely states, "ayer empezo." It is an *ayer* (yesterday) lying deep in the collective unconscious: a continuum of discrete moments that evoke a nearing present. Rather than a sense of time in which the present makes sense of the past, we have here a past that never fully arrives, but comes, nevertheless, to define our present. Viewers now experience the world with a transformed habitus immersed in a fluidity of unrepresentable time that nevertheless defines and seats in our memories the experience of self and world. The repetition of scenes and actors ground the significance of immediate and past frames. The recurrence of Antonio, of Bishop Samuel Ruiz, of anthropologist Andres Aubrey, of human rights activist Blanca Martínez Busto, of Maria, and of others pushes the narrative forward, but the interrupted and recurring testimonies also remind us that the documentary itself has a history of its production from clips that create a continuum of a past becoming and defining a never reached present. The film's time frame ends, as does its time of viewing, but viewers now carry its images, noises, music, voices, colors, and above all the gestures of those who gave testimony. We see gestures by those who can no longer see themselves.

We never see the eyes of the witnesses, with the possible exception of Antonio who looks at us from beneath the brim of a hat, a shaded face that allows us to intuit that he is looking at us and yet we never fully see his eyes. His look resembles that of a blind man, a visionary who transports us to the past with his voice, who sits facing us without gesture—which itself

Figure 7.3

Scene from *A Massacre Foretold* (courtesy of Nick Higgins and Lansdowne Productions)

is a form of gesturing. In his voice he carries the voices of others, most particularly of Alonso. Antonio tells us of the Zapatista uprising; indeed, as he relates, the Abejas knew the EZLN was an indigenous army struggling for the same causes, in the same condition of oppression, but one they would not join because they did not believe in violence. After a few seconds of silence, in voice-over, he goes on to tell us about the verbal exchange with Alonso on the eve of the massacre: "Había desplazados aquí en esta ermita y un hermano que se llama Alonso Gómez Vázquez, y el me preguntó, 'Toño,' dice—'¿qué?'—'¿estas seguron que nos van a matar?' Ahi comenzo a llorar. Ya nosotros tuvimos que esperar la muerte" ("There were refugees here in the small church and a brother named Alonso Gómez Vázquez, and he asked me, 'Toño,' he says—'what?' 'Are you sure they are going to kill us?' Then he started to cry. We had to await death"). Antonio barely moves, barely makes a gesture other than the inflection of the martyred Alonso's voice.

Otherwise the interviewees avoid our eyes, with only an accidental touching of our sight. This is the standard, the protocol in testimonial documentaries: never to address the viewers directly as if the insistence on credibility that would supposedly come from the gaze would betray a mask—indeed, expose the face to destruction. In these documentaries direct eye contact occurs only in the case of Zedillo, whose assurance seems to beg for credibility, and in that of the newscasters, who partake, precisely, of a setting that calls for a mask: we know they are reading a teleprompter. By looking to the side, witnesses avoid demolition by the iconoclast who would scream, "Look at the eyes, the face is a mask, it conceals a liar."

In the flow of time there is no time for such a fixing, unlike in still photography which inevitably calls forth and anticipates the death of the subject in the embalming of the face. Clearly, we can reproduce stills, as I am doing here, and stills may or may not appear in a given film. But when they do, they may serve an authenticating function, or even reproduce the semblance of the dead as in the capturing of the photographs of the massacred in the collective tomb in Acteal. And yet, the still will inevitably permeate the temporality of film with a rem(a)inder of what cannot be wholly mastered. Stills become actors with uncertain meanings that interact with the use of sound and silence to accentuate the sordidness of the events, to infuse nature with melancholy, or to anticipate the emergence of speakers, pilgrims, musicians. For instance, in Lacourse and Patry's use of freeze frames of the victims in the collective tomb of Acteal, one cannot but wonder at the ways in which the capture of stills in cinema furthers the martyrdom of the face. Whereas stills of landscapes or solitary dirt roads offer pauses for meditating on life lived, those of the dead and the living suggest masks that delimit the impenetrability of the faces.

To the stills we must add the use of slow-motion cinematography as a means of identifying and authenticating a landscape and capturing the movement of people: paramilitaries roaming the towns, military weaponry, the sadness of mourning. Stills and slow motion both provide images that penetrate our consciousness, depositing meaning and sensations deep in our unconscious and shaping our habitus. The past will now explore the world with new eyes, or, better, with a new sense of touch that affects all the senses, saturating them with haptic qualities.

In viewing films, not only our eyes and ears are touched, but through the various techniques of which stills and slow motion are a limit case we learn to touch the world with sight and listening. And listening to sound and silence in turn transforms the visual. In relation to the function of the face and speech, let me furnish an example of how gestures speak for themselves. In *A Massacre Foretold*, gestures emphasize the ironic tone in which the Mayor of Chenalho, Jacinto Arias, accuses Bishop Samuel Ruiz, and his catechists of the Diocese of San Cristobal de las Casas, of promoting the violence plaguing the municipality. As his pointing hand lectures us on the truth of the causes of violence in Chenalho, the film captures the posturing that betrays his attitude. Mayor Arias was shortly thereafter arrested for his intellectual participation in the massacre. Now let us contrast this scene with Maria's gestures in Higgins' film. If the inscrutability of the face could lead a viewer to see a mask disguising a liar (admittedly, a forced reading considering the pain her face expresses), Maria's credibility is secured in the constant wringing of her hands, in the nervousness that conveys the agony of having to recount the story one more time. Maria was not at the scene of the massacre but lost several members of her family, including her brother Alonso. We learn from Maria that the police kept them from entering Acteal and she tells of the struggle they faced to get the authorities to return the bodies for a proper burial.

Gestures in the video reveal character, not because of a body language that had to be pierced through to get at the truth, but because the truth itself is on the surface of the image. For the gestures touch the camera and touch us. While being touched by the request to answer questions and the camera's intrusion, those filmed—whether Maria, who speaks as a witness to the atrocity, or the Mayor of Chenalho, who speaks as a witness to the political activities of the Tzotzil catechists and Roman Catholic priests—must at once know the media, anticipate the effects on the viewer, and also remain unconscious, blind to their own gesturing. Gestures as such are mediated and yet spontaneous.

Sean Cubitt has further supported what Christian Metz understood (through the Foucauldian notion of the *dispositif*) as cinema's work of reproducing normalized subjectivities: "I would suggest, " writes Cubitt, "that cinema needs to be understood as a machine and an institution that promotes, if it doesn't determine, the erasure of difference through the promotion of a central, all translating, normalizing position for the spectator, rather in the way that perspective gives us a place in front of the picture."[18]

The diagnosis of an all encompassing machine, institution, normalizing position and perspective would seem to further the erasure of difference Cubitt intends to expose. In this theoretical understanding, there seems to be no room for citation, for the use of film stock or, for that matter, any perspective for purposes other than representation.

In early colonial works, indigenous painters would commonly deploy perspective as one more signifier rather than as the instrument to record a phenomenal (whether imaginary or real) occurrence in the world. Their perspective, for instance, could depict the colonizing gaze of inquisitors and confessors, rather than reproduce the semblance of a specific confessor or inquisitor.[19] In the same vein one may reference or draw on film archives to produce meanings other than those *intended* by the original cinematographer or inherent in the machine. The maleness of the apparatus could be further complicated by the fact that if the machine is an *actant*, it is also *acted* on by those it captures. In Higgins' juxtaposition of the Mayor and Maria, we certainly find the competing discourses, on the one hand, of patriarchy as fomented by state institutions and, on the other hand, of a feminine space that, if we cannot call it feminist, nevertheless carries its own force from within a patriarchal society where men might manifest openness while still reproducing a social order with clearly defined gender roles. Note that these roles are constantly subjected to negotiation in terms that escape our patriarchal categories. The Zapatistas are known for making gender a central issue in their examination of indigeneity by underscoring that patriarchy is not a determining element of Maya social institutions, just as the regime of *caciques*, the local political bosses that emerged after the conquest, is not. It is not simply a question of contending discourses but of multiple institutions with different histories. Urban middle-class feminists are often criticized for their assumption that the terms of their struggles apply universally, hence shunning the ways in which Maya women might be conducting their own struggles.[20] The Abejas are not unaware of the transformations in the Zapatista communities; they know that patriarchy and gender roles have histories that can be undone.

The dictating Mayor of Chenalho who wags his finger in our faces conveys a rhetorical expression of authority that competes with the equally rhetorical gestures of Maria's wringing hands that express genuine vulnerability. By rhetorical I don't want to suggest that Maria's expression lacks authenticity, but rather that she chooses to caress the camera with her equally genuine timidity before men from outside the community (that is, Higgins and his film crew). By comparison, in the video *Acteal. 10 Años de impunidad, ¿y cuantos más ...?* by Jiménez, Maria doesn't shy away from making forceful declarative statements in Tzotzil to the effect: "I declare that it is true that they came to massacre us." By this I want to suggest that the *dispositifs* belong to multiple institutions, and that the apparatus might appear less gender specific, at least less determining, once we remove it from a *visualism* that ignores and hence undermines other senses that in watching the video would include touch along with listening, as one possibility in a series of haptic impressions. Another form of touch involves the use of slow motion accompanied by avant-garde music and noise to convey, for example, the sordidness of paramilitaries surveying villages or the army invading territories. Indeed, as discussed above, we can find the filmmakers incorporating film stock that likely had other intended uses than the *factishes* a particular documentarist, Higgins in this case, produces by citing them.

High theory of the 1960s through the 1980s engaged the apparatus and the *dispositif* in an effort to unmask the ways in which power was exerted in film, but it was equally invested in tracking forms of resistance in viewers. Laura Marks has argued quite convincingly for a haptic criticism that would enable us "to 'warm up' [in the spirit of Marshall McLuhan's thermostatic lingo] our cultural tendency to take a distance."[21] For Marks not only argues against the determinacy of the apparatus but also offers an approach one might take toward documentaries such that we would no longer seek to subject them to our will. Marks is particularly interested in visual eroticism and the undoing of psychoanalytic perspectives that assume the male gaze as a given in the production and consumption of pornography instead of as one possible reading, even if it is a particular reading so integrated into our common sense, into our *critical* habitus, that we have to make an extraordinary effort to see and feel differently. By the same token, we can argue against the notion of the camera as an apparatus that reproduces an imperial eye, and we can resist the pull to generalize a colonialist objectification. We may appeal to the same theorists of the 1960s to 1980s, in particular Michel de Certeau, to invoke the oppositional practices of the everyday—including the undoing of the patriarchal and imperial gaze—that may be traced in the touching of the camera by the witnesses giving testimony. For the purpose of tracing instances of quotation, we may benefit from Certeau's dictum "memory does its work in a *locus* that is not its own," but also from the cultural practices he defines as "*poaching* in countless ways on the *property* of others."[22]

Filming as poaching can be traced to those instances when the documentarists cite the newscasts of addresses to the nation by then-president Zedillo, newscasts that seek to present him in the most authoritarian and patriarchal manner in order to secure the viewers' complicity. In citing such passages, the documentaries under discussion can and do create a contrary effect: the end is obviously not to confirm Zedillo's (or, for that matter, the newscasters') accounts of the events but to undo the force of his authoritarian posturing by means of an ironic use of the image and voice in a montage that reveals the absurdity and falseness of his communications to the nation. Note that at least in Higgins there is no voice-over drilling a message, but rather a poaching of the archive that *steals* the elements for an oppositional memory. Another instance of citation would be the use of stock footage of the paramilitary, soldiers, and police not just to represent their presence in the highlands of Chiapas, but to expose them as perpetrators of sordid violence. In one instance that I have discussed above, we find Faustina, along with her husband Alonso and their children, watching a video, pointing at paramilitaries that Danièle Lacourse and Yvan Patry turn into a citation through the work of cinematic montage. The slow-motion effect that transforms the handsome smile of a Tzotzil into the gesture of an arrogant murderer affects our sense of touch through the retina that receives the face, the composure, and the smile. And it affects our nervous system beyond the reception of a mere image. Faustina points at the video and identifies the paramilitaries. Her authority is drawn from her position of witness to the creation of paramilitary forces but also, perhaps even more importantly, from her historical condition as a refugee who cannot return to the highlands.

The gift of testimony in the documentaries can certainly be destroyed by an iconoclastic gesture that would *kill* the face of the witness in an attempt to silence the voice. But the wager of the filmmaker and the witness resides in the rhetorical force of audiovisual testimony to produce popular history for a long-term struggle against impunity—a struggle that seeks to dismantle the state and its repressive institutions, at least in their current forms.

notes

1. Pierre Vidal-Naquet, "'Inquiry into a Massacre' by Amnon Kapeliouk," in *The Jews: History, Memory, and the Present*, ed. and trans. David Ames Curtis (New York: Columbia University Press, 1996), 229.
2. Although Las Abejas shared the reasons for the insurgency and sympathized with the ends of the Ejercito Zapatista de Liberación Nacional (EZLN, Zapatista Army of National Liberation), they remained independent in their pacifist vocation. The EZLN took arms in 1994 on the eve of the implementation of the North American Free Trade Agreement (NAFTA). After twelve days of struggle a truce was signed between the insurgents and the Mexican state. While in the theater of dialogue all seemed to promise a peaceful negotiation, the army was conducting covert violence against the Zapatista bases and sympathizers. Given the truce and that neither the Mexican army nor the forces of Seguridad Pública could exercise violence directly, these entities trained paramilitaries to conduct low intensity warfare. Las Abejas organized themselves in 1992 to struggle by peaceful means to transform the social conditions of oppression in which the indigenous people of Chiapas live.
3. In a series of three articles between October and December 2007, Hector Aguilar Camín revived the once thought discredited accounts given by the Procuraduria General de la República (General Attorney of the Republic) and Gustavo Hirales: "Regreso a Acteal I. La fractura," *Nexos*, October 2007, "Regreso a Acteal II. El camino de los muertos (Segunda de tres partes)," *Nexos*, November 2007, "Regreso a Acteal III. El día señalado (Tercera y

última parte)," *Nexos*, December 2007, www.nexos.com.mx (accessed 23 April 2008). Aguilar Camín's articles have been echoed in the Mexican press by less well known journalists who underscore the professionalism of Aguilar Camín's journalism and historical vocation. Carlos Montemayor and Herman Bellinghausen have refuted these accounts in articles for the Mexican newspaper *La Jornada* (available on line at www.jornada.unam.mx, accessed 28 April 2008). Bellinghausen published twenty articles from 5 to 24 November 2007, tracing the history of the documentation of violence in Chiapas in numerous articles published in *La Jornada* during 1997–8. Montemayor's articles appeared in the 17–19 December 2007 issues of *La Jornada*. Bellinghausen and Montemayor write from a position committed to the Zapatista struggles.

4. Aguilar Camín, "Regreso a Acteal I."
5. Pierre Vidal-Naquet, "'Inquiry into a Massacre,'" 228–9.
6. Victoria Sandford and Asale Angel-Ajani, eds., *Engaged Observer: Anthropology, Advocacy, and Activism* (New Brunswick, NJ: Rutgers University Press, 2006), 5.
7. Aguilar Camín, "Regreso a Acteal III."
8. Two collections of verbal and photographic testimonies have been published: *Acteal: una herida abierta/Acteal: ipuc sc'oplal milel ta* (Acteal: An open wound) (Tlaquepaque, Jalisco: Instituto Tecnológico y de Estudios Superiores de Occidente, 1998) consists of a bilingual collection of photographs, testimonies, memorials for the dead, and essays by anthropologists, human rights activists, Jesuit priests, and prelates. The second testimony, *... esta es nuestra palabra ... Testimonios de Acteal* (This is our word: Testimonies from Acteal) (San Cristobal de las Casas: Centro de Derechos Humanos "Fray Bartolomé de las Casas," 1998), gathers verbal and photographic snapshots of the witnesses, of life in the refugee camps, and of the community in mourning; the ellipsis in the title captures well the collected fragments of testimonies. The black and white photographs by Jutta Meier-Weidenbach and Claudia Ituarte offer an aesthetic celebration of the martyrs and the strength of Las Abejas.
9. Aguilar-Camín, "Regreso a Acteal III."
10. See Stefan Mächler, *The Wilkomirski Affair: A Study in Autobiographical Truths*, trans. John E. Woods (New York: Schocken Books, 2001).
11. Beatriz Sarlo, *Tiempo pasado. Cultura de la memoria y giro subjectivo, una discusión* (Past tense. The culture of memory and the subjective turn: A discussion) (Buenos Aires: Siglo Veintiuno, 2005), 23; my translation. For a critique see John Beverley, "The Neoconservative Turn in Latin American Literary and Cultural Studies," *Journal of Latin American Cultural Studies* 17, no. 1 (2008): 65–83.
12. Sarlo, *Tiempo pasado*, 40.
13. Janet Walker, *Trauma Cinema: Documenting Incest and the Holocaust* (Berkeley: University of California Press, 2005), 19.
14. Bruno Latour, *Pandora's Hope: Essays on the Reality of Science Studies* (Cambridge, MA: Harvard University Press, 1999), 272 (original emphasis).
15. Jean-Luc Marion, *In Excess: Studies of Saturated Phenomena*, trans. Robyn Horner and Vincent Berraud (New York: Fordham University Press, 2002), 126.
16. http://www.us-army-info.com/directory/Installations/Fort_Bragg,_North_Carolina/index.html, accessed 14 November 2008.
17. On the concept of *elsewhere* and the undoing of the modern/premodern binary, see José Rabasa: "Elsewheres: Radical Relativism and the Frontiers of Empire," *Qui Parle* 16, no. 1 (2006): 71–94.

18. Sean Cubitt, *Videography: Video Media as Art and Culture* (New York: St. Martin's Press, 1993), 78. Also see Cubbit, *Cinema Effect* (Cambridge, MA: MIT Press, 2004).
19. José Rabasa, "Franciscans and Dominicans under the Gaze of Tlacuilo: Plural-World Dwelling in an Indian Pictorial Codex," in Morrison Library Inaugural Address Series 14, 1998, The Doe Library, University of California at Berkeley.
20. See Mariana Mora, "Decolonizing Politics: Zapatista Autonomy in an Era of Neoliberal Governance and Low Intensity Conflict" (PhD dissertation, University of Texas at Austin, 2007); Christine Eber and Christine Kovic, eds., *Women in Chiapas: Making History in Times of Struggle and Hope* (New York: Routledge, 2003); Rosalva Aída Hernández Castillo, *La otra palabra. Mujeres y violencia en Chiapas, antes y después de Acteal* (The other word: Women and violence in Chiapas, before and after Acteal) (Mexico City: CIESAS, 1998); Guiomar Rovira, *Mujeres de maíz* (Corn women) (Mexico City: Biblioteca Era, 1997).
21. Laura Marks, *Touch: Sensuous Theory and Multisensory Media* (Minneapolis: University of Minnesota Press, 2002), xiii. My observations on touch have benefited from Jacques Derrida, *On Touching—Jean Luc Nancy*, trans. Christine Irizarry (Palo Alto, CA: Stanford University Press, 2005).
22. Michel de Certeau, "The Oppositional Practices of Everyday Life," *Social Text* 3 (1982): 43; Certeau, *The Practice of Everyday Life*, trans. Steven Rendall (Berkeley: University of California Press, 1988), xii.

mediating testimony

broadcasting south africa's truth and reconciliation commission

eight

catherine m. cole

You always have to be prepared for the unexpected because that's the thing that I learned, that human beings are human beings. Once you put them under the glare of a camera and audience ... once a hearing started, you could control very few of the things.

Yasmin Sooka, TRC Commissioner, South Africa[1]

I had this strong perception that the cameras were seen as the ear of the nation.

Max du Preez, Executive Producer, TRC Special Report[2]

Truth commissions are state-appointed investigative bodies mandated to research and report on large-scale human rights abuses perpetrated during a specific time period or political regime. Designed as an alternative to trials, truth commissions are supposed to uncover "the truth about certain historical events rather than prosecuting specific defendants."[3] An alternative form of justice, they are part and parcel of an emerging field called transitional justice. There had been sixteen truth commissions in the world before South Africa's Truth and Reconciliation Commission (TRC) began its work in 1996.[4] But South Africa broke with precedent in two significant ways. First, it offered conditional amnesty to perpetrators who came forward to give statements, and if these statements met certain criteria, perpetrators could be deemed free from civil and criminal prosecution for their past violations of human rights forever.[5] Second, the TRC made the remarkable decision to hold its hearings publicly, with proceedings open to any spectator who wished to attend. Truth commissions before South Africa's made their work known to the public primarily through the publication of a final report. And South Africa's TRC, too, created a summary report, with the first five volumes appearing in 1998 and then two more in 2003.[6] However, this report should be, I argue, of secondary importance to our examination, analysis, and evaluation of the TRC. Rather, media coverage, though little studied thus far, was far more central to the national impact of the commission during its lifetime than any other representation, including the commission's own summary report, print journalism's coverage of the TRC, and the barrage of academic books that have followed in the TRC's wake.

Television and radio covered the TRC extensively during the two-year life of the Human Rights Violation Committee hearings (1996–8), as well as the four years of Amnesty committee hearings (1996–2000). Through these broadcasts, the TRC became a "media event" as defined by Daniel Dayan and Elihu Katz, that is, a historic occasion of state that was broadcast as it unfolded in time.[7] The media ensured not only that the TRC transfixed the nation and the world at large, but also that viewers were engaged actively in the process. Albie Sachs, presently a South African Constitutional Court justice and historically one of the key figures who assisted with South Africa's political transition from apartheid to democracy, says that when the truth commission was being considered, he opposed the idea of holding the proceedings in public. He told me in an interview, "I just couldn't imagine that the people who came to be called perpetrators would come up with the truth if they had to do so in public. And I felt that we would get far more information and material if it were done behind closed doors. They could really own up to what they had done."[8] During the transition to democracy, some civil society groups in South Africa opposed *any* version of a truth commission, for they contended such a commission would violate the principles of accountability central to the rule of law. Yet they agreed to a compromise solution: the TRC proceedings could go on if hearings took place in public. Sachs believes, "As it turned out, that [decision] resulted in the most significant feature of the whole truth commission ... far more important than the actual data, the facts, the information, that came out—and a tremendous amount did come out—was the fact that the story was being played out in public. It became a national drama."

As I posit in my forthcoming book *Performing South Africa's Truth Commission: Stages of Transition*, the TRC's public dimensions are one of its most significant and unexamined features.[9] I argue that the commission was a performance in many senses of the term: it was an embodied enactment with aural and visual signification, communicating through kinesthetic as well as affective registers; it was a time-based event that unfolded before an audience assembled in person, as well as spectators who witnessed remotely by listening to radios or watching on televisions; the media constituted simultaneously a representation and a performer in the process, enlisting a larger body politic to also participate in the TRC process. Of media events in general, Dayan and Katz said in 1992: "We are witnessing the gradual replacement of what could be called a theatrical mode of publicness—an actual meeting of performers and public in locations such as parliament houses, churches, convention floors, stadiums—by a new mode of publicness based on separation of performers and audiences, and on the rhetoric of narrative rather than the virtue of contact."[10]

South Africa's TRC bridged both of these realms: the theatrical, in-person and the media-transmitted, broadcast experiences. Each carried idiosyncratic "truth effects," and were fraught with biases the public held about format. For instance, there is an unexamined belief that live confrontation "can somehow give rise to the truth in ways that recorded representations cannot," as Philip Auslander has shown.[11] The TRC benefited from this common assumption, but it also suffered from it. Confidence in the veracity of liveness has a flip side, a Janus face known as "antitheatrical prejudice." This bias assumes that what transpires before an audience, especially on a stage, is inherently false and artificial.[12] The live and performative elements of the TRC triggered these twin and vacillating prejudices: on one hand, the unexamined confidence in the truthfulness of the live encounter; on the other, the inherent suspicion that acts done on stage, for show, are false—not something you want in a "truth" commission. The mediated and the theatrical dimensions allowed for multiple renderings and interpretations of the truths, lies, and everything in between which spilled forth at TRC public proceedings.

My focus in this chapter is primarily on television coverage of the TRC, and specifically one particular program, a weekly news digest aired nearly every Sunday for two years called *TRC Special Report*. Produced by the renegade liberal Afrikaner journalist Max du Preez, who was a gadfly of the apartheid state prior to its demise, *TRC Special Report* is an extraordinary representation of the commission. Among the questions to be asked of this series are: how did *Special Report* shape the TRC experience for audiences? How did the stylistic and structural conventions of the program create, position, and anticipate its audience(s), and by extension the experience of public witnessing of and participation in the TRC as national ceremony? How did

Special Report use narrative? In what kinds of storytelling did the program engage? How did the program negotiate the uncomfortable alliance between critical distance mandated by journalism and active promulgation of the TRC as public event? While answering all of these questions would exceed the space allotted, my chapter invites readers to consider some of the particular dimensions of the TRC video archive as "moving testimony," for this archive represents unique and distinctive features when considered next to some of the other video archives represented in this collection. The TRC's video archive also suggests the enormous potential of television and radio to enlist public participation in a process of transitional justice and the remaking of public memory in the aftermath of massive, state-perpetrated violations of human rights that were enacted in a context of denial, censorship, and repression.

From May 1996 to December 2000, communities throughout South Africa had the opportunity to attend TRC hearings which were generally of two types. First, there were those held by the Human Rights Violation (HRV) Committee, which had taken statements from 22,000 individuals who felt they were victims of gross violations of human rights. Of these, the HRV Committee chose 2,000 to be heard in public. These hearings were not intended primarily as fact-finding ventures, but rather were meant to honor and air the "narrative truth" of the witness, the truth as he or she had experienced it, and to enlist the community and the nation in the process of listening to these testimonies. Each witness was given thirty minutes of uninterrupted time to testify before a panel of commissioners, as well as the audience assembled in the hall. After that, the witness was often asked questions by the panelists. The tone of these events eschewed the protocols of a traditional courtroom where victims of crimes are cast in a passive role, in as much as they can only speak if spoken to by a lawyer or judge.[13] The point of the HRV hearings was to hear stories from those most directly affected by the past atrocities, and to hear those stories told on the victim's own terms and in his or her own language. The commission supported the principle of "parity of esteem" for all of South Africa's eleven official languages by providing simultaneous interpretation over headphones in multiple languages.

The second category of hearings comprised Amnesty hearings, which had a vastly different tone and style. Unlike the HRV hearings, these were held before three judges who were vested with the power to pronounce a perpetrator as having met or not met the criteria for amnesty. Thus this committee actually had *performative* power, in the sense of J.L. Austin's performative speech acts.[14] Since, at the end of the process, commissioners could pronounce perpetrators as either free or liable to prosecution for their crimes, Amnesty hearings tended to be much more like trials in a court of law. Even though guilt was not at stake (perpetrators came forward of their own accord), something else was at stake judicially, and profoundly so.

All hearings were recorded on video by the South African Broadcasting Corporation (SABC). While it had initially intended to broadcast the hearings continuously, the SABC realized very early in the TRC process that it did not have the fiscal capacity to sustain this level of coverage. Rather it could only afford regular news bulletins and weekly digests of TRC highlights. Yet the SABC devoted significant human and fiscal resources to seeing that the commission was comprehensively filmed. At each hearing there were between two and six cameras, and a producer who orchestrated a live edit. Hearings typically lasted from eight to ten hours a day. This raw footage now belongs both to the SABC (located in Johannesburg) and the Department of Justice (DOJ), the latter being the official owner of the TRC's archive. So there are two archives of video footage: one housed at SABC and the other with the government. The National Archives of South Africa in Pretoria, which is custodian for the DOJ holdings, has a collection of 7,101 videotapes (each two hours long) of TRC public hearings. This video collection alone is so enormous that if one researcher worked eight hours a day for seven days a week, it would take over four-and-a-half years to view the collection in its entirety.[15] The second, and parallel, visual archive of the TRC (for which the SABC holds exclusive rights) is a collection of the weekly news program called *TRC Special Report,* produced by Max du Preez. Broadcast on Sunday evenings from 1996 to 1998 for a total of 87 episodes, this program is remarkable for its documentary ingenuity, rigorous investigative journalism, and potent ability to convey the corporeal richness of testimony. The series was recently digitized by Yale School of Law Lillian Goldman Library, and is now available via streaming video online.[16]

Testimony heard before the TRC was recorded for reasons that contrast markedly with the reasons behind the creation of many of the other archives of filmed testimonies. Unlike the footage found at the Shoah Foundation Institute for Visual History and Education, for instance, the TRC's testimony was not given ostensibly "for" the camera or the documentarian, but rather for a state-sponsored investigative commission. Witnesses who appeared before the commission—rather than looking just slightly to the side of the camera (as one finds in the Shoah collection) at a single person or interviewer who has "called forth" the testimony—looked at a panel of commissioners, often placed directly in front of them or slightly to the side at an angle. While witnesses may have felt a documentary impulse when they chose to give a statement to the commission and then accepted the invitation to appear in public, they did so not primarily for the purpose of recording history or public memory, but rather so that the commissioners could eventually, by the end of the TRC process, make findings: the commission had to decide which perpetrators would receive amnesty, and which victims would be eligible to receive whatever reparations the government eventually decided to dole out.

While it is entirely true that the TRC's video archive was premised on instrumentalist objectives very much connected to state formation, as Richard Wilson contends,[17] to reduce this archive of testimony simply to the level of utility is to ignore the way public hearings were a complex "rainbow" genre that mixed ritual, law, media event, religious ceremony, confessional, theatre, therapy, storytelling, and politics. While South Africa's Truth and Reconciliation Commission was designed to contain and make manageable the effects of atrocity, the magnitude of that atrocity constantly exceeded the commission's bounds—and I argue that it was the domain of performance that was called upon to cope with this excess. Interventions that exceeded the instrumentalist goals of the TRC, or exceeded the narrow confines of "gross violations of human rights" that circumscribed its mandate (or even ran contrary to the commission's mandate), constantly erupted in the public hearings: witnesses challenged the commissioners, audiences interjected commentary and laughter, commissioners had to calm and rebuke unruly spectators, and both witnesses and commissioners took liberty to define the commission as they liked, irrespective of protocol. Chairperson Desmond Tutu, for instance, insisted on opening HRV hearings with Christian prayers and songs, even though South Africa is a secular state with a multireligious population. While hearings had a prescribed function and protocol, once audiences assembled in the halls, once the hearings began, and once the cameras started rolling, anything could happen. Commissioner Yasmin Sooka recalls:

> You always have to be prepared for the unexpected because ... human beings are human beings. Once you put them under the glare of a camera and audience ... I was always struck by how once a hearing started, you could control very few of the things. I mean I had this big thing about the whole sort of Christian theology issue. And I would say, "Well we're not going to have any prayers." And then I would arrive in the hall determined we would go straight to taking the oaths [where victims were sworn in] and the local priest or community would stand up and the hymn would be the same, and somebody would get up to pray and only then could you get back your hearing and it would start ... You have no control. You can just put in things, mechanisms, to make sure you manage it, but you have to be prepared for surprises.[18]

As persistent as those surprises were—the hearings' improvisational qualities, the way the format granted witnesses a degree of agency—this aspect of the TRC as live, public process is completely suppressed in the TRC's official record, its seven-volume summary report. But these very qualities of surprise, the unexpected, individual agency, and improvisational intervention are abundantly evident in the commission's television archive. One sees in the footage the unruliness of the process. I argue that through examining this unruliness, how the performative dimensions of the commission allowed for the unexpected, what emerges is a complexity of truth that is barely evident in the TRC's official textual self-representations, and indeed the burgeoning secondary literature on the TRC.[19]

Held on church daises, town hall stages, and community center platforms throughout the country, the commission was like a traveling road show. The TRC would roll into a metropolis, town, city, location, township, or *dorp* (small town) for a period spanning a few days to a week. Anyone was allowed to attend these proceedings, and many did, but far more participated in the process through radio and television broadcasts. Without international precedent or established protocols, microphones and television cameras sprang up in the spaces of transitional justice, making formidable technical and logistical demands on the commission, raising a host of ethical issues, and reaching millions more people than the few hundred who could be physically present at any particular hearing. At the start of the commission, television cameras faced intense opposition from the Amnesty committee, which "raised vociferous objections to the presence of TV cameras in hearings," according to former TRC Commissioner Wendy Orr. "The Amnesty Committee took the stance that their proceedings should be equated with those of a court of law—no TV cameras in court, therefore no TV cameras in Amnesty hearings."[20] In the TRC's summary report, the Amnesty committee articulated its reservations about television coverage, saying this might discourage people from applying for amnesty or giving testimony, or counsel might exploit the media for advantage. The TRC prevailed in the end, convincing the Amnesty committee to allow TV cameras, albeit with reluctance. Yet afterward even the Amnesty committee admitted that the media played a "constructive and important role" in covering the hearings: "The role of the media in communicating the essence of the amnesty process and involving the public in the proceedings cannot be underestimated," noted the committee report included within the TRC's summary report. "It must be said that the process was considerably enriched by this contribution."[21]

Through broadcast media, the public hearings became literally *hearings*, something that could be listened to, a sonic experience that communicated through orality: the cadence, inflections, rhythms, volume, accent, and grain of the voice. Television and radio transmitted the pauses, hesitations, revisions of sentences, dangling phrases, and silences that were sometimes filled with sighs, an inhalation, a wail of grief, or sometimes nothing at all, just silence. Extra-linguistic features of testimony were central to many who participated in the process. For instance, Victor Doyesa, a victim who publicly opposed an Amnesty application, cited the aural tone of the perpetrators' testimony as being key to his decision: "I hear the manner in which they [the perpetrators] address the commission, and I hear the manner in which they tell their story. They show no remorse."[22] Of course, remorse or contrition was not one of the criteria for granting amnesty under the TRC mandate: perpetrators had only to give full disclosure and prove that their deeds were politically motivated. But remorse *was* important to Doyesa: his perception of the subtext and tone of perpetrators' testimony—elements that could only be conveyed by actually *hearing* the hearings—was central to his own participation in the process. Audiences also experienced through sound broadcast the multilingual texture of South Africa, for witnesses gave testimony in any of the country's eleven official languages. For instance, audiences could hear the clicks and pops of a female Zulu-language witness intermixed with the English-language translation from a male interpreter, reflecting the way the embodied performance of the commission expressed South Africa's dense linguistic tapestry and complicated clear gender binaries.

To the sonic dimensions of the hearings that were captured by radio, television added visual signification. Through television, the commission could be heard and *seen* by millions. Audiences could see the minute facial expressions of those who gave testimony, their emphatic hand gestures or sullen, affect-less demeanor. Audiences also experienced the intercut perspectives of a witness speaking and someone in the audience listening. Broadcast media invited audiences to evaluate for themselves how particular words came out of particular mouths, enticed them to consider what complexities and shades of other truths might be submerged in a facial tic, an averted eye, or an unfinished phrase. "See for yourself," the TRC public hearings seemed to say.

"Transitional justice," the nascent field out of which truth commissions emerge, was designed to address certain failings of traditional jurisprudence. When addressing crimes against humanity, the law is often called upon: (a) to place those crimes into the public record, (b) to convey to the public both the documentary facts of what happened and the historical context of those crimes, and finally (c) to perform the restoration of the rule of law. International law in the wake of the Nuremberg trials had traditionally assumed that "both didactic and individual goals can be met in the same proceeding," says Stephen Landsman.[23] Yet it is precisely this elision of personal responsibility and didacticism on a national scale—and the theatrical devices used to accomplish grand didactic ends—that made critics such as Hannah Arendt most acutely uncomfortable. "The purpose of a trial is to render justice and nothing else," she argues, elaborating that even the noblest of ulterior motives for making a historical record of Nazi crimes "can only detract from the law's main business: to weigh the charges brought against the accused, to render judgment, and to mete out due punishment."[24] The need to memorialize, dramatize, and document crimes against humanity—and to engage a larger public in that reflective process—is enormous and of paramount importance. And yet trials may not be the best forum to accomplish such ends. Many believe that truth commissions are far better venues for memorializing "controversial, complex events," to use Martha Minow's words.[25] This goal of public engagement with the process was central to the decision to have South Africa's TRC happen in public. Yet without television and radio, the TRC's national reach would have been a tiny fraction of what it eventually achieved.

While much has been written about South Africa's TRC, relatively little has been written about its coverage on television and radio.[26] A host of scholars have analyzed and written about the TRC's seven volume summary report as the most important and authoritative representation of what the commission did, said, and found out. However, for many people in South Africa the summary report is completely irrelevant: too expensive, dense, poorly distributed, and laden with rarified quantitative data to be accessible even to those who actually worked on the commission. Yet the ample broadcast media coverage of the TRC *as the process was unfolding* meant that this media coverage became synonymous with the commission in many people's minds, however erroneously.

The TRC's Media Department targeted radio as the "most effective communication medium for its proceedings to the widest number of people."[27] The geographic distribution of radio in South Africa exceeds that of all other media, especially in rural areas, and radio transcends barriers of language, literacy, and technology. At the time of the TRC, the multilingual SABC radio stations reached 3.3 million Zulu-speaking listeners and 1.6 million Xhosa speakers, 1.5 million seSotho, 1 million seTswana, 700,000 Afrikaans, 450,000 English, and 116,000 speakers of Venda (357). On many of these stations, the public hearings were broadcast continuously throughout the day.[28] Unfortunately radio coverage of the TRC was not preserved in archives, and this lack of preservation, combined with the limited language skills of researchers, has meant there has been no substantive analysis of radio coverage of the TRC to date.

While it is worth noting that television reached far fewer people than did radio, it is also true that television was much more experientially rich. To the sonic dimensions of the TRC it added visuality, embodiment, and the potency of re-broadcast and re-contextualized archival footage, as well as location shots, and a whole range of techniques of communication not available through radio. "Without a doubt," writes former Commissioner Orr, "the TV images which appeared during the Commission's lifespan were compelling and conveyed the magnitude of our work with an impact which neither print nor radio could achieve."[29] Even the TRC's summary report acknowledged television's role in promulgating its proceedings: "The images relayed to the nation through television news bulletins and the SABC-TV weekly programme 'TRC Special Report' were probably the single most important factor in achieving a high public profile for the Commission."[30]

TRC Special Report, which was created by a team of journalists with extensive experience covering during the apartheid years many of the prominent stories featured at the TRC, provided a level of contextualization and analysis that far surpassed most journalistic coverage of the TRC. In its first year, *Special Report* achieved an estimated viewership of 1.2 million people weekly.[31] The program eventually topped TV ratings across all channels, surpassing even the obsessively watched soap opera *The Bold and the Beautiful*.[32] For its quality, *Special Report* garnered critical acclaim: a Pringle Award and the Foreign Correspondent Association's 1996 Award for Outstanding Journalism.

As Dayan and Katz argue of all media events, television coverage of the commission compensated viewers for what they were missing in person by giving them an experience that they *could not* have had in person: close-ups, contexts, intercutting of perspectives, and editorial commentary.[33] As is true of many of the media events studied by Dayan and Katz, television coverage of the TRC played an ambiguous role as witness, performer, and surrogate of the truth commission—a position that, I argue, the entire commission cast anyone who came within its orbit. There was no place outside the commission: once you had witnessed it, you were implicated, like it or not. In the way of all media events, *TRC Special Report* walked a fine line between journalism and participation, between reporting the event and actively propagating it (78–118). An episode shown in May 1997 ended by telling viewers that if they were considering applying for amnesty, "here are the phone numbers. Please don't write to *Special Report*. We are a completely independent agency. We just report on the commission."[34]

Anxious though the producers were to create a distinction between *Special Report* and the truth commission, the conflation of the two in public perception was unavoidable. *TRC Special Report* performed an act of surrogation, functioning as a secondary, shadow commission that, similar to the TRC, took statements, conducted investigations, aired confessions (including confessions *not* heard before the TRC), made findings, and even made retractions bordering on apology. The show remunerated viewers for the direct participation of which they were deprived by rather giving them, as its motto claimed, the "stories behind the stories." The substitute offered for "being there" was being in multiple theres across space and time: the producers wove together the "then," as seen in archival footage from the former regime, with the "now" of the TRC hearings and interviews conducted in local communities. It sutured together propaganda from the old apartheid South African Broadcasting Corporation (SABC, which tightly controlled public access to the country's evolving political situation) with a program broadcast by the rehabilitated new SABC, a state media apparatus of the fledgling new South African democracy. Now the SABC was serving, essentially, as a co-producer of the Truth and Reconciliation Commission by transforming it from a localized into a national experience.

In order to provide the context and explanatory narratives so often missing at the public hearings, *Special Report* intercut TRC hearing testimony, which had the potency of embodiment, with other kinds of footage and narratives: the program used voiceovers, freshly commissioned interviews with TRC deponents often shot in their own homes, interviews with bystanders and other witnesses, and location shots where incidents narrated before the commission had happened. The rigorously edited episodes mixed the formality of TRC testimony given in public spaces, such as churches, schools, and government buildings, with the intimacy of interviews conducted in kitchens and living rooms, or at the gravesites where loved ones had been buried, or at the places where those same loved ones had been tortured and killed. *Special Report* had a highly ambiguous role: it had to maintain separation from the commission in order to ensure journalistic objectivity, and yet it was also a performer, participant, and, indeed, documenter of the commission as it unfolded in time.

The Truth and Reconciliation Commission had an independent investigative team that worked behind the scenes before and after public hearings in order to uncover documents, verify statements, and corroborate evidence. The television program *Special Report* was also immersed in investigative processes, and key members of its staff (Du Preez and Jacques Pauw, in particular) had made their careers as hard-bitten investigative journalists during the apartheid years. So when *Special Report* began covering the TRC, its journalists sometimes rivaled and shadowed the commission's investigators, conducting independent, parallel investigations into cases that were being researched, or cases that were *not* being investigated (but which *Special Report* felt were being erroneously overlooked), or cases that were not being investigated properly, in the opinion of the journalists.

Sometimes the journalist's findings, when broadcast on television, had dramatic implications for the Truth Commission. For instance, the very first episode of *Special Report*, which aired on April 21, 1996, broadcast an exclusive interview with Joe Mamasela, the notorious black policeman who had worked undercover with the clandestine enterprise Vlakplass to entrap, torture, and kill many anti-apartheid activists. The segment on Mamasela, shot in a tight close-up (so close that one can rarely see Mamasela's full face), aired directly after *Special Report*'s inaugural images of the first TRC hearings, which had begun that week. The TRC's Human Rights Violation Committee had heard testimony by "victims" in a particularly famous case known as the "Pepco Three," a case long haunted by unanswered questions. What *Special Report* promised these families was something that surpassed what the TRC could at that point deliver: answers. "Tonight we *will* give the Pepco families some answers," says Pauw, the producer of this segment. Mamasela's testimony on *Special Report* had implications for the TRC, for it placed certain knowledge in the public record, information that the TRC could not ignore. Many confessions and revelations followed in the wake of Mamasela's exclusive testimony on *Special Report*, and footage from this single interview was woven consistently into subsequent episodes throughout the two-year life of the program.

Special Report thus functioned at times as a shadow commission, a surrogate truth-seeking and truth-exposing entity, one that made its own findings and revelations. *Special Report* also took a leadership role in educating the public about the TRC process, how it was organized, what the mandate of the commission entailed, and how individuals could come forward to participate in the process.[35] And while it transmitted each Sunday what it considered the key TRC stories from the previous week, *Special Report* was not merely a mouthpiece for the commission. Its journalists were also critical of the commission, even publishing chastisements of what it considered the commission's excesses or failures. When HRV Committee member Pumla Gobodo-Madikizela behaved in a publicly censorious way at a special hearing held on an incident known as the Bisho Massacre, Du Preez rebuked her on that week's *Special Report*:

> We think it is legitimate to ask the truth commissioners tonight, Is it your role to force suspected bad guys to eat humble pie, to humiliate them in public? Is it not more important to elicit the truth than to try and force people to say how sorry they are? Commissioners should be very careful not to undermine the credibility of the TRC especially to IFP, NP and FF [key political parties] who already call the TRC a witch hunt. But those are our feelings and opinions. Let's get back to the program.[36]

Special Report simultaneously promoted the TRC process, conducted its own parallel investigative processes, and actively criticized the commission. *Special Report* was an active performer and mediator of testimony, an entity that was both bystander and active participant in the process, a difficult position but one that perhaps anyone who came within the TRC's orbit was forced to occupy.

If one compares the complete daily footage from the hearings (which could total from ten to twenty-five hours) with *Special Report*'s weekly one-hour digest, one is first struck by how little actual hearing footage is used. Since *Special Report* specialized in providing "the stories behind the stories," each of the several segments that made up any one program devoted much footage to contextual interviews, location shots showing where past events narrated before the commission (killings, abductions, torture, discovery of dead bodies, etc.) had transpired or the larger local context for the story, archival footage, and commentary by the segment's producer. Having watched all 87 episodes of *Special Report*, I would estimate that, for any typical segment, less than 20 percent of the footage comes from the actual hearing. Yet I would also assert that *how* the program incorporated that hearing footage is of paramount importance to our interpretation of this show. Interestingly, *Special Report* rarely showed commissioners listening to testimony. If you watch the original footage, you see a fair amount of intercutting between the witness giving testimony and the commissioners listening. Often witnesses and commissioners were placed at tables directly facing each other, so even the physical staging of the live event suggested that the primary "drama" of the hearings was between these two constituencies, with the larger audience in the hall being cast as passive spectators. Only occasionally in the rushes (comprised of the live edit conducted on site) does one see cutaways to the audience. But *Special Report* rarely broadcast footage of commissioners speaking or listening. Instead the program made witnesses and the audience central to their coverage of the hearings. Images of witnesses were intercut with shots of "ordinary" people who had come to listen in the hall. Sometimes we saw long shots from the back of the house, but often cutaways were of unidentified individuals listening, perhaps with chin in palm, or wiping a tear from the eye, or conferring with a neighbor, or gesticulating in reaction to the testimony. Through this method of editing, *Special Report* portrayed TRC hearings as a storytelling experience aimed primarily at the public—not the commission.

In this regard, *Special Report*'s tone, style, and mode of address *implicated* its audience, both the live audience and the television audience. Witnesses came before the commission to say what they had heard and seen. Through the media event of the TRC, especially via television, the country was called upon to become a secondary witness. Television demonstrated the implications of witnessing by itself serving as exemplary witness: what the cameras "saw" they turned around and *testified* about by broadcasting the story, transmitting it to others. Like a chorus in an ancient Greek play, *Special Report* was simultaneously witness, narrator, and commentator on the action, giving editorial opinions and interpretations, shaping our experience and guiding our focus. Occasionally television even intervened in the action. But above all, television cast the general public—not the state or a state-appointed commission—as the key recipient of the unfolding process of the Truth and Reconciliation Commission.

Thus, while *Special Report* amplified the commission's reach exponentially and served as a goad, I would argue that *Special Report*'s most notable transformation of the TRC process was its repositioning of the audience. Through *TRC Special Report* the primary audience became not the commissioners, to whom most testimony was directed, but rather the public—the public assembled in the hall, and, by extension, the public assembled around radios and televisions throughout the nation.

Special Report executive producer Du Preez contends that witnesses themselves interacted with the camera in a way that indicated they were well aware of the role of the camera as audience, or surrogate audience, for their testimony. Recalling his years as executive producer of the program,

Du Preez notes, "I had this strong perception that the cameras were seen as the ear of the nation," a statement that oddly conflates cameras with hearing. "The ear, not the eye?" I asked during our interview, to which he responded, "The ear and the eye."[37] Through the cameras, witnesses could be both seen and heard. Those who gave testimony used the cameras to imagine particular audiences. According to Du Preez, witnesses often told him they knew they were speaking to the "whole nation" through his cameras. Simultaneously, they were also speaking to very specific imagined audiences though. Perpetrators, for instance, "addressed their peers and their families through the cameras," according to Du Preez (ibid.).

For some of those who testified at the HRV hearings, the cameras may have been more about what the witnesses received *from* the cameras than what the cameras conveyed to a particular audience. So-called victims may have told their stories before, but to family members, furtively, in private. If they told their stories to the police or to other public entities, they were often not believed. But here in the public TRC hearings, they could speak openly, freely, uninterrupted for thirty minutes, and they were speaking not just to family or community members, or to a small group of government officials, but to the entire nation. As they gave their stories to the camera, *the camera gave them recognition.* As Du Preez explains, under apartheid these stories "couldn't be told publicly because of fear. You don't stir up more [trouble] if you're already in trouble. And the government made them out to be liars, or said, 'You deserved it [whatever bad thing happened] because you are an enemy of the state.' And for the first time now they could come again and tell the story, but not only to their closest friends, but to everybody. And that was justice. That was recognition—because of the cameras" (ibid.). Those who came before the TRC seemed to be aware of the cameras and their potency for communicating to a larger world. "Even traditional people from deep rural areas who have never seen a television camera before knew" what the camera was and what it meant, says Du Preez. But he is quick to add that witnesses before the TRC did not act as politicians, who often search for and look directly into the camera to establish the feeling of eye contact with the viewer. "You never saw that," says Du Preez, "never once" (ibid.). The cameras were witnesses. They gave recognition to victims while at the same time reproducing the images and sounds of the commission to larger audiences, imagined as both an anonymous entity, the "nation," and as specific individuals implicated in the story being told. The cameras helped shape, create, and define the commission's audience.

The recognition the cameras conferred was not limited just to "victim" testimony before the HRV hearings. Perpetrators appearing before the Amnesty committee also got their moment in the full glare of the television cameras' attention, and with this constituency as well *Special Report* often edited stories in such a way as to suggest that the real drama of the event transpired not between witness and commissioner, but rather between perpetrator and specific (though unidentified) spectators in the hall. To give just one example, warrant officer Hendrick Steyn was featured in the September 1, 1996 episode giving testimony before the Amnesty committee in Durban. A white Afrikaner police officer serving a 19 year prison term for illegally killing suspects during a police action, Steyn's testimony is remarkable: it is one of the few occasions when a white perpetrator appearing before the TRC actually apologized in public and expressed remorse. While popular belief sometimes erroneously attributes apology as part of the TRC's mandate, it was not. And if one does word searches on the thousands of pages of TRC testimony transcripts for words like "forgive," "sorry," and "apologize," one finds them appearing repeatedly in HRV hearings as victims were asked if they might be prepared to forgive perpetrators, and yet such words hardly ever appear in Amnesty hearing testimony. *Special Report*'s five-minute segment on Hendrick Steyn (which begins 27 minutes into the program) included extensive footage of Steyn giving testimony before the TRC. At first this is intercut with archival footage of the aftermath of the police raid during which Steyn perpetrated the murders. But halfway through his testimony, just as Steyn begins to describe in detail the actual killing, the editors of *Special Report* cut away not to commissioners, but to the audience. A very small crowd was assembled in a largely empty hall that day, the last day of Amnesty hearings in Durban, but once the camera has established this low attendance, it focuses in on two black male spectators, then an elderly black couple (perhaps the parents of one of the deceased?), then a single man listening intently using the TRC's language interpretation equipment. They witness and watch as Steyn utters words so rarely heard at Amnesty proceedings: "I am very sorry about the incident ... I don't want to condone what I've done ... I have remorse about the fact that I ever chose the police as a career and I ever became so involved in the political struggle because in the end it wasn't worth it." Steyn apologizes, says he is sorry about the suffering he has caused, that his actions are a disgrace. The *Special Report* editors cut back and forth between Steyn and his audience: a forlorn looking white couple, three men (two black and one Indian) in police uniforms watching a fellow police officer confess. We never see the commissioners at all. The entirety of Steyn's testimony was scripted and he read it out, face buried in his pages of Afrikaans, as an unseen female voice translated his words into English, but he eventually looks straight ahead as he apologizes. While the footage never conveys the exact layout of the room, it is quite possible based on the customary arrangement of the hall for TRC hearings that when Steyn looked up and ahead, he was looking at the judges who presided over his Amnesty hearing. Yet we never see them. *Special Report*'s editing constructs the testimony as an utterance whose audience is the public—those in the hall and those watching *Special Report* from home. "We" are the focus of this speech act, and our response, like Steyn's speech, is being watched by everyone.

While *TRC Special Report* struggled to maintain critical distance from the TRC, a perspective it needed for journalistic credibility, the program's status was inevitably liminal and conflicted. This conflict, I argue, is one of performative witnessing, and it was a conflict all participants in the TRC process faced. The hearings were performances predicated on the foundational notion of *ubuntu*, a Zulu philosophical principle that translates as "a person is a person through other people." To experience the public, embodied, human dimensions of the TRC—either theatrically by attending hearings in person or by watching or listening to their broadcast via television or radio—was to be a participant in the process. There was no place outside the event: to witness was to perform, to be implicated in the event and its ramifications. The media coverage of South Africa's Truth and Reconciliation Commission implicated its viewers in a way that print journalism and the publication of the summary report never would have: the report's style was not particularly inviting to a general reader; the report favored quantitative assessments of patterns of violence over a more humanistic, qualitative analysis of the content, style, and meaning of testimony. The report also favored findings and concrete results: by the report's conclusion, witnesses were granted the status of "victim," and hence were entitled to reparations, should there be any. The report quantified patterns of violence, such as how many deaths from police torture happened in one region or another, or in certain decades. But what one finds very little of in the TRC's summary report, despite its sprawling length, is qualitative analysis of testimony that captures the performative richness of that testimony. Nor does one find a rendering of the TRC as an ongoing, multi-year *process* in which the entire nation engaged.

The TRC testimonies captured on video and then broadcast in excerpted form on the Sunday program *Special Report* were indeed "moving," in as much as many found them emotionally compelling. But more importantly this televised testimony was spatially mobile, carrying the embodied life of the commission on a human scale across geographic distances, from Kimberly to Durban, from Port Elizabeth to Gautang. Videotaped TRC testimony also moves the embodied life of the commission across time, for it is now one of the only records of the commission that documents the complexity of what transpired in the TRC's public hearings. The visual archive of the TRC is large, neglected, and, I would contend, absolutely central to any appraisal of what the commission might have meant to a larger public in the late 1990s in post-apartheid South Africa.

acknowledgments

I am deeply indebted to the many individuals in South Africa who granted interviews and helped me gain access to archival materials. For their generous funding of the project, I am indebted to the National Humanities Center (Hurford Fellowship), the National Endowment for the Humanities, the University of California Regents Humanities Fellowship, and University of California, Santa Barbara's Interdisciplinary Humanities Center and Academic Senate. The final phases of the chapter received financial support from the University of California, Berkeley, my new academic home.

notes

1. Yasmin Sooka, interview with the author, Pretoria, 26 July 2006.
2. Max du Preez, interview with the author, Napier, Western Cape, 18 December 2006.
3. Stephen Landsman, "Those Who Remember the Past May Not Be Condemned to Repeat It," *Michigan Law Review* 100, no. 6 (2002): 1589.
4. Priscilla Hayner, *Unspeakable Truths: Confronting State Terror and Atrocity* (New York: Routledge, 2001), 305–19.
5. See Charles Villa-Vicencio and Erik Doxtader, *The Provocations of Amnesty: Memory, Justice, and Impunity* (Trenton, NJ: Africa World Press, 2003).
6. Truth and Reconciliation Commission, *Truth and Reconciliation Commission of South Africa Report*, vols. 1–5 (Cape Town: Truth and Reconciliation Commission, 1998); Truth and Reconciliation Commission, *Truth and Reconciliation Commission of South Africa Report*, vols. 6–7 (Cape Town: Truth and Reconciliation Commission, 2003).
7. Daniel Dayan and Elihu Katz, *Media Events: The Live Broadcasting of History* (Cambridge: Cambridge University Press, 1992), 1.
8. Albie Sachs, interview with the author, Johannesburg, 29 June 2007.
9. Catherine M. Cole, *Performing South Africa's Truth Commission: Stages of Transition* (Bloomington: Indiana University Press, forthcoming 2009). While the current chapter was written expressly for this volume, many ideas and some sentences were drawn from passages throughout my forthcoming monograph.
10. Dayan and Katz, *Media Events*, 118.
11. Philip Auslander, *Liveness: Performance as Mediatized Culture* (New York: Routledge, 1999), 128–9.
12. Jonas Barish, *The Antitheatrical Prejudice* (Berkeley: University of California Press, 1981).
13. See Marie-Bénédicte Dembour and Emily Haslam, "Silencing Hearings? Victim-Witnesses at War Crimes Trials," *European Journal of International Law* 15, no. 1 (2004): 151–77. See also Peter Brooks and Paul Gerwitz, eds., *Law's Stories: Narrative and Rhetoric in the Law* (New Haven, CT: Yale University Press, 1996). The term "victim" to connote those who appeared before the South African truth commission to testify about violations of human rights they experienced or witnessed was a contested word, for it did not highlight the agency and resistance that the alternate word "survivor" suggests. But for a host of reasons, including the language of the law that authored the commission, the word "victim" was widely adopted by the TRC. See also Shoshana Felman, *The Juridical Unconscious: Trials and Traumas in the Twentieth Century* (Cambridge, MA: Harvard University Press, 2002); Judith Lewis Herman, *Trauma and Recovery: The Aftermath of Violence—From Domestic Abuse to Political Terror* (New York: Basic Books, 1997); Shoshana Felman and

Dori Laub, eds., *Testimony: Crises of Witnessing in Literature, Psychoanalysis, and History* (New York: Routledge, 1991).

14. J.L. Austin, *How to Do Things with Words*, 2nd edition (Cambridge, MA: Harvard University Press, 1975). While in theory those not granted amnesty by the TRC were liable to future prosecution, in actuality there have been very few prosecutions in the wake of the commission. Much of this is due to lack of "capacity," that is, the fiscal ability to pursue such litigation. There have been a few notable exceptions, though these have tended to be about high profile cases.
15. The status of the TRC archive is fraught and contested, for reasons too complicated to detail here. Suffice it to say that the TRC archive was *intended* to be publicly accessible, and national acts promoting freedom of access to information would suggest that this archive *is* accessible. Yet, in reality the majority of the TRC archive is *de facto* inaccessible to researchers, and even to those who gave testimony before the commission. However, the video and audio portions of the TRC archive are fully accessible, vast in scope, and grossly underutilized. Hardly any researchers are using this valuable resource at all. The only study to date to have made extensive use of this video collection is Anne Fleckstein, "Performing Truth: Performative Aspekte der öffentlichen Anhörungen der Wahrheitskommission in Südafrika" (masters thesis, Humboldt-University of Berlin, 2006).
16. See www.law.yale.edu/trc/index.htm (accessed 1 November 2008). Note that some episodes are missing, and not all of the cataloguing is accurate. But this is nevertheless an enormously valuable online collection.
17. Richard Wilson, *The Politics of Truth and Reconciliation in South Africa: Legitimizing the Post-apartheid State* (Cambridge: Cambridge University Press, 2001).
18. Sooka, interview.
19. The bibliography on South Africa's TRC is extensive. For an overview, see the following review essays: Olayiwola Abegunrin, "Truth and Reconciliation," *African Studies Review* 45, no. 3 (2002): 31–4; Richard Dale, "The Politics of the Rainbow Nation: Truth, Legitimacy, and Memory in South Africa," *African Studies Review* 45, no. 3 (2002): 39–44. Key secondary sources include: Kader Asmal, Louise Asmal, and Ronald Suresh Roberts, *Reconciliation through Truth: A Reckoning of Apartheid's Criminal Governance* (Cape Town: David Philip Publishers, in association with Mayibue Books, University of the Western Cape, 1996); Wilmot Godfrey James and Linda van de Vijver, eds., *After the TRC: Reflections on Truth and Reconciliation in South Africa* (Athens: Ohio University Press, 2001); Deborah Posel and Graeme Simpson, eds., *Commissioning the Past: Understanding South Africa's Truth and Reconciliation Commission* (Johannesburg: Witwatersrand University Press, 2002); Fiona C. Ross, *Bearing Witness: Women and the Truth and Reconciliation Commission in South Africa* (Sterling, VA: Pluto Press, 2003); Mark Sanders, *Ambiguities of Witnessing: Law and Literature in the Time of a Truth Commission* (Palo Alto, CA: Stanford University Press, 2007); Charles Villa-Vicencio and Wilhelm Verwoerd, *Looking Back, Reaching Forward: Reflections on the Truth and Reconciliation Commission of South Africa* (New York: St. Martin's Press, 2000); Charles Villa-Vicencio and Erik Doxtader, *The Provocations of Amnesty*; Wilson, *The Politics of Truth and Reconciliation in South Africa.*
20. Wendy Orr, *From Biko to Basson: Wendy Orr's Search for the Soul of South Africa as a Commissioner of the TRC* (Saxonwold, South Africa: Contra Press, 2000), 90–1.

21. Truth and Reconciliation Commission, *Truth and Reconciliation Commission of South Africa Report*, vol. 6 (Cape Town: Truth and Reconciliation Commission, 2003), 30.
22. *TRC Special Report*, episode 15, 18 August 1996. Note: the episode numbers listed here correspond with the Yale digitized collection of this series available online. However, the Yale numbering is not entirely reliable; Yale does not have a complete collection, for they are missing episodes. Furthermore the digital links do not always correspond with the correct episode; hence when viewing links online with Realplayer or similar software, users should confirm that the date scrolling at the bottom of the screen corresponds with the date chosen from the summary listing. Finally, some episodes are wrongly catalogued altogether. However, to the best of my ability, I have tried to ease user access to the online collection by following Yale's current episode numbering.
23. Landsman, "Those Who Remember," 1571.
24. Hannah Arendt, *Eichmann in Jerusalem: A Report on the Banality of Evil* (New York: Penguin Books, 1963), 253.
25. Martha Minow, *Between Vengeance and Forgiveness: Facing History after Genocide and Mass Violence* (Boston: Beacon Press, 1998), 47.
26. The scholar Annelies Verdoolaege has made the most extensive analysis of *Special Report* to date, but her work examines just 34 of 87 episodes, or roughly 39 percent of the series. See Annelies Verdoolaege, "Reconciliation. The South African Truth and Reconciliation Commission: Deconstruction of a Multilayered Archive" (PhD thesis, Universiteit Gent, Belgium, 2005); Annelies Verdoolaege, "Media Representations of the South African Truth and Reconciliation Commission and their Commitment to Reconciliation," *Journal of African Cultural Studies* 17, no. 2 (2005): 181–99.
27. Truth and Reconciliation Commission, *Truth and Reconciliation Commission of South Africa Report*, vol. 1, 357.
28. See Truth and Reconciliation Commission, *Truth and Reconciliation Commission of South Africa Report*, vol. 1, 356. The following radio programs carried weekly TRC programs: Lasedi (seSotho) on Sunday evenings, SA FM on Friday mornings, Ukhozi (isiZulu), Umhlobo Wenene (isiXhosa), Thobela (Sipedi), Ikwekwezi (Ndebele), Motsweding (Setswana), Munghana Lonene (xiTsonga), and Ligwalagwala (Siswati) on Friday evenings, and Radio Sonder Grense (Afrikaans) on Monday mornings. These programs are mentioned at the end of the *TRC Special Report* program broadcast on 19 October 1997.
29. Orr, *From Biko to Basson*, 90–1.
30. Truth and Reconciliation Commission, *South Africa Report*, vol. 1, 358.
31. Max du Preez, "When Cowboys Cry," *Rhodes Journalism Review*, special edition: The Media and the TRC (1997), available at www.rjr.ru.ac.za/no14.html (accessed 4 August 2004).
32. Verdoolaege, "Media Representations," 191. See also Zubeida Jaffer and Karin Cronjé, *Cameras, Microphones and Pens* (Cape Town: Institute for Justice and Reconciliation, 2004).
33. Dayan and Katz, *Media Events*.
34. *TRC Special Report*, episode 46, 4 May 1997.
35. See *TRC Special Report*, episode 1, 21 April 1996, and episode 5, 26 May.
36. *TRC Special Report*, episode 29, 24 November 1996.
37. Du Preez, interview.

mediating genocide

producing digital survivor testimony in rwanda

nine

mick broderick

Films should haunt the soul and inspire new hope

Gilbert Ndahayo, 2007

People are still hurting. When someone tells you that they have been unhappy for ten years, they mean it. Ten years later, life is still tough and it is still too soon

Yves Kamuronsi, 2004

The genocide that caused approximately one million deaths in Rwanda in 1994 was aided and abetted by media and cultural representations, compelling the Hutu majority to demonize and dehumanize the Tutsi minority as loathsome "cockroaches" requiring extermination.[1] In 100 days from April to July 2004, between 800,000 and a million Tutsi and moderate Hutu were slain by extremist Hutu. The legacy and historical antecedents of this national barbarism are profound and complex. Resentment against the Tutsi, promoted by the Belgian colonialists as a superior caste, simmered for decades and informed earlier attempts by Hutu at ethnic cleansing (forced expulsions to tsetse fly-infected marshlands) in the late 1950s and other periodic pogroms in Rwanda's regional areas.[2]

At the time of writing, the annual April remembrance commemorations in Kigali and elsewhere across Rwanda have been marred by several murders (a grenade and machete attack and a deliberate "hit and run") at, or near, a number of genocide memorial sites.[3] That the previous genocidal ideology is reappearing across the nation is alarming. Equally troubling is the small but growing number of genocide deniers, mostly expatriate Rwandans in neighboring African states, or in Europe and America, and the controversial Francophone authors who were forced to cancel an academic conference in Montreal as a result of the backlash against their publicly articulated skepticism toward the genocide.[4]

Indeed, prior to the recent violence, several commentators have expressed concern over influential figures residing outside the country who are inflaming tensions, such as Paul Rusesabagina, the person who inspired the film *Hotel Rwanda* (dir. Terry George, UK/US/Italy/South Africa, 2004) and is the recipient of multiple international human rights awards, including the US Freedom Medal from President George W. Bush.[5] Irrespective of Rusesabagina's past actions, the film's hero in real life is "linked to extremist elements dedicated to the violent overthrow of the

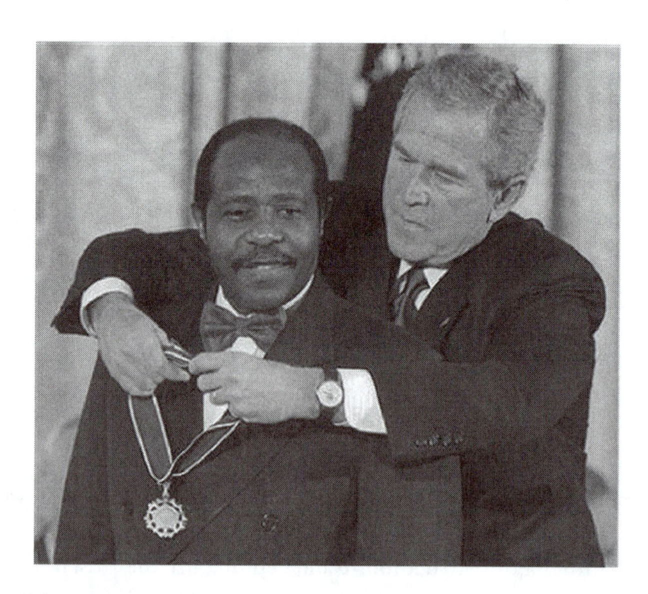

Figure 9.1

President George W. Bush awards Paul Rusesabagina with the US Freedom Medal, November 2005

Rwandan government," according to William Church, the director of the Great Lakes Centre for Strategic Studies.[6]

Based on field research conducted in Rwanda during 2007, this chapter suggests that a number of grassroots Rwandese digital media initiatives, eschewing Hollywood-style cathartic drama/horror, are aimed at ameliorating the absence of local and parochial (self-)expression. Whereas these Hollywood genres generally reconcile their screen traumas by violent reprisal and punishment, where evil is destroyed, African folkloric narrative articulates reconciliation and coexistence while foregrounding the process of attaining knowledge and wisdom.[7] Technological leapfrogging via regional Internet access, GPS, mobile telephony, and portable media technology is enabling new modes of communication between the Rwandese and the global community.[8] Cheap and portable digital cameras and computer-editing software are providing survivor groups, community organizations, and commemorative centers such as Ibuka, the Kigali Memorial Centre, and the SURF Humura Centre in Kamonyi with the capacity to record testimony and evidence at local judicial tribunals (gacaca), as well as to fashion short narrative dramas, documentaries, and recorded performances for local and international distribution (on DVD and online).

However, this chapter recognizes that while such technological capacities provide opportunities, they also raise a number of dilemmas for the critical evaluation of these projects and their production output. For example, the proliferation of Rwandan genocide narratives might best be approached by recognizing the problematic "situatedness" of their construction and delivery. The institutional contexts of their preservation or promulgation, as well as the fundamental desire of survivors and victims to self-preserve and self-present their own experience, need consideration.

Rwandan digital testimony, with its dramatic narrativization and its circulation, draws from a number of indigenous traditions, such as folkloric and poetic storytelling.[9] But as the emerging talents of Rwandan new media establish reputations overseas, might this success translate into an exilic or diasporic "accented" media (as Hamid Naficy might have it) that bypasses notions of National Cinema and Third Cinema? Also, how might the globalized circulation of user-created content across social networks, as opposed to highly integrated mechanisms of distribution and exhibition, serve to ameliorate the tragedies of mass human suffering?[10] And what of Rwandan media producers eschewing stories of genocide and survival to pursue international careers in Hollywood? What is their perceived cultural legacy and moral burden?

rwandan film

In the lead-up to the tenth anniversary of the genocide a number of Western filmmakers and documentarians eventually turned their attention to the

Rwandan catastrophe and, to a lesser degree, its legacy. Following the impasse on distributing the first feature film concerning the genocide shot in Rwanda, *100 Days* (dir. Nick Hughes, UK/Rwanda, 2001), the initial cinematic response, *Hotel Rwanda*, gained three Academy Award nominations, including one for its co-producing star Don Cheadle. However, the movie created significant agitation amongst the survivor NGOs in Rwanda, especially Ibuka, the peak agency representing the myriad genocide survivor groups around the country, as well as the international (mostly Tutsi) Rwandan diaspora.[11] The discontent was threefold. Firstly, and commonly, the historical plotting and characterizations were presented via the conventions of Hollywood narrative truncation and distortion in order to convey the events as entertainment for a mass audience, to satisfy the domestic US box office before an international release.[12] Secondly, the heroic elevation of Rusesabagina, the Hutu manager of the Hotel Mille Collines in Kigali who saved hundreds of lives, ostensibly by "his resourceful use of contacts in the regime, money and alcohol," was strongly contested and seemingly discredited by multiple survivor-witnesses.[13] If nothing else, as Darryl Li has commented, this "bourgeois" hotel manager's "resistance of the genocide on its own terms and from within its own structures required a degree of trust in the system itself and in his ability to manipulate it."[14] Thirdly, the film was shot outside of Rwanda in South Africa with a foreign cast and crew. Little economic benefit flowed back to Rwanda, let alone the genocide survivors, from the expenditure on a major international film production. So aggrieved was Ibuka that they mandated a protocol for filmmakers to comply with when the Rwandan government negotiated offshore productions in the country on genocide topics.[15]

The few mainstream Western attempts to mediate this mass trauma and horror adopt conventions of feature-length narrative docudrama (e.g., *Hotel Rwanda*, *100 Days*, *Sometimes in April* [dir. Raoul Peck, France/US/Rwanda, 2005], *Shooting Dogs* [dir. Michael Caton-Jones, UK/Germany, 2005]). Other transient international visitors produce often powerful but conventional generic documentary works for a global or transnational television market (e.g., *Shake Hands with the Devil* [dir. Roger Spottiswoode, Canada, 2007]), not a domestic Rwandan audience.[16] As the entrepreneurial director of the Rwandan Film Centre, Eric Kabera asserts the pattern for most international filmmaking in Rwanda is: "People come. They shoot, they go."[17]

Yet the principal cultural modes of representation in Rwanda remain traditional—music, dance/performance, and fine arts. It is somewhat ironic that the French and Belgian colonialists failed to instill a culture of cinema-going and its craft/praxis and as a result generations of Rwandese have grown up with poor electronic media literacy, apart from state-run television and radio—both of which were implicated in the genocidal propaganda of the early to mid-1990s.[18] Unlike the French cinema projects in former African colonies that consistently generated a diverse range of (often auteurist) films from the 1960s to the 1980s, it remains curious as to why Rwanda was not assisted by the French Ministry of Cooperation in this regard.[19] Similarly, the political pan-African cinema movement and emergence of various national and transnational African film organizations during the same period operated chiefly outside of Rwanda's creative orbit and its postcolonial, politico-cultural consciousness.[20]

Today it is still a surprising aspect of Rwandan life that a country of nearly eight million people does not have a single, purpose-built cinema. However, a small band of dedicated locals and émigrés have been engaging with the community to challenge this paradigm and a 300-seat auditorium is currently under construction in Kigali's new 2020 Estate. Rwandan filmmaker-entrepreneur Eric Kabera is one such advocate of film culture. Although he spent most of his life in exile in eastern Zaire, Kabera is best known for developing "Hillywood," the annual Rwandan Film Festival that has been operating since 2005. After working as a "fixer" for foreign journalists in the 1990s, Kabera acted as producer for British filmmaker Nick Hughes on his feature *100 Days*, a project that struggled to get broad release for four years.[21] Kabera is as much involved in digital media production training and touring films as he is in producing his own projects. Using an inflatable screen to travel into the rural townships, Kabera has taken a band of emerging filmmakers' works to a cine-illiterate populace, attracting remarkably large audiences. This cultural out-reach and screen promulgation is crucial for Rwanda's future viability, according to Kabera: "One of the catalysts for the genocide was that people had no idea what life was like outside their own village ... We were too insular."[22]

With limited equipment and funds Kabera has also been successful in helping mentor a number of young Rwandans, occasionally relying on visiting international "guerrilla" filmmakers from Europe and the US, such as Lee Isaac Chung, to train these aspirational auteurs.[23] Many productions have now been shown at multiple overseas film festivals. Despite the exposure, Kabera has found that along with international success comes the inevitable industry typecasting: "These films are sending a message about Rwanda, so at least people know where we are from, but it means that everybody ... sees the genocide and nothing else."[24] Kabera and his cohort of filmmakers want to "present a new face of Rwanda" by creating alternative projects, such as a romantic comedy, but potential investors have been dubious, failing to equate "Rwanda" with the comic genre.

Cameroon-born filmmaker François Woukouache operates a small digital media production house, Kemit, established in 2001, which he runs from a converted warehouse in Kigali. Woukouache is an African pioneer in community media training, working principally in the Great Lakes region. Like Kabera, he has deployed his filmmaking skills collaboratively both to train locals as well as to instill a *cineaste* culture among the population. With sparse resources at his disposal Kemit has worked with the European Union in developing a local appreciation of cinema and documentary form and history.

According to Woukouache, the role of Kemit is

> ensuring the emergence of a new generation of film-makers who are aware of the need to become involved in thinking about the big issues in their countries and who have the technical and artistic means at their disposal to show these realities through the cinematic medium. There is a fundamental difference between making a film and creating cinema: creating cinema means constructing a viewpoint, articulating a vision of the world.[25]

Woukouache raises community consciousness regarding genocide and trauma through participatory digital video and public testimony, as well as recording artistic responses, especially Rwandan song and dance. Through Kemit, Woukouache works with primary and secondary schools and tours film programs to provinces outside of Kigali, such as Butare and Nyamata, which bore much of the brunt of the genocidaires' wrath. During 2003 and 2004, touring Kemit productions reached thousands of patrons—no small feat considering the general ambivalence toward cinema amongst a largely illiterate populace. Recent films by Woukouache and his collaborators include the documentary *Humura* (Rwanda, 2005), which showcases the performance "Yrio Nabonye" by fifteen Rwandan and Congolese artists at the Rwandan University Centre for the Arts, and *Testimony of Astérie, Genocide Survivor* (Rwanda, 2005), where the octogenarian Astérie recounts the painful memory of escaping blows from machetes and militiamen killing his family. Like Kabera, Woukouache recognizes the importance of local knowledge and capacity building, and Kemit helps young Rwandans to craft indigenous projects that "draw on their sources of inspiration in the culture, memory and experience of the people, as no film industry has developed anywhere in the world without a solid foundation in its home territory, among its own people."[26]

In the end Woukouache's desire for a sustainable local media industry infrastructure in Rwanda may be overtaken by rapid developments in, and the ubiquitous roll-out of, portable media technologies and broadband capacity. Similarly, Kemit's grassroots training and education may need to bypass current DV recorders and computer editing and move toward mobile content capture and uploading to blogs and social networks in order to work in tandem with public health educators and transnational telcos.[27] These transitions occur with such speed and with so little lag between First and Third World that even relatively recent critical observations about "first" cinema expression in Africa via the "video boom" and "video revolution" may seem *passé* for the online generation of media makers.[28]

trauma, memory, and testimony

The ascendancy of trauma studies from the early 1990s within the humanities was coeval with the constellation of a number of discrete, yet interrelated historical events and movements. These included the catastrophic war in the Balkans and renewed "ethnic cleansing," the Rwandan genocide, debates surrounding "recovered/false memory," and the fiftieth anniversary celebrations of the Allied victories in Europe and Japan. These wartime commemorations saw corresponding controversies over the unfinished business of reparations for the Shoah and how to represent the atomic bombings of Hiroshima and Nagasaki, with the latter evident in a number of museum exhibitions as well as mainstream and independent film productions.

As Susannah Radstone has indicated, the literature evaluating and critiquing artistic modes of expression and representation of "trauma" is relatively new within the humanities but, after more than two decades of investigation, is now burgeoning and promoting certain orthodoxies in methodology and assumptions.[29] It conforms to what Andreas Huyssen has elsewhere described as a "memory boom of unprecedented proportions."[30] As a neophyte discipline, trauma studies draws from, overlaps with, and informs a range of pre-existing, tangential, and emerging loci of inquiry, including Holocaust studies, memory work, testimony, and genocide studies. Yet many of these domains share certain fundamentals, such as the primacy of witnessing, remembering, articulating, and representing the traumatic experiences and affects of mass and individual human suffering.

Critical theory on trauma incessantly returns to Freud, who associated traumatic neurosis with both an external event and an intrapsychic conflict.[31] Importantly for Freud, according to Cathy Caruth, that which "returns to haunt the victim ... is not only the reality of the violent event but also the reality of the way the violence has not been fully known."[32] This is certainly apposite for Rwandan genocide survivors, as either child-witnesses who were too emotionally immature in 1994 or as adults grappling with fragments of memories and histories who desire narrative reconstruction, resolution, and reconciliation. But unlike the unexpected shock of an accident informing Freud's paradigmatic clinical studies, the violence of genocide is not unplanned, or random, or contingent upon chance. Just as the context and impact of "battle fatigue," "shell shock," and modern "post-traumatic stress disorder" informing (post)Freudian concepts of trauma vary depending on the individual and social experience, so too the annihilating ideologies perpetrated against (and by) civilian populations appear to differ (e.g., the Ottoman "Young Turks" in Armenia, Nazis in Europe, and Khmer Rouge in Cambodia). Genocide is deliberate, organized, systematic, and executed on a scale of mass human suffering only surpassed by catastrophic "acts of God" such as the 2006 Boxing Day tsunami.[33] Hence, genocide—its traumatic affect and legacy—requires for survivors a comprehensible (and ideally simple) narrative to explain the unthinkable and the unbearable. To make sense of the (in)human agency responsible for their plight. To know its truth.

The following survivor case studies and their digital media representation practices do not necessarily conform to definitions of "trauma cinema" or concepts of the modern "atomized individual" stripped of historical agency, nor display the binary of "acting out/working through" of trauma.[34] Certainly Rwandan new media producers may offer insights for trauma studies and extend the field beyond some of its current limitations, such as the tendency to locate trauma's genesis in, and homogenize it as, accidental shock. However, it would be critically irresponsible to expect these emerging Rwandan media producers—mostly autodidacts long denied a democratic media culture and largely ignorant of First World media history—to produce nuanced, postmodern filmic works of "disremembering" and to recuperate digital memories that "remain self-critically unsettling," which often draws the critical attention and valorization of Western analysis.[35] The paradigms of Third Cinema consistently demonstrate that those nations and practitioners historically starved of the capacity to produce films "progress" through a staged evolution in competency and aesthetics (while often embracing "revolution"). But such historicism is largely based on Victorian-era technology and early twentieth century industrial modes of national production and consumption.[36]

Furthermore, as Radstone suggests, the political dimension of what receives critical attention in the humanities also needs redressing—why the disproportionate number of volumes published on 9/11 and not "the recent suffering of those in Rwanda"?[37] The cultural specificity of the Rwandan genocide and its local mediation by emerging survivor-practitioners may also contribute new knowledge and inform debates over testimonial practices as well as trauma cinema. For instance, entirely new digital archives will become available, recorded increasingly by survivors themselves and often in situ, for public access. Another aspect somewhat unique to Rwanda is the recording of ongoing community commemorative practices (and the further associated trauma of remembrance and public mourning), recording which is regarded as crucial to national reconciliation and continued genocide prevention. Research and study into how the effects of such new media production and global exposure will manifest amongst survivors, communities, and audiences are a necessary corollary, as is the evaluation of these narratives within educational, archival, and public health domains.

digital testimony case studies in rwanda

yves kamuronsi, digital producer and online archivist, kigali memorial centre

The Kigali Memorial Centre (KMC) sits atop one of the hills surrounding the Kigali township in Gisozi. Purpose-built by the mayor of the capital on land donated by the city, the KMC was commissioned after Rwandan officials visited a Holocaust memorial center in Nottinghamshire in central England, operated by the British not-for-profit Aegis Trust. Opened for the tenth anniversary of the genocide in 2004, the KMC is home to the single, major repository of human remains from the tragedy. Well over 300,000 bodies are interred beneath the compound's Garden of Peace. Adjacent to these concrete crypts is a large but empty Wall of Names, painted black with names in white, that runs at right angles for well over fifty meters. The immensity of the tragedy—where over one quarter of the nation's genocide victims lay quite literally underfoot—is amplified by the bucolic setting, the barrenness of the wall, and the minuscule quantum (less than 1 percent) of names identified for public display.

Within the KMC a team of young genocide survivors act as both tour guides and interpreters, shepherding visitors through the compound and interior displays. Some, like Yves Kamuronsi, are employed to record and archive the history and ongoing testimony of the genocide, or acquire and assemble texts for the library and research center currently under development. Kamuronsi's personal video testimony and that of his KMC peers play continuously inside the interpretation center, where the graphic details of the Rwandan genocide are displayed for locals and international visitors. The KMC guides' testimony is also available anthologized in book form, in a manner similar to that used in the many official commemorative spaces around the world that stand as witness to mass human suffering, torture, and trauma.

Significantly, however, Kamuronsi currently works on a large project collating gacaca records (local truth and reconciliation tribunals), digital video testimony gleaned from door-to-door interviews, and GPS location data to "map" the genocide in an integrated, multilingual (Kinyarwanda, English, and French) archive and online web resource that will soon be accessible to visitors and online browsers from all over the world. This digital repository is a substantial venture for the KMC and for Rwanda. In the fourteen-plus years since the genocide Rwanda has received appreciable foreign aid and infrastructure assistance and the country is changing rapidly as a result. Kamuronsi is keenly aware of the need to record interviews with survivors (in situ, and with the aid of global positioning technologies) as quickly as possible since the topography at the thousands of sites of violence across this small nation is being inexorably altered by roadworks, new buildings, sewers, and electricity towers. Hence, a decade-and-a-half later, the capacity for survivors to recall the details of traumatic events at specific locales is swiftly diminishing.

Yves was thirteen at the time of the genocide, is the second-born son, and has two younger sisters. The following testimony is taken from the digital survivors video at the KMC, expanded as transcribed text in *A Time to Remember: Rwanda, Ten Years after the Genocide*, and a personal interview conducted at the KMC digital archive office in January 2007.[38]

Figure 9.2

Yves Kamuronsi, Director of Documentation, Kigali Memorial Centre (photo by Mick Broderick)

Although an adolescent at the time, Kamuronsi recalls that the global community should have been more alert to the dangers facing his nation and the Tutsi minority.[39] As Darryl Li indicates in relation to the function of Rwanda's hate radio in advance of and during the genocide, "it is often noted that the road to genocide is paved with smaller massacres."[40] Kamuronsi relates that in the lead-up to the 100 days of slaughter his family sensed unease. His parents warned the children that the entire family might be killed. To minimize that outcome the family split into two groups—"perhaps then some of us would survive," he says—with Kamuronsi traveling to his grandmother's home in Gitarama. Urban Kigali was considered too unsafe. Yves Kamuronsi's reflections will be familiar to those acquainted with the many Jewish tales of encroaching and imminent doom during the Shoah, and the role of parents as heralds of pragmatic wisdom for a future *in absentia*:

> My strongest memory of my mother is of a time before the genocide. She took me aside and told me that there was a war going on, that no-one knew what was going to happen. She told me that she and my father might die, and we had to be strong ... My mother told me how I should behave in her absence. She told me, "You should love people and always think of living peacefully with people." I wondered why she said that to me, but later on, when she was no longer there, I thought about it again and realised how important it is.

Kamuronsi's testimony of his family's eventual plight is constrained emotionally by the absence of direct witnesses. It is understandably tinged with sadness, regret, and impotence. As far as his parents and siblings are concerned, Kamuronsi's melancholy story is relayed secondhand and attests to his own incapacity to help. Like many sufferers of trauma, those affected find themselves mentally rehearsing events over and over again, and returning to what the absent or unassimilable scenario must have imaginatively entailed:

> The thing that hurts me most is the way my parents were killed. I was told that the attackers came to get them, and my mother had been sick with malaria. She didn't have any medication and she had been shivering and vomiting all night. When they came that morning, my older brother was mopping the floor and listening to the radio, even though they were hiding ... People told me how my mother was killed. It was on the morning of 27 April, two weeks after the genocide started. She was ill and feeling weak. There were about 60 people together. She sat there for about two hours and some people were begging them not to kill them. They got her to lie face down on the floor and shot her with a bullet to the head.

When Yves Kamuronsi describes his father's demise, he displays the relevant file on the KMC database of genocide victims. Hence, Kamuronsi's own work in digitally restoring the public memory frequently returns him to the source of his suffering (parental and familial loss) but also directly usurps and mitigates the genocidal ideology of Tutsi annihilation in his daily practice of recording, identifying, archiving, and networking:

> What hurts the most is that they shot five bullets at my father and he lay there in agony for two days with no medication ... [W]hen he was starting to feel better, they came back and finished him off. That hurts me and I always feel it would have been better if he'd died right away without suffering so much pain ... My father was murdered by a soldier we didn't know. But I know that one of my dad's very good friends betrayed them ... He was head of the *interahamwe* [Hutu militia] in Kicukiro. He didn't help my dad at all; he betrayed him. We even used to hide in that man's house when it was getting less secure before the genocide ... When he was wounded and sick after they shot him, Dad sent someone to ask his friend if he could do anything to help. Still he did nothing. In fact he was the one that went ahead and told the other perpetrators that

Dad was still alive. He told them to kill him, and his wife and children ... so he sent a second group of attackers who killed Dad.

Kamuronsi's narrative articulates a discourse of pain and suffering akin to Freud's "cry from the wound"[41] and affirms the common traumatic requirement to revisit the past, to rehearse and repeat scenarios in order to obtain a satisfactory cognitive congruence and/or emotional closure:

I didn't find out what happened to my parents until after the genocide. I was so convinced they were still alive. I learnt about it later on in August. The people that knew what had happened didn't know how we would handle it (my sister and I had a long conversation and she told me what had happened). We spent some months living on our own without any other members of the family.

The experience and its subsequent cognitive dissonance is comparable to the "psychic numbing" noted by Robert Lifton in his landmark 1967 study of the *hibakusha*, the people directly affected by the atomic bombings at the close of World War II. Lifton aptly named his book *Death in Life*, in recognition of the overriding physical and emotional responses to the abject horrors of that calamity and the survivors' residual sense of (non) existence afterwards.[42] Similarly, Kamuronsi's retrospective testimony foregrounds his fears, dislocation, despair, alienation, guilt, and disbelief. He speaks of the paradoxical desire to forget whilst simultaneously feeling compelled to remember and comprehend:

I was still a child but I felt very sad inside. I was also scared—although it reached a point where all the fear disappeared. I reached a point where I felt as if I didn't know what was happening or where I was. Seeing human beings killing other human beings, or run after them, or with machete wounds all over their bodies—those are things I wasn't capable of grasping or fully understanding ... I just can't get out of my mind how my parents were killed, the ways in which people were killed. And yet they were innocent children, innocent women, innocent parents. And then surviving by jumping over dead bodies, not being able to sleep, and having to steal a jacket from the dead—all these are things I can never forget. I can't go to bed without thinking about them and remembering how my family and other people I knew were killed. It's not something I can ever forget.

Both aspects of surviving—witnessing the sustained violent onslaught and the necessity to live by any means—are tainted with abhorrence, and regret.[43] The continual return to these events, whether in conscious life or via nightmares, reveals the immutability of the psychic mechanisms in operation to (re)negotiate trauma and its seemingly unassimilable nature. Yves Kamuronsi's testimony speaks to the disjuncture of survivance, a traumatic mode described as "the oscillation between a *crisis of death* and the correlative *crisis of life*: between the story of the unbearable nature of an event and the story of the unbearable nature of its survival."[44] For Yves Kamuronsi:

> The most difficult thing of being a survivor is remembering what happened to you. Sometimes you remember so many bad things that it could destroy your life and stop you from doing anything. You could become a very wicked person because of the things you saw or went through. Being a survivor can make life very hard because of what you saw. It may change the way you look at people and can even stop you from loving anyone. You saw so much evil that you no longer fear anything. You may be woken by nightmares about people with machetes who want to kill you. Or you may remember a child you saw being killed. Those are the challenges for the survivors. It affects them for the rest of their lives.

Simple acts of identification and burial, their rituals and rites of passage, were denied and "stolen" from most genocide victims. In this context, exhumation and re-burial enable survivors previously robbed of this experience the opportunity for materially witnessing and participating in the interment of their loved ones with dignity:

> In Rwandan culture, when someone dies, people come and mourn with you. But they killed my family and threw them into some garbage. To me they were not buried: that is one of the things that really hurts about the genocide. I wish we had at least buried them as a family. They were respectable and innocent people. Even my sister who was with them saw the way they were killed. Afterwards, some people showed me the place they were killed and we decided to exhume their bodies and bury them in a better way—no matter how hard that was. At least we buried them like everyone else is buried, in a way that honours them.

Unexpected triggers of trauma come in many forms for survivors, unwittingly and unexpectedly returning them to the incomprehensible scene. As Gilbert Ndahayo relates when confronting his parents' killers in the case study to follow, Kamuronsi correspondingly admits confusion and resignation at his cravenness when encountering a man implicated in his family's murder:

> I once saw someone who was present the day they were murdered—even though he wasn't the one who killed them. I was so overwhelmed that I didn't know what to say. I felt that if I talked to him, I thought that I might say or do something wrong out of anger. So I chose to leave. He was going to be questioned in a gacaca court. I didn't have the strength even to approach him and ask him anything. There was nothing to talk about. He knew who I was and I also knew him. Should I have greeted him? I didn't know what to do so I left there.

Kamuronsi finds refuge and solace in his digital recording and archival work at the KMC:

> I want to work hard and achieve something in life. I'm not a sad person; I'm not sorrowful. Even when something saddens me, I look for a reason to be happy. I want to work hard and get somewhere in life. I know no-one will have pity on me just because I'm an orphan.

However, his constant professional immersion in the aftermath of genocide takes its toll. But he "does it because who else is there; not everyone is capable of doing it." Kamuronsi recounts the recording and data management are a burden but he also feels privileged to honour the dead in this way:

> It's very sad spending all your time looking into the lives of people who were killed and looking at their pictures. But I do it—and I do it with all my strength because it needs to be done—so that even the people who want them to be forgotten will have failed. When the project is completed, I think it will have a lot of impact. It is even very helpful for us. When you want to remember your friends or family, you will be able to go there. That's why I give myself fully to that project because it will be a big help. It will even show the international community that the genocide really happened.
>
> After ten years, life is still very difficult. Some people think that the genocide is over and there's absolutely no problem. In fact, now after ten years, some people are starting to realise the consequences of the genocide. They are beginning to understand what genocide is. People are still hurting. When someone tells you that they have been

> unhappy for ten years, they mean it. Ten years later, life is still tough and it is still too soon ... We survivors need each other. Very few people who aren't survivors can actually help a survivor.

Kamuronsi is a firm believer in the gacaca process and the rebuilding of Rwanda through careful, targeted assistance and education. As he says, "every day you are reminded by those around you who are implicated [in the genocide]. They may sit next to you on a bus or be in a bar or at work. You might not like them, but we have to live together." Yves Kamuronsi accepts the need for a pragmatic and compassionate national reconciliation, one that cares as much for the children of the tens of thousands of incarcerated perpetrators as it does for the survivors:

> Surviving. Living. That is our "revenge." It's not a revenge of violence or hate. It's just that we *exist*. We live. The best revenge is to get education.

gilbert ndahayo, independent filmmaker, new jersey

Gilbert Ndahayo migrated to the United States in January 2008. He is one of the emerging talents of Rwandan filmmaking. As a teenager, he witnessed the brutal and horrific death of his parents—his father a lawyer and politician, his mother a civil servant. A decade after the genocide Ndahayo received his training from Swedish filmmakers as part of the program initiated by Eric Kabera's Rwandan Film Centre. He received further training in Uganda at Hollywoodian Mira Nair's film lab. Ndahayo's debut short drama *Scars of My Days* (2006) won the inaugural local film award.[45] His other films have subsequently toured at international festivals and screened on overseas networks, including Al Jazeera. Now part of the large international Tutsi diaspora, he currently resides in Newark, New Jersey, completing a novel and looking for an inspirational educational institution to further hone his impressive digital filmmaking skills. The following testimony comes from Ndahayo's films, media interviews, online correspondence and a telephone interview conducted in May 2008.[46]

In his March 2008 address to the Shoah Foundation at the University of Southern California, Ndahayo eloquently outlined his personal witness of the genocide and his approach to media-making:

> I remember two months before the genocide ... I saw a young man raising his nail-club to hit my mother on her head. Mum was on her knees and when she was hit, she felt onward [*sic*] without a single scream. I was coming from school ... three days after the genocide started on April 10th my mother, my youngest sister and about 200 people in the village were burnt alive in a pit in

> my courtyard. They were hit with nail-clubs and hacked with machetes before they were thrown into a pit. The killers burnt down our home with fuel and then proceeded to inflame the pit. Those who barely lived, suffocated.
>
> On the 17th of April, 1994 my father was discovered from the convent where he was hiding. His body was hit with nail-clubs and then beheaded. Three other men perished with him.

But Ndahayo's horror did not end with the "100 days of madness," it continued into his teens:

> There were numerous scary experiences ... I hardly find sleep. For twelve years, I lived in a state of death. I turned to drinking, trying to push away anger. To destroy a recent past, I would drown the painful sadness. My vision became blurred and my hearing got distorted, but yet, only in this condition could my mind gather some rest.

Like Kamuronsi, Ndahayo is deeply affected by the seemingly irreconcilable nature of the events he has witnessed and participated in. Common to victims of mass human suffering, discourse often fails in its attempted recounting. The capacity to express meaning orally is frequently impeded to such an extent that a "knowing silence" is a familiar trope among survivors and trauma artists.[47] This ploy is not so much a denial of discourse as a recognition of its total inadequacy to encapsulate the immensity of the events and their associated feelings and emotions:

> I have no name to my suffering. I have no language to speak of it. I struggle with the words to describe it.

Yet, conscious of Rwandan oral tradition, where storytelling is often deployed to act as a social or cultural warning, usually by establishing a generic prologue in verse to "set the scene," Ndahayo has turned to filmmaking and infused it with a distinctly Rwandan mode of narrative, a gift he considers "inherited from his ancestors":

Ngucire umugani	Let me tell you a tale,
Nkubambuze umugani	Let me wake you up with a tale,
... harabaye, ntihakabe	... there was, but never again,
Harapfuye, ntihagapfe	There was death, but no more

Interestingly, in this traditional Rwandan poem we find a transcultural marker of mass suffering, memory, and trauma, evident from before the Shoah and Hiroshima, embedded in the ancient verse of local storytellers—"never again."

As Ndahayo relates:

> The testament of our ancestors cautioned the youth to be vigilant and careful. "There was" is a warning with caution in regards to evil. "But never again" is a remembrance of the evil that should not be repeated. Civilization endures in consequence to memory. The evil we forget, will be repeated.

Gilbert Ndahayo's pedigree in this domain is prominent. His mother's uncle, Felicien Ntagengwa, mentored Gilbert in the arts while on regular visits to his native rural village, and according to tradition he became Gilbert's grandfather. Felicien and other ancestors were poets and storytellers at the former king's court. Felicien survived the genocide and earlier mass deportation of the Tutsi following the chaos of Rwanda's 1959 independence. His grandfather's poignant words are displayed in the national Kinyarwanda language at all the memorial sites in Rwanda:

> If you knew me
> and you really knew yourself,
> you would not have killed me.

Felicien inspired Ndahayo to channel his creativity and education in order to articulate his traumatic experiences. As Ndahayo relates, his grandfather

Figure 9. 3

A banner with Felicien's words hangs outside the church in Nyamata, home to over 38,000 interred bodies (photo by Mick Broderick)

"taught me the good traditions of Rwanda and storytelling. The devices that I use in my poems and scripts of my films, I have learnt them from him. I owe him so much."

Despite his pain at personal recollection, the filmmaker feels compelled to utilize the new medium he has worked hard to master:

> In Rwanda, a saying goes "*ujya gukira indwara arayirata*"; that is "if one wants to be healed from a sickness, he must talk about it to the world." For twelve years, I lived with the remains of my parents and 200 unpeaceful dead in my backyard.
>
> The way my parents were is the way people are. I wanted to tell a story about their death ... a story that has not been shown on film.

Ndahayo's own experience in making his feature-length documentary *Behind this Convent* (Rwanda, 2008) was simultaneously traumatic and cathartic. With a small crew he filmed the community gacaca where the accused Hutu militia killers of his family appear before the local villagers. It is harrowing to watch as "director" Gilbert Ndahayo confronts the murderers of his parents and sister in this public space, determinedly and powerfully asking the two men (who wear the traditional and unmistakable pink uniforms of Rwandan convicts) to account for their actions. These are the men who clubbed, hacked, decapitated, and incinerated Ndahayo's immediate family and nearly two hundred others at the same time and place.

Figure 9.4

A roadside billboard promoting the gacaca process in regional Rwanda (photo by Mick Broderick)

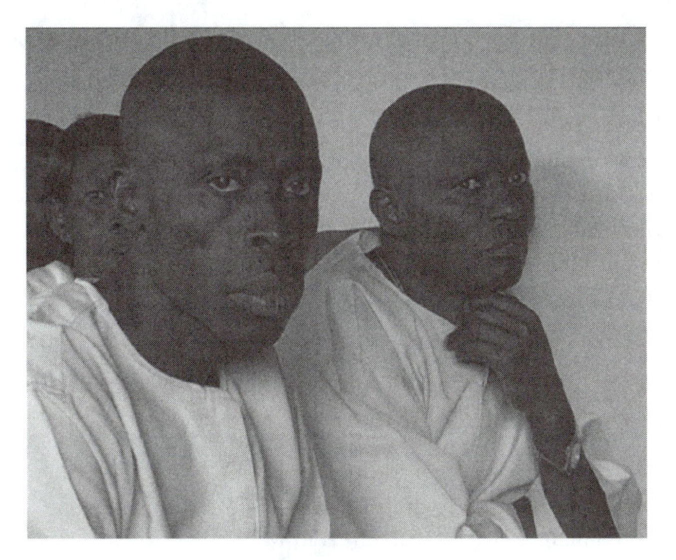

Figure 9.5

Two of the accused killers at a gacaca hearing (from Gilbert Ndahayo's documentary *Behind this Convent*)

In the film's key sequence, viewable on YouTube, lilting and haunting African birdsong fills darkened images. The camera tilts and pans around the exterior crypt of the Nyamata church, which holds over 38,000 bodies.[48] As the camera slowly pans left to right across a barren convent school ground, we hear the as-yet unidentified Ndahayo speaking, his words translated and subtitled into English:

> My name is Gilbert Ndahayo.
> My father is among the three people he killed.
> I'd like to know how he killed them.
> Did you choke them?
> Did you poison them?
> Did you burn them alive like others?

Ndahayo is shown in close-up and in profile, questioning the accused. The mostly static camera, though occasionally roving, is trained to capture Gilbert Ndahayo's delivery. It combines verité-style with an equally ethnographic attention to the proceedings. This narrative space and limited *mise-en-scène* enables the power and increased conviction of Ndahayo's at times banal but forensic questioning to build momentum and pathos:

> Bear with me, I've spent the last 13 years waiting for this truth.
> I have no other way to attain it.
> That's my first question.
> I have a second question.

The gacaca hearing is depicted in wide shot, with a slow zoom-in on the judges at the front of a classroom.

> I have a second question.
> As we exhumed bodies in the bush,
> it dawned on us that
> they were executed,
> not just meagre killings.
> We exhumed four corpses,
> not three like he confessed.

The two accused are shown in medium close-up and in profile, at one point both staring directly into the camera lens. Ndahayo continues:

> Why doesn't he mention the fourth person?
> I might have forgotten things,
> but I remember we needed four coffins.
> There were four dead bodies.
> I have a third question.
> You denied being present at the first attack.

Ndahayo's voice waivers and he sheds a tear.

> My youngest sister perished
> along with my mother and those 150 people.
> All slaughtered.

Ndahayo wipes away another tear. As he pauses, a cutaway reveals one of the killers and a slow pan to the right shows the gacaca audience listening intently and respectfully.

> You said you had left, what
> happened when you came back?
> How long did it take to kill 153 people?
> How long were you absent?

Ndahayo raises a finger and lowers it emphatically:

> Were they alive when you arrived? Were they dead?
> If they were dead, were they already burnt?
> How much fuel did you use to burn those 153 people?

Gilbert Ndahayo raises his other hand and finger, waving it up and down, then alternating, pointing accusingly as his determination and confidence grow.

> Where did you get the fuel?
> Did you use the fuel of your own vehicle
> or did you have to leave to get more?

Figure 9.6

Gilbert Ndahayo confronts those accused of his parents' murder (from Ndahayo's documentary *Behind this Convent*)

> You are now confusing us, saying they were already dead
> and burnt when you came.
> Even worse, you are denying any knowledge of where the pit is located.

At this point the video fades to black over non-diegetic birdsong and quickly fades into a group of men in a pit exhuming bodies. They dig conscientiously while townsfolk stand and look on in silence, as one corpse after another is removed. The camera POV lingers on the scene in long-take, shot from above, as the gruesome work of digging and brushing away dirt from the remains continues, while more and more villagers gather to watch. The scene echoes Kamuronsi's recovery of his own parents in the previous case study.

Ndahayo's gacaca experience—literally, his day in court—is recorded in all of its raw emotional display, yet the sequence remains incongruously respectful and dignified given the heinous charges and evidence. Equally surprisingly, Ndahayo admits finding empathy with the family of the accused:

> In the gacaca court, I was sitting with a daughter of a (Hutu) killer; she was crying tears of a rain. I first thought she is a survivor and she couldn't stop crying. In the editing, I realized that my cameraman did an incredible job to capture the killer with his family and "drinking buddies"

> (as the judge said in the film), greetings and the joy of seeing his family after 13 years in jail.
>
> When we talk of forgiveness in Rwanda, we mean "kubabarira," a word with two kuba-barira, kuba (being) and barira (crying). I guess the readers will also be crying as well as the author, crying for Rwanda and for ourselves to see and hear the indescribable.

Ndahayo maintains that it was important to hold his composure during the questioning. He maintains he did not cry, although his voice is choked with emotion, and he appears to wipe away the occasional tear. It was an ordeal that drained him physically and emotionally, leaving him totally incapacitated for 12 hours. The experience was shared by his collaborators, with his cameraman unable to speak with Ndahayo for two days after filming.

During this gacaca hearing, one of the Hutu admits ultimately to the killings and apologizes to Ndahayo and those present for his role in the genocide. The other accused remains defiant, challenging Gilbert Ndahayo over the purpose of his audiovisual recording to the point of disputing the role and efficacy of all such recordings. It is a provocation that Ndahayo does not take lightly and still wrestles with today as he continually develops his craft and storytelling skills.[49]

However, as many Rwandans understand, the gacaca process is about truth and reconciliation, not necessarily justice or recompense. With characteristic poesis, Ndahayo asserts:

> A Rwandan saying goes *ukuri guca mu ziko ntigushye*, meaning the truth passes through the fire and does not burn. The truth relieves the man and enlightens the world.

Pragmatically this inviolable truth, and its public enunciation and performance via the gacaca, lead directly (but not necessarily immediately) to emotional and psychological relief, unburdening both perpetrator and victim alike. Enlightenment comes with the admission of guilt, and the well of information that springs from its public revelation, association, and action. Previously suppressed details emerge that enable survivors and the community to pinpoint atrocities, implicate others, exhume and identify loved ones from the masses of still anonymous dead. Ndahayo's personal documentary and Yves Kamuronsi's systematic gacaca archiving and genocide mapping inform one another in an evidential accrual of histories and truths that not only recount past events but also testify to their continued impact and legacy.

It is clear Gilbert Ndahayo regards himself an artist, not a documentarian. The implicit requirement for an indigenous Rwandan cinema to emerge, with all of its success and failures, as in any other national cinema, should be supported at the local and international level:

> As an artist, I think there would be no classification in telling audiovisual stories. As soon as Africans will be able to take cameras in their hands, film themselves in their local environment and speak their own language, edit on Final Cut Pro or Avid; all the theories will be dismantled. A story is a story, it has plots, it has signs, language and portrays values and culture of a community.

Recently a BBC News journalist/reviewer complained that the low-budget, guerrilla work of Ndahayo's peers in Rwanda and their international collaborators ultimately fails since it will not find "mainstream" audiences.[50] But this dismissive global arbiter of taste does not understand the dynamic of socially networked connectivity and the advent of consumer-producers. His observation also overlooks the tradition of Third Cinema as a necessarily "imperfect" cinema, in contrast to Western hegemony and industrial practice. While Ndahayo and his peers may aspire to Hollywood budgets and resources, they are succeeding in reaching their own community and can connect intimately with global audiences online who offer instant feedback, ratings, and comments. Already on YouTube, MySpace, Facebook, Flickr, and various blogs, Rwandan digital testimony of the genocide is reaching an international audience through Web 2.0 social networking and end users uploading content. The reaction of the BBC reviewer is merely symptomatic of what Kaplan and Wang describe as "cultural memory being subjected to relentless erasure by the transnational media driven by the logic of commodity and consumption."[51]

As a new generation of Rwandans becomes increasingly digital media-savvy, such sites and cultural practices will go a long way to ensuring and sustaining audiences for these narratives of witness, memory, and testimony of the Rwandan genocide. However, cheap, portable technologies and democratizing media practices can also espouse the reviled genocidal ideology of annihilation both from within the country and from without. On this matter Gilbert Ndahayo is cautious and urges vigilance:

> The post-genocide situation in Rwanda bothers me, however. The evil is not going to stop. One young survivor participant in the video says "the extermination of Tutsi is not yet over" and his view is supported by an elder who "fears even a whistle since it was used to hunt down the Tutsi."

Ndahayo is similarly wary of the potential for unethical or ambivalent uses to which such digital testimony may be put, whether by the government, the KMC, Ibuka, or SURF.[52] Despite gifting some key works for posterity, he remains a fiercely independent artist and filmmaker:

> I value and cherish this important work since it is the only weapon we have to keep the memory of survivors while they ... are still alive as well as to combat the final phase of genocide. This made me not to affiliate with them and produce independent work that I donated to the memorial center as educational materials.

Ultimately, Ndahayo offers some salient advice for any researcher-academic-filmmaker (such as myself) who ventures into Rwanda. Despite the best of intentions:

> The material you are assisting to collect should have both the aim to preserve the history as well as foster awareness and genocide education. They should not be used as political propaganda, nor incite more hatred ... but encourage unity among citizens. I am afraid that our friends might take into hostage these voices and faces for non-humanitarian references. I believe, however, that without testimonies of genocide, there is no history of it. Without the history of genocide, the final stage, which is denial, becomes even more ugly.

conclusion

The two case studies above demonstrate that the generation who were adolescents, children, or infants during the Rwandan genocide of 1994 (now teenagers and young adults) continue to confront their horrific memories and associated trauma. Yet some of these tormented individuals seek reconciliation with perpetrators, in part by crafting their own digital narratives of resistance, survival, persistence, and forgiveness. As Yves Kamuronsi records, plots, and archives thousands of gacaca testimonies and Gilbert Ndahayo struggles to express the incomprehensible through his artistic media, both seek to honour the plea, according to Ndahayo, of "making 'never again' not a slogan but reality," particularly in view of continuing events in Darfur and escalating atrocities in Kenya and Zimbabwe.[53]

The recent capacity of Rwandan genocide survivors to employ mobile digital media, not available to earlier generations of mass suffering, in order to record their evolving self-expressions as personal testimony or narrative fiction, provides an opportunity for reconsidering the existing parameters of traumatic representation, its scholarship and shifting political dimensions. Hence, Rwandan survivor-media makers embrace the cultural specificity of their own local experience and traditional modes of discourse while recognizing the contexts of other forms of collective suffering that occurred before and continue after April 2004.[54]

Rather than homogenizing "genocide," it is important not only to foreground the antecedents and shared histories of exterminism but also to recognize and articulate significant historical variations from genocide to genocide and their evolving or pluralist processes of representation and memorialization. For example, the latent and protracted physiological and psychological effects of HIV-AIDS infection, used *en masse* as a deliberate genocidal act of extinction in Rwanda (which builds on the all-too-common crime of wartime rape), deserves scholarly consideration and reflection as well as its discrete media representation.[55]

One potential approach might evaluate the founding principles underlying much psychological trauma (accidents and battlefield experience) and related memory work to address the more cognitively and philosophically complex aspects of surviving genocide, specifically its perceived *incomprehensibility* and resistance to dissemination and transmission beyond fellow survivors. In other domains (e.g., apocalyptic and millenarian theology, the nuclear *episteme*) such manifest cognitive dissonance has invoked consideration of the "sublime" in its absence of the comprehensible and presence of the manifestations of terror.[56] Hence, it may be appropriate to speak of the *genocidal sublime*.[57]

This is a key concern for artists and critics—ostensibly due to genocide's literally "inconceivable" human agenda, though one repeated throughout history, to expunge an entire category of *Homo sapiens* dictated by essentialist and seemingly arbitrary criteria (e.g., race, religion, class, or caste). Anecdotally, amongst genocide survivors the shock, impact, disorientation, and cognitive readjustment are profoundly intensified as a crisis of epistemology—where victims only *later* comprehend their personal experience of violence and suffering as having resulted from *deliberate* and *politically systemic* crimes against humanity. Such recognition is evident amongst the new generation of Rwandans, no longer infants or children, now attempting to reconcile the lasting impact (and potential recurrence) of the genocide in testimony; their ongoing encounters with perpetrators; the accrual of "official" and "amateur" digital evidence; and the production of narrative dramas informed by indigenous tradition. Making sense of their experiences and histories inevitably requires a return (not only metaphorically) to the sites of trauma but also to comprehension and healing through gacaca and public witness, *in situ* and mediated online.

While the recently emerging works of these remarkable and resilient survivors "speak" for themselves, they demand broader circulation and exhibition. As Gilbert Ndahayo implores: "I only have these two requests to this world: please help survivors to recover and move forward. Please stop the genocides."

notes

1. See Alison Des Forges, *Leave None to Tell the Story: Genocide in Rwanda* (New York: Human Rights Watch, 1999); and Linda Melvern, *Conspiracy to Murder: The Rwandan Genocide* (London: Verso, 2004).
2. *Encyclopedia Britannica Online*, "Rwanda," britannica.com/EBchecked/topic/514402/Rwanda (accessed 20 May 2008).
3. James Muntaneza, "Grenade Attack at Genocide Memorial Kills Policeman," *New Times*, 12 April 2008, newtimes.co.rw/index.php?issue=13498&article=5519 (accessed 20 May 2008).
4. Kennedy Ndahiro, "Rwandans Overwhelm Revisionists in Montreal," *New Times*, 31March 2008, newtimes.co.rw/index.php?issue=13486&article=5255 (accessed 20 May 2008).
5. Arthur Asiimwe, "Hotel Rwanda Hero in Bitter Controversy," *Reuters*, 4 April 2007, reuters.com/article/worldNews/idUSL0420968620070404 (accessed 4 July 2008).
6. William Church, "Rwanda: Hate Speech and Paul Rusesabagina," *American Chronicle*, 31 January 2007, americanchronicle.com/articles/19908 (accessed 9 May 2008).
7. See Manthia Diawara, "Oral Literature and African Film: Narratology in *Wend Kuuni*," in *Questions of Third Cinema*, eds. Jim Pines and Paul Willeman (London: British Film Institute), 199–211.
8. On "leapfrogging," see Amanda Third and K.T. Kao, "ICT Leapfrogging Policy and Development in the Third World," in *Encyclopedia of Information Ethics and Security*, ed. M. Quigley (Hershey, PA: Information Science Reference, 2008), 326–34.
9. On African tradition and Third Cinema, see Teshome H. Gabriel, "Third Cinema as Guardian of Popular Memory: Towards a Third Aesthetics," in *Questions of Third Cinema*, 53–64; and Diawara, "Oral Literature and African Film: Narratology in *Wend Kuuni*."
10. For a discussion of "accented cinema" and its modes of address, see Hamid Naficy, *An Accented Cinema: Exilic and Diasporic Filmmaking* (Princeton, NJ: Princeton University Press, 2001).
11. *Ibuka* means, literally, "remember."
12. David Bordwell, Janet Staiger, and Kristin Thompson, *The Classical Hollywood Cinema: Film Style and Mode of Production to 1960* (New York: Columbia University Press, 1985), 367–70.
13. See Darryl Li, "Echoes of Violence: Considerations on Radio and Genocide in Rwanda," in *The Media and the Rwandan Genocide*, ed. Allan Thompson (London: Pluto Press, 2007), 90–109, also at www.idrc.ca/openbooks/338-0/ (accessed 28 February 2008); and Felix Muheto, "Rusesabagina Entangled Himself in His Own Lies," *New Times*, 16 April 2008, newtimes.co.rw/index.php?issue=13502&article=5596 (accessed 20 May 2008).
14. Li, "Echoes of Violence," 78, pdf at www.idrc.ca/openbooks/338-0/ (accessed 28 February 2008).
15. Ibuka Director Benoît Kaboyi, interview with the author, Kigali, January 2007.

16. Michael Dorland, "PG—Parental Guidance or Portrayal of Genocide: The Comparative Depiction of Mass Murder in Contemporary Cinema," in *The Media and the Rwandan Genocide*, 389–402.
17. Steve Bloomfield, "Welcome to Hillywood," *Independent*, 20 August 2007, independent.co.uk/news/world/africa/welcome-to-hillywood-how-rwandas-film-industry-emerged-from-genocides-shadow-463541.html (accessed 9 May 2008).
18. See H.L. Gulseth, "The Use of Propaganda in the Rwandan Genocide: A Study of RTLM" (Master of Political Science dissertation, University of Oslo, 2004), digbib.uio.no/publ/statsvitenskap/2004/19095/19095.pdf; and Thompson, ed., *The Media and the Rwandan Genocide*.
19. On the French cooperation program in Africa, see Roy Armes, *Third World Film Making and the West* (Berkeley: University of California Press, 1987), 214–25.
20. See Paulin Soumanou Vieyra, "African Cinema: Solidarity and Difference," in *Questions of Third Cinema*, 195–8.
21. Hughes was a cameraman working in Rwanda during the early days of the genocide and shot the famous telephoto footage depicting Hutu militia in the act of a roadside killing by machete. He recounts the experience in Nick Hughes, "Exhibit 467: Genocide through a Camera Lens," in *The Media and the Rwandan Genocide*, 231–4, pdf at www.idrc.ca/openbooks/338-0/, 78 (accessed 28 February 2008).
22. Bloomfield, "Welcome to Hillywood."
23. Lee Isaac Chung's collaborative film *Munyurangabo* (Rwanda/US, 2007) was shot in Kinyarwanda over ten days and produced with a small multinational crew and local nonprofessional Rwandan actors. It cost US$60,000 and has played at several international film festivals, including Berlin, Toronto, and Cannes. Several clips and interviews can be viewed at youtube.com.
24. Bloomfield, "Welcome to Hillywood."
25. Woukouache quoted in Judith Basutama, "Cinema in Burundi and Rwanda: Still a Long Way to Go," *Africalia* 10–11, January 2008, africalia.be/download/en/newsletter/newsletter_10_en_04.pdf (accessed 15 June 2008).
26. Quoted in Basutama, "Cinema in Burundi and Rwanda."
27. On the penetration of mobile telephony and next generation capacity in Rwanda and Africa, see Ericsson, "Upwardly Mobile Rwanda," press release, 19 March 2007, ericsson.com/solutions/news/2007/q1/20070319_rwanda.shtml, and "Ericsson Announces Delivery of First Telecom Services to Millennium Village in Rwanda," ericsson.com/ericsson/press/releases/20071029-1163745.shtml (accessed 20 May 2008).
28. N. Frank Ukadike, "Video Booms and the Manifestation of 'First Cinema' in Anglophone Africa," in *Rethinking Third Cinema*, eds. Anthony R. Guneratne and Wimal Dissanayake (New York: Routledge, 2003), 126–43.
29. Susannah Radstone, "Trauma Theory: Contexts, Politics, Ethics," *Paragraph* 30, no. 1 (2007): 9–29.
30. See Andreas Huyssen, "Present Pasts: Media, Politics, Amnesia," *Public Culture* 12, no. 1 (2000): 21–38.
31. Freud's key works on trauma include *Beyond the Pleasure Principle* (1920) and *Moses and Monotheism* (1939).
32. Cathy Caruth, *Unclaimed Experience: Trauma, Narrative, and History* (Baltimore, MD: Johns Hopkins University Press, 1996), 6. Even professionally trained

observers such as international news cameraman Nick Hughes—whose film of genocidal murderers in Rwanda is one of the few actual images of the atrocity recorded at the time—recalls how "only later" did the slow process of understanding the genocide "as it happened" become a retrospective act of comprehension. Hughes, "Exhibit 467."

33. This is not to suggest that the experience of genocidal violence is not shocking and perceived as random or chaotic despite earlier massacres, warnings from parents, and prognostications by media or politicians. The experience/reception of such acts differs from subject to subject, just as there is no universal or monolithic experience of trauma or genocide. Context is everything.
34. "Trauma cinema" is defined by Janet Walker, *Trauma Cinema: Documenting Incest and the Holocaust* (Berkeley: University of California Press, 2005), 19–29. For atomization, the individual, and agency, see E. Ann Kaplan and Ban Wang, eds., *Trauma and Cinema: Cross-cultural Explorations* (Hong Kong: Hong Kong University Press, 2004), 8. For concepts of working out and through, see Dominick LaCapra, *Representing the Holocaust: History, Theory, Trauma* (Ithaca, NY: Cornell University Press, 1994).
35. On "disremembering" see Janet Walker, *Trauma Cinema*, 16–19, and on unsettling, self-critical remembering, see Lisa Yoneyama, *Hiroshima Traces: Time, Space, and the Dialectics of Memory* (Berkeley: University of California Press, 1999), 5.
36. See, for example, Armes, *Third World Film Making and the West*; Robert Stam, "Beyond Third Cinema: The Aesthetics of Hybridity," in *Rethinking Third Cinema*, 31–48; and Teshome H. Gabriel, "Towards a Critical Theory of Third World films," in *Questions of Third Cinema*, 30–52.
37. Radstone, "Trauma Theory: Contexts, Politics, Ethics," 24.
38. Aegis Trust, *A Time to Remember: Rwanda, Ten Years after the Genocide* (2004).
39. The failure of the international community to intervene, unlike the multiple UN Security Council resolutions and NATO forces operating in the former Yugoslavia, is charted in William Ferroggiaro's dossier for the National Security Archive, "The U.S. and the Genocide in Rwanda 1994: Information, Intelligence and the U.S. Response," 24 March 2004. Gleaned from the declassified State Department, White House, Defense Department, CIA, and NSA documents, the attitude of the Clinton administration can be summarized thus: "The story of Rwanda for the US is that officials knew so much, but still decided against taking action or leading other nations to prevent or stop the genocide. Despite Rwanda's low ranking in importance to US interests, Clinton Administration officials had tremendous capacity to be informed—and were informed—about the slaughter there; as noted author Samantha Zower writes 'any failure to fully appreciate the genocide stemmed from political, moral, and imaginative weaknesses, not informational ones.'" Ferroggiaro, "The U.S. and the Genocide in Rwanda 1994: Information, Intelligence and the U.S. Response," http://www.gwu.edu/~nsarchiv/NSAEBB/NSAEBB117/index.htm (accessed 28 February 2008). Writing from the vantage of a decade's hindsight, Ferroggiaro's indictment of US policy makers, and by implication the entire West, over the serial failure to intervene in Rwanda is similarly evinced by the entertainment industry's eschewal of the issues until comparatively recently.
40. Li, "Echoes of Violence," 139. Frequent atrocities were committed long before 1994, mostly by Hutu against the Tutsi. Gilbert Ndahayo describes

how his grandparents and mother were forced into internal exile: "Nyamata is known as having been used as a pilot area for genocide long before it officially unfolded on April 7, 1994. My mother's parents were deported there in 1959 to die in the hands of wild animals and tsetse but survived to die in 1994." Gilbert Ndahayo, "Hi-Jacked Easter, 1994," RWANDALESSON TIGBlog, 2 April 2008, rwandalesson.tigblogs.org/ (accessed 12 May 2008).

41. The "crying wound" relates to Freud's retelling of Tasso's story from the Crusader epic *Gerusalemme Liberata* in *Beyond the Pleasure Principle*, foregrounded by Cathy Caruth as representing the enigma of trauma's repetition and the "witness of the crying voice." See Caruth, *Unclaimed Experience*, 2–3.
42. Robert J. Lifton, *Death in Life: Survivors of Hiroshima* (London: Pelican, 1971), 26–37. The death-in-life phenomenon is also articulated by Ndayaho, who, according to Stefanie Carmichael, "began drawing on the death he felt inside of him to create new life through his films." Stefanie Carmichael, "From Hillywood to Hollywood: One Rwandan Makes His Major Motion Picture Dreams Come True," *Rwanda Sunday Times*, 24 February 2008, globalventure.blogspot.com/2008/02/from-hillywood-to-hollywood-one-rwandan.html (accessed 20 May 2008).
43. On the "death taint" of survivors, see Lifton, *Death in Life*.
44. Caruth, *Unclaimed Experience*, 7, original emphasis.
45. Clips from Ndahayo's films are available on YouTube: *Scars of My Days*, youtube.com/watch?v=lVw1fCXl7ek; *Growing Roses on a Bed of Skeletons* youtube.com/watch?v=SBfE5UH5e88; and a teaser/trailer for *Dirty Wine* (Uganda/Rwanda, 2008), youtube.com/watch?v=QE_14yQ1slg. For more information about the films, see Ndahayo's website at ndahayofilms.wordpress.com/.
46. Ndahayo's text is taken verbatim from written and recorded sources in English, including my own correspondence and telephone interview with him. I have not grammatically amended it for publication.
47. On survivor/artistic "silence" and "knowing," and cultural prohibitions concerning mass suffering's unrepresentability, see Peter Schwenger, *Letter Bomb: Nuclear Holocaust and the Exploding Word* (Baltimore, MD: Johns Hopkins University Press, 1992); Mick Broderick, ed., *Hibakusha Cinema: Hiroshima, Nagasaki and the Nuclear Image in Japanese Film* (London: Kegan Paul International, 1996); Jean-Luc Nancy, "Forbidden Representation," *Poesis* 6 (2004): 6–23; and Stephen K. Levine, "Editor's Introduction," *Poesis* 6 (2004): 4–5.
48. To see the clip I refer to here, see youtube.com/watch?v=SBfE5UH5e88. Coincidentally, Ndahayo's choice of emphasizing the birdsong and images from the Nyamata crypt echoes my own experimental digital installation work *Exhale* (2007), filmed on location at this same site and employing a similar aural soundscape.
49. In a blog, Ndahayo recalls the scene in the film. After one of the killers admits that his father was "his friend," the other murderer rankles him, saying: "A film is not really that important." Ndahayo continues: "I had only wanted to have a normal conversation as a civilized citizen. He told me this after I asked him 'have you ever been filmed in your life?' Now, I am much more concerned by this profession I just discovered. What is the value of making films? I would like to challenge filmmakers of this world to help me to respond to him. This is the journey I want to undertake. I have a serious question to respond. The floor is ours and the ball is in our court, we the filmmakers of the world." Ndahayo, "Hi-Jacked Easter, 1994."

50. BBC News, "Talking Movies," 2007, youtube.com/watch?v=Qhs7ATvXPNY (accessed 9 May 2008).
51. Kaplan and Wang, *Trauma and Cinema*, 11.
52. It is not just the potential genocide deniers that re-interpret history to re-create their own official narratives. As Allan Thompson has asserted, "an authoritarian regime in Rwanda continues to justify censorship and propaganda as a necessary safeguard against the recrudescence of genocide ... after the RPF stopped the genocide and took control in July 1994, it retooled the previous regime's information agency and the official media to disseminate its own propaganda." Allan Thompson, "Introduction," *The Media and the Rwandan Genocide*, 15, www.idrc.ca/openbooks/338-0/ (accessed 28 February 2008). See also former Human Rights Watch staffer Lars Waldorf, "Censorship and Propaganda in Post-genocide Rwanda," in *The Media and the Rwandan Genocide*, 417–32, www.idrc.ca/openbooks/338-0/ (accessed 28 February 2008).
53. Ndahayo's warning is pointed. *Behind this Convent* starts with the following introductory titles: "VIEWER DISCRETION ADVISED FOR SCENES OF DEATH AND DYING. Since 2002, the government-supported Janjaweed enjoy complete immunity as they commit genocide and crimes of genocide in Darfur, Sudan till this day. From 1995 to January 2008, about 170 survivors of the 1994 Tutsi genocide have been murdered by machetes and other traditional weapons." For another transhistorical and transcultural reading of "never again," see Yoneyama on *hibakusha* memories and their difference from "conventional historical narratives." Yoneyama, *Hiroshima Traces*, 30.
54. The broader international context and history of genocide are foregrounded at the Kigali Memorial Centre. The museum layout graphically describes earlier acts of genocide around the world and the official literature available on site also articulates the lineage of genocide globally.
55. For an account of rape in Rwanda as an act of genocide, see Banifer Nowrojee and Regan Ralph, "Justice for Women Victims of Violence: Rwanda after the 1994 Genocide," in *The Politics of Memory: Truth, Healing and Social Justice*, eds. I. Amadiume and A. An-Na'Im (London: Zed Books, 2000), 162–75.
56. On the various sublimes, see Morton Paley, *The Apocalyptic Sublime* (London: Yale University Press, 1986); and Frances Ferguson, "The Nuclear Sublime," *Diacritics* 14 (Summer 1984): 4–11.
57. See Mick Broderick, "Waiting to *Exhale*: Somatic Responses to Place and the Genocidal Sublime," *IM: Interactive Media* 4 (Summer 2008), wwwmcc.murdoch.edu.au/nass/issue4/pdf/IM4_broderick.pdf(accessed20December 2008).

ten

between orbit and the ground

conflict monitoring, google earth and the "crisis in darfur" project

lisa parks

This chapter builds upon a series of earlier studies about the use of satellite and aerial imagery to represent world conflicts: the 1990s pogroms in Rwanda, the civil war in former Yugoslavia, and the ongoing US war against Iraq.[1] In each study I explored how particular satellite images of conflict zones became part of mass media culture and how they were used by different agencies to draw world attention to historic events. Through these analyses, I set out to show that high-resolution satellite images, initially designed for military intelligence purposes, could become useful to world citizens in their efforts to understand the complexities of world conflicts and political violence and, in some cases, to contest the claims of those in power and insist upon alternate interpretations. More to the point, I explored whether the satellite could be appropriated as a technology of witnessing, and how we might use the satellite image to hold states and corporations with enormous visual capital accountable for what they see and know and how they act (or do not act) based on that vision and knowledge.

In 2005 Google corporation released a new web application called Google Earth, which repurposed decades of satellite imagery to represent the world as a digitally mosaic'ed and navigable domain. Where in the earlier incidents mentioned the circulation of satellite images was an exception—that is, US officials or agencies singled out particular satellite images as part of an urgent call for world attention—Google Earth has made the circulation of satellite images the norm. Composites of satellite images form the optical platform from which a user initiates each act of global navigation or investigation. With Google Earth satellite images have become more widely available to the public and have been used for a variety of purposes including conflict monitoring and humanitarian intervention.

On April 10, 2007 representatives of Google and the United States Holocaust Memorial Museum (USHMM) held a joint press conference in Washington, DC announcing the release of a new "Global Awareness" layer in Google Earth entitled "Crisis in Darfur." Given the paucity of investigative reporters and television news crews generally working in Africa,[2] the US Holocaust Memorial Museum and Google had a unique opportunity to draw attention to a serious crisis underway and did so by pooling together audiovisual and written materials from a variety of sources, geo-referencing them and integrating them within the Google Earth system. The Crisis in Darfur, they claimed, would make it "harder for the world to ignore those who need us most." The project was also designed to highlight the humanitarian potentials of new information technologies. As Google Earth's Elliot Schrage explained, "At Google, we believe technology can be a catalyst for education and action" and, because of this, his company decided to join "the Museum's efforts in responding to this continuing international catastrophe."[3]

In recent years traumatic events from the Holocaust to the Darfur conflict have become part of Google Earth's global digital archives, and visual technologies that extend from orbit to the ground are increasingly implicated in our understanding of them. That humanitarian uses of Google Earth are on the rise suggests that we need to evaluate how satellite images and terms such as suffering, testimony, and witnessing are being reconfigured within such projects. Given the tendency to align the intelligibility of suffering and the credibility of testimony and witnessing with the proximate, I suggest that the satellite image, with its remote, abstract qualities, can become productive in its visualization of more structural and geopolitical dimensions of world conflicts. The Crisis in Darfur interface is structured as a dynamic interplay of remote, orbital, and close-up, grounded perspectives. This alternation of distant and proximate views creates the potential to represent and understand the more psychic and embodied details of suffering, testimony, and witnessing in relation to a particular geographic context. Indeed, the capacity to geo-reference suffering, testimony, and witnessing is one of the distinguishing characteristics of Google Earth. The Crisis in Darfur interface thus has the potential to foster understandings of these terms not only within a temporal logic of the historic, but in relation to the spatial logics of the territorial and geopolitical as well.

This technical potential to inscribe situated knowledges within cartographic perspectives is an important feature of Google Earth, but it demands careful analysis. As Irit Rogoff suggests, "By introducing questions of critical epistemology, subjectivity and spectatorship into the arena of geography we shift the interrogation from the center to the margins, to the site at which new and multi-dimensional knowledge and identities are constantly in the process of being formed."[4] In this chapter I question whether such multidimensional knowledge and identities can be formed in relation to the Google Earth/USHMM Crisis in Darfur project. The analysis begins with a discussion of the Crisis in Darfur project's history, proceeds to analyze some of the press coverage of the project, and then moves to a critique of the layer using four categories: 1) the shifting role of satellite image; 2) the temporality of the interface; 3) the practice of conflict branding; and 4) the practice of information intervention. Throughout the chapter, I explore how the presentation of Darfur-related materials through Google Earth reproduces problematic Western tropes of African tragedy, and misses an opportunity to generate public literacy around satellite images. I also consider how the project's humanitarianism is intertwined with digital and disaster capitalism, and suggest that this instance of information intervention makes patently clear that high visual capital alone cannot resolve global conflicts. In this way, the chapter challenges the notion that change will come if we simply raise awareness with ever more powerful techniques of seeing and knowing. The Darfur atrocities have been widely publicized and documented in a multitude of media forms in recent years. And though a veritable media industry has emerged around the Darfur conflict, the killing continues. This analysis ultimately suggests that we may need new ways of communicating about and understanding what political violence is and where it comes from before we can help to stop it. The satellite image, I want to suggest, can play a crucial role in this process.

"crisis in darfur" background

In 2005 Google began providing free downloads of its basic version of Google Earth software, offering an interface for navigation of a burgeoning collection of geo-referenced databases. In this way, Google Earth builds upon earlier geospatial projects such as GIS, Terraserver, and the Digital Earth.[5] The interface presents the world as a globe that has been mosaic'ed together as a patchwork of satellite and aerial images acquired by different sources at different times and provides people who have computers and high-speed Internet access with the opportunity to "fly" around and explore the planet as a "collaboratively produced" digital domain. Google Earth functions as a kind of "world player" or "globe browser" in that it facilitates access to content/databases uploaded by agencies, companies, and individuals from around the world. The capacity to produce the world in such a way depended in part upon Google's 2004 acquisition of Keyhole Corporation, a digital mapping company with a multi-terabyte database of mapping information fused with aerial and satellite imagery.

Since its launch in 2005 Google Earth has been used to circulate information about various conflicts around the world, including the wars in Iraq and Afghanistan. "Crisis in Darfur" has been its most high profile conflict layer. In 2004 the USHMM began concerted efforts to draw public attention to the Darfur conflict and, along with the Committee on Conscience, became one of the first US organizations to describe the conflict in Darfur as "genocide." As an institution with a mission to broaden "understanding of the Holocaust and related issues, including those of contemporary significance," the USHMM has attempted to generate awareness about the conflict in Darfur, claiming: "To date about 2,500,000 civilians, targeted because of their ethnic or racial identity, have been driven from their homes, more than 300,000 people killed, and more than 1,600 villages destroyed by Sudanese government soldiers and government-backed militias, known as the 'Janjaweed.'"[6]

"Crisis in Darfur" became the first project in the museum's "Genocide Prevention Mapping Initiative." From 2004 to 2007 a team of museum staff members began gathering materials related to the Darfur conflict and building a database that included reports and information from Amnesty International, Human Rights Watch, and the US State Department, written or quoted testimony from victims, professional photographs, video clips, and data about displaced persons and refugees. USHMM director, Sara Bloomfield, indicated the museum approached Google after learning Google Earth software had been downloaded by 200 million people worldwide. Museum staff working on the Crisis in Darfur project felt that partnering with Google would allow them to present evidence of genocide on "the world's biggest billboard."[7] As Michael Graham, coordinator of the museum's Genocide Mapping initiative indicated, "We had all this information [about Darfur] from human rights groups, the State Department, and others, but it wasn't accessible, because the vast majority of people don't read 80-page human rights reports."[8] Thus one of the goals of the Crisis in Darfur project was to transform long investigative reports into formats that would facilitate public engagement with the important findings they contained.

On April 10, 2007 Google and the USHMM held a high profile press conference in Washington, DC to announce the public launch of the Crisis in Darfur project. Representatives of Google and the USHMM spoke, as did Darfurian refugee Daowd Salih, who witnessed the widespread atrocities in his homeland. In his statement Salih thanked the museum and Google for "recognizing that people around the world need to see what genocide looks like," and insisted, "it's not about numbers. It's about the people—like my brothers and sisters who are still in Darfur in internally displaced camps and refugee camps in Chad ... My village is completely destroyed." He then pointed to a Google Earth frame representing the Sudanese territory as covered with red flame icons and said, "It is not easy to mention the name of my village (even though it is on the map) for fear that my family could be put in danger." Salih closed with the suggestion, "We need the perpetrators to understand that they are being watched" and went on to thank the media "for covering this for Darfur. Our voice only comes through the media."[9]

Salih's press conference testimony is significant for several reasons. First, his remarks position Google Earth not only as a mechanism for informing the Western world about genocide in the region, but also as an observational platform that can be used to monitor the perpetrators and deter their violence in the region. In other words, he imagines Google Earth as a technology for tracking political violence with the intention of stopping it. In this sense, Google Earth is figured as a testimonial apparatus designed to raise awareness, and is also understood more urgently, at least by this eyewitness, as a technology of direct intervention. Second, Salih suggests how very important the news media are in conveying the voices and experiences of Darfur's displaced persons and refugees. News media do not simply represent, they also carry, project, and re-distribute trauma so that it is not simply "localized," but becomes part of a shared system of global circulation. Indeed, Google Earth plays a role in projecting and redistributing the affect of trauma and suffering within systems of digital exchange. Finally, the ability to *hear* Salih's testimony is all the more important given that Google Earth does not yet have a sonic dimension. Audible testimonials and the sounds of suffering and violence from Darfur, which for some might be as vivid and compelling as the corresponding imagery, reverberate far beyond the global digital corporate archive. The only testimony accessible at the interface is textual and it has been carefully selected, translated, and transcribed by the database developers. Testimony is embedded within Amnesty International and Human Rights Watch reports, but is not presented as an array of audible voices recounting their traumatic experiences.

Nevertheless, the press conference speeches by Salih and others insisted that using the Google Earth platform to present evidence of "genocide" would make it more difficult for the world to turn the other way, as had happened in the case of Rwanda during the 1990s and, as Samantha Power suggests in her book *A Problem from Hell*, in other conflicts throughout the twentieth century.[10] At the press conference USHMM director Sara Bloomfield declared, "When it comes to responding to genocide, the world's record is terrible. We hope this important initiative with Google will make it that much harder for the world to ignore those who need us the most."[11] Google's Vice President of Global Communications and Public Affairs, Elliot Schrage, also spoke at the press conference, proclaiming: "'Crisis in Darfur' will enable Google Earth users to visualize and learn about the destruction in Darfur as never before" (ibid.). Both presented the project as a kind of "information intervention" that relied upon new technology to expose ongoing political violence in a region largely ignored by the international community.

To explore the project in Google Earth the user must click on the "Global Awareness" layer and select "USHMM: Crisis in Darfur," which exists alongside other projects such as the World Wildlife Federation Conservation Projects, UN Environmental Program's Atlas of Our Changing Environment, and a handful of others that have been approved by Google Earth. After clicking on the Crisis in Darfur the user encounters a view of the Darfur region made from US satellite images acquired between 2004 and 2007. This view is inscribed with an array of small icons including tents, flames, cameras, and quotation marks. As the USHMM website explains, the layer is designed to allow users to "zoom down and see what a burned village looks like from above, the vast tent cities of people displaced from their homes, and photos on the ground of refugees struggling to survive." By clicking on the various icons, the user can link to frames that contain data about the numbers of refugees and internally displaced persons in certain locations, images of destroyed and partially destroyed villages, quotes from those whose villages were destroyed, photographs of sites and people throughout the region, and video of foreigners discussing what they witnessed while working in the region. Testimony excerpts and photographs are presented at the interface as emerging from the specific locations in which they transpired.

Clicking on a camera icon will lead to a photograph taken by one of several professional photographers including Jerry Fowler, staff director of Committee on Conscience; Mark Brecke, a professional photographer/filmmaker who also worked in Rwanda, the West Bank, Kosovo, and Iraq; Ryan Spencer Reed, a photojournalist; Ron Haviv, a professional war photographer who also worked in Yugoslavia and Afghanistan; and Brian Steidle, former US Marine who became a monitor for the African Union Monitoring Force. Photographs taken by Hollywood actress Mia Farrow, who made several trips to the region, are also included in the database. As the Crisis in Darfur interface explains, "The imagery allows any user to see the systematic destruction of tens of thousands of homes, schools, mosques and other structures" and invites the user to "witness destruction for yourself ... See more than 1,600 villages that have been damaged or completely destroyed. Zoom to more than 133,000 homes, schools, mosques and other buildings burned to the ground."

The interface draws on and combines the visualizing conventions of cartography, the National Geographic photo essay, war photography, and human rights monitoring in an effort to arouse "global awareness" about the conflict in Darfur. Yet what is missing in the layer is a history of the (post)colonial geopolitics of the region, including historical details about events such as the Berlin Conference of 1885, the so-called "Scramble for

Africa," which divided up the continent among European powers and had the effect of introducing animosities in the region derived from colonial policies and the biopolitical constitution of majorities and minorities.[12] It would also be important to provide information about the various cease-fire treaties that have been signed and violated, extensive testimonials from victims, details about aid workers and peacekeepers killed in the conflict, and information about the perpetrators of violence and their resources and maneuvers.[13]

into the heart of dark press coverage

Despite the paucity of historical information in the Crisis in Darfur interface, the project's launch and press conference were met with a congratulatory press. Even though the USHMM initiated the project, headlines tended to recognize and praise Google and emphasize the corporation's benevolent efforts to draw attention to the violence in Darfur. A BBC headline announced, "Google Earth Turns Spotlight on Darfur"; the *SF Gate* proclaimed, "Google Earth Zooms in on Darfur Carnage"; and *Tech News World* read, "Google Earth Zooms into Heart of Darfur's Darkness."[14] Such headlines not only invoke problematic Western tropes of Africa as a "dark continent" in need of "exposure" and "close examination," they also position the Google corporation and the Google Earth application as an assemblage of resources and technologies that can be mobilized to "spotlight" and monitor trouble spots and promote civil society. In its own descriptions of the project Google interpellates users as if global peacekeepers, explaining: "Improving rapid access to satellite imagery has the potential to enable citizens worldwide using Google Earth to play a part in monitoring areas at risk of genocide, and to strengthen organizations' ability to respond effectively. Expanding the use of remote imagery might help convince potential perpetrators that their actions against civilians will not go unnoticed by the international community."[15]

The press coverage also stressed Google's humanitarianism, positioning the company as hero of digital capitalism. *Wired* claimed the Crisis in Darfur project demonstrated that Google Earth could be "a life-saving humanitarian tool."[16] *PC World* pointed out that the project was consistent with the Google corporation's mantra "Do No Evil," and suggested that by making the Crisis in Darfur available "Google takes it one step further."[17] A senior advisor to the International Crisis Group, John Prendergast, proclaimed, "No one can any longer say they don't know. This tool will bring a spotlight to a very dark corner of the earth, a torch that will indirectly help protect the victims. It is David versus Goliath and Google Earth just gave David a stone for his slingshot."[18]

While the press focused on Google's humanitarianism (and ironically less so on that of the USHMM), there was little discussion of the complexity of the Darfur conflict itself, not to mention the challenge of visually representing it. Instead, most of the coverage promulgated the idea that the information contained in the Crisis in Darfur project is simply "true" or would "expose the truth." Even before the Crisis in Darfur project was released, an online publication entitled *Ogle Earth* posted a comment about satellite images of Darfur that were added to Google Earth in January to March 2006, describing them as "an unequivocal indictment of the Janjaweed, and of the Sudanese government whose implicit support it has enjoyed, because in these new images each and every burned-out gottia is visible."[19] *The Register* in the UK reported: "The Crisis in Darfur project offers stark evidence of the true scale of the carnage, including the location of more than 1,600 destroyed and partially destroyed villages, plus audio and pictorial evidence."[20]

While it may be accurate to say that many villages have been destroyed by the Janjaweed, the "truth" status of satellite images and of other visual materials presented in Google Earth needs to be evaluated and contextualized more carefully rather than simply adopted as "the real." Using satellite images alone, it may not be possible to determine exactly who burned certain villages. One of the only press articles to recognize the precariousness of representation in the Crisis of Darfur layer appeared in the *Telegraph*. In it David Blair remarked that Google Earth "unquestionably labels the war a 'genocide' even though the United Nations investigation ruled in 2005 that the term did not apply to events in Darfur," and continued, "the atrocities detailed on Google Earth are overwhelmingly attributed to the Janjaweed ... Rebel armies have also committed atrocities in Darfur, but these are not detailed on the website. Sudan's regime may also ask why Google has chosen to highlight this war and not other crises."[21]

Blair's observation serves as an important reminder of the need to be wary of the mantra that "seeing is believing," even when it seems that such a position is the most ethical and just one to take. Though the USHMM went to great lengths to acquire materials from reputable and credible organizations such as Human Rights Watch and Amnesty International among others, there are many ways of presenting and interpreting this information. In the digital age even the most seemingly incriminating visual evidence must be examined closely and considered in relation to broader institutional, technological, and geopolitical strategies.[22] Phrases such as "the image speaks for itself" are no longer tenable. Not only do different users/viewers have radically different ways of interpreting the same visual information, the status of the digital image is itself uncertain and is often subjected (sometimes undetectably) to practices of doctoring and spinning.

The press doled out high praise for the Crisis in Darfur project without mentioning that there is limited historical contextualization at the interface, there is a ready embrace of both the satellite and other imagery as "truthful evidence," and there is little sense that the packaging of information in the Google Earth platform has impacted policy making and/or led to meaningful intervention. The project has perhaps helped spread awareness of the violence in Darfur, but the violence itself has not ceased. Further, it is worth asking what kind of "awareness" the layer raises. As a writer for the ICT (Information Communication Technology) for Peacebuilding blog astutely observed, "Although this [Google Earth] technology ... tries to galvanize global political actors and policy to act urgently against a further deterioration of conditions in Darfur, it's unclear how earlier attempts at using technology have succeeded in raising and sustaining the level of awareness and compassion necessary to address such crises."[23] Indeed, US information technologies and awareness initiatives have limits and are not in themselves sufficient to thwart a civil war in Sudan. This war and other wars have their roots in colonial pasts, pasts that the West remains deeply implicated in. An interesting way to navigate the Crisis in Darfur layer might be to hold in the other hand Sven Lindqvist's book *Exterminate All the Brutes*, a geographic meditation on the history of European genocide in Africa.[24]

In general, the press coverage and discourse surrounding the Crisis in Darfur project tended to reduce the political to the visual and encourage a "seeing is believing" logic, deputize the user/citizen as a monitor on global patrol situated at a strategic interface, celebrate the humanitarian potential of a US corporation and information technology, and demonstrate a preoccupation with the power to visualize rather than to develop coherent policies that may lead to peace in the region. In the following sections I question these tendencies further by offering a critical analysis of the interface that focuses upon the shifting role of the satellite image, the temporality of the interface, the branding of the Darfur conflict and the meanings of "information intervention."

eclipsing the satellite image

During the past fifteen years US satellite images have appeared in news media on various occasions, whether to draw attention to displaced persons in central Africa, mass graves in Bosnia, or alleged weapons facilities in Iraq.[25] In these previous instances the satellite images that circulated had been declassified by the US Department of Defense and presented by different news agencies as either novel, horrifying, or strategic views of events related to conflicts on the ground. In Google Earth, the satellite image takes on a different function. Rather than being a site/sight of focus in the context of a print or broadcast news story, the satellite image is positioned as an entry point or gateway to closer—typically anthropomorphic and, hence, more easily relatable—views. The Crisis in Darfur interface is structured in a way that encourages users to zoom through and bypass the satellite image—as opposed to scrutinize it—in search of closer and presumably more meaningful perspectives. In this sense, the satellite image becomes a kind of throwaway, even despite its prominence and ubiquity in Google Earth. Unfortunately, the potential for satellite image literacy may ironically be diminished at the very site at which it could be enhanced and extended.

As I have argued elsewhere, the satellite image is useful as a site/sight of focus because its abstraction and indeterminacy keep acts of interpretation and practices of knowledge dynamic. The satellite image is a site/sight that must be read.[26] Yet, at the Crisis in Darfur interface, satellite images are traversed in favor of closer views and anthropomorphic representations, many of which feature injured bodies and/or displaced women and children. For instance, by clicking on a camera icon one can view a photo with the caption, "A malnourished girl in the MSF therapeutic feeding center. Inba, Chad, May 2004," or another featuring "Mihad Harrid, a year old girl, whose mother had attempted to escape an attack from helicopter gunships and Janjaweed marauders on their village, Allet, in October 2004," or yet another with the caption, "Girl with traumatized baby sister. The baby has not made a sound since the day their parents were slaughtered and the village burned." As illustrated in Figures 10.1, 10.2, and 10.3, the Google Earth interface is structured in a way that eclipses the satellite image and fills it in with closer views that are consistent with Western tropes of African tragedy and the representation of refugees. The images spotlight the frail and wounded bodies of innocent young girls. Figure 10.1, for instance, shows a photo of a baby girl who is so small that she is barely visible while cradled in the arms of a woman preparing to nurse her. Figure 10.2 reveals a close-up designed to focus attention upon an infected open wound on

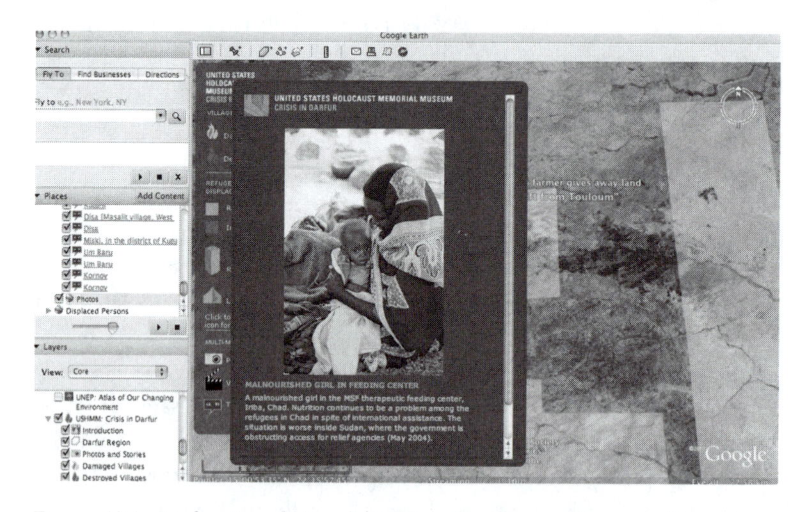

Figure 10.1 At the Google Earth/Crisis in Darfur interface satellite images are overlaid with closer views of victims. This screen capture reveals a photograph with a caption that reads, "A malnourished girl in the MSF therapeutic feeding center. Inba, Chad, May 2004."

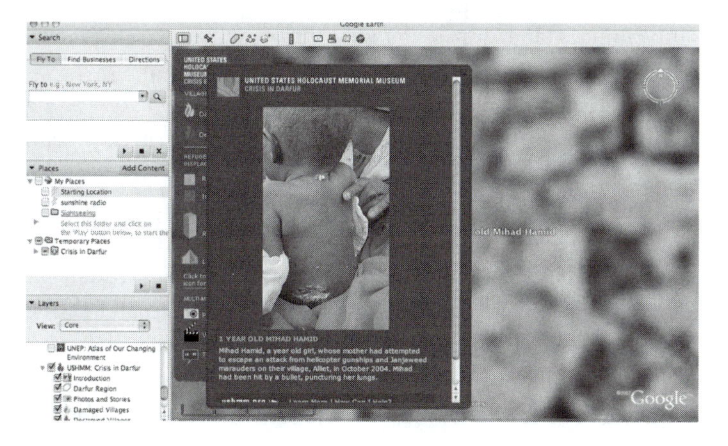

Figure 10.2

In this screen capture the satellite image is once again eclipsed by a photograph, this time of an infant victim. As the caption explains, "Mihad Harrid, a year old girl, whose mother had attempted to escape an attack from helicopter gunships and Janjaweed marauders on their village, Allet, in October 2004."

the lower back of a tiny infant. Figure 10.3 features two young sisters gazing directly into the camera after losing their parents and home in an attack. These figures illustrate how the territorial perspective of the satellite image is overlaid with close-up photographs that are mobilized to *affectively* pinpoint feminized bodily injury and trauma. While the Darfur conflict has

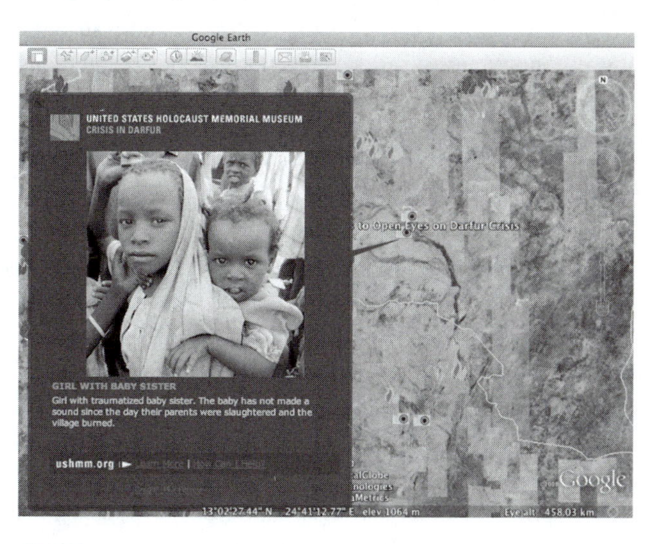

Figure 10.3

Yet another screen capture reveals how the Google Earth/Crisis in Darfur interface positions the satellite image as a backdrop or gateway to closer views rather than as the site of focus. This one features a photograph of "Girl with traumatized baby sister. The baby has not made a sound since the day their parents were slaughtered and the village burned."

certainly injured and displaced many innocent women and children, I wonder what it is that we see in these close-up photographs exactly.

Such closer views rely on what Michael Shapiro refers to as the "personal code" and focus on individual bodies rather than the complex dynamics of political violence in the region.[27] As David Campbell suggests in his analysis of newspaper photographs of the Darfur conflict, such images may reify Africans as victims as much as they draw attention to conflict. Similarly, the photographs integrated within the Crisis in Darfur layer may not trigger the kind of awareness and education that the USHMM intended. As Campbell writes, "Although many of the individuals who are producing and publishing such images are hoping that we feel moved and responsible and driven to act, the affective responses engendered by these symbolic statements of conflict can—because of their familiar forms—just as easily lead to inattention and indifference."[28]

While the repetitive circulation of such images in news media may make some citizens/viewers indifferent to the violence they register, several authors throughout this book convincingly show that images of victims and video testimonies have also been used very effectively to document and bear witness to the embodied and psychic effects of traumatic events ranging from environmental disasters to civil wars. Indeed, some such representations are at the core of activist movements for peace, justice, and social change. Here, I want to suggest that the satellite image has a unique role to play in the representation of political violence as well, and that it can be used to support such movements. Its cartographic and abstract qualities position it as more evocative than definitive and as such it may set off chains of inquiry, investigation, reflection, as well as questions about position and perspective. In other words, rather than being used to resolve questions of activities on the ground, this medium is most useful when it is used to stage inquiries concerning the complex dynamics of political violence which cannot simply be "seen" and "understood." While historically some images have successfully encapsulated or served as icons of violent conflicts around the world, there is a need to imagine and develop *different* ways of using and engaging with images in efforts to account for political violence. Satellite images could be used to represent aspects of the conflict that are more territorial and geopolitical and that cannot be reduced to images of the wounded body alone. They can expose territorial dimensions of atrocities such as burned villages, encampments of displaced masses, and perpetrators' maneuvers and hideouts. Their abstraction, and their dynamic interplay with other kinds of images, may help sustain a sense of the complexity of the conflict rather than reduce it to familiar, yet apparently unresolvable, tropes of "ethnic cleansing" and "tribal warfare" that are as much inventions of the Western imaginary and ways of understanding world conflicts as they may be accurate descriptions of conditions on the ground.

interface of the past perfect

The second point I wish to address involves the issue of temporality and, in particular, the tense of the Crisis in Darfur interface. One of the stated goals of the USHHM has been to "intervene" in the conflict and this has been emphasized in the project's publicity—to change things on the ground. If intervention is about the "now," then it would seem that the dates of satellite and other imagery that make up the layer would be highly significant. Yet many images available at the Crisis in Darfur layer are dated either only by year (between 2004 and 2007) or not at all. Updated satellite images can be acquired by Google Earth, but such refreshed views are not regularly integrated in the layer. Moreover, some of the professional photographs in the database are not dated precisely. This limited or missing temporal data is problematic because it plays into and perpetuates imaginings of the African continent as perpetually in strife, an ahistorical logic that presumes there are never changes to the conditions there.

While the Crisis in Darfur provides individuals with access to a wider array of sources and viewpoints than that of television news, it functions more as a medium of the past than of the present. The layer has a quite different temporal status than that of television news, which, in its claims to be "live" or "up-to-the-minute," typically provides the dates of visual materials it presents. The project may have been developed with the intention of fostering interventions on the ground, but the lack of temporal data is problematic in that it may prevent the interface from being useful to those for whom timing is everything—whether those aiding in refugee relief efforts, tracking human rights violations, or developing news reports. Ultimately, the Crisis in Darfur functions as *an archive of violent conflict that unfolded while being observed but without intervention.* It is an accumulation of information, a database of documents and images being used to represent and produce knowledge about a conflict site/sight that *could have been* intervened in. In this sense, the Crisis in Darfur project is a visual display of the *past perfect subjunctive* and perhaps as much as anything it *exemplifies the power to see/know and not act.* Thus even as Google Earth generates awareness and attempts to compel intervention, the project may, ironically, participate in the twentieth century pattern Power describes so powerfully in her book *A Problem from Hell* of knowing genocidal atrocities are occurring but not acting to stop them.

It is this paradox and conundrum that perhaps prompted Amnesty International to begin working on a project which tracks attacks in the region online *as they happen.* The *All Eyes on Darfur Project* was launched in June 2007 and uses commercial satellite imagery from the companies Digital Globe, Geoeye, and Imagesat to monitor 13 villages in Darfur and Eastern Chad at imminent risk of attack. In this project, not only are satellite images the featured sites/sights of investigation, they are also clearly dated.

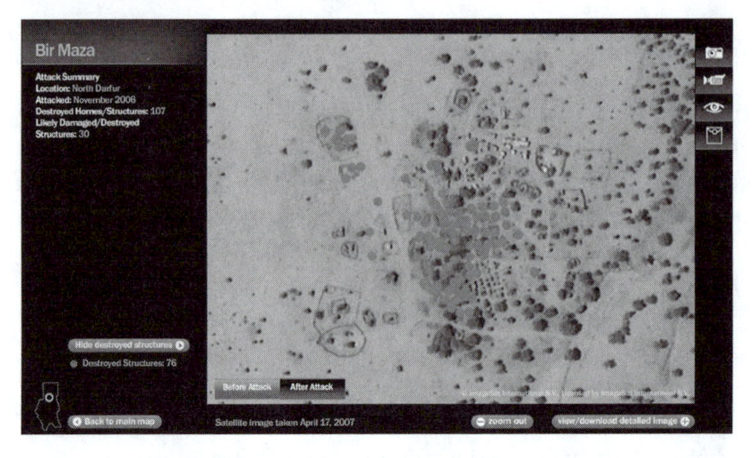

Figure 10.4 This screen capture reveals the way satellite evidence is presented at the Amnesty International Eyes on Darfur website. Featured is a satellite image of the Sudanese village of Bir Maza and in the color version of the image destroyed buildings and structures are identified with red dots.

Furthermore, there is an attempt to use them to analyze and predict other villages at risk given analysis of locations already attacked and the spatial patterns of the attacks. For instance, by clicking "view destroyed structures" one can get a spatial sense of the attacks in different villages as red and/or yellow dots are graphically inscribed in the satellite image to indicate the locations of destroyed or partially destroyed structures. Figures 10.4 and 10.5 contain satellite images that were used to identify destruction in the villages of Bir Maza and Bornyo.

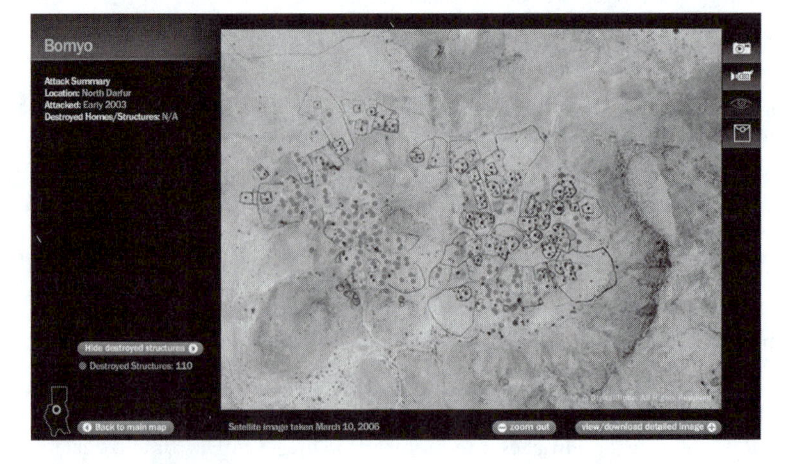

Figure 10.5 The "satellite evidence" presented at Eyes on Darfur is the site of focus at the interface, and can be used to initiate forensic investigations. This screen capture reveals a satellite image of destroyed buildings in the Sudanese village of Bornyo.

While Amnesty International does not have the funding to provide constantly updated satellite imagery, I want to emphasize the importance of its efforts as well as its intention to foreground "satellite evidence." The Eyes on Darfur website significantly presents satellite images as catalysts for forensic investigation since they can be used to initiate questions such as: who conducted the attack? From which direction did it occur? How many people were killed? How were they killed? How many buildings were destroyed and how? Were nearby villages also attacked? In other words, a strong focus on the satellite image itself can create an interrogatory position for the viewer, as well as a sympathetic one. Such a position confronts issues of temporality in that forensic investigations are designed to reconstruct the order of events and to use this knowledge to prevent them from happening again in the future. The Eyes on Darfur project is thus suggestive of the way that a *satellite forensics*—an investigative disposition or practice—can take shape in relation to the satellite image and be used to impact events on the ground whether through a process of historic reconstruction or future deterrence. This satellite forensics emerges through the interplay of far and near logics, through the orbital view's provocation of close-up curiosities. Though the Eyes on Darfur project has the potential to inspire such investigative practices, it has not had nearly as much publicity as Crisis in Darfur, likely because it does not have the Google brand name behind it.

conflict branding

The third issue I would like to discuss is the relationship between the digital corporation and global conflicts. Google Earth software has been used by many people for many purposes around the world and in the process has arguably generated a more fully elaborated form of digital capitalism. Google Earth transforms the sovereign territories of all of the world's nation-states into visual, digital, navigable, and privatized domains (largely) owned by one US corporation, Google. When the user navigates the Crisis in Darfur database (as well as others) with Google Earth software, the Google logo appears in the bottom right corner of every frame. Google claims copyright ownership of all of these frames unless they contain images originally classified as public domain. (NASA satellite images, for instance, remain public domain when they are part of Google Earth's databases.) In Google Earth the satellite image may be obscured or undated, but the Google brand is never lost.

The corporation's involvement in the Crisis in Darfur project and use of it to market and extend its brand name is a perfect example of neoliberalism. As David Harvey explains, neoliberalism is a set of "political economic practices that proposes that human well-being can best be advanced by liberating individual entrepreneurial freedoms and skills within an institutional framework characterized by strong private property rights, free markets and free trade."[29] One of the aims of neoliberalism is to convert "various forms of property rights (common, collective, state, etc.) into exclusive property rights" (159). In this case, intellectual property that has been classified as public domain (whether state department or UN documents, NASA satellite images, reports from Amnesty International and Human Rights Watch) has been compiled as a database that is accessible through the privatized interface of Google Earth. *The digital corporation*, as opposed to the state, international agencies, or NGOs, becomes the primary mechanism for distributing information about the Darfur conflict. *Public* reports and documents are rearranged and presented alongside *privatized* information owned and branded by the Google corporation. Google, of course, does not own all content in the Crisis in Darfur database, but it does own the means to distribute it and thus has the power to control and regulate access to the information. What is also significant here is the way public and private intellectual properties are intermixed within Google Earth so that their ownership status is unclear and becomes relatively indistinguishable. This is reinforced when Google Earth imprints its brand name across and around public domain materials about Darfur because it owns the means to distribute them. Thus as Google Earth participates in the global circulation of public and privatized information about the Crisis in Darfur, it also lays corporate claim to the conflict.

In addition, Google Earth assumes responsibilities of global imaging once administered by the US National Reconnaissance Office and the Central Intelligence Agency. Satellite images have been gathered by federal agencies for nearly fifty years and Google Earth has now taken on the function of making this information accessible and valuable within the global economy. The very production of Google Earth software is symptomatic of a global economy in which most nation-states are unable to control the production and circulation of representations of their own territories and those transnational corporations that own and operate satellite and computer technologies—the technologies of high visual capital—are able to generate huge profits from such a condition of disparity. Google did not request formal permission from states to include satellite and other images of their territories in its proprietary interface/databases. In fact, countries such as India, South Korea, and Morocco have registered complaints against the company, alleging privacy invasions and concerns about national security.

Finally, the Crisis in Darfur interface is also symptomatic of an economic shift that Naomi Klein identifies as "disaster capitalism," in this case a condition defined by global security and information industries' rapid privatization and expansion after 9/11. As she explains, disaster capitalism involves "orchestrated raids on the public sphere in the wake of catastrophic events, combined with the treatment of disasters as exciting market opportunities."[30] Comparing this shift to the high-tech bubble economy, Klein writes that the, "disaster capitalism complex is on a par with the 'emerging market' and information technology boom of the nineties ... the disaster economy may well have saved the world market from the full-blown recession it was facing on the eve of 9/11."[31] Google Earth has become part of this complex to the extent that it produces systems of planetary visualization that have been used for conflict and disaster management. In addition to representing the conflict in Darfur, Google Earth interfaces have featured disasters ranging from Hurricane Katrina to the war in Iraq, from the tsunami in Indonesia to wildfires in California. When discussing how aspects of disaster capitalism have played in different parts of the world, Klein poses the rhetorical question, "Why deploy UN peacekeepers to Darfur when private security companies like Blackwater are looking for new clients?"[32] We could similarly ask, why have Human Rights or Amnesty International distribute their own reports on Darfur when Google can do it? The point here is that Google is part of a global economic system that has been organized to allow the US digital corporation to profit from the erosion of public, state, NGO funding for all kinds of programs, but especially conflict, disaster, and security-related services. In short, Google Earth is not "a view from nowhere"—it is the view from a company with enormous visual capital. And it, like other US corporations, whether security firms or media cartels, stands to profit from disaster and conflict.[33]

information intervention and the google earth effect

In their book *Forging Peace*, Monroe Price and Mark Thompson identify "information intervention" as a crucial aspect of contemporary warfare, explaining that it involves "the extensive external management, manipulation or seizure of information space in conflict zones."[34] Practices of "information intervention" range from radio jamming to peace broadcasting and involve "actions taken by a powerful state or a combination of states sometimes in the name of the 'international community.' The actions may be taken to prevent conflict, as part of conflict, or as part of post-conflict reconstruction" (8). Military organizations use information interventions not only to win wars, but also to "democratize" and "liberalize" media systems, and increasingly, particularly in the age of neoliberalism and disaster capitalism, the digital corporation is implicated in these efforts. Google Earth can certainly be described as participating in the "external management," "manipulation," and "seizure" of Sudan's information space with the intention of preventing further violence and killing in the region. In this sense, Google Earth can be understood as yet another technique in the arsenal of information intervention.

While the Crisis in Darfur project alone could not deter violence in the region, a Google Earth spokesperson has emphasized its other successes, claiming: "The reaction to this project has been immediate: it has stimulated extensive worldwide media coverage, traffic to the USHMM website has quadrupled, and reporters and human rights organizations have used the information in these layers to ask more pointed questions."[35] What is striking here is that success is measured by an increase in world media attention to the Crisis in Darfur project itself and traffic to the USHMM website as opposed to an impact upon international policy or a change in conditions in Darfur. Moore's statement is a testament to the Google public relations campaign that underpins the project. This is all the more clear when one realizes that the Sudanese themselves cannot even access the Crisis in Darfur project using Google Earth, given that US export controls and economic sanctions against Sudan prohibit people in that country from downloading US software.

Another issue to consider is whether this increase in traffic to, and the alleged impact of, Google Earth are analogous to the CNN's expanded influence when the network globalized throughout the 1990s. In other words, it is worth considering how a project such as Crisis in Darfur relates to what has been called the "CNN effect." This term emerged during the 1990s when it became clear that the representation of news events on the 24-hour global cable news network CNN was beginning to impact the foreign policies of nation-states. Steven Livingston suggested in 1997 that "the extent, depth, and speed of the new global media have created a new species of effects" that differed from earlier ones.[36] Whether the Crisis in Darfur (or any other database in Google Earth for that matter) has impacted foreign policy in a way that warrants the designation "Google Earth effect" is open to discussion and may be too early to determine. I raise this question here simply to suggest that Google Earth may, because of its capitalistic underpinnings and global ambitions, end up operating more like CNN than digital enthusiasts would like to imagine. While the Crisis in Darfur presents information in a different format than that of a television news report, it relies upon similar practices in that it draws upon and combines evidence from different sources, privatizes public records, brands conflicts, and presents multimedia accounts of world historical events. Furthermore, it has reproduced some of the conventions of representing African displacement and victimization often seen in the coverage of CNN and other news networks.

Perhaps a good indicator of things to come is to be found in CNN's frequent use of Google Earth imagery in its news coverage such that the two brands are positioned as competing within the same frame. Yet just as one can glimpse the Google Earth brand in the video flow of CNN, one can find icons and a pop up window revealing CNN's corporate logo and Atlanta headquarters in the digital terrain of Google Earth, as shown in Figure 10.6, which is consistent with what Siva Vaidhyanathan calls the "Googlization of Everything."[37] Indeed, both companies not only use their brands to attract and compete for consumers, but also hold the power to shape knowledge about and impact interventions into world affairs. In this sense,

Figure 10.6
Just as Google Earth frames have been increasingly integrated in CNN news reports, this Google Earth screen capture reveals how the software can also be used to pinpoint the location of CNN's headquarters in Atlanta, Georgia.

they are major players within the global media economy and the geopolitical condition. Because of this, it is vital that critical analyses of their world-visions, whether they come in the form of the Crisis in Darfur layer or in the form of live reports from other conflict zones, continue.

conclusion

While Google Earth presents exciting new possibilities for integrating and accessing documents and audiovisual materials and providing them in geo-referenced fashion, information interventions such as Crisis in Darfur need to be discussed and evaluated carefully. The project compels us to reflect upon the visual representation of political violence as a serious challenge and to ask what kinds of representations might lead not only to more awareness, but also to better policy making as well. As Power reminds us, "History has shown that the suffering of victims has rarely been sufficient to get the US to intervene ... Humanitarian intervention came about only on the rare occasions when the shorter term political interests of US policymakers were at stake."[38] Perhaps there has been too much congratulatory discourse around Google Earth and too little scrutiny and discussion of the implications of its visual capital. Should the accumulation of visual capital come with the responsibility of developing accountability for and appropriate responses to the horrific acts that imaging technologies might be used to see? This is a question that deserves further deliberation.

Rather than operate in the past perfect subjunctive—that is, *observe what could have been intervened in*—we need a visuality that is linked to acknowledgment, accountability, and intention as opposed to regret and lament. This mode of looking might also have built within it a recognition of the very great challenge of representing global conflicts—whether from the satellite or the ground—and an inherent sensitivity to the tensions, disparities, inequities, and traumas that have resulted from the histories of colonialism, the Cold War, and the war on terror. These historical contexts are not merely backdrops, but are themselves constitutive of modern visualities. Adopting sensitivity to such historical conditions in our visual encounters is especially important when the views of global conflicts are generated and experienced through the privileged platforms of high visual capital.

The satellite image, whether it appears in news media or Google Earth, remains a useful tool in the representation and discussion of global humanitarian crises. It is useful because it displaces the familiarity and authority of the proximate view and, in so doing, challenges the all too easy assumption that a closer view leads to better understanding. This point is especially important in relation to the visual representation of historical violence and trauma, since, in some cases, proximity literally clouds or obscures vision.[39] And yet the distant view of the satellite image comes with its own baggage. Its historical alignment with military strategy and scientific objectivity compels us to be wary of its paternalistic associations with "humanitarian" over-sights and super-visions. In the end, the structural interplays between the far and the near that undergird Google Earth's Crisis in Darfur project are helpful in that they represent the potential to refigure key terms of humanitarianism. The iconographies of suffering are not reduced to the anthropomorphic photograph alone, but are placed in dynamic alternations with satellite images and graphics that emphasize the territorial and the geopolitical. Testimonials are translated, transcribed, and geo-referenced but they remain inaudible and unheard. Witnessing is figured across a continuum of technologized far and near perspectives rather than fetishized as the physical bystander or "eyewitness." The satellite image can function as an "information intervention," then, in that it fosters different ways of visualizing and conceptualizing these key terms of humanitarianism—suffering, testimony, and witnessing.

Finally, the intense energy and motivation to "do something" about the Darfur conflict could be accompanied by further critical thinking about the relationship between images and political change. Since research shows that Westerners have become increasingly desensitized or immune to images of victims' suffering and displacement, this approach to communicating about world conflicts and their effects (used by news agencies and NGOs alike) may need to change. Google Earth represents the possibility of visualizing some of the geopolitical, territorial, and structural conditions that set the stage for political violence in the first place. For instance, it offers the potential to overlay historical maps of colonial occupation, highlight areas of desertification, and identify networks of transportation. While the human dimensions of the conflict are no doubt extremely important, political violence stems from structural conditions and it seems useful to find ways of better communicating and understanding them. For instance, we might consider what the transit routes of the Sudanese and Janjaweed weapons trade are. What are the spatial patterns of Janjaweed attacks? Where are the region's water and agricultural resources located? Treating the satellite image as a field in which to initiate and answer these questions might be a good place to start. Armed with such information, world citizens might be more apt to pressure their governments to formulate proactive as opposed to reactive foreign policies, to understand world conflicts as the result of more than the primitivism or pathology of tribal warfare, and to help push the historical forces and power hierarchies that shape the planet into bold relief.

acknowledgments

I would like to thank those who gave feedback on earlier versions of this text when I presented it at the University of Michigan Human Rights Lecture Series, the Conference on the Planetary in Cologne, Germany, and the Beaverbrook Scholar in Residence public lecture at McGill University in Montreal. Thanks also to Bhaskar Sarkar and Janet Walker for their very helpful comments and encouragement.

notes

1. Jo Ellen Fair and Lisa Parks, "Africa on Camera: Televised Video Footage and Aerial Imaging of the Rwandan Refugee Crisis," *Africa Today* 48, no. 2 (2001): 35–57; Lisa Parks, "Satellite Witnessing: Views and Coverage of the War in Bosnia," in *Cultures in Orbit: Satellites and the Televisual* (Durham, NC: Duke University Press, 2005), 76–107; and Lisa Parks, "Planet Patrol: Satellite Images, Acts of Knowledge, and Global Security," in *Rethinking Global Security: Media, Popular Culture, and the "War on Terror,"* eds. Patrice Petro and Andrew Martin (New Brunswick, NJ: Rutgers University Press, 2006), 132–50.
2. Jo Ellen Fair, "The Body Politic, the Bodies of Women, and the Politics of Famine," *Journalism and Mass Communication Monographs* 158 (1996): 1–42.
3. Google Earth, "U.S. Holocaust Memorial Museum and Google Join in Online Darfur Mapping Initiative," 2007 press release, www.google.com/intl/en/ press/pressrel/darfur_mapping.html (accessed 30 July 2007).
4. Irit Rogoff, *Terra Infirma: Geography's Visual Culture* (London: Routledge, 2000), 20.
5. Lisa Parks, "Satellite and Cyber Visualities: Analyzing 'Digital Earth,'" in *Visual Culture Reader 2.0*, ed. Nicholas Mirzoeff (New York and London: Routledge, 2003), 279–94. Translated into Dutch and reprinted in *Journal of Dutch Gender Studies*, 2003.
6. "Crisis in Darfur" Interface, Google Earth (accessed 30 July 2007). This information is also available at http://www.ushmm.org/conscience/alert/darfur/contents/01-overview/ (accessed 15 March 2009).
7. Desmond Butler, "Google Earth Focuses on Sudan Atrocities," MSNBC, 10 April 2007, www.msnbc.msn.com/id/18045002/ (accessed 30 July 2007). This partnership has facilitated other museum projects as well. For instance,

the USHMM is using Google Earth to map key Holocaust sites such as Auschwitz, Dachau, Bergen-Belsen, Treblinka, Warsaw, and Lodz with historic content from its collections.

8. Stefan Lovgren, "Photos, Video Expose Darfur Activities in Google Earth," *National Geographic News*, 25 April 2007, news.nationalgeographic.com/news/2007/04/070425-google-darfur.html (accessed 15 August 2007).
9. Video of the press conference, including Salih's testimony, is available on YouTube, www.youtube.com/watch?v=EgdFHoyJD6Y&feature=PlayList&p=457CE3DBD8B79672&index=7 (accessed 7 December 2008).
10. See Samantha Power, *A Problem from Hell: America and the Age of Genocide* (New York: Harper Perennial, 2002).
11. Elise Labott, "Google Earth Maps out Darfur Atrocities," CNN, 15 April 2007, edition.cnn.com/2007/TECH/04/10/google.genocide/index.html (accessed 30 July 2007).
12. Peter Bloom, *French Colonial Documentary: Mythologies of Humanitarianism* (Minneapolis: University of Minnesota Press, 2008).
13. Setting the Crisis in Darfur project into dialogue with the specificities of the colonial past could also offer a useful corrective to trauma theory's overarching psychologism, a tendency that is often carried through in testimonies and, more so, in their reception. I thank Bhaskar Sarkar and Janet Walker for making this point.
14. Laura Smith-Spark, "Google Earth Turns Spotlight on Darfur," *BBC News*, 11 April 2007, newsvote.bbc.co.uk/mpapps/pagetools/print/news.bbc.co.uk/hi/Africa/6543185.stm (accessed 30 July 2007); Verne Kopytoff, "Google Earth Zooms in on Darfur Carnage," *SF Gate*, 11 April 2007, sfgate.com/cgi-in/article.cgi?file=/c/a/2007/04/11/MNGPNP6D1.DTL&type=printable (accessed 30 July 2007); Chris Maxcer, "Google Earth Zooms into Heart of Darfur's Darkness," *Tech News World*, 11 April 2007, www.technewsworld.com/story/56827.html# (accessed 30 July 2007).
15. Michael Graham, "United States Holocaust Memorial Museum *Crisis in Darfur*," Google Earth Outreach Case Study website, 2007. Available at http://earth.google.com/outreach/cs_darfur.html (accessed 15 January 2008).
16. Scott Gilbertson, "Google Earth Zooms in on Darfur Genocide," *Wired*, 27 June 2007, www.wired.com/techbiz/it/news/2007/06/google_darfur (accessed 15 August 2007).
17. Tom Spring, "A Closer Look: Google Earth Darfur Awareness," *PC World*, 11 April 2007, blogs.pcworld.com/staffblog/archives/004070.html (accessed 30 July 2007).
18. N. Boustany, "Museum, Google Zoom in on Darfur," *Washington Post*, 14 April 2007. Available at www.washingtonpost.com/wp-dyn/content/article/2007/04/13/AR2007041302189_pf.html (accessed 30 July 2007).
19. "Darfur," *Ogle Earth*, posted 3 October 2006, www.ogleearth.com/2006/10/darfur.html (accessed 30 July 2007).
20. Lester Haines, "Darfur Genocide Mapped from Space," *The Register*, 11 April 2007, www.theregister.co.uk/2007/04/11/crisis_in_darfur/print.html (accessed 31 July 2007).
21. David Blair, "Google Earth Maps 'Genocide' in Darfur," *Telegraph*, 13 April 2007, www.telegraph.co.uk/core/Content/displayPrintable.jhtml?xml=/news/2007/04/12/wdarfur12.xml&site=5&page=0 (accessed 30 July 2007).
22. See William J. Mitchell, *The Reconfigured Eye: Visual Truth in the Post-Photographic Era* (Cambridge, MA: MIT Press, 1992); Parks, "Satellite Witnessing"; and Parks, "Planet Patrol."

23. Sanjana Hattotuwa, "Darfur through Google Earth: The Reality of Conflict through 'Crisis in Darfur,'" ICT for Peacebuilding, 12 April 2007, ict4peace.wordpress.com/2007/04/12/darfur-through-google-earth-the-reality-of-conflict-through-crisis-in-darfur/ (accessed 7 December 2007).
24. Sven Lindqvist, *"Exterminate All the Brutes": One Man's Odyssey into the Heart of Darkness and the Origins of European Genocide* (New York: The New Press, 1996).
25. Fair and Parks, "Africa on Camera"; Parks, "Satellite Witnessing"; and Parks, "Planet Patrol."
26. Parks, "Satellite Witnessing"; and Parks, "Planet Patrol."
27. Michael Shapiro, *The Politics of Representation: Writing Practices in Biography, Photography, and Political Analysis* (Madison: University of Wisconsin Press, 1988).
28. David Campbell, "Geopolitics and Visuality: Sighting the Darfur Conflict," *Political Geography* 26, no. 4 (2007): 380.
29. David Harvey, *A Brief History of Neoliberalism* (Oxford: Oxford University Press, 2005), 2.
30. Naomi Klein, *The Shock Doctrine: The Rise of Disaster Capitalism* (New York: Metropolitan Books, 2007), 6.
31. Ibid., 14.
32. Ibid., 13.
33. International diplomacy has been outsourced not only to Google, but also to Hollywood as well. There is a veritable media industry that has emerged in relation to the conflict in Darfur. Feature documentaries such as *Darfur Now* (Braun, US, 2007) and *The Devil Came on Horseback* (Stern and Sundberg, US, 2007) have had wide theatrical release. Independent films such as *A Journey to Darfur* (George and Nick Clooney, US, 2006) and *Darfur Diaries: Message from Home* (Bain, Shapiro and Marlowe, US, 2006) have been released on DVD. The book *They Poured Fire on Us from the Sky: The True Story of Three Lost Boys from Sudan* (Alphonsian Deng et al., Public Affairs Press, 2005) has been on a number of best-seller lists. And Hollywood spokespersons from Mia Farrow to George Clooney have been actively involved in generating awareness about the conflict and have spoken before the United Nations. Finally, there is a "game for change" related to the Darfur conflict entitled *Darfur Is Dying*, available at www.darfurisdying.com.
34. Monroe Price and Mark Thompson, eds., *Forging Peace: Intervention, Human Rights and the Management of Media Space* (Bloomington: University of Indiana Press, 2002), 8.
35. Rebecca Moore, "Raising Global Awareness with Google Earth," *Imaging Notes* 22, no. 2 (2007), available at www.imagingnotes.com/go/article_free.php?mp_id=97&cat_id=18&Udo (accessed October 2007).
36. Steven Livingston, "Clarifying the CNN Effect: An Examination of Media Effects According to Type of Military Intervention," research paper for John F. Kennedy School of Government's Joan Shorenstein Center on the Press (President and Fellows of Harvard University, 1997), www.ksg.harvard.edu/presspol/research_publications/papers/research_papers/R18.pdf (accessed 10 January 2008).
37. Siva Vaidhyanathan, "The Googlization of Everything Blog," www.googlizationofeverything.com/ (accessed 14 March 2009).
38. Power, *A Problem from Hell*, 512.
39. Kyo MacLear, *Beclouded Visions: Hiroshima-Nagasaki and the Art of Witness* (Albany, NY: SUNY Press, 1998).

contributors

Deirdre Boyle is a media historian, critic, and curator and Associate Professor in the Department of Media Studies and Film at The New School in New York City. She is the author of *Subject to Change: Guerrilla Television Revisited* (Oxford UP, 1997) and *Video Classics: A Guide to Video Art and Documentary Tapes* (Oryx Press, 1986), among other books. She has new essays forthcoming in *Challenge for Change/Société Nouvelle: The Collection*, edited by Thomas Waugh, Michael Baker, and Ezra Winton (McGill-Queen's University Press); *The Tin Drum Trilogy: Paul Chan* (Video Data Bank); and *50 Years of Bay Area Experimental Film and Video*, edited by Steve Seid (Pacific Film Archive). She is currently writing about the films of Errol Morris.

Mick Broderick teaches Media Analysis at Murdoch University in Western Australia. He is author of *Nuclear Movies* (1988, 1991) and editor of *Hibakusha Cinema: Hiroshima, Nagasaki and the Nuclear Image in Japanese Film* (1996, 1999) and has been researching and writing on the cultural manifestations of the nuclear era and the apocalyptic for the past 25 years. His experimental new media installation representing the "aura" of Rwandan genocide sites, *Exhale*, was premiered at the 2007 Perth International Film Festival, "Revelation10." In 2008 Broderick co-convened the international conference "Interrogating Trauma: Arts & Media Responses to Collective Suffering."

Hye Jean Chung is a doctoral candidate in the Department of Film and Media Studies at the University of California, Santa Barbara, and is writing a dissertation that analyzes transnational cinema by integrating theoretical concepts of mediated space with postcolonial approaches to history. She is the recipient of a Fulbright Graduate Study Fellowship and a UC Santa Barbara Regents Special Fellowship. Her main interests include cultural translation, the historicization of memory, the multiple layering of time and space in cinema, and the triangular relation among filmmaker, subject, and spectator in documentary films.

Catherine M. Cole (PhD, Northwestern University) teaches African performance, field methods, postcolonial studies, and disability studies in the Department of Theater, Dance and Performance Studies at the University of California, Berkeley. She is the author of *Ghana's Concert Party Theatre* (2001), which received a 2002 Honorable Mention for the Barnard Hewitt Award from the American Society for Theatre Research, and was a finalist for the Herskovitz Prize in African Studies. She is editor of *Theatre Survey*, co-editor of *Africa after Gender?* (2007), and the author of *Performing South Africa's Truth Commission: Stages of Transition* (2009). Her dance theater piece *Five Foot Feat*, created in collaboration with Christopher Pilafian, toured North America in 2002–5. She has published articles in *Africa*, *Critical Inquiry*, *Disability Studies Quarterly*, *Research in African Literatures*, *Theatre*, *Theatre Journal*, and *TDR*, as well as numerous chapters in edited volumes. Cole's research has received funding from the National Humanities Center, National Endowment for the Humanities, Fund for U.S. Artists, American Association of University Women, ELA Foundation, and University of California Institute for Research in the Arts.

Bishnupriya Ghosh received a doctorate from Northwestern University and teaches postcolonial theory, literature, and media studies in the English Department, University of California, Santa Barbara. She has published essays on literature, film, and visual culture in *boundary 2*, *Postcolonial Studies*, and *Screen*; a monograph on the literary political imagination in new global markets, *When Borne Across: Literary Cosmopolitics in the Contemporary Indian Novel* (Rutgers UP, 2004); and a co-edited volume, *Interventions: Feminist Dialogues on Third World Women's Fiction and Film* (Garland, 1997). She has recently completed *Moving Technologies: Global Icons in South Asia* (forthcoming, Duke UP), a monograph on mass mediated icons as magical technologies of the popular, as she embarks on a third book, *The Great Vanishing: The Spectral Modern in South Asia* and a longer collaborative project on risk and uncertainty ("Speculative Globalities").

Lisa Parks is Professor of Film and Media Studies at UC Santa Barbara, where she is also an affiliate of the Departments of Art and Feminist Studies. She is the author of *Cultures in Orbit: Satellites and the Televisual* (Duke UP, 2005) and co-editor of *Planet TV: A Global Television Reader* (New York UP, 2003). She is currently writing two new books: *Coverage: Media Space and Security after 9/11* (forthcoming, Routledge) and *Mixed Signals: Media Infrastructures and Cultural Geographies*. She is also co-editing *Down to Earth: Satellite Technologies, Industries and Cultures* with Jim Schwoch (forthcoming, Rutgers UP).

José Rabasa teaches in the Department of Romance Languages and Literatures at Harvard University. He received a PhD in History of Consciousness from the University of California, Santa Cruz, in 1985, and is author of *Inventing America: Spanish Historiography and the formation of Eurocentrism*, *Writing Violence on the Northern Frontier: The Historiography of New Mexico and Florida and the Legacy of Conquest*, and *Without History: Subaltern Studies, the Zapatista Insurrection, and the Specters of History*. He has recently completed *Elsewheres: Radical Relativism and the Limits of Empire*, a study of how the *tlacuilo* of Codex Telleriano-Remensis created a pictorial vocabulary (consistent with Mesoamerican pictographic forms) for depicting missionaries, conquistadors, Spanish institutions—in brief, a pictorial vocabulary that enables us to reflect on the colonial world from a native perspective.

Bhaskar Sarkar is Associate Professor of Film and Media Studies at the University of California, Santa Barbara. His primary research interests include postcolonial media theory, political economy of global media, subalternity and representation, and visual cultures of crisis. He is the author of *Mourning the Nation: Indian Cinema in the Wake of Partition* (Duke UP, 2009), a critical exploration of the cinematic traces of a particular historical trauma. He has published essays on philosophies of visuality, and Indian and Chinese popular cinemas in anthologies and journals such as *Quarterly Review of Film and Video*, *Rethinking History: Theory and Practice*, *Cultural Dynamics*, and *New Review of Film and Television Studies*. At present, he is working on a comparative study of India and China's repositioning within the global cultural economy, as a way of tracking "plastic nationalisms" within a world-historical frame.

Noah Shenker received his doctorate in Critical Studies at the University of Southern California School of Cinematic Arts. He is the recipient of a 2006–7 Charles H. Revson Fellowship for Archival Research at the Center for Advanced Holocaust Studies at the United States Holocaust Memorial Museum, a 2007–8 USC Annenberg Graduate Fellowship, and a 2007–8 Distinguished Dissertation Fellowship from the Council on Library and Information Resources. His research explores the institutional and cultural mediations of audiovisual Holocaust testimony across archives in the United States. In fall 2009 he will begin a two-year post-doctoral fellowship at McMaster University awarded by the Council on Library and Information Resources.

Bjørn Sørenssen is Professor of Film and Media at the Department of Art and Media Studies at the Norwegian University of Science and Technology (NTNU) in Trondheim. His main research interests focus on film history, documentary film, and new media technology. He has published on these and other film-related subjects in numerous international journals and anthologies. He has also published books in Norwegian, most recently *Å fange virkeligheten. Dokumentarfilmens århundre* (Catching reality: A century of documentary, 2nd edition, Oslo, 2007).

Janet Walker is Professor of Film and Media Studies at the University of California, Santa Barbara, where she is also affiliated with the Feminist Studies Department, the Comparative Literature Program, and the Environmental Media Initiative of the Carsey-Wolf Center for Film, Television and New Media. Her essays in the areas of film feminism, documentary, historiography, and trauma studies have been published in journals including *Screen* and *Signs*, and she is the author or editor of *Couching Resistance: Women, Film, and Psychoanalytic Psychiatry* (1993), *Feminism and Documentary* (co-edited with Diane Waldman, 1999), *Westerns: Films through History* (2001), and *Trauma Cinema: Documenting Incest and the Holocaust* (University of California Press, 2005). She directs an ongoing project, *Video Portraits of Survival*, to create expressive documentary shorts about local residents who are survivors and refugees of the Holocaust, and, along with co-editing the present volume, is working on a book about "documentaries of return."

index